The
Felt Meanings
of the World

The
Felt Meanings
of the World

A Metaphysics of Feeling

Quentin Smith

Purdue University Press
West Lafayette, Indiana

Published in 1986
Printed in the United States of America

Book and jacket design by Lynn Gastinger

Library of Congress Cataloging in Publication Data

Smith, Quentin, 1952-
    The felt meanings of the world.

    Bibliography: p.
    Includes index.
    1. Emotions (Philosophy) 2. Metaphysics. I. Title.
B105.E46S65   1985   128'.3   85-9532
ISBN   0-911198-76-8

In the clear night of the nothing of anxiety the primordial openness of beings as such emerges: that there is being—and not nothing.

—Heidegger, *Was ist Metaphysik?* 1929

One particular experience presents itself to me which is therefore in a sense my experience *par excellence*. I believe the best way of describing it is to say that when I have it *I wonder at the existence of the world*. And I am then inclined to use such phrases as "how extraordinary that anything should exist" or "how extraordinary that the world should exist."

—Wittgenstein, *Lecture on Ethics* 1929

Contents

Acknowledgments

The thoughts expressed in this treatise began to take form in 1969 and since then have been developed in several drafts, the last of which was finished except for some minor additions and deletions in June 1983. I would like to thank the people who over the years have read and commented upon a portion of one or the other of the rough drafts, especially Richard J. Fallon, Gordon G. Globus, James Manns, and Howard P. Smith. I would also like to thank the three readers for Purdue University Press for their helpful suggestions about revising some of the drafts. Most of all, I would like to express my gratitude to three people who have extensively commented upon and discussed several of the drafts, and who have influenced equally the book's final form: Peter Heron, Susan Ament Smith, and William F. Vallicella.

Preface

The assumption that reasoning can be the only means of discovering a meaning of the world has been the guiding idea of philosophical investigations since the time of Plato. But for over a century now it has been apparent that this assumption leads to a nihilistic conclusion. Reason has been demonstrated to be incapable of comprehending such a meaning, and thus, if the only meaning the world is capable of possessing is a rationally discernible meaning, the conclusion becomes unavoidable that the world is meaningless. It is this situation that makes it particularly urgent at this time to explore the possibility that there is another mode of access to a meaning of the world. It is the aim of the present treatise to develop the idea that feelings provide such an access, and that the world possesses a felt meaningfulness. It will be shown that feelings are distinctive in this regard, in that felt meanings are the only kind of meanings the world can be known to possess.

The development of this idea begins with an introductory analysis of the failure of the metaphysics of reason, and of the need for its replacement by a metaphysics of feeling.

INTRODUCTION

The Metaphysics of Reason and the Metaphysics of Feeling

Metaphysics is the study of the meaning of the world as a whole. A metaphysics of reason endeavors to discover the rational meaning of the world-whole, and a metaphysics of feeling its felt meaning. The development and decline of the metaphysics of reason is discussed in the first two sections of the Introduction, and the groundwork for a metaphysics of feeling is laid in the last three sections.

Intro. 1. The Metaphysics of Rational Meaning

Rational meaning is what provides an answer to the question "Why?" The question "Why?" aims at an answer that begins with a "Because . . . " An answer in terms of a "Because . . . " always asserts a reason: it asserts that something exists, or has a certain nature, because of a specific reason. *Reasons* are the meanings discovered by rational thought. The questions about the rational meaning of the world thus ask about the reasons for the existence and nature of the world; they ask "Why does the world exist?" and "Why does the world have this nature?" Both of these questions are answered in terms of a first and final reason for the world. The first reason for the world is its cause, and the final reason its purpose. The cause and purpose of the world lie outside of the world; they do not belong to the causal and teleological series within the world. The series within the world consists of conditioned causes and purposes; every cause is an effect of a prior cause, and every purpose is for the sake of a further purpose. But the cause and purpose of the world itself are unconditioned; they neither are effects of a prior cause nor are for the sake of a further purpose. They are an uncaused cause and a purposeless purpose, such that the causal series within the world is an effect of the uncaused cause, and the teleological series is for the sake of the purposeless purpose.

1

The unconditioned cause and purpose of the world are usually thought of as *God* and *goodness*. The world is the effect of God, and the world exists for the sake of realizing goodness. God and goodness are interconnected as the rational meanings of the world in that God caused the world for the purpose of realizing goodness.

The belief in such a meaning of the world has provided the underpinning of a substantial area of human culture for more than two thousand years. This belief emerged in disparate cultures at different times; its first recorded expression appeared before 1500 B.C. in Books 1 and 10 of the *Ṛg Veda*, but it was not until the fifth century B.C. in Athens that this theory was articulated in a logically demonstrative form. This articulation appears primarily in Plato's middle and late dialogues, the first indication of it being traceable to his *Phaedo* 97C-99D. Plato here outlines a theory of the cause of the world as Mind (*Nous*) and of its purpose as the good (*ta agathon*), but asserts that he as of yet is unable to verify such a theory. The following statement, which indicates the essence of this theory, has a historical significance of great moment:

> It seemed to me correct that Mind is the cause of everything, and I thought if this be so, then Mind sets everything in order and arranges each thing in the way that is best for it.[1]

Plato was later able to develop some of the aspects of this theory, particularly in Book 6 of the *Republic*, the *Timaeus*, and in Book 10 of the *Laws*. The unconditioned cause of the world is argued to be a self-moved mover,[2] and the unconditioned purpose to be the imitation of or participation in the Idea of the Good.[3] In the *Timaeus* he connects the cause and purpose by asserting that the purpose for which the Demiurge ordered the world is to make the world better.[4]

Plato's ideas and arguments for a rational meaning of the world were developed and modified by subsequent philosophers, until they finally reached their culmination in the philosophy of Georg Hegel. Some of the major landmarks along the route from Plato to Hegel can be briefly pointed out, as they will further explain the nature of a metaphysics of rational meaning. The development of the concept of an unconditioned purpose can be discussed first.

One of Aristotle's most significant contributions to the development of this theory was to propound a doctrine of the concrete nature of the world's purpose. The unconditioned purpose of the world is the goodness of the world as a whole. Every thing in the world aims at this end in its own specific way; one thing is for the sake of another, until the teleological series culminates in the purpose of the highest thing (the human race). The circular motion of the first heaven imparts motion to the sun, and the sun's motion is for the purpose of maintaining the physical processes of becoming and passing away. The plants grow for the sake of nourishing animals, and animals exist for the sake of humans. Humans have their final purpose in theoretical contemplation, particularly in the contemplation of divine things. Through such divine contemplation humans become, in their own fashion, like God, and in such likeness the teleology of the world achieves its unconditioned completion.[5] The idea that every non-human part of the world was made for the sake of man, and man for the sake of serving God through loving and contemplating Him, became the nucleus of the later conceptions of the purpose of the world.[6]

The next major development in the conception of this purpose was made by Boethius in the sixth century A.D. Boethius was the first to make explicit the distinction between the goodness of a thing in its existence (*esse*) and the goodness of the thing in its action.[7] The implication of this distinction is that the purpose of the things in the world has a twofold aspect; things realize goodness in virtue of simply existing (what Thomas Aquinas later conceived as the "relative goodness of a thing's first actuality"[8]), and in virtue of performing the actions proper to them (what Aquinas conceived as the "absolute goodness of a thing's complete actuality"[9]).

But the consequences of this distinction for the theory of the unconditioned purpose of the world were not fully recognized and formulated until the late seventeenth century, when Gottfried Leibniz made them a basis of his philosophy. Leibniz distinguished between a purpose of the existence of the world and a purpose of the nature of the world; this distinction enabled a complete teleological explanation of the world to be achieved. In Leibniz's words, there is both "a complete reason why there is any world at all, and why there is this world rather than some other."[10] Why any world exists at all is that existence is better than nonexistence.[11] The existence of a world is good, and this is the reason God brought a world into existence. The reason for the existence of this world, rather than some other world, is that a world with this nature is better than a world with some other nature. This world is the most perfect of all possible worlds because it contains rational souls; these souls are the most perfect of substances, and it is for the sake of them that all other substances (the sun, plants, animals, etc.) exist. The final purpose of rational souls is their own perfect state, which is happiness. Happiness is perfectly achieved in knowing and loving God. In this achievement of happiness, the supreme perfection of the world is achieved; the attainment of this perfection is a purpose that is for the sake of no further purpose. It is the final reason for the nature of the world.

In Leibniz's philosophy we can see with the greatest clarity what was already present in previous theories of the rational meaning of the world. This is the idea that the first and final reason for the world's nature are not connected in a linear manner, but circularly. The final reason for the world is a reversion to the first reason, in that the final reason, man's happiness, consists in knowing and loving the first reason, God. And the first reason reverts to the final reason in that the first reason, God, causes the world for the sake of the final reason, man's knowledge and love of Himself.

The culmination and completion of this theory of the teleological meaning of the world in the system of Hegel is the next and final major stage in its development, but to understand this stage in its full significance it is necessary to first return to the conception of the causal meaning of the world.

The causal meaning of the world is more fundamental than the teleological meaning, in that the ultimate intelligibility of the rational meaning of the world lies within the causal meaning rather than the teleological one. The explanation of the existence of the final reason is found in the first reason, but the explanation of the existence of the first reason is found within itself. The question, Why is there a purpose of the world? is answered: Because God ordered the world in a purposive fashion. But the further question, Why is there a God? can only be answered in terms of God Himself, namely, that God necessarily exists, i.e., that it is of the essence of God to exist. It is the conception of the uncaused cause of the world as an existent whose essence is identical with His existence that is the ultimate foundation of the theory of the rational meaning of the world.

But it was not until several centuries after Plato that this conception of the uncaused cause as a necessary existent was developed. The rational explanation of the world by the Greek and early Christian philosophers remained incomplete. The different conceptions of the uncaused cause, Plato's *demiourgos*, Plotinus's the One (*to hen*), Augustine's and Boethius's *Deus*, were unable to provide an answer to the question, Why does the uncaused cause exist? The breakthrough was made in the eleventh century by Avicenna. Avicenna was the first to make an explicit distinction between essence (*mahiyya*) and existence (*wujud*), and this distinction enabled him to form a concept of the uncaused cause as having an essence which is identical with its existence.[12] Since it is of the essence of the uncaused cause to exist, this cause is a necessary existent.[13] This conception of the uncaused cause as being essentially identical with its existence was adopted by the scholastic philosophers, and became a central idea in the theories of René Descartes, Baruch Spinoza, Nicolas de Malebranche, Leibniz, and finally in Hegel.

Prior to the culmination of the theory of rational meaning in Hegel's system, the foundations of this theory had been seriously attacked, but subsequent philosophers were able to account for these criticisms to their satisfaction in various reformulations of the theory. David Hume's sceptical reflections were accounted for in Immanuel Kant's transcendental philosophy in a way that enabled later philosophers to continue espousing the theory of rational meaning. Of course Kant himself denied to theoretical (but not to practical) reason a knowledge of this meaning, but due to a contradiction in his system, first made public to the philosophical world by Friedrich Jacobi,[14] Johann Fichte was able to resurrect the theory of rational meaning along transcendental lines. This led to Friedrich Schelling's Identity Theory and Hegel's system, which represents the final and completing stage of the theory of rational meaning.

Hegel is the last figure in the philosophical epoch of rational meaning in two respects; he completed the theory of rational meaning, and he was the last thinker to propound a theory of rational meaning before the epoch of rational meaning declined and gave way to a belief in rational meaninglessness. Hegel's completion of the theory of rational meaning lies in the *Encyclopedia of the Philosophical Sciences* and in the series of lectures and books elaborating the ideas in this work. Hegel's completion of this theory lies in his endeavor to explain everything in the world in terms of the first and final reasons for the world. Previous theories had asserted that various kinds of existents that constitute the world are connected in a logical manner to the first and final reasons for the world, but apart from a few general observations, they made no attempt to deduce each kind of thing in the world from the world's reasons. It is true that significant attempts in this direction had been made by Karl Reinhold and Fichte, and particularly by Schelling, but it was not until Hegel that this endeavor was brought to completion. Hegel deduced everything in the spheres of the world, Nature and Spirit, from the first reason of the world, the Absolute Idea, and explained how everything in these two spheres is logically related to the final reason of the world, the philosophical contemplation of the Absolute Idea and of its realization in Nature and Spirit. Every phase of Nature and Spirit is explained as a necessary consequence of the Absolute Idea, and as a necessary condition of philosophical contemplation. The particular work of Hegel's that stands as the culmination of his system, and thus as the culmination of the epoch of rational meaning, is his *Lectures on the History of Philosophy*. These lectures represent the elaboration of the final section of the *Encyclopedia*, which explains the unconditioned purpose of the world as the activity of philosophical contemplation. Philosophical contemplation has a purpose of its own, namely absolute philosophical knowledge, and this purpose—which is thus the final purpose within the unconditioned purpose—is ultimately realized, according to Hegel, in his own system. The realization of this final stage of the unconditioned purpose at the same time brings to complete actualization the first reason of the world, inasmuch as the first reason achieves complete actualization when its necessary consequences have one and all become realized. This complete realization of both of the unconditioned reasons for the world is indicated in its final moment in the very last section of the *Lectures on the History of Philosophy,* and this section accordingly can be understood as the last and culminating piece of philosophical literature in the epoch of rational meaning. The following quote from this section is the historically significant one; it describes how the Absolute Spirit becomes actualized through the elevation of finite self-consciousness to absolute self-consciousness, which has occurred through the philosophical comprehension reached in Hegel's system:

> It appears that the World-spirit [*Weltgeiste*] has finally succeeded in removing from itself all alien objective essence [*Wesen*], and in apprehending itself at last as Absolute Spirit [*absoluten Geist*], in producing out of itself whatever is to be its object, and holding this serenely in its power. The struggle of the finite self-consciousness [*endlichen Selbstbewustseins*] with the absolute self-consciousness [*absoluten Selbstbewustseins*], which seemed to the former to lie outside of itself, has now come to an end. The finite self-consciousness has ceased to be finite, and in this way the absolute self-consciousness has achieved its own realization. It is the whole history of the world up to the present time, and the history of philosophy in particular, that represents this struggle. It now appears to have reached its goal, when this absolute self-consciousness, which it had the task of depicting, has ceased to be alien, and where Spirit is accordingly realized as Spirit.[15]

Intro. 2. *The Metaphysics of Rational Meaninglessness*

With the completion of the epoch of rational meaningfulness in Hegel's system, came its decline. By the middle of the nineteenth century, the belief in a rational meaning of the world had been superseded by a prevailing conviction of its rational meaninglessness. In the 1850s an empathy with Arthur Schopenhauer's pessimistic irrationalism[16] acquired precedence over adherence to Hegelian and neo-Hegelian systems; this in turn led to the cultural dominance of Eduard von Hartmann's irrationalism of the unconscious in the 1870s and 1880s, and finally to Friedrich Nietzsche's more extreme irrationalism and diagnosis of nihilism, which took hold as the prevailing philosophy in the 1890s. Meanwhile in France and England the reductivist and avowedly mundane spirit of positivism and empiricism reigned, which claimed that questions about the reasons for the world are without sense.

The decline of the epoch of rational meaning in the nineteenth century and the consequent emergence of the epoch of rational meaninglessness, which still flourishes today, is not confined to the area of philosophy. The arts and sciences have forms that, interpreted philosophically, can be seen to express analogues to the philosophical theories of rational meaning and meaninglessness. The decline of the belief in a rational meaning that occurred in the nineteenth-century philosophies can also be seen in the arts and sciences of this period.

In *poetry*, rhymed and metrically symmetrical verses are the analogues of a theory of rational meaningfulness in philosophy. Rhymes and metrical symmetry manifest a law of the harmonic recurrence of sounds in the poem, culminating in the final line in which the progression of sounds is brought to a pleasing rest. Such verses can be understood as symbolizing by virtue of their form a telic order in the world that aims at the final good. The emerging disbelief in such a meaning of the world is first expressed in the form of the poems in Walt Whitman's *Leaves of Grass* (1855), whose unrhymed and metrically asymmetrical verses became the predominant pattern of twentieth-century poetry.

In *fiction*, an omnisciently narrated plot consisting of events which build up teleologically to a climax, the happy ending, is the analogue of a philosophical theory of a rationally meaningful world. The expression of a rationally meaningless world-view first appeared in fiction in the novels of Gustave Flaubert, particularly in *Madame Bovary* (1855-57), *Salammbo* (1862), and *Sentimental Education* (1869). Flaubert initiated what James Joyce and Marcel Proust would bring to completion in the early twentieth century: a relatively plotless novel, consisting of largely disconnected scenes, the absence of a happy ending that resolves the various problems in the story, an antihero in the place of a hero, and a narration by an author who knows no more than the characters in the story.

In *music*, consonance, expressed in tonality and in rhythmical order, is the analogue of a philosophical theory of a rationally meaningful world. For instance, in tonal compositions there is a home key which is the analogue of a purpose in rational metaphysics; in these compositions there is an ordered progression of related tonalities that finds its goal and resolution in the home key. When the home key is reached, there is a sense of rest, of purpose attained. Atonal compositions through lacking a home key convey no such sense. The period of dissonance in music was ushered in by the single harmonic cluster at the opening of Richard Wagner's *Tristan and Isolde* (1859), the noted *Tristan-Akkord*. However, this period did not achieve its more mature expressions until the last movement of Arnold Schoenberg's String Quartet No. 4 (1907), which except for its final cadence in F-sharp major is the first entirely atonal music, and Igor Stravinsky's *Rite of Spring* (1913), which is the first work to emphasize irregular rhythmic patterns.

In *painting*, the representational depiction of an objective order of the world is the analogue of a theory of rational meaning. The idea that there is an objectively ordered reality that is there to be accurately represented in painting held sway over painters until the impressionist movement in France; Édouard Manet's *Déjeuner sur l'herbe* (1863) lay at the beginning of this movement, and manifested the first influential move towards nonrepresentationalism, a tendency that would be developed in such early twentieth-century schools as Fauvism and Cubism and which would reach full bloom with Abstract Expressionism.

The *sciences* manifest their own kind of analogue to the philosophical theories of rational meaning and meaninglessness. The most significant event in nineteenth-century science occurred in 1859, with the publication of Charles Darwin's *The Origin of Species*. Darwin's theory of the evolution of species through chance mutation gradually replaced Georges Cuvier's catastrophic explanation of the differences between primitive and contemporary forms of life, and thereby put an end to the widespread acceptance of the plausibility of interpreting life in terms of a teleological meaning and biblical creation. The scientific developments in the twentieth century exhibit an increasing acceptance of the scientific forms of rational meaninglessness. This appears most noticeably in quantum mechanics; Werner Heisenberg's principle of uncertainty entails that the laws of causality are inapplicable to subatomic events, and that the construction of a statistical probability is the closest approximation to an effective explanatory device.

The foregoing remarks indicate the emergence of the epoch of rational meaninglessness in western culture, an epoch which is in full flower today.[17] The philosophical basis and presuppositions of the epoch of rational meaninglessness deserve a closer scrutiny, as it is only through examination of them that the possibilities of transcending this epoch can be clearly understood. To this end I shall in the following explicate the arguments upon which the philosophy of rational meaninglessness is based.

The demonstrations that the belief in a rational meaning of the world is erroneous can be divided into material demonstrations and formal demonstrations. The material demonstrations involve criticisms of the specific conceptions of the first and final reasons for the world, and the formal demonstrations aim to prove that any possible reason for the world is intrinsically unknowable.

A significant number of material demonstrations have been developed, but in the following I will confine myself to mentioning the four most widely accepted arguments, two of them being criticisms of the concept of the first reason for the world, and two being criticisms of the idea of the final reason.

Two ideas were prominent in the conception of the first reason for the world, that it is a first cause and that it necessarily exists. It was inferred that there must be a first cause from the premises that an infinite series of causes is impossible, and a series of causes exist. But the first premise, that an infinite series of causes is impossible, has been subjected to a number of criticisms in the nineteenth and twentieth centuries. One of the principal sources of these criticisms lay in Georg Cantor's pioneering studies in the nature of infinite sets,[18] which revealed that the difficulties usually associated with the idea of infinity are pseudo-difficulties. The logical and metaphysical implications of Cantor's theories made it evident that there is no intrinsic impossibility in there being an infinite series of causes, be this series temporally regressive (the series of causes *in fieri*) or temporally simultaneous (the series of causes *in esse*). As Bertrand Russell,[19] Paul Edwards,[20] John Hick,[21] Wallace Matson,[22] Joel Kupperman,[23] and numerous others have pointed out, there are no *a priori* grounds for assuming that the world either does or does not have a first cause.

The idea that the first reason for the world is a necessary existent, in the sense that it belongs to its essence to exist, has been argued to be incoherent by a number of different philosophers, including Gottlob Frege,[24] J. J. C. Smart,[25] William Alston,[26] Jerome Shaffer,[27] P. F. Strawson,[28] Richard Swinburne,[29] Martin Heidegger,[30] and others.[31] One of these arguments can be presented by way of illustration. According to Strawson, the concept of a necessary existent analytically includes the concept of existence, which is equivalent to saying that the concept of a necessary existent analytically entails its own instantiation. But this is an incoherent notion, for a concept can analytically entail only another concept, and cannot be related in such a way to its own instance(s). "Logical or analytical necessity relates solely to the connexion of concepts with one another. No concept can logically guarantee its own instantiation. . . . "[32] Whether a concept is instantiated cannot be known *a priori*, through an analysis of the concept, but only *a posteriori*, through examining what lies beyond the concept.

The concept of a final reason for the world is mainly criticized from one empirical viewpoint and one logical consideration. Empirically, the evidence is overwhelming that all things in the world are not teleologically constructed so as to serve the end of human happiness. This evidence is primarily derived from the sciences, originally and most strikingly from Darwin's *The Origin of Species* and *The Descent of Man*.

Logically, it is pointed out that the idea that human happiness (specifically, the knowledge and love of the first reason for the world) is good, i.e., is something that ought to be, is based on an illegitimate fact-value argument. The goodness of such contemplation is a value, and as such cannot be deduced from the factual structure of this contemplation. Generally speaking, moral judgments cannot have a universal and absolute truth, but are culturally or individually relative (Nietzsche,[33] Jean-Paul Sartre,[34] E.A. Westermarck)[35] or are but expressions of emotions, wishes, or suggestions (A. J. Ayer,[36] Charles Stevenson,[37] Rudolph Carnap),[38] to name a few of the contemporary views that imply the falsity of traditional rational-metaphysical ethics.

Criticisms such as these relate to the specific conceptions of the first and final reasons for the world. The formal criticisms, on the other hand, do not aim at the specific formulations of a first and final reason, but at the very assumption that reasoning is capable of demonstrating a rational meaning for the world. These criticisms assert that a rational demonstration, even though valid in its logical form, remains unverifiable and empty unless it is grounded in an observation or intuition. Since rational demonstrations of the existence and nature of unconditioned reasons cannot in principle be grounded in an observation or intuition, the endeavor to demonstrate rationally a reason for the world is doomed *a priori* to failure.

The idea that all verifiable propositions must be grounded in empirical observation is the basic tenet of the logical positivist movement; the principle that all true propositions must be fulfilled in a phenomenological intuition is the foundation of the phenomenological movement. Although these two movements are not the only directions that have been taken in the theories of rational meaninglessness, they are the main ones, and hence an analysis of their representative figures will provide the most appropriate illustrations of the basis for the formal criticisms of the theory of rational meaning.

The principles of logical positivism are largely based on Ludwig Wittgenstein's *Tractatus Logico-Philosophicus*. The conclusion of the *Tractatus* is that what makes the world nonaccidental, the reasons why the world is and is as it is, lie beyond the world. These reasons are God and value (goodness).[39] They constitute the meaning of the world; thus Wittgenstein writes: "The meaning of the world [*Der Sinn der Welt*] must lie outside the world."[40] In this respect Wittgenstein adopts the underlying assumption of the theory of rational meaningfulness, viz., that the reasons for the world cannot be found in the series of conditions that are within the world. But the essential difference lies in this: Wittgenstein argues that since the meaning of the world is outside of the world, it cannot in principle be known or expressed in language. Only what is within the world can be known and linguistically expressed. This is necessitated by the requirements of knowledge and language; in order for propositions to be true or false representations of reality, they must be capable of analysis into elementary propositions, all of which represent the existence or nonexistence of a state of affairs (*Sachverhalt*) within the world. Elementary propositions are representations of the combinations of objects—the irreducible simples of the world—in states of affairs. Since all propositions, in order to have a determinable sense, must be reducible to elementary propositions about the combinations of objects, it is in principle impossible for a proposition to make sense if it asserts the existence of a God or value beyond the world.

The reconstruction of Wittgenstein's elementary propositions as observation or protocol statements by Carnap, Moritz Schlick, Herbert Feigl, Ayer, Carl Hempel, and others provided the basis for the development of logical positivism. All propositions that have a sense, and which are not tautologies or contradictions, must be capable of verification by the empirical observation of something (primarily sense data) within the world. Thus a proposition asserting the existence of a rational meaning for the world lacks sense. As Ayer says, "it cannot be significantly asserted that there is a non-empirical world of values, or that men have immortal souls, or that there is a transcendent God."[41] But this does not mean that it is "verifiable" that the world is rationally meaningless; such a meaninglessness cannot be empirically observed, and consequently it is just as cognitively senseless to talk about a lack of meaning of the world as it is to talk about a meaning of the world. All statements in the whole "field of metaphysics," as Carnap emphasizes, are "entirely senseless."[42]

Heidegger's *Being and Time* can be considered as the major work in the phenomenological school of thought. For Heidegger, the world in its *a priori* structure, in its worldhood, belongs to the *a priori* constitution of *Dasein*.[43] *Dasein* is characterized as thrown into its existence, without being able to comprehend the "whence and whither" (*Woher und Wohin*) of its existence. "This character of Dasein's Being, this 'that it is' [*Dass es ist*], is veiled in its whence and whither, but disclosed in itself all the more unveiledly; we call it the thrownness [*Geworfenheit*] of this being into its 'there'."[44] "*That* it is factically may be hidden in regard to its *why* [*des Warum*], but the '*that*' itself [*das "Dass" selbst*] has been disclosed to Dasein."[45] There is no answer to the "Why? For what reason?" as this question pertains to *Dasein*'s Being-in-the-world.[46] Prior to all theoretical-logical cognition, *Dasein* is disclosed to itself as "reasonless [*abgründigen*]."[47] The hiddenness of a reason does not pertain only to *Dasein*'s mode of Being, to existence (*Existenz*), but to Being itself. As Heidegger indicates in his draft for the unpublished division 3 of part 1 of *Being and Time*, "the reason for Being is obscure [*der Grund des Seins ist dunkel*]."[48] The reason for *Dasein*'s Being-in-the-world and for Being itself is inaccessible both to *Dasein*'s unthematic modes of disclosedness and to the thematizing disclosedness achieved in phenomenological investigation.

The assertion of apparent reasonlessness expressed in *Being and Time* remained, although in varying senses, at the core of subsequent existential and phenomenological metaphysics. Karl Jaspers laments at the very end of his *Philosophy* that "there is no answer in the vast silence, no justification for what is, and for the way in which it is."[49] The metaphysical implications that Sartre draws at the end of his ontology are that being-in-itself "is without reason [*sans raison*], without cause, and without necessity";[50] the upsurge of being-for-itself may, Sartre adds, have a reason, and hypotheses can be formed about this reason, but "these hypotheses will remain hypotheses since we cannot expect them to be subsequently confirmed or disconfirmed."[51] And Maurice Merleau-Ponty adopts an analogous metaphysical stance when he writes: "the contingency of all that exists and all that has value is not a little truth for which we have somehow or other to make room in some nook or cranny of the system; it is the condition of a metaphysical view of the world."[52]

The positivists and phenomenological/existential philosophers share in common the belief that the world has no knowable rational meaning, even though they differ in the exact sense they give to "knowable" and "rational meaning."[53] A reason for the world, however this "reason" be characterized, can be neither empirically observed nor phenomenologically intuited.[54] This belief is an instance of the basic tenet of the theory of rational meaninglessness, which may be generally stated as the thesis that *there is no knowable reason that explains why the world exists and has the nature it does.* This tenet is comprehensive: it includes both the *formal* criticisms of the very possibility of knowing any sort of reason for the world, and the *material* criticisms of the specific conceptions of a first and final reason that had been developed during the epoch of rational meaningfulness.

It is not this tenet that the present treatise wishes to challenge. Rather, I am concerned with criticizing an additional tenet implied in the theory of rational meaninglessness, the tenet that a meaning of the world can only be a rational meaning, such that if the world lacks a rational meaning, it can have no other meaning. This claim cannot be explicitly asserted by these philosophers, for to assert it implies an awareness of the possibility that the world could have an extrarational meaning. A denial of all kinds of meanings but rational meanings implies an awareness that there is a question of whether or not there are different possible kinds of global meaning. And it is precisely this question of which philosophers had no awareness; they assumed, without further reflection, that a meaning of the world must be a reason for it. This can only be illustrated indirectly in the writings of these philosophers, by showing that their discussions of the meaning of the world presupposed a conception of this meaning as rational. I will illustrate this briefly in the work of the two major philosophers of this epoch, Wittgenstein and Heidegger.

Wittgenstein defined the meaning of the world as "what makes it nonaccidental."[55] What makes the world nonaccidental can only be an unconditioned reason that entails the world as a necessary consequence of itself; it is because of this unconditioned reason, or reasons (God and value), that everything in the world is and is as it is. These reasons would be the solution to the "problem" that is posed by everything in the world.[56] But that this problem could be something other than a need for rational necessity, and that the solution to "the problem of the world" could be something other than reasons that supply such a necessity, is not considered by Wittgenstein. Metaphysical problems are tacitly presupposed to be set up by rational considerations and to be soluble (supposing they make sense) by rational considerations.

A different but nevertheless somewhat analogous presupposition can be found in Heidegger's writings from 1927 to 1935. It is instructive to analyze Heidegger in this regard, for in some respects he overcame the presuppositions of the rational metaphysical tradition more than any other philosopher. However, at the very deepest level, Heidegger's "overcoming" of the rational metaphysical tradition still remains *within* this tradition. It can be shown that although Heidegger characterized "reasons" (*Grundes*) in a different way than did traditional metaphysicians, and although his manner of questing after or "thinking" (*Denken*) about reasons is different, Heidegger still held the presupposition that metaphysics is at bottom *an inquiry about reasons*.

In *An Introduction to Metaphysics*, Heidegger asserts that the most fundamental metaphysical question is "Why is there being (*Seiendes*) at all and not rather nothing?"[57] Heidegger wishes to differentiate himself from the preceding metaphysical tradition by not asking about a reason for being that is itself another being, but through asking about a "reason for the Being of being."[58] This means, for one thing, that the reason sought for cannot be God,[59] for God is a being, albeit the highest being (if He exists). The ultimate reason Heidegger is seeking is something other than the supreme ontical cause of beings. Moreover, although "the reason in question must *explain* the Being of being,"[60] this explanation is not to be represented as a logico-deductive explanation, such that the Being of being can be logically deduced from this reason. For Heidegger, the authentic metaphysical "thinking" about this reason is not a "logical" thinking. But Heidegger does not wish to commit himself to determining what this reason could be, or how it could "explain" the Being of being. The fundamental metaphysical question is deliberately left "undeveloped" and the issues "undecided."[61] For a preliminary matter must be inquired into first: "How shall we inquire about, not to say discover, the reason for the Being of being if we have not adequately considered and understood Being itself?"[62] This consideration motivates Heidegger to devote most of his attention to the question about Being itself, rather than to the more fundamental metaphysical question about the reason for the Being of being.[63]

The basic presupposition shared by Heidegger and other philosophers in the rational-metaphysical tradition from Plato and Aristotle onwards is that the central metaphysical question is a *Why-question*, and is about the reason or reasons that explain why everything is and is as it is. Metaphysicians from Plato to Hegel presupposed the most fundamental metaphysical truth to be *the answer* to this question, and metaphysicians from Schopenhauer onwards presupposed the most basic metaphysical truth to be *the unanswerability* of this question.

The nature of these presuppositions can be more fully characterized if we recognize them as an expression of human spirituality. Spirituality can be understood as a need for and quest after a meaning of the world. Rational spirituality is the need and quest for a rational meaning of the world. Over the past two thousand or more years, human spirituality has become so closely identified with rational spirituality that human and rational spirituality have come to seem to be the same thing. This has resulted in nihilism, which is the particular form of the human spirit's sickness. Nihilism occurs when the human spirit finds itself in a situation where it is incapable of being fulfilled, and it can be understood as a need for a meaning of the world coupled with a conviction that such a meaning cannot be grasped. Contemporary nihilism is the need for a reason for the world coupled with the belief that such a reason is unknowable. Now the only avenue out of the contemporary situation of nihilism in which human spirituality finds itself is to draw into question the fundamental presupposition of this spirituality, which is that global meaning must be rational in nature. If there is no other kind of global meaning than global reasons, then nihilism is the last and definitive attitude of the human spirit, and spiritual self-consciousness can only resign itself to a fatalistic understanding of its destiny. "There is no way out. Lie and wait, lie still and be quiet."[64] But if it is possible that the world has another kind of meaning than a reason, then the task which lies before the human spirit is to explore this possibility to the limit. Only this holds out the chance for the birth of a new and different kind of human spirituality, a spirituality that is based on something other than reason. The possibility that the kind of meaning the world possesses is a *felt meaning*, and that *feeling* is the mode of access to this meaning, is what I intend to explore in this work.

Intro. 3. Critique of the Rationalist Theory That Feeling Cannot Be a Source of Metaphysical Knowledge

In order to show that we do have an access to meanings of the world in our feelings, and hence that a metaphysical study of feeling is a viable project, the traditional rationalist theory of feeling must first be shown to be false. The metaphysics of reason brought with itself a certain viewpoint on feeling, one that denied the proper nature of feeling and rendered nonsensical the idea of a metaphysics of feeling. This viewpoint flourished during the epoch of rational meaning, from Plato to Hegel, but its consequences remain in effect today in various and often implicit forms, as is evinced in the fact that a positive conception of the metaphysical nature of feeling has not yet been developed. Rationalist metaphysics is based on the idea that the part of human nature that relates to the meaning of the world, and that also realizes this meaning, inasmuch as the rational contemplation of God is the unconditioned purpose of the world, is reason. Human nature is conceived as centered around its rational part, and every other part, including feelings, is conceived from the viewpoint of its relation to reason. This theory has two consequences that pertain specifically to feeling: feelings are true inasmuch as they are rational, and the nature and function of feelings is to serve reason. The import of these consequences is that a metaphysics of feeling is impossible. In the following, the argumentative basis of this theory is set forth and then criticized.

The main idea in the rational theory of human nature, that reason is the essence of man, was first stated in its traditional form in Aristotle's *On the Soul*, when he abandoned Plato's tripartite psychology and asserted that man's substance (*ousia*) is reason (*logos*). This idea appears recurrently in rational metaphysics, e.g., in Aquinas's theory, man's substantial form is the *principium intellectualis*; in Descartes's theory it is termed the *substantia intellectio*; and in the nonsubstantial theories of the subject in Kant and Fichte, reason is asserted to be the noumenal or absolute *Ich*. The mode of argumentation developed by Aristotle is that the soul's essential nature can be inferred from the kind of activity proper to the soul. Reasoning, so it is assumed, is the proper activity of the human soul; therefore man's substance or subjectivity is a rational one. Feelings belong to human nature through participating in its rationality; thus with respect to feelings it can be asserted, with Descartes, that "in their formal concept some type of reasoning [*intellectio*] is contained."[65]

The first of the two consequences of this theory is that feelings possess no truth that is not possessed in a superior way by reason. Since reason is the essence of the soul, it is the standard by which the soul's apprehension of truth is to be measured. If feelings are to possess a true relation to the world, this relation can only be a rational one. But the truth possessed by feeling is necessarily inferior to the truth possessed by reason. This inferiority manifests itself in two ways:

1. Feelings not based on reason are confused thoughts (Descartes),[66] inadequate ideas (Spinoza),[67] or confused perceptions (Leibniz);[68] that is, they know in a confused or inadequate way what reason knows clearly or adequately. According to Spinoza, they are *ideis inadaequatis* in that their knowledge of their causal reasons is partial and individual, not complete and universal.[69] Malebranche, who propounded another version of this theory, explains that "the mind never apprehends clearly what is not universal";[70] emotions are confused since they are not cognitions of universals, these universal cognitions being at their highest level cognitions of God and goodness. It is through comprehending universal truths about metaphysical reasons and their consequences that the mind has clear ideas. Hegel articulates this rational inferiority of feeling as follows: "Immediate feeling

which has not been purified by rational knowing is laden with the character of the natural, the contingent, the outside-of-itself and apartness."[71]

2. If feelings do bear a relation to an adequately and clearly conceived truth, they can do so only indirectly, through being effects of the rational cognition of such a truth. The rational cognition relates to the truth directly, through knowing it, and the feeling relates to it indirectly, through being an effect of the rational cognition. Such effects are the "higher feelings" discussed in the rational-metaphysical tradition. For instance, the rational pleasures discussed in Book 9 of Plato's *Republic* have a relation to something true only through being based on a rational cognition of essences (*eidei*); the intellectual appetites discussed in Aquinas's *Summa Theologica* are related to universals only through these universals being apprehended by the intellect;[72] and the feeling of respect that is treated in Kant's second critique is related to the universal law stating the unconditioned purpose of human existence through being an effect of reason's cognition of this law.[73]

This theory of the "truth" possessed by feeling entails that a metaphysics of feeling is an untenable notion. Feeling cannot have a true relation to the world that reason cannot have in a more clear and direct way; hence a metaphysics of feeling by definition can be no more than an inferior version of a metaphysics of reason.

The theory that rationality is the essence and metaphysical aspect of human nature leads to a second conclusion about feeling that puts to rest in a different way the possibility of developing a viable metaphysics of feeling. The essential self of man, which is reason, actualizes what it is potentially through acquiring a rational knowledge of the world and through governing its practical conduct in accordance with rational principles. The actualization of this rational self ultimately has the significance of contributing to the realization of the final reason for the world, viz., realizing the goodness of the world through rationally knowing the world's cause. Feelings belong to man as properties of his rational self in order to aid this self in the realization of its nature; it is the function of feeling to serve and obey reason in reason's endeavor to realize the unconditioned purpose of the world.

This function that rational metaphysics assigns to feeling can be understood more exactly if it is explained in terms of the practical syllogism. The practical syllogism was first explicitly conceived by Aristotle in chapter 7 of *The Movements of Animals*. The major premise of this syllogism is universal; it states an apparent or real good that is the purpose of the action; the minor premise is the intuition of a particular that instantiates the universal concept in the major premise. The conclusion of the syllogism is the ensuing action itself. Now the function of feeling (which includes wish or will, *boulasis* or *voluntas*) is to aid in moving the rational agent to undertake the action specified in the syllogism. This entails that the feeling itself be elicited by and in accordance with the syllogistic reasoning. If the syllogism indicates that something is desirable, a feeling of desire should arise that disposes the agent to engage in an action aimed at possessing the desirable object; likewise, if the syllogism asserts that a particular course of action is dishonourable, and ought to be feared, then a feeling of fear should be elicited.

Although the function (*ergon, opus*) of feeling is thought to be its obedience to reason, feeling is recognized to be capable of resisting reason and thereby of malfunctioning. This is possible, as Aquinas explains, because feeling is not only naturally moved "by the cogitative power which the universal reason guides, but also by the imagination and sense."[74] Feeling can thereby prevent a person from pursuing the purpose he rationally ought to pursue, or induce him to pursue an irrational purpose that he ought not to pursue. Feeling malfunctions by preventing a person from conducting his life in accordance with the dictates of the practical syllogism. This can occur in five ways, all of which were first enumerated by Aristotle. Feeling can prevent: (1) the major premise from being known, (2) the minor premise from being known, (3) the knowledge of the minor premise from being exercised, (4) the conclusion of the syllogism from being carried out in an action, and even (5) the very formulation of a syllogism itself, thereby inducing a person to act without first deliberating about the rational purpose.[75]

This interpretation of the functioning and malfunctioning of feeling implies that a metaphysics of feeling is impossible. A "metaphysics of feeling" would be no more than an explanation of how feeling serves or fails to serve reason in the latter's endeavor to realize the unconditioned purpose of the world. Feeling has metaphysical significance only insofar as it aids reason, and a theory of feeling that aimed to produce metaphysical knowledge would accordingly be confined to explaining the purpose that feeling enabled reason to achieve. But the explanation of this purpose belongs properly to the metaphysics of reason, and consequently a theory of feeling in truth has no distinct metaphysical content of its own. What can only be known by analysing feeling, namely the manner in which feeling serves or fails to serve reason, is a psychological fact about feeling, and says nothing about the meaning of the world. Investigations of feeling can only be psychological; they must be "treatises on the passions," or the psychological parts of Ethics.

The above is an account of the rationalist theory that feeling is unable to be a source of metaphysical knowledge. This theory can be brought into question in the first instance through observing that it is developed from the perspective of reason, a perspective that the proponents of this theory did not recognize to be a perspective but tacitly assumed to be the absolute human standpoint. This assumption blinded these metaphysicians to the perspective of feeling. If feelings are understood in terms of themselves, from the perspective inherent in feelings themselves, they do not appear as inferior versions of reason that are in the service of the latter, but as phenomena with a positive nature of their own. They relate, not to rational meanings but to *felt meanings*, to the ways in which things are *important*. They are *appreciations* of things for being important. This positive character of feelings as appreciations of importance will be described more fully in the next two sections. Here I shall simply note that appreciations of the ways in which the world as a whole is important are the metaphysical feelings, and constitute the distinctive metaphysical nature of humans as this nature is understood from the viewpoint of feeling.

This implies that the standard of metaphysical truth cannot be understood solely in terms of "rationality" and its opposite, "irrationality," but that a distinct standard must also be recognized, the standard proper to metaphysical feelings.[76] Metaphysical feelings, understood in terms of themselves, are neither rational nor irrational but extrarational. This does not mean they are "mystical feelings," for the rational/mystical dichotomy falls within the sphere of reason no less than does the rational/irrational dichotomy. Mystical feelings are not "irrational" but "suprarational"; they (paradoxically) violate the laws of reason in order to relate immediately and positively to the ultimate meaning that reason relates to mediately and by the *via negativa*, this ultimate meaning being God, the first reason for the world. Mystical feelings are ineffable experiences that are thought to possess their own certainty and truth, a truth that, being suprarational (e.g., "God is both One and Many"), cannot be evidentially communicated to people who have not experienced them but must be taken on "faith." This gives rise to the related dichotomy between "reason" and "faith," a dichotomy that is also relative to the rational perspective.

But metaphysical feelings, understood from what is genuinely the perspective of feeling, do not relate to reasons for the world but to its ways of being important, and they do not relate ineffably but effably—but their effability is not that of reason. Metaphysical feelings have their own ways of evident knowing and of communicating this knowledge, and such appreciative knowing is what "extrarational" means, rather than "mystical" or "to be taken on faith." Thus, to say that metaphysical feelings are "extrarational" is to say that they are neither inferior to reason (and are "irrational") nor superior to reason (and are "suprarational") but fall outside the sphere of rational evaluation altogether. Appreciative knowings of the world-whole cannot be measured in relation to the rational-metaphysical standard of truth in any way whatsoever.

But these remarks are not to be taken as implying that there are two *real* standards of metaphysical truth inherent in human nature, such that man *really is* irreconcilably split into a rational-metaphysical aspect and an appreciative-metaphysical aspect. What I am contrasting here is the appreciative-metaphysical standard of truth with what is purported to be a rational-metaphysical standard of truth by the metaphysicians of rational meaning. The fact of the matter is that this rational standard of metaphysical truth is not a standard at all but a chimera. This statement should not come as a surprise, since it is precisely this that was demonstrated in the metaphysics of rational meaninglessness. The main thrust of this metaphysics was that *a priori* rational demonstrations of the existence and nature of God and goodness are invalid as a method of obtaining truths about the world. And if this method is invalid, then there is no *real* standard for obtaining knowledge of rational metaphysical meanings that can be found in human nature and that can be opposed to the appreciative-metaphysical standard.

It is in this manner that the rational theory that feeling cannot be a source of metaphysical knowledge is to be ultimately criticized. This theory is not to be *limited* by opposing to it another perspective, but *rejected* by showing that it is false. Specifically, we are to judge as false the basic thesis of the rational-metaphysical theory of human nature, that the essence of man is a rational self in the sense of a *principium intellectualis* or *absoluten Ich*, etc., that is capable of knowing *a priori* the rational meanings of the world. In terms of the two rationalist interpretations of feeling discussed above, this means that there are no clear and direct veridical *reasonings* about the rational meanings of the world in relation to which feelings could be metaphysically interpreted as epistemically inferior, and there are no true practical and syllogistic *reasonings* asserting an unconditioned purpose, in relation to which feelings could be interpreted as having the metaphysical function of obeying. Feelings are not metaphysically inadequate in these two respects because there exists nothing in relation to which they could be inadequate.

The task of defending feelings against the traditional theory of their metaphysical incapacity is only the first step on the way to validating the idea of a metaphysics of feeling. The next step is to outline in a positive way the distinctive nature of a metaphysics of feeling.

Intro. 4. The Metaphysics of Felt Meaning

In this section the idea of a metaphysics of feeling is developed by elaborating upon the respects in which it differs from a metaphysics of reason.

It was noted in the last section that the *meanings* relevant to these two metaphysics are different. From the perspective of reason, it is *reasons* for the world that are meaningful, whereas from the perspective of feeling, it is the ways in which the world is *important* that are meaningful. Importances are the felt meanings, and have the same fundamental role in the metaphysics of feeling that causes and purposes have in the metaphysics of reason.

Felt meanings of the world do not provide answers to the question, "Why does the world exist and have the nature it does?" but to such questions as "In what ways are the world's existence and nature important?" While rational metaphysics is concerned to discover the unconditioned reasons that are reasons for every other reason, the metaphysics of feeling inquires about the ultimate importances. The world has different ways of being important, and the aim is to discover which ways are more fundamental, and ultimately, which is the basic way of being important that underlies every other way.

The relation of reasoning to the world is *explanative*; the world is regarded as an *explanadum*, as something-to-be-explained. But the relation of feeling to the world is *appreciative*; the world is appreciated for being important. This appreciation involves an awareness of the world's importance, and a sensuous pleasure or pain that redounds from the importance of which one is aware.

If the world has a rational explanation, this is known through reasoning, but if the world is important, this cannot be known by any process of reasoning, but only through appreciative feeling. If the world has the importance of being fulfilled, this can only be discovered through appreciating the world in the mood of euphoria or the affect of joy.

Importances are not values. Values, what ought to be and what ought not to be, are only some of the phenomena that are important, and which can be known to be important through appreciative feeling. I will indicate in the course of this work that the presupposition that feelings relate to values is one of the ideas that prevented the meaningful nature of feeling from being recognized. That feelings relate to importances and not values entails that a theory of the felt meanings of the world is not an Ethics but a Metaphysics. It deals, not with how the world ought to be, but with how it actually is in its ultimate aspects.

But if importances are not values, that does not mean they are "facts." The customary division of reality into felt values and neutral facts is inapplicable to the reality that appears in appreciative feeling. No "facts" can be found in this reality. This means, for one thing, that the controversy about whether felt values are "projected upon" or "intrinsically attach to" facts cannot be applied to the importances studied in the metaphysics of feeling. For if there are no facts, and only importances, then there is nothing upon which importances could be "projected" or to which they could "intrinsically attach."

The importances with which the metaphysics of feeling is primarily concerned are not to be found as realities within the world. The metaphysics of feeling shares with the metaphysics of reason the desire to transcend this or that part of the world and to discover the meaning of the whole. But in this quest for meaning, the metaphysics of feeling does not transcend to the same realm to which the metaphysics of reason transcends. The metaphysics of reason transcends not only the parts of the world but the whole world itself; it aims to go *beyond* or *outside* the world to the ground (reason) of the world. Specifically, it aims to transcend "the world," in the sense of the whole of created being, to the Creator, and to transcend "the world," in the sense of the whole of what is the case and of what is relatively good, to the ideal of absolute goodness, of what absolutely ought to be the case. But if these world-transcendent realms are empty of any knowable meaning, as has been argued in the metaphysics of rational meaninglessness, there still remains another locus of metaphysical meanings (meanings of the world as a whole), namely, the *wholeness* of the world itself. And this is precisely the realm to which the metaphysics of feeling transcends when it transcends this or that part of the world. The felt meanings of the world which are the theme of the metaphysics of feeling are ways in which the world as a whole is important; they are the important features of the whole of all that exists. To understand the precise sense in which the world is a whole, and specifically, an important whole, is a fundamental aim of the metaphysics of feeling.

Since the metaphysics of feeling transcends to a different realm than the metaphysics of reason, the problems that are dealt with in the metaphysics of reason acquire a transformed sense in the metaphysics of feeling. For example, the problem of whether or not there is an ultimate truth is not whether there are divine Ideas to which our ideas can correspond, but whether there is an important appearance of the wholeness of the world that makes possible all other important appearances. Such an important appearance would be the ultimate "felt truth." And the problem of whether there is a meaningful reality that is independent of human awareness is not whether causal inferences to a noumenal or divine ground of the world are justified, but whether it is possible to appreciate an important feature of the world-whole that can exist as an important feature irrespective of whether or not it is being appreciated.

These and related problems concerning the rational or felt meanings of the world are dealt with at the terminus of metaphysical inquiry. In order for these problems to be treated adequately, their treatment must be preceded by more formal studies of the nature of meaning in general, and of the ways in which we can know or relate to meanings. The metaphysics of reason approaches these preliminary issues from a rationalist viewpoint; it aims to understand the nature and types of causality and teleology, the principles (such as the principle of sufficient reason) that enable the causal and teleological orders of the world to be comprehended, and the kinds of rational knowing (the methods of inference) in which this comprehension is achieved. The metaphysics of feeling, on the other hand, aims to understand the nature and types of importance, the principles that express the basic appreciative knowledge of the world (e.g., each thing and each feature of a thing is an importance), and the kinds of feelings (sensuous feelings/feeling-awarenesses, moods/affects, etc.) in which these importances are appreciated.

The difference in the sense of the problems and preliminary studies of these two metaphysics, as well as every other difference discussed so far in this section, is an expression of one underlying difference, the difference in the *spiritual needs* that motivate these two metaphysics. A discussion of this underlying difference will be the most appropriate way to complete and conclude this section's introductory elucidation of the metaphysics of feeling.

The difference between the two spiritual needs is revealed in a fundamental way in the different approaches that are taken to the primordial state of affairs of the existence-but-possible-nonexistence of the world. Rational spirituality is well exemplified in Leibniz's approach to this state of affairs. He asks: "Why is there something rather than nothing? For nothing is simpler and easier than something [*Car le rien est plus simple et plus facile que quelque chose*]."[77] Leibniz's concern is not to appreciate the importance of this state of affairs, but to find a reason for it. The attitude into which he wishes to bring himself is an explanative attitude, an attitude of knowing the explanation of this state of affairs by inferring to its reason. In the knowledge that God exists, and that God created the world for the sake of realizing goodness, Leibniz's spirituality achieves its fulfillment. But if Leibniz, instead of trying to explain why there is existence rather than nonexistence, had appreciated the importance of this state of affairs, he would have found the world's existing-even-though-it-could-not-have-existed to be miraculous and astounding. "Nothing is simpler and easier than something"—but nevertheless there is something! To appreciate this miraculous existence of the world fully and without reservation is to allow oneself to be overwhelmed by marvelling. In this affect of marvelling, the spirituality of appreciative feeling finds one of its satisfactions, for here the miraculous importance of the world achieves its appreciation. Just as explanative reasoning is fulfilled in discovering the rational meaning of this state of affairs, so appreciative feeling is fulfilled in discovering its felt meaning.

The historical contrast between these two spiritual needs is not absolute, however. Although metaphysics has always been based on rational spirituality, some philosophers have partly expressed a spirituality of appreciative feeling. This can be found in particular in Wittgenstein and Heidegger; both of these philosophers identify the raising of the question of the reason for the world with a definite spiritual feeling. But the emphasis still remains on the rational spirituality; the feeling is assumed to be of significance only insofar as it provides a vehicle for raising the question about reasons. Thus Wittgenstein, in a passage from his "Lecture on Ethics," states that the experience of wondering at the existence of the world leads him to use such phrases as "how extraordinary that anything should exist" and "how extraordinary that the world should exist."[78] Although Wittgenstein places a central emphasis on this feeling of wonder at the extraordinary existence of the world, he does so not because he is concerned with this experience as a fulfillment in itself, i.e., as an appreciation of a felt meaning of the world, but because he is concerned with this experience in the respect in which it can be interpreted as pointing beyond the world to a God and an absolute value. Hence Wittgenstein asserts that his verbal expressions of this experience are nonsensical, as "all I wanted to do with them was just *to go beyond* the world and that is to say beyond significant language."[79] Wittgenstein interpreted these expressions as having an ethical-theological import; they are attempts to refer to an absolute value and to God.[80] A remark Wittgenstein made to Frederick Waismann, that "Good is what God orders,"[81] may be understood as the transcendental meaning to which he interpreted the wonder as referring. But what must be emphasized is that Wittgenstein failed to realize that he could, from a different perspective, have interpreted the *extraordinariness* of the world's existence as a felt meaning of the world, and the wonder as an appreciation of this meaning. By interpreting them as pointing to a God and Goodness, he revealed that he was interested in them only from the viewpoint of a metaphysics of reason.

The possibility of developing a metaphysics of feeling was even more available to Heidegger, but, like Wittgenstein, he was unable to achieve the requisite metaphysical perspective. Heidegger had achieved the awareness that the primordial revelation of being takes place not in logical cognition, but in spiritual feeling. Heidegger discusses this idea especially in *What is Metaphysics?* In this work he attempts to answer the metaphysical questions he raises solely through a description of what is disclosed in certain moods, specifically, anxiety. In this respect, *What is Metaphysics?* comes closer than any other work to realizing the idea of a metaphysics of feeling. However, at bottom it still remains within the perspective of the metaphysics of reason. For the metaphysical import of anxiety for Heidegger is not that it reveals the felt meaning of the Being of being, but that it makes possible the question about the reason for the Being of being. To make this clear, it should be noted that in *Being and Time* Heidegger describes moods as being disclosive of (amongst other things) the ways in which phenomena "matter."[82] Anxiety discloses the way of "mattering" of the "indefinitely threatening."[83] Such ways of "mattering" can be interpreted as felt meanings. Thus a metaphysics of feeling could interpret anxiety as an appreciation of the "indefinitely threatening" way in which the primordial phenomenon—that there *is* being and not nothing—"matters." This interpretation would represent a possible way of answering one of the basic questions of the metaphysics of feeling: the felt meaning of the "indefinitely threatening" is the answer to the question: "In what way does it ultimately matter that there is being and not nothing?" But in Heidegger's metaphysical interpretation of anxiety in *What is Metaphysics?* he does not mention this felt meaning; rather, anxiety is significant for Heidegger because it enables the question about the reason for the Being of being to be raised. Anxiety awakens *Dasein* to the "basic question of metaphysics,"[84] the question "Why is there being at all and not rather nothing?"[85]

Although Wittgenstein and Heidegger came closer than the traditional philosophers to adopting the metaphysical perspective of feeling, they ultimately operated within the confines of the presupposition that a metaphysics is concerned with reasons. They believe that if feeling has a distinctive metaphysical capacity, it is a capacity to relate in some sense to unknown rational meanings, rather than to known felt meanings.

This reference to "known felt meanings" highlights the fact that there is a unique kind of *knowing* proper to feelings. The character of this knowing has been generally intimated in this section by saying that feelings are appreciations of importances, but we have as yet no exact understanding of this knowing. This lacuna in our understanding shall be filled in the next section, where I will describe a method of obtaining metaphysical knowledge that is unique to feelings.

Intro. 5. The Appreciative Method of Metaphysical Knowing

In this section I will introduce a method of metaphysical knowing, the appreciative method, that is to replace the invalidated method of rational metaphysics, viz., rational inferences to God and goodness.

The appreciative method of metaphysical knowing is not a method that is imposed on feelings from the outside, but is found in feelings themselves. There is a method of knowing through feeling, and there is the possibility of developing a metaphysical theory of feeling, only because there are *methodological feelings*. Since the knowing in question is metaphysical, i.e., concerns the world as a whole, the methodological feelings to be discussed are global rather than mundane in nature.[86] These global methodological feelings not only lie at the origin of metaphysical knowledge, but also, in their higher levels, account for the theoretical development of this knowledge. It will be seen that these methodological feelings exhibit a three-tiered stratification, with the feelings on the higher strata being ways of reappreciating the importances appreciated by the feelings on the lower strata.

At the lowest level of this stratification, there are the *intuitive feelings of global importances*. These feelings are "intuitive knowings" in the sense that in them the presence of a global importance is felt. A world-importance is manifest in an immediate way, without appearing through the intermediary of verbal significations, mental imagery, or any sort of discursive or inferential thought. These intuitive feelings may vary from a suspenseful and anxious contemplation of an all-pervading ominousness, to a captivated marvelling at the miraculous presence of the whole, to a joyous feeling of global fulfillment. In these intuitions and others, there is a direct sense of a meaningful whole, a whole to which I respond with sensations of feeling.

These intuitive feelings and their sensuous accompaniments eventually begin to decline and dissipate, and the global importance begins to lose its immediate presence. But there lingers an "afterglow" of the feeling and of the appearance of the importance, and I experience a vivid retention of the importance as it appeared during the height of the feeling. Through experiencing this retentive afterglow, there arises the possibility of reliving in immediate memory the intuition of the importance, and of reappreciating this importance on a second-order level. I could reappreciate the importance by allowing its vividly retained presence to evoke in me thoughts and linguistic formations that capture and articulate its nature. In the reappreciative afterglow of a marvelling affect, for instance, the global importance of miraculousness could evoke in me the verbal significations that are appropriate for expressing and conveying its felt importance. I could be moved to exclaim inwardly, "It is amazing that the world exists! It is a miracle!" These significations are felt to capture the very tension and vibrancy of the intuited importance; in them the world's importance reverberates and rekindles my sensuous feelings, although in a subtle and diminished way.

Often these verbal significations are metaphorical, and often they are vague in their sense but rich in connotations. For example, the global importance that is reappreciated in a rejoicing-afterglow may inspire the expressions, "The world-whole is fulfilled! Everything joyously radiates with its fullness!" This points to the fact that these original linguistic articulations of the global importance are meant to be intimative, suggestive, and evocative of the importances, and to express neither precise and rigorous descriptions nor complicated theoretical analyses. The aim of these articulations is to capture the intuitively felt meanings *as* intuitively felt meanings, and not to misrepresent them by articulating them from the very beginning in a dispassionate and technical language.

The reappreciative afterglows gradually burn themselves out, and as they do so a new and higher-level methodological feeling is able to evolve from them. This is a feeling of *concentrative interest*, which is moved to reappreciate the remembered importance through making explicit its implicit content. This implicit content is felt to be of fascinating interest, in that it belongs to the global importance and yet had not been explicitly appreciated in the intuitive feeling or its afterglow. In the intuitive feeling, what explicitly appeared was the unitary phenomenon comprised of the various aspects and structural articulations inherent in the global importance; the various structural contents themselves appeared only in a tacit way. The significations evoked in the afterglow of the intuitive feeling were evoked by this explicitly appearing unitary phenomenon, and were designed to capture this unitary phenomenon rather than its various structural constituents. It is these structural contents, which fell outside of the explicit appreciative focus of the intuitive feeling and its afterglow, that now appear to be of fascinating interest and worthy of being attentionally appreciated in their own right. They inspire me to concentrate upon them, to single out and analyze them in successive acts of attention, and to capture them in linguistically articulative thoughts.

The difference in the reappreciative focus of the afterglowing and concentrative reappreciations requires a corresponding difference in the significations formed in these feelings. The afterglowing reappreciations form suggestive and vague significations that are designed to evoke the global importance as a unitary phenomenon, and the concentrative reappreciations form exact and strict significations that are designed to articulate the structural constituents of the importance in a precise and detailed way.

The structural content of the global importance is usually too complex to be made completely explicit in the concentrative feeling that originally evolves from the afterglow. The desire to make this content completely explicit motivates subsequent concentrative reappreciations to emerge on their own; this emergence is possible in that the memory of the intuitively felt importance can be recalled and concentratively reappreciated on different and separate occasions, long after the intuitive feeling and its afterglow have subsided.

The concentrative feelings do not in these later emergences distort or eliminate the original contributions of the afterglowing reappreciations. The evocative significations formed in the afterglows are preserved as a basis upon which the exact significations are built and integrated. The two kinds of significations are interrelated in that the exact significations make explicit what is implicitly but not explicitly suggested by the evocative significations, and the evocative significations in their turn explicitly signify the unitary phenomenon the constituents of which the exact significations explicitly signify. In this way an organic synthesis of the two kinds of significations can be achieved, and the global importances can thereby be fully described. The complete outcome of this synthesis, an outcome inspired by the global importances themselves, is a metaphysical theory of the felt meanings of the world.

This outline of the three levels of methodological feelings completes my introductory description of the appreciative method of metaphysical knowing. Further descriptions of these levels of feeling will be offered in the course of this work; at the present stage of this inquiry the most instructive task is to highlight the distinctive nature of the appreciative method by contrasting it with certain aspects of the rational method of metaphysical knowing it is designed to replace. Further contrasts can be made here that were not made in previous sections, contrasts that serve to differentiate in a more strictly methodological way the metaphysics of felt meaning from the metaphysics of rational meaning.

The method of rationally explaining the world-whole commences with intuitive cognitions of self-evident propositions, and proceeds through inferring further propositions from these self-evident propositions. This method has been practiced in two ways in the metaphysics of rational meaning.

One way has been to begin with evidential cognitions of formal rational principles (e.g., the principle of sufficient reason), and then proceed, with the help of additional premises (e.g., "a causal series can be found in the world"), to infer mediately propositions asserting the existence of God and goodness. Such was the rational method practiced by Aristotle, Avicenna, Aquinas, William of Ockham, Leibniz, Christian von Wolff, and others.

The second way has been to introduce self-evident propositions that explain the world as the logical consequence of God or goodness. Plato, Proclus, Bonaventura, Descartes, Spinoza, Fichte, and Schelling[87] are examples of philosophers who practiced the rational method in this way.

Among the numerous differences between the rational and appreciative metaphysical methods, three can be mentioned.

First, the *intuitions* that lie at the basis of the rational metaphysical knowledge are cognitions of propositions or, as they also have been characterized, cognitions of principles, axioms, universals, essences, or Ideas. The intuitions that comprise the foundations of appreciative knowledge, on the other hand, are feelings of omnipresent importances. These felt importances are neither propositions nor universals nor Platonic Ideas; rather, they are individual and concrete features of the empirically existing world-whole. Accordingly, eidetic intuitions or the cognitions of "clear and distinct ideas" must forever remain blind to these importances; global importances can make their appearance only in global feeings.

This difference between the rational and appreciative intuitions entails a further difference in the kinds of *evidence* relied upon in these two methodological procedures. The intuitively cognized propositions are comprehended as being rationally self-evident; that is, the reason for their truth lies within themselves, and not in more basic propositions from which they can be inferred. In contrast, the evidence that appears in the intuitive feelings is an extrarational and nonpropositional felt evidence. For example, a person experiencing an affect of awe tacitly and nonpropositionally feels it to be evident that the world is stupendous and immense. It is irrelevant to this evidential feeling that a corresponding proposition about the world, e.g., "The world is stupendous," cannot be cognized to contain the reason for its truth within itself. A global state of affairs has felt evidence in that it is immediately present in intuitive feeling.[88] But this does not imply that the knowledge obtained in these feelings is "subjective" or "individually relative." There are criteria specific to intuitive feelings, to be developed in the course of this work, that enable us to determine which appreciations are veridical and which are not, and these criteria enable the community of appreciators to reach agreement about the nature of the world's felt meanings.

A third difference concerns the relationship of the intuited evidences to the knowledge based upon them. The rationally self-evident propositions function as the logical reasons for further propositions that are inferred from them. These propositions can function as the major or minor premise of syllogisms, and thereby function as logical reasons for the conclusions, or they can be the theses or antitheses of dialectical arguments, and thereby provide the logical reasons for the syntheses.[89]

The intuitively felt meanings, however, are not propositions that provide logical reasons for inferred propositions, but importances that evoke afterglowing and concentrative reappreciations. Whereas the relationship between the different levels of rational knowledge is an inferential relationship, the levels of felt knowledge are interconnected through an evoked appreciative relation. The global importances originally evoke intuitive appreciations, then afterglowing reappreciations, and finally concentrative reappreciations. Through inspiring these appreciations and reappreciations, the global importances become articulated and explicated in a body of theoretical knowledge.

However significant the above-mentioned differences between the rational and appreciative methods may be, they pale before the ultimate factor that differentiates them. The rational method, as I indicated in Section 2 of the Introduction, is fundamentally defective and is thereby incapable of providing a knowledge of the meaning of the world-whole, whereas the appreciative method is free of the former method's defects. The crucial rational-metaphysical propositions and arguments, those asserting the existence and nature of God and goodness, are invalid, false, or simply nonreferential, and accordingly in inferring from one of these propositions to another we remain confined within the sphere of our own thoughts, closed off from the reality of the world. But the appreciative method of metaphysical knowing enables us to break out of this self-enclosed realm of thought and to open ourselves to the felt presence of the important whole of which we are a part.

But we have so long been used to thinking in the categories of rationalist philosophies that it is extremely difficult for us to free ourselves from them and to open ourselves to the important world-whole. To begin with, we virtually have no understanding of feelings, or of how the world appears to us in our feelings. Accordingly, the prerequisite for achieving an understanding of the felt meanings of the world is to clear away the rationalist obstacles and prejudices that prevent us from understanding feelings, and to allow feelings and felt reality to put themselves into their own words and to reveal themselves as they are in themselves. This preparatory task was initiated in a partial fashion in this Introduction and will be completed in Part 1 of this treatise, entitled "Feelings and the World as Felt."

These clarifications shall prepare the way for a detailed examination of the specific nature of the various felt meanings of the world, particularly of the three fundamental meanings: fulfillment, closeness, and supremacy. The explication of the fulfillment of the world will reveal to us the felt meaning of both time and existing; the explication of its closeness will bring to light the intuitively felt ultimate truth; and the understanding of supremacy will point us towards the importance of the human-independent absolute reality. These explications are undertaken in Part 2, "The Basic Felt Meanings of the World."

PART ONE

Feelings and the World as Felt

*T*he nihilism of our current spiritual-historical situation is due to our interpretation of reality in terms of the category of reason and consequence; feelings and everything else in the world are interpreted as reasons or consequences of reasons, and the world itself is interpreted privatively as failing to manifest itself as a consequence of any reason. Nihilism can be overcome if such an interpretation is shown to be false, and is replaced by a true understanding of feelings and the world as felt. This understanding is developed in the three chapters of Part 1.

The first step is to understand the real nature of feeling-sensations and the world as sensuously felt. Each concrete experience of feeling consists of a feeling-sensation and a feeling-awareness, and the correlated world-as-felt consists of a sensuously felt aspect and an important aspect that is apprehended in the feeling-awareness. Although feeling-sensations and the sensuously felt aspects of the world never occur in reality apart from feeling-awarenesses and apprehended importances, they can for purposes of descriptive explication be considered separately. This shall be done in Chapter 1, "Feeling-Sensations and the World as Sensuously Felt."

In the next chapter the other aspects of feeling and the world as felt are considered, the feeling-awarenesses and importances. Each awareness is a feeling-awareness, and each part of the world is an importance. The erroneous idea that some parts of the world are unimportant, and some awarenesses are not feeling-awarenesses, is traced back to a certain degenerate type of feeling that misinterprets itself as a "disinterested act of reasoning." (Cf. Chapter 2, "Feeling-Awarenesses and the World as Important.")

In Chapter 3, I focus exclusively on the importances that belong to the world in its wholeness, and on the global feeling-awarenesses in which these importances are revealed. The moody and affective awarenesses of the world as a whole are described and distinguished from the other feeling-awarenesses that may be thought to be global in nature but really are not, viz., mystical, existential, essential, and natural feeling-awarenesses. (Cf. Chapter 3, "Global Feeling-Awarenesses and Global Importances.")

CHAPTER I

Feeling-Sensations and the World as Sensuously Felt

*T*he first step in achieving an appreciative understanding of the world as felt is to make explicit the metaphysical nature of sensuous feelings. The ultimate point of the present chapter is to show that sensuous feelings are not only feeling-sensations of the I, but are also sensuously felt features of the world, these features being termed "feeling-tonalities." This will contravene the traditional presupposition that sensuous feelings are but "sensations or emotions of the soul which are related especially to it,"[1] as Descartes says, and thus as phenomena related solely to the soul have no global metaphysical significance. I wish to show in particular that some feeling-tonalities have sources in the world as a whole, these sources being global importances.

As culminating my descriptions in this chapter, the discussion of feeling-tonalities occupies the last three sections (I.8-10). This discussion is preceded by preparatory analyses of the feeling-sensations of the I to which the worldly feeling-tonalities are correlated (I.6-7). I begin in I.6 with a critical and historical analysis of the rationalist theory of feeling-sensations that prevented their correlation with feeling-tonalities of the world from being recognized. This historical critique will uncover a further rationalist misinterpretation of feeling not discussed in the Introduction.

In this chapter, sensuous feelings rather than global importances are the phenomena that are being made explicit in significations. This signifies that the appreciative method of knowing discussed in the Introduction is here being directed upon feelings rather than global importances. In this case, the reappreciative afterglows and concentrations are inspired to make explicit the sensuous aspect of the feelings in which the global importances are appreciated.

I will also discuss the sensuous aspect of mundane feelings in this chapter, an aspect that is made explicit in mundane reappreciative feelings, these being afterglowing and concentrating reappreciations that are inspired by important parts of the world or by the feelings in which these world-parts are appreciated.[2]

I. 6. *The External Characterization of Feeling-Sensations as Consequences of Reasons*

An *internal* characterization of a feeling-sensation explicates it solely in terms of determinations found in the feeling-sensation itself. Specifically, the feeling-qualities of pleasure or pain found in the feeling-sensation are allowed to become manifest solely in reference to other feeling-determinations also found in the feeling-sensation and with which the feeling-qualities of pleasure or pain are united. Such an internal characterization allows one to recognize the feeling-tonalities of the world that correlate to the internal determinations of the feeling-sensations.

An *external* characterization of a feeling-sensation defines it as a quality of pleasure or pain that is related to something external to the feeling. An external characterization is *rational* if the external phenomena in reference to which the pleasurable and painful sensations are defined are reasons that explain these sensations, specifically, causal reasons. As so characterized, a feeling-sensation is a pleasurable or painful consequence of a reason, i.e., a pleasurable or painful effect of a cause.

The result of an external and rational characterization of feeling-sensations is that the concept of the world as sensuously felt becomes replaced by a concept of a world of causal reasons to which the feeling-sensations are externally related. By this means, the world we experience as correlating to our feeling-sensations becomes represented as the world *as reasoned about*, and the sensuously felt features of the world that correlate to our feeling-sensations, the feeling-tonalities, are left unrecognized.

The above remarks can be developed and substantiated by presenting a historical analysis and critique of the external and rational ways of characterizing feeling-sensations. The origin of these ways of defining and classifying feeling-sensations can be understood from an examination of the first systematic classification of feelings, which Aristotle developed in Book 2 of *Rhetoric*.

In the second book of the *Rhetoric*, Aristotle is concerned with classifying affective-sensations rather than with other types of feeling-sensations, such as mood-sensations,[3] and in this tendency he is followed by virtually every subsequent author of a "treatise on the passions." Affects (*pathe*) are "movements of the soul" involving pleasure or pain, and as such are distinguished by Aristotle from the pleasurable or painful complements of a function, such as the pleasure associated with seeing.[4] Affects are distinguished from one another primarily by three external factors: 1) the cause of the affect, which is a good or evil phenomenon, 2) the people about whom the affect is felt, and 3) the states of mind that are the mental preconditions of the affect.[5] In regard to the internal nature of the affects, nothing more is said than that they are qualities of pleasure and pain. This is illustrated in Aristotle's definitions of pity and envy. Of pity Aristotle writes: "Pity is definable as a feeling of pain caused by the sight of a destructive or painful evil that happens to a person who does not deserve it."[6] Note that Aristotle's remark that pity is a "feeling of pain," which is the only reference he makes to the internal nature of pity, is insufficient to demarcate the individual essence of pity or to distinguish it from the other affects, for a number of these other affects, such as envy, fear, and shame, also have this very same internal characteristic. Aristotle thus is forced to differentiate pity from these other affects by pointing to differences among the things to which they are related. For example, envy, like pity, is a "pain," but it differs in that: "Envy is a pain caused by the sight of such goods as the aforementioned ones, riches, power, aristocratic birth, etc., and it is felt about people who are our equals."[7] Pity and envy also differ in the predispositions of the people who feel them; pity is felt by elderly or weak men, etc., and envy by small-minded or ambitious men and the like.

These definitions are prototypes of the future definitions of the qualities of feeling-sensations, although the form of these definitions was modified in two ways. Aristotle's emphasis on the external aspects of feeling was retained, but his theory of the three kinds of external phenomena underwent a number of changes. To begin with, his conception of the predisposing state of mind was abandoned. Aristotle's classification was undertaken in the context of a theory of rhetoric, and he wished to describe the predisposing states of mind of the different affects in order that a speaker may recognize and attempt to instill them in his audience. In the subsequent "treatises on the passions" the feelings were examined in other contexts, and the need to investigate their predisposing states of minds was no longer deemed to be of prime significance. Aristotle's distinction between the causes of the affects and the people to whom the affects are related had a more significant influence. It was not adopted as such, but in two modified forms. The first modification, the less popular one, lay in extending the category of the "people" to which affects are related to the larger category of "objects" in general, such that affects are defined as related to *causes* and *objects* rather than *causes* and *people*. The second modification, adopted by most of the subsequent writers on affects, was to extend the category of "people" to that of "objects," and then to identify the objects of the affects with their causes, so that affects are defined as related to only one external phenomenon, the *objective cause*.

The classification of affects in terms of causes and objects received its most famous and influential expression in Book 2 of Hume's *A Treatise of Human Nature*. Pride and love, for example, are described by Hume as types of pleasure that differ in terms of their objects and causes. The object of pride is myself, and its cause is something good which is related to myself; the object of love, on the other hand, is another person, and its cause is a good quality of the person. Hume's classification of affects is of especial significance in that it was the first classification using the cause/object distinction to achieve an explicit insight into the external nature of its principles. Hume's insight into this feature of his classification is expressed in the following passage, in which he indicates that feeling-sensations, exemplified by pride and humility, are "simple" and so cannot be defined. All that can be done is to describe the objects and causes (the "attendant circumstances") to which the feeling-sensations are externally related:

> The passions of PRIDE and HUMILITY being simple and uniform impressions, 'tis impossible we can ever, by a multitude of words, give a just definition of them, or indeed of any of the passions. The utmost we can pretend to is a description of them, by an enumeration of such circumstances, as attend them.[8]

The classification of affects by means of the single concept of their "objective cause" was practiced by most of the stoic, patristic, scholastic, and modern philosophers. The predominance of this method of externally defining feelings is exemplified by the fact that the treatise on passion that most influenced Hume's treatise, Francis Hutcheson's *An Essay on the Nature and Conduct of the Passions and Affections*, and the treatise that was most influenced by Hume's theory, Thomas Reid's theory of passions in the third essay of *Essays on the Active Powers of the Human Mind*, both used the single "causality" principle in their definitions of the passions. Some of the other philosophers who used it are Cicero, Plotinus, Augustine, Aquinas, Descartes, Spinoza, Kant, and Hegel. Among these philosophers, the one who achieved the greatest clarity about this external principle of definition and classification was Spinoza. In Book 3 of *Ethics*, Spinoza distinguished pleasure, pain, and desire as the three basic types of affects (*affectibus*) and proceeded to distinguish their various subtypes by aligning these affects with different causes. The nature of his external definitions may be gleaned from two examples: "Love is pleasure accompanied by the idea of an external cause [*idea causae externae*]."[9] "Pleasure, accompanied by the idea of an internal cause [*idea causae internae*] is named honour."[10]

It can be gathered from these two definitions that Spinoza's principle of external definition and classification is none other than one of the traditional principles of causality. The principle that where there is a difference in the cause, there will be a difference in the effect, entails that "there are as many species of pleasure, pain and desire . . . as there are species of objects that affect us."[11] Spinoza explains this further in a passage which explicitly states the principle which has been used — mostly in an implicit manner — in a majority of the traditional classifications of affects:

> . . . the pleasure which is an effect, for example, of the object A involves the nature of that object A, and the pleasure which is an effect of the object B involves the nature of that object B, such that these two pleasurable affects [*affectûs*] are by nature different inasmuch as the causes from which they originate are different.[12]

Since the affective sensations of pleasure and pain are defined and differentiated in reference to their external causal reasons, it follows that the world as affectively experienced is to be defined accordingly, viz., as a world of causal reasons. The sensuously felt features of the world that are correlated with the internal differentiations of the feeling-sensations are unrecognized because these internal differentiations are themselves unrecognized. The world as causally reasoned about becomes substituted for the world as sensuously felt, and the global-metaphysical nature of sensuous feeling remains hidden from view.

This external and rational theory of feeling-sensations predominated in the epoch of rational meaning that extended from Plato to Hegel, but was expounded with less frequency in the subsequent epoch of rational meaninglessness. This is due to several factors, one being that in the middle and late nineteenth century, attention began to be turned toward the physiological disturbances accompanying feeling-sensations. In the nineteenth century, with the works on emotion by William James and Carl Lange, attention was turned towards visceral physiological disturbances; in the twentieth century, following the publication of Walter Cannon's *Bodily Changes in Pain, Hunger, Fear and Rage* (1916), attention was predominantly directed towards cortical events. Such thinkers showed less concern with classifying types of feeling-sensations than with classifying the types of their accompanying visceral or cortical physiological occurrences. Feeling-sensations themselves were differentiated in terms of these disturbances, e.g., a recent proponent of the peripheral or "visceral" theory, M. A. Wenger, writes that we "distinguish between emotion per se only insofar as we can differentiate patterns of visceral change."[13] Insofar as the traditional "causal reasons" of the feeling-sensations are discussed in these theories, they are conceived as "external stimuli" of the physiological disturbances.

A second basis for the declining preponderance of the external-rational classifications of feeling-sensations is that a second major group of thinkers who were interested in feelings, the phenomenologists, were less interested in classifying feeling-sensations than in studying "feelings" in the sense of the acts of awareness that accompanied feeling-sensations. Many of these thinkers, like Franz Brentano, Alexius Meinong, Max Scheler,

Dietrich von Hildebrand, and others, were concerned to describe the "feeling-acts" or "intentional feelings" of ethical and aesthetic values, whereas others were concerned with feeling awarenesses in a nonaxiological context, e.g., Sartre was interested in the emotional "consciousnesses" of magically pursued purposes, and Heidegger in the moody "disclosedness" of *Dasein*'s thrownness into the world. In the few cases where feeling-sensations were mentioned, e.g., in Brentano's reference to "sensuous pleasures and displeasures" in *The Origin of Ethical Knowledge*,[14] Scheler's discussion of "feeling-states" (*Gefuhlszustande*) in *Formalism in Ethics and the Material Ethics of Value*,[15] Sartre's theory of "coenesthesia" in *Being and Nothingness*,[16] and Frederik Buytendijk's mention of "emotional sensations" in "The Phenomenological Approach to the Problem of Feelings and Emotions,"[17] feeling-sensations are described in their qualitative aspect as pleasures and pains, without further internal typological determinations being mentioned. And in the few instances where they are typologically differentiated from one another, they are differentiated externally and rationally; e.g., Scheler differentiates feeling-states in terms of their different "causal objects" (understood phenomenologically); each bodily feeling-state, for instance, is distinguishable as "a state that corresponds to the agreeableness of a food, a scent, or a gentle touch, etc."[18] "Agreeableness" is understood here as a value-property that belongs to the causal object (the food, etc.) of the feeling-state.

Other approaches to feeling besides the physiological and phenomenological ones shared this general disinterest in feeling-sensations. Gestaltists were concerned with the *forms of conduct* exhibited in affects, psychoanalysts with their *unconscious motivations*, ordinary language philosophers with the *words* we use to express or refer to feeling-sensations, to name a few of these other approaches.

This systematic neglect of feeling-sensations and a concern with other phenomena that are associated with feeling-sensations reflected in different ways the traditional view that feeling-sensations cannot be studied *in themselves*, in an internal fashion, and that a theory of feeling must occupy itself with external phenomena that are correlated in some way with feeling-sensations. However, if the presupposition that feeling-sensations have no internal typological determinations apart from their pleasurable and painful qualities had been questioned, a further internal and typological character of feeling-sensations could have been found, their character of *flowing in a certain direction and manner*. The discovery of these feeling-flows could have led in turn to the recognition that there are sensuous features of the world correlating to these flowing feeling-sensations, such that the world has a sensuously felt reality of flowing in a certain direction and manner. And the discovery of these sensuous world-flows could have led in its turn to the further discovery of the *sources* of the world-flows, the world-importances or felt meanings from which the flows emanate. The world *as felt* could therein have revealed itself, not as a world of "causal reasons" in the traditional sense of good or evil objects, or a world of physical "stimuli," or of phenomenological "causal objects" to which values attach, but as a world of *important sources of feeling-flows*. On this basis a metaphysics of feeling could have been developed, a metaphysics based on the insight that the world can and does have meanings other than reasons, meanings that come to appearance *as* the sources of sensuous feeling-flows.

Such in outline is the course of the descriptive explications to be followed in this chapter and the next two chapters. These explications must begin with the first and crucial descriptive demonstration that every further description is dependent upon — the demonstration that feeling-sensations do have a complex internal nature that is describable in terms of the category of feeling-flow.

I. 7. *The Internal Characterization of Feeling-Sensations as Qualitative-Flows*

Feeling-sensations are the sensuous feelings adhering to the I; they appear in the marginal or attentional reflexion that "I feel," or more fully, "I sensuously feel." The first step in elucidating the feeling-sensations of the I is to say a few words about this "I that sensuously feels."

The I that feels is not itself a sensuous phenomenon. But this does not mean that it is a concept or an act of awareness. It is to be observed, first of all, that the I that appears in the "I feel" does not appear as a concept or idea *of* something; specifically, it does not appear as an I-concept that would be something different from an I of which it is a concept. Instead, the I appears as a "something" itself, i.e., as a "something" of which a concept can be formed, but which is not itself a concept. It is a nonsensory "something" (or rather "somebody") that appears immediately in reflexive awarenesses. It is to be observed secondly that this "somebody" is not an "awareness of" something; rather, it is that which is aware of things. "Awarenesses of" are features of the I.

Feeling-sensations are also features of the I, but they are not "awarenesses of." Instead, feeling-sensations are some of the phenomena of which the I is aware. The I's awareness of its feeling-sensations is what is expressed by the phrase "I sensuously feel."

An elucidation of the "I that feels" can be achieved by a brief contrast of this "I" with the "empirical ego" conceived by Sartre. For Sartre, the "ego is nothing outside of the concrete totality [*totalité concrète*] of the states and actions it supports."[19] The ego is not a "one and many," a "one" that has "many" states and actions, but is the "many" states and actions themselves. In this vein Sartre writes about the ego and its qualities (which are the substrates and potentialities of its states and actions):

> . . . we do not finally know the ego as a pure creative source [*une source créatrice pure*] besides the qualities. It does not appear to us that we could find a skeletal pole [*un pole squelettique*] if we removed one after the other all the qualities. . . . at the end of this plundering, there would remain nothing, the ego would have vanished.[20]

As a description of the phenomenon of the ego that appears to us in our reflexive awarenesses, this does not seem to be accurate. Sartre mentions "love" as an example of a state of the ego. When there is an awareness that "I love Jane," the "I" that loves is not given, as Sartre would have it, as an "infinite totality of states and actions." "I love Jane" does not appear in the phenomenal form of "an infinite totality of states and actions loves Janes." Sartre articulates this awareness as a fulfilled intuition of the love as the present state of the infinite totality of states and actions, and as an empty consciousness of the infinity of past and future states and actions.[21] But the "I" that loves is not reducible to the love *qua* present state of the infinite totality of states and actions. If it were so reducible, there would not be the phenomenon of an "I" that loves, but only the phenomenon of the love and the other states and actions with which the love is synthesized. "I love" would then mean no more than that "there is a love that is synthesized with an infinite totality of other states and actions." But surely it is intuitively felt to be evident that *I* love. It is true that the love belongs to the totality of states and actions, but this totality, like the love itself, is given as belonging to the I. It is *my* totality of states and actions, not *your* totality or *his* totality. The "I" that is given in reflexive intuitive feeling is a unique and unitary "somebody" who, although related to his states and actions, is not reducible to them.

Much more could be said about this "I that feels," but at present I wish to mention only one further point, a point I will endeavor to establish in Chapter 6, that an "I" which is irreducible to its experiences is not by that fact a transcendental-constitutive ego. The "I that feels" is the personal unity of experiences, the single person who has the many experiences and who is not constituted by these experiences (and thus is not an empirical ego), but who nevertheless is not constitutive of the world he experiences (and thus is not a transcendental-constitutive ego). The "I that feels" is rather a *part* of the world he experiences, an *appreciative part*.[22]

With this last remark we can terminate our preliminary descriptions of the "I that feels" and commence our descriptions of the feeling-sensations felt by this "I." We can begin by comparing these feeling-sensations with the so-called "visceral physiological disturbances" that occur during our feelings, e.g., the muscular contractions and distensions that occur in the stomach, chest, face and throat, the blushing, and the increase of bodily

temperature. According to James, feelings *are* these physiological disturbances, insofar as these disturbances are observed by us:

> *Every one of the bodily changes, whatsoever it be, is FELT, acutely or ob-*
> *scurely, the moment it occurs.* If the reader has never paid attention to this
> matter, he will be both interested and astonished to learn how many dif-
> ferent local bodily feelings he can detect in himself as characteristic of his
> various emotional moods. . . . Our whole cubic capacity is sensibly alive;
> and each morsel of it contributes its pulsations of feeling, dim or sharp,
> pleasant, painful, or dubious, to that sense of personality that every one
> of us unfailingly carries with him. It is surprising what little items give accent
> to these complexes of sensibility. When worried by any slight trouble, one
> may find that the focus of one's bodily consciousness is the contraction, often
> quite inconsiderable, of the eyes and brows. When momentarily embarrassed,
> it is something in the pharynx that compels either a swallow, a clearing of
> the throat, or a slight cough; and so on for as many more instances as might
> be named.[23]

James is here confusing biological and anatomical categories with
categories of feeling. It is true, as he points out, that a "bodily consciousness" is experienced in our feelings. But the body does not appear
in this consciousness *as* a "biological body" consisting of muscular contractions and resolutions, obstructions in the pharynx, and so on. For example, the muscular contractions in the eyes and brows do not appear *as*
muscular contractions in the eyes and brows. A "contraction of the eyes
and brows" is an affectively neutral category; it describes this bodily occurrence not *as* it appears to a worried person but *as* it would appear to
a biologist or anatomist observing the changes in his body and catalogu-
ing them in terms of scientific categories. A conceptualization of this "contraction" as it appears to the worried person must employ categories proper
to feeling-sensations manifested in a prescientific "I feel."

Such categories include, first of all, the traditionally recognized category of the *quality* of feeling, the *pleasurable* and *painful* qualities and
their subtypes, as pleasure divides into pride-pleasure, joy-pleasure, love-
pleasure, etc., and pain into fear-pain, humiliation-pain, anger-pain, etc.
Besides the qualitative category there are the *nonqualitative categories.*
These include categories of several *nontypological characters* of feeling,
characters which do not vary with each variation in the qualitative type
of feeling, as well as one *typological character* of feeling, a character that
does vary in correspondence with the qualitative types of feeling. The nontypological characters of feeling-sensation are inessential characters, as they
are not determinative of the individual types of feeling and thus do not
enter into the internal definition of each type of feeling. Because of their
inessentiality, I will not discuss them here, but will briefly explicate them
in Section 9 of this chapter. The one typological character of feeling-
sensations besides their qualitative character is, like the qualitative char-

acter, an essential feature of feeling-sensations, since it is determinative of and enters (along with the qualitative character) into the internal definition of each type of feeling-sensation. This nonqualitative typological character is the *flow* of the feeling-sensation, which can be formally elucidated in the following way.

Each qualitative sensation of pleasure or pain *flows in a certain direction and manner*. The *direction* of the flow can have one of several modes, it can be an upwards flow, or a downwards, forwards, or backwards one, or it can be some combination of these, such as backwards and downwards. The directionality of the flow can also be experienced in certain privative or negative ways, as a feeling can be "suspended" before a downward flow. The direction of the flow is always characterized by a certain *manner* in which the feeling flows in that direction. The manner could be one of radiating, cringing, sinking, plummeting, etc. Each specific quality of pleasure or pain has its own distinctive feeling-flow; the feeling-flow of fear-pain is different than the feeling-flow of humiliation-pain, and so on for the other qualities of feeling.

Before some of the specific qualitative-flows are described, I should point out what may already be obvious to many, namely that the terms being used to describe the direction and manner of the feeling-flow are being employed in a metaphorical way. The word "upward," for instance, is not being used to refer literally to a spatial direction, but metaphorically to suggest a character of feeling that in some respects is analogous to an upward spatial direction. The metaphorical language of feeling-flows is evoked by the reappreciated feeling-sensations themselves, and captures these feeling-sensations as they actually were experienced. In this language, feeling-sensations *put themselves into words*, and the metaphorical words they evoke are such that they *cannot* be "translated" into literal statements that are their equivalents. The connection between feeling and metaphor is further discussed in later sections, and no more need be said for the present.

In the following, I describe the feeling-flows of the sensations of pride, humiliation, anger, love, hilarity, fear, anxiety, sadness, and some bodily feelings like fatigue and tactile pain.

The direction in which the feeling-sensation of pride flows is *upwards*. It flows upwards in the manner of an *inflated rising*. In reference to pride it is said that one's ego is "inflated"; with regard to the feeling-flow of pride this designates the sensation of rising upwards in an inflated manner. This sensation of rising provides a determinate reference to the phrase that one feels "puffed up" in pride, and that in intense pride one's self-esteem "shoots sky high."

The direction in which the feeling-sensation of humiliation flows is *downwards*. It flows downwards in a *plummeting* manner. The downward flow of humiliation is not the slow, sagging flow of sadness, but the quick and violent emotional "drop" that occurs when one's self-esteem has received a sudden blow. One plummets downwards in humiliation, and one continues to plummet downwards in this violent and painful way as long as one is feeling the sensation of humiliation.

The feeling-sensation of angry retaliation is different from the initial "outrage" one feels when first affronted; angry retaliation is an angry "striking back" at something or somebody, and as such flows *forwards*, towards the person or thing at which one is angry. It flows forwards in a *violently attacking* manner. In this respect, the feeling-flow of retaliatory anger differs from the feeling-flow of love, which also has a forwards direction, for in love I experience a sensation of flowing forwards in a manner that *gently binds me together* with the other person or thing.

The feeling-sensation of hilarity is present in hilarious laughter. The flow of this feeling-sensation is *upwards*, and it flows upwards in a manner of *quick, staccato surges*. Hilarious laughter is not the polite social laughter that one engages in voluntarily, but the genuine laughter that one is affected by and that one has no control over. In this laughter, one's feeling springs upwards in quick, discontinuous surges. This feeling-flow constitutes the feeling of "shaking with laughter." The vocal expressions of laughter—the "Ha! Ha! Ha!"—are expressions of the staccato surges of feeling that are uttered in the same rhythmic pattern as the staccato surges themselves. However these vocal expressions are not necessary to this feeling-flow, as it is possible to laugh silently.

The distinction between fear and anxiety is the most widely discussed distinction between types of feelings made in this century. It has been discussed by Sigmund Freud, Heidegger, Ludwig Binswanger, Paul Tillich, Sartre, Karen Horney, Rollo May, and a number of others, but in these discussions only differences between fear and anxiety *other than* the differences between their feeling-sensations were mentioned. The feeling-sensations of fear and anxiety are both painful in their quality, but these pain-qualities flow in different directions and manners.

The flow of the feeling-sensation of fear is *backwards*; it has the directional sense of retreating backwards and away from the existent that is threatening me. It flows backwards in a *shrinking* and *cringing* manner; I have the sensation of "shrinking and cringing back from" the threatening existent.

But anxiety is not felt as a "retreat from"; it does not flow backwards but has the directional sense of being *suspended over an inner bottomlessness*. In fear my ego is felt to have a bottom to it, and the backward direction of the feeling-flow manifests a feeling of security in this respect. But in anxiety my ego is felt to have no foundation; the directional sense of the flow consists solely in the precarious "being suspended" over the abyss of my ego. The onrush of anxiety is identical with the sudden crumbling of the secure foundation my ego had been felt to be resting upon. The more intense the anxiety, the further down this inner void is felt to go. There is always the feeling that I am about to fall helplessly down this void, and become extinguished as a self, but I never do; anxiety is only the precarious feeling that it is imminently possible for me to fall into the abyss. This sensation of being suspended over an inner bottomlessness is in the strict sense not a direction in which the anxiety is flowing. Rather than flow in a direction, anxiety is a flow that is suspended before the possibility of flowing in a downward direction.

The feeling-flow of anxieties that are less intense have a different directional sense. The anxiety of a low degree, the feeling of *nervousness*, does not manifest a sensation of bottomlessness, but only of the coming-into-question of the foundation of my ego. What is felt as imminently possible is not my falling down an inner void, but the very opening up of this void. My ego is still felt to rest on a foundation, but this foundation is under stress and strain, and it is felt as possible that this foundation may give way.

The manner in which the suspended flow of anxiety flows is also different from the manner in which fear flows. Anxiety is suspended in a *quavering* manner. Anxiety is a feeling of quavering and quivering over the bottomless void that has opened up in my ego. This is what we refer to when we say that in anxiety "we are coming apart at the seams"; in anxiety we can no longer "hold ourselves together." We cannot "get a grip on ourselves," but are helplessly quavering over the abyss.

The feeling-sensations so far described immediately adhere to the "I that feels." Other feeling-sensations present themselves as immediately adhering to the whole of my body, and as only mediately adhering to the I. Such feeling-sensations are fatigue, vigor, feverishness, drunkenness, and so on. The difference between these two kinds of feeling-sensations appears in our linguistic expressions. We say "I am inflated with pride" but not "my body is inflated with pride," thus expressing the fact that the feeling-sensation of pride immediately adheres to the I and not to my body. On the other hand, we say "my body is tired," expressing that the feeling-sensation of tiredness immediately adheres to my bodily-whole, and by virtue of this body being *my* body, mediately adheres to my I (and thus we also say "I am tired").

I will describe one such feeling-sensation, tiredness or fatigue. The feeling-flow of fatigue permeates my whole body; it flows *downwards* in a *dragging* manner. As such, it is similar to the feeling-flow of sadness, which flows downwards in a sinking and sagging manner. But they differ in several respects; one difference is that the feeling-sensation of fatigue flows through my body as a whole, whereas the feeling-sensation of sadness does not. Another is that the flow of fatigue appears to "drag down" the ego from below, while the flow of sadness appears as a "sinking down" of the ego under its own weight. In fatigue, the body "weighs down" the ego, but in sadness, the ego "sags down" under its own weight.

It should not go unnoticed that some of the feeling-sensations which mediately adhere to the I immediately adhere to one part of the body rather than to the bodily-whole. Such are the gustatory, olfactory, and localized tactile feeling-sensations. Feeling-flows are also exhibited in these feelings, e.g., a feeling-flow can be felt in my leg as a painful *wincing back and away* from something that is cutting me.

We are in a position now to draw some conclusions about the nature of the "I's" immediate and mediate feeling-sensations. First, the relation between the flow of feeling-sensations and physiological disturbances can be exactly determined. Negatively speaking, it is clear that metaphorical statements about the flow of feeling-sensations are not translatable into literal statements about physiological disturbances in the body. The statement that in retaliatory anger "I feel a sensation of flowing forwards in a violently attacking manner" is not literally understandable as the statement that "I feel a muscular hypertension in my chest and throat, an increase in bodily temperature, and blood rushing to my face." These statements do not have the same referents, one of the statements referring to an item in a literal way and the other statement referring to the same item in a metaphorical way; they refer to two different items. For the feeling-flow *is not* the physiological disturbances. But the feeling-flow and the disturbances are integrally connected. The feeling-flows are sensuous appearances *presented to* the "I that feels" by the physiological disturbances. These appearances neither are the physiological disturbances that present them, nor are appearances wherein the physiological disturbances appear *as* physiological disturbances. Rather, they are appearances wherein the physiological disturbances appear *as* qualitative feeling-sensations flowing in a certain direction and manner. While the physiological disturbances can be described in the literal language of biology and anatomy, the sensuous appearances they present are describable only in the literal language of feeling-qualities and in the metaphorical language of feeling-flows.

These qualitative feeling-flows essentially constitute the complex internal nature of feeling-sensations. It is through describing them that we are able to formulate the "just definitions" of the feeling-sensations that Hume declared to be impossible. It is true, as Hume pointed out, that the *qualities* of feeling-sensations are simple phenomena, and that a description of them alone is insufficient to distinguish one feeling-sensation from another. Both fear and humiliation, qualitatively described, are *pains*, and thus cannot be descriptively differentiated from one another on that basis. However, rather than differentiate them externally, by describing the external things to which these pain-qualities are related, it is possible to differentiate them internally by describing other internal determinations of the feeling-sensations with which these pain-qualities are united. The pain-quality of fear is internally united with a feeling-flow that *flows backwards in a cringing manner*, and the pain-quality of humiliation is internally united with a feeling-flow that *flows downwards in a plummeting manner*.

It is true that in describing these feeling-flows it is sometimes helpful to refer to some external existent to which they are related. Angry retaliation is describable as a flowing towards the person at whom one is angry, and fear is describable as a cringing backwards from the existent that is threatening one. But these external references are neither necessary to nor part of the internal characterization of these feeling-sensations. Strictly speaking, the internal nature of retaliatory anger is characterized as a *painful sensation of flowing forwards in a violently attacking manner*, and the internal nature of fear as a *painful sensation of flowing backwards in a cringing manner*.

The metaphysical implications of these internal characterizations of feeling-sensations shall be developed in the next three sections. We shall see that these characterizations enable us to recognize and typify the different sensuously felt features of the world (in Sections 8-9) and that this in turn enables us to comprehend that sensuous feelings of the world have sources in the world, these sources being the felt meanings or importances of the world (cf. Section 10).

I. 8. *Feeling-Tonalities of the World*

The next step in the development of the understanding of sensuous feelings and of the world as sensuously felt is to show that the qualitative-flows of the I's feeling-sensations are correlated with qualitative-flows that permeate the world. These latter qualitative-flows are constitutive of feeling-tonalities. It is in the internal structure of these feeling-tonalities that the world is sensuously felt. These feeling-tonalities are not felt by the world but by the I; nevertheless, unlike feeling-sensations, they are not felt to be features of the I but of the world. They appear to be relational features of the world, features the world possesses through being felt by the I. The world is imbued with feeling-tonalities when it is being apprehended by an I that feels, and the world has its tonal-features only insofar as and as long as it is being apprehended by this feeling I. It is not the case that feeling-tonalities seem to be features the world possesses independently of the I, and really are not such features; it is the case rather that feeling-tonalities seem to be features possessed by the world dependently upon and in relation to the I, and really are such features. This will become evident, I believe, as descriptions of these tonalities are developed in the following.

It is instructive to note by way of an introductory remark that although the flowing feeling-tonalities have not been described in philosophical or psychological studies of feeling, they have been portrayed in literature and the arts: orchestral music and painting, especially the musical compositions of Ludwig van Beethoven and the paintings of Vincent van Gogh, contain many auditory and visual depictions of flowing tonalities. I will offer some examples of these depictions below, after I have first articulated some of the general characteristics of these tonal-flows in philosophical categories.

The nature of the feeling-flow that belongs to feeling-tonalities can be initially explicated by contrasting it with "flowing" aspects of the world in the usual sense of this term, as when we speak of the "flowing" of water or air. In this ordinary sense of the word, what we have in mind is a natural flow. A natural flow has three characteristics whereby it differs from a tonal-flow. The first of these characteristics is that the natural existent which is flowing is constantly changing its position in space. Secondly, the natural flow is not a sensuous aspect of the existent that is flowing, but a synthetic interrelation of the different spatial positions that the existent assumes through time. The consciousness of the existent's present spatial position in connection with the consciousness of its immediately past and immediately expected spatial positions constitutes the awareness of the existent's "flow" through space. Thirdly, the flowing of the existent does not involve the whole of the thing, but only its boundaries. The existent's flow is nothing other than the steady changing of the boundary relations between the flowing existent and the existents it is flowing past.

Now a feeling-flow that belongs to a feeling-tonality differs from a natural flow in that it has none of these three characteristics. This is illustrated most clearly in the feeling-flows of the perceptual feeling-tonalities. The perceptual feeling-tonalities that "flow" do not change their position in space; rather, they are feeling-tensions that animate and vitalize the perceptual existents they permeate. They enliven these existents with an emotional energy and "bring them to life" with feeling. This emotional energy does not move from one existent to the next, but remains in the same existents, animating continually the same spatial regions. And unlike the natural flow, this flow of feeling-tension is not a temporal connection of the different spatial positions of an existent it is enlivening. Instead, it appears as a sensuous character of the existent, and it appears as such to each perception of the existent, without needing to be "constructed" out of the succession of the existent's appearances. Furthermore, this tensional flow does not involve only the boundaries of the existent; it animates the entirety of the existent, the bounded areas of the existent as well as its boundaries. And since the existents in the background can be animated with the very same feeling-flow, the foreground existent does not necessarily appear in its flowing as something that is in contrast with its background.

If the feeling-flow of tonalities could not be described further than this—as a nonnatural flow of feeling-tension—it would be impossible to differentiate the different types of tonal-flows that correlate to the different types of sensational-flows. However, the tonal-flow does admit of a further description; like the sensational-flows, the tonal-flows have a direction and manner in which they flow. In fact, this direction and manner of the tonal-flows is so essential to them that it is through flowing in a direction and manner that *corresponds* to the direction and manner of a coexperienced sensational-flow that the feeling-tonalities are recognizable in the first place as typological *sensuous feelings that adhere to the world*. I recognize that typological sensuous feelings adhere to the world because I apprehend phenomena in the world—qualities flowing in a direction and manner—that exactly correlate in their structure to the typological sensuous feelings that are adhering to my "I."

In the following, I will exhibit by way of illustration the tonal-sensation correspondences that obtain in the feelings of joy, sadness, fear, repugnance, and love.

The feeling-sensation of joy flows *upwards* in a *radiated* manner. In joy, I feel uplifted and elevated, as if I were "on top of the world" or "on cloud nine." The expression that in joy "we feel in high spirits" and that "we are radiant or beaming with joy" captures the direction and manner of this sensational-flow. This feeling-sensation is experienced as correlating with a similar feeling-tonality that imbues things in my environmental surroundings. The things around me seem to be infected with a joyousness that springs out of them and gives them an "uplifted" momentum. In a joyful perception of a landscape, the trees and pond appear to be radiated upwards with this joyous vitality; the pond appears to be shimmering upwards, the trees appear to be almost springing out of the ground with a joyful momentum, and the branches seem to be reaching towards the heavens. Everything in my view is expanding and leaning upwards, radiating from itself a joyous energy. This joyful radiation has been effectively portrayed by Van Gogh in some of his paintings, particularly in *The Orchard*, and musically in the first, third, and fourth movements of Beethoven's Seventh Symphony and the last movement of his Ninth Symphony.

The feeling-sensation of sadness flows *downwards*, in a *sinking* manner. In sadness, I feel downcast, in low spirits. Likewise, the things in the world appear to be forlornly sinking and sagging downwards; a sad and gloomy landscape is one wherein everything appears to be sadly drooping to the ground. The branches of the trees are permeated with a sadness that makes them appear to be listlessly drooping downwards, and the sky is infected with a sadness that makes it seem to be a vast canopy sagging downwards towards the earth. Van Gogh has captured this sad drooping of existents in a number of his paintings, such as *The Church at Auvers* and the *Quay at Antwerp*. The auditory feeling-flow of sadness has been expressed in the slow and melancholic movements of a wide range of works, e.g., the sounds in the slow movement of Beethoven's Hammerklavier Sonata are thoroughly infected with the sagging and downward sinking flow of sadness.

The sensuous feelings of joy and sadness are similar in that the directions and manners of their sensational and tonal flows correspond to each other in a *parallel* rather than *reverse* fashion. The sensational and tonal flows of joy both flow upward in a radiated manner, and the sensational and tonal flows of sadness both flow downwards in a sinking manner. The direction and manner of other sensational and tonal flows, however, correspond to one another in a reverse fashion, as is exemplified in fear, repugnance, and awe.

The feeling-sensation of fear, we know, flows *backwards* in a *cringing* manner. But the feeling-tonality that imbues the worldly existent does not flow backwards in a cringing manner, but *forwards*, towards me, in a *looming and menacing* manner. The existent I fear seems to loom towards me menacingly, as I cringe and shrink from it in fear. The animal or person of whom I am afraid seems larger than life, he seems to dominate my spatial field, and to be encroaching upon my vital space in a threatening way. The closest Van Gogh came to painting a fearful feeling-flow is in his *Cornfield with Crows*. A more exact depiction of this tonal-flow can be found in some expressionist paintings, particularly in Franz Marc's *Tigers*. Musically, it is most clearly expressed in certain passages of Béla Bartok's *Concerto for Orchestra* and *Music for Strings, Percussion and Celeste*.

The feeling-sensation of repugnance flows *backwards*, away from the disgusting existent, and it flows backwards in a *repelled* manner. The feeling-tonality of repugnance has a reverse flow; it flows *forwards*, towards me, and it flows forwards not in a repelled manner but in a *repelling* manner. A repugnant thing is one that affectively repels me; it seems to be flowing *at* me with an emotional energy that thrusts me away from itself. When I encounter a disgusting existent, such as a pool of vomit that suddenly greets me as I open a restroom door, I feel repelled by it. The revolting pool of vomit seems to be discharging a feeling-flow that obtrudes upon me and thrusts itself into my awareness in an unpleasant manner. The feeling-tonality of the repugnant vomit has an offensive flow that pushes me back, so that, if I want to examine the vomit more closely,

I have to make an *effort* to bring myself closer and look at it, instead of instinctively backing away from it and turning my head. It is an aim of a contemporary painter, Francis Bacon, to endow many of his paintings with such a repugnant feeling-flow, although he aims to make the repugnant effect more subtle, and thus more quietly disturbing, as in his *Study of George Dyer* (1971). Karlheinz Stockhausen introduces a repugnant auditory-flow in some of his works, e.g., in certain passages in *Contact* and *Kommunion*, although most of his sounds express the tonal-flow of the uncanny and dreadfully strange.

The sensational-tonal correspondence in the feeling-flow of awe is more complicated, in that it involves all four flow-directions. The feeling-sensation of awe flows *backwards and downwards* in a *shuddering* manner. In its feeling-tonality, the awesome existent is felt to be flowing *forwards and upwards*, and to be flowing in the manner of *towering above me and swelling over and dwarfing me*, rendering me diminutive and insignificant. This tonality is visually depicted in some of John Turner's paintings, e.g., his *Snowstorm: Hannibal and His Army Crossing the Alps*, and auditorily in Anton Bruckner's symphonies and in the first two symphonies of Jean Sibelius.

It is not to be thought that all forward or backward feeling-flows exhibit a reverse correspondence. Some, like love, have a parallel correspondence. The direction of the sensational-flow of love is *forwards*, towards the loved existent, and it flows forwards in a *gently binding* manner. The forward flow of love is a mild and soft diffusion that gently spreads towards the other and attaches me to the other. As endowed with a loving feeling-tonality, the thing I love is also felt to flow *forwards*, towards me in a *gently binding* manner. The sensational-tonal flow of love is thus an intertwining flow. During this feeling, there is no longer a felt "gap" between myself and the other, but a "bridge of loving feeling" that links us together. The visual appearance of this flow is depicted in Rembrandt van Rijn's *Return of the Prodigal Son*, to give one example, and auditorily it appears quite distinctively in the Romance of Wolfgang Mozart's Piano Concerto No. 20.

Besides its visual and auditory forms, the tonal-flow also appears in gustatory, olfactory, and tactile guises. One such instance can be mentioned, that of a painful tactile flow. When a sharp object is painfully cutting me, I experience a feeling-sensation of *wincing back and away* from the object, and in correlation with this sensational-flow the sharp object is felt to have a tonal-flow of flowing *forwards*, towards and into me in a *piercing* manner.

Tonal-flows are no less present in images and signs that I apprehend in imaginative and signitive awarenesses than they are in the perceived things I apprehend in perceiving awarenesses. I can imagine a sadly drooping and sagging landscape no less than I can perceive one. In my use of words there also can be found an inflectional feeling-flow: if I talk in a sad and depressed tone of voice, my words will sound sad and downcast; they are inflected with a downward sagging flow. The words I read, write and use in thinking have a less noticeable feeling-flow, but a flow is nevertheless present. If I am reading a poem that makes me joyful, the words on the page marginally appear to me to be tinged with the vibrant and radiant tonal-flow of joy.

These descriptions of tonal-flows lead us to conclude that the rational-metaphysical tradition is in error in believing that sensuous feelings are features only of the self and not of the world. A feeling, said Kant, is but a "subjective sensation"[24] (*subjektive Empfindung*), echoing the view espoused since Aristotle that *pathe* are merely "movements of the soul,"[25] or, in Cicero's more telling language, *perturbationes*[26] that take place in the rational soul's "lower half." In opposition to this rational-metaphysical tradition, it must be asserted that every feeling-sensation of the "I" is experienced as corresponding to a feeling-tonality of the world, such that through my feeling-sensations I am connected to a sensuously felt reality of the world. This world is not a world of causal reasons but a world that tonally flows in a certain direction and manner. By virtue of these correlated tonal and sensational flows, the world and I are joined together in an extrarational and sensuously appreciative way.

This conception of the tonally flowing world can be placed in a broader perspective, and my criticisms of other theories of sensuous feelings can be stated in a more refined way, if the explication of sensuous feelings is extended to uncover a series of internal determinations in addition to the quality and flow determinations.

I. 9. *The Nontypological Internal Characteristics of Sensuous Feelings*

The internal characteristics of sensuous feelings besides the qualities and flows are inessential characteristics in that they are not determinative of the individual types of sensuous feeling and thus do not enter into the internal definitions of these types. Because of this they are called "nontypological characters" of sensuous feeling. For this consideration, and for another consideration I shall mention below, they are not of central interest to a metaphysics of feeling. However, a short description of some of these nontypological characters, and an indication of the extent to which they have been noticed by philosophers and psychologists, will enable me to specify both the metaphysical significance of the qualitative-flows and the precise respects in which other theories of sensuous feelings are inadequate.

One nontypological character of sensuous feelings is their *intensity*. Although tonal-intensities have been overlooked, thinkers since Plato[27] have often noticed that feeling-sensations display a greater or lesser degree of intensity. They have also correctly but tacitly realized that a description of feeling-intensities is inadequate to define and classify the individual types of feeling-sensation. This is because feeling-intensities admit only of a relative and twofold distinction between *high* feeling-intensities and *low* feeling-intensities, and such a distinction is obviously insufficient for purposes of distinguishing among all the individual types of feeling-sensations. This recognition is expressed in an implicit manner in Hume's theory, wherein feeling-sensations are divided into the "calm" and the "violent"[28] but are nevertheless indicated to be indefinable in a "just" way in terms of this and the qualitative divisions alone. The most ambitious attempt to typify feeling-sensations in terms of feeling-intensities was made by Wilhelm Wundt,[29] who endeavored to distinguish the characters of tension/relaxation from excitement/depression, and to associate these feeling-characters with specific physiological occurrences, an attempt, however, that was shortly and appropriately shown to be unsuccessful.[30]

Feeling-intensities are similar to feeling-qualities in that they are describable in a literal way; the phrase "a feeling of great intensity" is no more metaphorical than the phrase "a feeling of pain." Other non-typological feeling-characters, however, are similar to feeling-flows in that they are describable only in untranslatable metaphorical terms. Three examples of these characters are *feeling-colors, feeling-weights*, and *feeling-temperatures*.

Feeling-colors are nontypological characters of feeling that are referred to metaphorically by color words. These are not simply ways of talking about feelings, such that these color words "actually have no referents" when they are used to refer to feelings. Nor are feeling-colors simply "associations" between feeling-qualities and natural colors, such that, for instance, the feeling-quality of sadness "makes me think of the color blue." Rather they are felt characters of feeling-sensations and feeling-tonalities. In sadness, *I feel blue*. This does not mean that I visualize the color blue while I am sad, nor that I somehow sense this color in the sad feeling. Rather, I feel, as an aspect of my feeling-sensation and feeling-tonality, a feeling-character that is analogous to the color blue. There is a feeling-character of the sadness to which no word literally corresponds, but which can best be described as the analogue in the realm of feelings to what blueness is in the realm of colors. Some other qualities of feeling also possess their own feeling-colors. They are usually referred to by certain stock phrases. In anger, *I see red*. In joy, everything about me seems to be bathed in a *rosy gleam*. Envy is fused with a feeling-green; *I feel green with envy*. To feel cowardly is to *feel yellow*. In boredom, everything seems *gray*.

However, feeling-colors do not vary with every feeling-quality. Not every distinct feeling-quality is fused with a distinct feeling-color. What, for example, are the feeling-colors that are fused with pride, humiliation, repugnance, fear, awe, anxiety, etc.? This is not to say that these qualities have no feeling-color, but that they have no clearly distinguishable type of feeling-color that is fused with them and them alone. It is true that humiliation is a slightly "darker" feeling than pride, but beyond this general difference not much more can be said. Pleasurable feelings usually are "lighter" or "brighter" than painful feelings, but the particular types of colors (red, blue, green, etc.) are fused in a clearly distinguishable manner only with some of the particular types of qualities.

Feeling-qualities are also fused with *feeling-weights*. Sadness, grief, and fatigue are *heavy* feelings: I am "weighed down" with sadness, I am "burdened" with grief, I am so tired that my shoulders sag, my head is bent over, my feet drag along the ground, my limbs are so heavy I can barely move them. Joy, gaiety, and vigor are *light* feelings. I feel "light-hearted" in gaiety, my "burdens are lifted" in joy, I walk with a "lighter step" when I feel invigorated. The variations in feeling-weight show less differentiations than those of feeling-color. Beyond the distinction between heavy and light feelings, very little can be said.

Feeling-temperatures are also present in every feeling. Sadness is a cold feeling. So is the feeling of arrogance and haughtiness ("He has an icy manner"). The feelings of love and friendliness, on the other hand, are warm feelings. Anger is hot ("He is hot under the collar." "His temperature is rising"). Feeling-temperatures also show less variations than feeling-colors.

Of these three feeling-characters, it is only the feeling-colors that have been referred to in philosophical or psychological literature in a way that is worthy of comment, for the feeling-colors have been referred to as characters, not of feeling-sensations, but of feeling-tonalities of the world. Thus these references express at least a tacit recognition that there *are* feeling-tonalities of the world, a recognition that is unusual and remarkable when considered against the background of the traditional presupposition that sensuous feelings are not features of the world but only of the self. However, in most of these references to tonal-colors, such as in Anthony Kenny's statement that "the objects of depression are . . . things which seem black"[31] and Stephan Strasser's remark that "if I have an elevated disposition, all appears to me 'in a rosy light,' "[32] there is no express indication that these metaphorical descriptions of how things appear in feelings are references to *sensuous* feeling-determinations of the world. Color metaphors are used in describing how the world appears in feelings, but the nature of the referents of these metaphors is not made explicit.[33] But there is at least one reference to these tonal-colors in which we can find an explicit recognition and statement that these tonal-colors are sensuously felt features of the world. Edmund Husserl writes in his *Logical Investigations* of the pleasure-sensation belonging to joy:

> . . . attaching to the presentation [*Vorstellung*] there is a pleasure-sensation [*Lustempfindung*], which at the same time is located and apprehended as a feeling-excitement [*Gefuhlserregung*] in the psycho-physical feeling sub-ject and also as an objective property [*objektive Eigenschaft*]: the event ap-pears as if it were bathed in a rosy gleam.[34]

This passage represents the nearest thing we have in philosophical or psychological literature to an overthrow of the traditional presupposition that sensuous feelings are not features of the world. However, Husserl did not develop his insight or realize its significance, nor, more crucially, did he recognize the nonqualitative *typological* determinations possessed by the tonal features of the world. Husserl was unaware of feeling-flows, and as such was not in a position to offer the traditionally omitted "just defini-tions" of feeling-tonalities or of sensuous feelings in general.[35] It is only the feeling-flows that vary with each of the variations in the quality of a feeling, and that through these variations enable each and every quality of feeling to be internally defined as a quality that is united with its own unique type of feeling-flow.[36]

More significant, however, on the metaphysical level than the typo-logical nature of feeling-flows, is that feeling-flows are the characters of sensuous feelings *that refer to the felt meanings or importances of the world*. The feeling-flows of the world come to appearance as flowing from *sources* in the world, and these sources *are* the world-importances. It is through experiencing the flowing of the feeling-tonality, and not its in-tensity or color, etc., that I feel the tonality to have a source. For example, to experience in depression a tonal blackness of things is not to be pointed towards a source of the black tonality, for a character of blackness does not in and by itself refer to a source wherefrom this blackness comes. "To be black" is "to be black," and it is not "to be a blackness *coming from.* . . . " But to experience a tonality that flows downwards in a sinking man-ner is to be referred by the flow to a source of the flow, for to flow down-wards is to flow downwards *from* somewhere, from a source.

The source from which the tonality is felt to flow is not to be con-fused with that which imbues the world with the tonal-flow. The I that feels imbues the world with the tonality, such that the tonality is, as it were, "painted on the world" by the I *as* flowing from the importance the I is apprehending. The character of *flowing from a source* requires two items, the I that bestows the tonality as flowing from the source, and the importance that so to speak "demands" or "invites" the I to appreciatively respond to the importance by imbuing the world with a tonality that flows from the importance. The feeling-sensation is the manifestation of my appreciative response *in myself* (as a feature of myself), and the feeling-tonality is its manifestation *in the world* (as a feature of the world).

The importances or felt meanings of which the I is aware are the subject of Chapter 2; in the following section we will lay the groundwork for bringing these importances into view by examining the manner in which feeling-tonalities refer to them by flowing from them as from their sources.

I. 10. *The Depth and Breadth of the World-Emanation of Feeling-Tonalities*

To show that feeling-tonalities permeate the world is only one step on the way to uncovering the full metaphysical significance of these tonalities. The next and final step is to make it manifest that some feeling-tonalities are felt to flow from meanings of the world as a whole. This can be done by describing the depth and breadth of the world-emanation of the tonal-flows, where "emanation" refers to the felt character of the tonalities as flowing from a source.

A feeling-tonality has a *deep* world-emanation if it flows from the *interior* of the world (and conversely, has a *shallow* world-emanation if it flows from the *surface* of the world). A feeling-tonality has a *broad* world-emanation if it flows from the *whole* of the interior or surface of the world (and has a *narrow* world-emanation if it flows from one *part* of this interior or surface). These different world-emanations combine to produce four basic modes of world-emanation: i) narrow and shallow, ii) broad and shallow, iii) narrow and deep, and iv) broad and deep. An explication of these four modes of world-emanation will indicate that the fourth mode, the broad and deep world-emanation, manifests a relation of feeling-tonalities to meanings of the world as a whole.

Before I begin these descriptions, it is necessary to become clear about the nature of the verbal significations in which these world-emanations are to be articulated and made explicit. The significations, "interior," "surface," "emanation," "source," etc., are to be understood in a metaphorical way that corresponds to the felt characters of the world. The felt "interior" of a sensible phenomenon, for instance, is not to be understood in a literal sense as being the spatial interior or the physical matter that is located inside the physical surface of the phenomenon. Rather, a felt "interior" is a nonspatial and nonsensible reality that is intuitively felt to be "inside" a sensible phenomenon in a way that *is not* but *is somewhat analogous to* the way in which space or matter can be spatially inside a physical surface. Moreover, it should be emphasized that unlike some metaphorical descriptions, these metaphorical descriptions cannot be translated into literal terms and sentences. "He is a pig" can be literally translated as "He has a voracious appetite, is ill-mannered and unrefined," but "a tonal-flow that is emanated from the whole interior depths of the world" has no literal translation. This also implies that these metaphorical categories cannot be interpreted in light of the traditional rational-metaphysical categories. The surface/interior distinction, for example, cannot be understood in terms of the properties/substance distinction (Aristotle), the nominal essence/real essence distinction (Locke), or the phenomena/noumena distinction (Kant), etc. This distinction can only be understood outside of the sphere of rational-metaphysical categories, and in terms of the reality that one immediately feels.

It must not be thought that this metaphorical knowledge of the world is inferior to a literal knowledge, as has been maintained in a rational-metaphysical tradition beginning with Plato and Aristotle, and including such recent exponents as Frege, Russell, and Carnap. Aristotle asserted that in a perfect philosophical language there are no metaphors, and that the presence of metaphors is indicative of a defect and unclarity in one's understanding of the world.[37] According to this view, truths about the world are expressable only in literal terms, ultimately in the literal categorical terms of rational metaphysics, "cause and effect," "substance and accident," and so on. The untenability of this view is revealed in an evidentially felt manner in the reappreciative feeling-afterglows and concentrations, in which a substantive metaphorical knowledge of the world is obtained. In these feelings, and originally in the feeling-afterglows, the felt realities of the world are allowed to "speak for themselves," to inspire their own verbal articulation, and in many cases these realities inspire metaphorical formulations that capture what is inexpressible in literal terms, or what is expressible only in an inadequate and inferior way in literal terms.[38] The felt truth of these metaphors is immediately experienced in the reappreciative afterglows, wherein the felt realities in their vanishing intuitive presence *evoke* the metaphors and in this evocation appear as *truly intimated* by these metaphors.

It is such an intimative truth that is communicated in the following descriptions of the four modes of the world-emanation of feeling-tonalities.

I. 10.i. Narrow and Shallow World-Emanations

Feeling-tonalities that have a narrow and shallow world-emanation flow from one part of the surface of the world. The surface that is felt to be the source of the flowing is the sensible appearance of the world. It is the "look," "taste," "smell," etc., of the world that emanates the feeling-flow. An enchanted feeling-tonality, for example, may flow upwards and outwards in a shimmering and dreamlike manner from the colorful look of a sunset; or a feeling-tonality of repugnance may be flowing towards me repellingly from the odor of a corpse. These feeling-flows seem to emanate from the world's outer aspect, the bodily surface of the world that is exhibited to my senses, and do not emanate from a source deeper in the interior of the world. And they seem to emanate from only one part of this surface; e.g., the piercing pain in my toe flows from the thumb-tack I am stepping on, and does not flow from the remaining surface of the world.

I. 10.ii. Broad and Shallow World-Emanations

Feeling-tonalities with a broad and shallow world-emanation flow from the whole world-surface. When I arise in the morning groggy and only half awake, everything around me appears to be enshrouded in a sleepy haze; the furniture and contours of my room, as well as everything else I am perceiving, seems to be emanating a thick veil of sleepiness. The same is true for the delirious explorer wandering in circles in the jungle: everything appears to him infused with a feverish glow. And to the old wino, stumbling through the streets at night, everything appears permeated with a drunken fog. These are feeling-tonalities that the whole world-surface seems to have when my body is in this or that state of feeling (such as illness or fatigue). These tonalities flow from the way everything looks, sounds, tastes, emanating from the entire bodily surface that the world exhibits to my senses.

I. 10.iii. Narrow and Deep World-Emanations

These tonalities emanate from one part of the world-interior. The most common instances of these tonalities are those emanating from the people I relate to and respond to with feeling. The soft binding-together flow of love is not felt as a binding-together between the other person's bodily surface and myself, but between the other's ego and myself. In such a case, although the feeling-tonality appears to imbue the other's bodily surface, it does not seem to arise there, but from further within. What I intuitively feel is not that the other's eyes and face are lovingly-bound-together-with-me, but that the other himself is, and that the loving-bindingness is merely flowing through his eyes and face from the interior reality of his ego. But since I do not sensuously perceive this interior, I do not perceive the loving flow emanating from it. Rather, prior to all explicit judgment and cognition, I have an immediate intuitive sense that the sensuously apparent flowing of the other's body stems from and emerges out of an imperceptible source that is within the other's body.

Phenomena other than people can manifest a feeling-tonality that seems to emerge from the depths behind their sensory surface. A painting can be viewed superficially as consisting only of "aesthetically arranged colors and shapes," but it also can be interpreted more profoundly, as a sensuous manifestation of a deeper reality. For instance, the *Pieta* from Villeneuve-les-Avignon, by an unknown fifteenth-century painter, can be imaginatively interpreted and felt as a sensuous manifestation of the solemn presence of God. In such a case, the solemn and holy tonal-flow that infuses the painting is felt to emanate from a reality beyond the sensory surface of the painting.

Even a bone can seem to emanate a tonal-flow from deep within itself. An archeologist may feel overawed upon finding the femur of a smilodectus. He does not feel the femur to be emanating an awesome feeling-tonality from its sensible appearance, but from deep within itself, from its historical reality as a several million year old femur of a smilodectus.

I. 10.iv. Broad and Deep World-Emanations

The tonal-flows that have a broad and deep world-emanation have their source in the whole interior of the world, and not just in one part of this interior, such as in the interior of a person or bone. They emanate from deep *within* the *whole* sensible surface of the world. Such tonal-flows are experienced in global moods and affects. For example, in a serene mood I am oriented towards the whole in serene contemplation. In this contemplation, there is felt to emanate from far within the whole sensible surface of the sky, the field, the trees and the strollers, a profound calmness, an all-embracing serene feeling-flow that gently glides upwards. I contemplatively feel adrift in a vast ocean of serenity that diffuses *through* the whole surface of the world, and gently buoys and lifts everything upwards in one peaceful motion. All the many things in my surroundings are united in an ocean of calm. I am not oriented in this contemplation to the surface appearance of the world, to the look, sound, and smell of the whole, but to the one inner reality that is behind the surface, the reality that cannot be perceived but is felt to be within the whole of what is disclosed to my senses. But the source of this serene-flow is not felt to be *all of the individual* inner identities of the sensible phenomena, not their inner identities as my friends, my beloved, this age-old oak tree, and the like; the source is rather the *one* inner identity possessed by the entire sensible surface that is exhibited to me, its identity as a surface *of the world as a whole*. This inner global identity of the entire sensible surface is the *whole interior* of the world, the global interior. In the serene contemplation, I feel the intuitive omnipresence of a vast whole that extends far beyond this whole sensible surface and that at the same time encompasses this surface and myself in respect of our imperceptible identities as parts-of-this-whole. It is from this imperceptible whole that the serene tonal-flow calmly emanates.

I am present to this whole in global affects and moods. This whole is not something to which I rationally infer, but something to which I am sensuously connected by virtue of interconnected sensational and tonal flowings. Globally flowing expansions and contractions embrace me from within the global interior and make me sensuously expand and contract with the globe itself.

The global interior emanates through the world-surface different types of flows. Through this surface, I feel that the world-whole is awesomely towering over and above me, or is disseminating a softly binding flow of love that intimately ties me together with the whole itself, or is beckoning me from afar, into the wondrous felt distances deep within itself. Or I feel it flowing towards me fearsomely, looming towards me and contracting around me through the whole surrounding surface.

Through these flowings, I am carried into the great *sensuous metaphysical regions* of the world. In global joy, I am radiated to the celestial region of the world, the tonal peak of the world. I feel myself and everything else to be "on high," to be elevated to the very *top of the world*, and to be radiated there by the vast global interior itself.

In global despair, I am cast down to the nethermost region of the world, the world-abyss. Global despair differs from global sadness, for in global sadness I and everything else are sinking downwards, towards the bottom of the world, but we haven't yet reached bottom. In global despair, on the other hand, everything and myself have been hopelessly sunken to the very *bottom of the world*. We have "hit bottom" and can go no further downwards.

The middle region of the world is occupied by global equanimity. Global equanimity although somewhat similar to global serenity, is nevertheless different; serenity is more positive, more pleasurable, more affirmative; it is an upwardly directed feeling, belonging in the upper tonal half of the world, near to, but not at, the joyous top of the world. Equanimity, by contrast, is an absolutely still feeling; it flows neither forwards nor backwards, neither upwards nor downwards, and is not suspended before or oriented towards any direction at all. It is perfectly directionless. In equanimity, everything about me is utterly stilled and brought to a complete rest; everything becomes like an endless, still and rippleless pond. Everything is frozen in the motionless silence that obtains in the absolute *center of the world*.

The existence of such sensuous metaphysical regions as these puts into question the traditional rational-metaphysical opposition between the *sensuous* and the *metaphysical*. In the metaphysics of rational meaning, the sensuous, the irrational, and the nonmetaphysical are associated with one another. This was first argued in a substantial way in Plato's *Phaedo*, wherein Plato advises the philosopher to transcend the sensuous and to "free himself from feeling" (*Phaedo* 69b-c) as much as possible, as it is only in *nonsensuous ratiocination* that the philosopher can climb to the *metaphysical regions*, the regions of the *eide* and the *theion*, the essences and the divine, these being the regions of *the reasons, the aitiai*, that explain the world. These metaphysical regions are *nonsensuous regions*. It is because of this, as Hegel concluded at the end of the epoch of rational meaning, that there is an ultimate "contradiction between the spiritual [*geistigen*] and the sensuous."[39]

However, if the spiritual and the metaphysical are viewed from a different perspective, from the point of view of feeling, it can be seen that the sensuous has its own spirituality and its own metaphysical import. This spiritual-metaphysical nature is manifested in the *global tonal-flows*, for these flows are constitutive of the sensuous metaphysical regions of the world. In fact, it is not through being *rational beings*, but through being *sensuous beings*, that we are *metaphysical beings*, for it is by virtue of our sensuous feelings that we can be carried to the *top* of the world, the *bottom* of the world, the *center* of the world, and the like. It is these sensuous metaphysical regions, and not the nonsensuous regions of global reasons, that can be known to exist, as is evinced both by the positive descriptions in this chapter and by the negative arguments developed in the epoch of rational meaninglessness.

But these sensuous regions are not the *only* metaphysical realities we know to exist. They make manifest a nonsensuous metaphysical reality, but not a nonsensuous reality of *reason*. Rather, they make manifest a reality of *importance*. The metaphysical importances are the *regional sources* from which these sensuous regions flow. The tonal-flows constitutive of these regions flow from sources deep in the whole interior of the world, and these sources in the global interior are the importances of the world as a whole. Each different type of tonal-flow has its source in a different importance of the world-whole. One global importance is the source of the despairingly-sunken-to-the-bottom-of-the-world, a different one is the source of the joyously-radiated-to-the-top-of-the-world, and likewise for each type of tonal-flow that is emanated from the whole interior of the world.

It is true that the other three modes of world-emanation also have sources in importances, these sources being importances of a part or of the whole of the surface of the world, or importances of a part of the interior of the world.[40]

But what are these important sources? They are not *causal reasons* of tonal-flows, not good or evil substances in the traditional sense. Nor are they to be identified with *values*. And certainly they are not *facts*, or *facts-that-have-values*. But then again, importances are not to be identified with *feelings*. The possibilities of characterizing them in any familiar way seem exhausted.

This question about the nature of importances can only be answered by allowing the sources of tonal-flows to come to a pure appearance in afterglowing and concentrative reappreciations, and by allowing these sources to therein evoke their own verbal significations, significations that uniquely capture their nature. It is the task of the next chapter to offer an introductory exposition of these significations, and to therein elucidate the general nature of importances and of the feeling-awarenesses in which they are appreciated.

CHAPTER II

Feeling-Awarenesses and the World as Important

Feelings, as I pointed out in the introduction to Part 1, are concretely experienced as sensuous feelings (feeling-sensations and feeling-tonalities) conjoined with feeling-awarenesses of importances. In this chapter, the feeling-awarenesses and importances are considered by themselves, with a view to understanding their general nature and their principal mundane types. In the following chapter, the major types of global feeling-awarenesses and importances are examined.

My general aim in the first three sections (II.11-13) is to show that every awareness is a feeling-awareness, and that every feeling-awareness is an awareness of an importance. The intention is to establish the falsity of the traditional dichotomization of humans into feeling/nonfeeling aspects, and the world into important/neutral aspects.

In the fourth and final section (II.14), I will uncover the origin of the feeling/nonfeeling and importance/neutral dichotomies in a degeneration of concentrating feelings. At the basis of these dichotomies is the degenerated feelings' misinterpretation of themselves as disinterested acts of reasoning, and misinterpretation of the world as a whole of causal and teleological reasons and consequences.

The outcome of these four sections shall be that the nature of human beings is *appreciation*, not reason, and that the world is a whole of *importances*, not of causal and teleological reasons and consequences.

II. 11. The Feeling-Awarenesses of Importances, and Their Distinction from the "Feeling of Values"

My descriptions in the last section of Chapter 1 enable me to offer a preliminary characterization of the feeling-awareness of importance. Every sensuous feeling is accompanied by a feeling-awareness, and the feeling-awareness is an awareness of an importance that is the source of the sensuous feeling. The importance is directly the source of the tonal feeling-flow, and thus indirectly of the sensational feeling-flow, which is flowingly connected with the tonal-flow. Briefly put, then, a feeling-awareness of an importance is an *awareness of a source of a sensuous feeling-flow*.

However, an importance is not *the feature* that something has of being a source of a feeling-flow. Rather, an importance is apprehended to be the concrete something that has this feature. For example, a child is not felt to be important in that he is the source of an affectionate and caring feeling-flow; instead, he is the source of such an affectionate feeling-flow as a result of his importance, his importance *as* a child.

An importance, then, can be provisionally characterized as whatever has the feature of being a feeling-flow source.[1] *But each and every thing of which we are aware is the source of a feeling-flow, and thus every thing that appears to us appears as an importance.* There is nothing that appears to us as being absolutely unimportant and neutral. This can best be shown through examining only the cases in which we would normally say that we feel "indifferent" to something, or that something is "unimportant" and "neutral."

I feel "indifferent" to a particular thing if I apprehend it as lacking some kind of importance that "makes a difference" to me. Inasmuch as the thing lacks this kind of importance, it is unimportant. But it is not absolutely unimportant, only relatively so. It is relatively unimportant in that it lacks the kind of importance that "makes a difference" to me, but it has some other kind of importance. For example, it has at least the importance of being *noteworthy*, of being worthy of notice and attention. For if it were not noteworthy, I would not even bother to direct my attention towards it or to engage in grasping *what it is* that is thrust before my awareness. I find it to be noteworthy in that it is worthy of being apprehended and examined to see if it has a further kind of importance that "makes a difference" to me.

If the word "noteworthy" is used in a suitably broad sense, then it can be said that everything we apprehend is noteworthy; the noteworthiness of something is that whereby it attracts and holds our attention.

It is within the framework of this basic noteworthiness that things can appear relatively unimportant and neutral. The feeling of indifference that is experienced in regard to these relatively unimportant things is a feeling of *relative* indifference; the thing is felt to "not make a difference" to me in respect of its nonpossession of a certain kind of importance, but it is felt to "make a difference" in that it is worthy of being noticed and examined in respect of its possession or nonpossession of the kind of importance that especially concerns me. Such relatively unimportant things, then, are at least a source of a type of interested feeling-flow, wherein I feel attentionally attracted to the thing. It is true, however, that this feeling of attracted interest is often very weak and is accompanied by a stronger feeling of indifference to the thing in respect of its nonpossession of the kind of importance for which I am looking.

Similar considerations arise in regard to the global feelings which we may express by such phrases as "everything is devoid of importance" and "nothing matters at all." In a feeling of profound boredom and world-weariness, I may be tempted to articulate what I feel with the phrases· "The world matters to me not one whit. All that happens within it is without any importance whatsoever. The world is a monotonous and un-differentiated mass of existences that is incapable of inspiring me to act or respond in any way." However, I am not aware of the world as absolutely neutral; rather, I feel its global monotonousness and dullness to be the way in which the world is important to me. The world is felt to have a negative and dislikeable importance in that it is monotonous and undif-ferentiated. My boredom is a feeling of appreciating, or better, of "de-preciating," the world for having this negative importance.

A metaphysician of rational meaninglessness may express a feeling of global despair in the following words: "There is no knowable God or absolute goodness; therefore, nothing can be really important. It is all but a play of meaningless events." However, an interpretation of these phrases as signifying that the world is absolutely unimportant would be incom-patible with what intuitively appears in the despairing affect. This despair is an intuitive feeling that everything is really pointless, empty, and wor-thy of despair, and it is this global importance of pointlessness and emp-tiness that is apprehended as the source of the despairing feeling-flow. From this global pointlessness there emanates a hopelessly-sunken-to-the-bottom tonal-flow that permeates everything.

It is possible to distinguish a feeling of global indifference from that of boredom, the former being truly "indifferent" and lacking even the negativist and depreciatory attitude of boredom. In global indifference, I feel indifferent to the world as a whole in that it does not have the kind of importance that "makes a difference" to me. I already pointed out that this feeling is accompanied by a feeling of minimal interest in that towards which I am indifferent; the world is felt to be at least noteworthy with regard to its lack of the kind of importance that "makes a difference." But the feeling of indifference itself involves a feeling-flow that has a source in an importance of the world, viz., the privative importance of *lacking the kind of importance that makes a difference*. The world's privative character is the source of a basically directionless feeling-flow that is static, lifeless and inert, but that has a slight downward orientation; it hangs down from things lifelessly. It is manifest that this global privation of what "makes a difference" is an importance, for otherwise I would not respond to the world by *feeling* this inertial indifference towards it. I would not respond at all—the world would not even provoke a feeling of indifference.

In the above, I have considered the mundane feeling of indifference and three global feelings that may be expressed by phrases that seem to, but do not really, imply that the world is absolutely unimportant. All of these feelings are focal and attentional feeling-awarenesses. What of our horizonal and marginal awarenesses, and of the things that appear to us in these awarenesses? Are not these things, which are not even worthy of attention, absolutely unimportant?

First of all, it should be observed that although these things are not attentionally noteworthy, they are nevertheless marginally noteworthy. I would not apprehend them and tacitly "pick them out" on the fringe of my awareness if they were *absolutely* devoid of noteworthiness.

Horizonally apprehended things, moreover, are felt to have importances above and beyond their marginal noteworthiness. In moods, there is a horizonal awareness of everything as being important in some way; in an anxious mood, for instance, there is a horizonal and diffused awareness of everything as being vaguely ominous and threatening.

Even in affective reactions, when my attention is riveted on one thing, there is a background awareness of other things as being important. In fearing a dangerous drunk who is advancing towards me with a knife, I horizonally apprehend other things as having the importance of being the setting or scene of the dangerous event; the ground is important as the-ground-over-which-the-dangerous-drunk-is-advancing-towards-me, the sky is important as the-sky-under-which-the-danger-is-occurring, etc.

The above descriptions of some of the ways in which things appear to be important serve to illustrate the thesis that each thing of which we are aware is apprehended in a feeling-awareness as being important. This thesis can be interpreted in a weak or strong sense. Interpreted in the weak sense, it would mean: "Each appearing thing is important in that, among its various appearing features, there is at least one feature that constitutes the way in which the thing is important." In a strong sense, it would mean: "Each appearing thing is important in that each and every one of its appearing features is a way in which the thing is important."

An examination of how things appear to us shows that the correct interpretation is the strong one. Consider that I would not notice any feature of a thing unless that feature represented some respect in which the thing was noteworthy. The pencil with which I am writing is noteworthy in respect of its features that are pertinent to my usage of it; it is easy to hold and manipulate, it is able to trace letters clearly, etc.

But noteworthy features of things are not the only ways in which things appear to be important. In a mood of irritability, to take another instance, each thing in respect of each of its appearing features is felt to be annoying, oppressive, and to grate on my nerves. Things appear to be annoying in that they are in my way or out of my way, in that they are too talkative or too untalkative, too bright or too dim, uncomfortably hard or uncomfortably soft, etc.

In a loving affective response to another person, the loveworthy person is not felt to have some important features and other neutral features; rather, each feature of the person I apprehend in my loving-awareness appears to be a way in which the person is loveworthy, e.g., the person's kind behavior, intelligent remarks, the sensitive look in her eyes, her winsome smile, etc. And the features of other things I horizonally apprehend are felt to be ways in which these things contribute to the setting or situation of the loveworthy person, and to be important in this respect; e.g., the bright light of the room is a way in which this room is important as her situation in that it illuminates her beautiful face.

Other examples could be given of the ways in which appearing features of things are importances,[2] but further understanding of the strong interpretation of my thesis can best be achieved by contrasting it with another theory, the theory of the "feeling of values" that was developed by the philosophers in the twentieth-century British school of ethical intuitionism (Moore, Prichard, Ross, Raphael, Broad, Ewing, Laird, et al.), and by the thinkers in the twentieth-century Geman-Austrian school of ethical intuitionism (Meinong, Scheler, Husserl, Hartmann, Hessen, Reiner, Von Hildebrand, et al. — a school, however, that was founded in the nineteenth century by Brentano). The "feeling of values" was conceived in different ways by the thinkers in these two schools, and accordingly I shall contrast their conceptions separately with my concept of the feeling-awareness of importances.

G. E. Moore and Scheler are considered to be the leading representatives of the British and Geman-Austrian schools of ethical intuitionism. Moore's conception of the "feeling of values" was developed in his *Principia Ethica* (1903), *Ethics* (1912), and in several articles.[3] He argues that certain things, primarily people's emotional attitudes towards natural and artistic objects, and towards other people, are bearers of a nonnatural and nonsensible property of being good or evil. A person's attitude toward something is good in the sense that his attitude *ought to exist*, and his attitude is evil in the sense that it *ought not to exist*.[4] These value-properties of people's attitudes are intuited in feelings of approval or disapproval; when "we *approve* of a thing" we are "feeling that it has a certain predicate — the predicate, namely, which defines the peculiar sphere of Ethics [this predicate being the predicate *good*]."[5]

I believe Moore is in some sense right in believing that we experience feelings in which we approve or disapprove of something as being good or evil, although the specifics of his ethical theory need not be accepted. The notions of good and evil will be examined more fully in Section 14 of this chapter; here I wish to point out that the connection between the feelings of approving/disapproving of good/evil things and the feeling-awarenesses of importances is that the former are *one type* of the latter. Being good or evil are features of things which represent some of the ways in which some things are important. The feeling-of-importance has a far wider range than the feelings of what ought to be or ought not to be. For example, I can feel the world as a whole to be important in that it is mysterious, but it is not the case that the world-whole ought or ought not to be mysterious. And I can fearfully apprehend a threatening hurricane, without feeling the hurricane to be morally evil in that it is threatening me. And a person can be admired for being talented or noble of birth without it being the case that he ought to be talented or noble of birth. The good and the evil relate to persons, and do not include the ways in which nonpersonal things are important or the ways in which people are nonethically important.

The theory of the "feeling of values" developed by Scheler is considerably different than Moore's. In his *The Essence and Forms of Sympathy, Ressentiment, Formalism in Ethics and the Material Ethics of Value, "Ordo Amoris," On the Eternal in Man*, and other works written in his middle period (1912-21), Scheler developed the theory of an emotional intuition of value-facts (*Werttatsachen*).[6] These value-facts, unlike Moore's positive and negative values (the good and the evil), are not properties that constitute the "ought to exist" or "ought not to exist" of something, but are *facts*, like physical, psychological, or mathematical facts. Just as a star, a red color, or an act of willing are facts, so the beautiful, the noble, the holy, and the just are facts.[7] Propositions about values are ontological propositions that assert what *is* the case, not normative propositions that assert what *ought to be* the case.[8] Value-facts, however, are facts of a unique sort; they are not thingly properties of things, but value-properties of things of value (*Wertdinge*) and complexes (*Sachen*).[9] Moreover, they bear a distinctive connection to the ought-to-be and the ought-not-to-be: positive values ought-to-be and negative values ought-not-to-be, and a higher positive value ought to be preferred to a lower positive value, and other normative relations such as the foregoing hold.[10] These value-facts are intuited in feeling-functions, in acts of preferring (*Vorziehen*) and placing-after (*Nachsetzen*), and in acts of love and hate.[11]

Can we say that these emotional intuitions of value-facts are one type of the feeling-awarenesses of importances, as we said in regard to Moore's feelings of approving and disapproving? The answer must be negative; I believe there are no such phenomena as value-facts or the emotional intuitions in which they appear. I shall argue this in regard to two examples.

According to Scheler, if I am enchanted with a sunset, this is because I am intuiting the value-fact of "beauty" that belongs to the sunset. This value-fact is a nonsensuous property of the sunset, something distinct from its sensuous colors. But is this really what I am intuiting? Is the *beauty* that enchants me really an *unseen* property of the sunset? Am I not enchanted with the visually seen colors, the brilliant stripes and patterns of red, orange, and yellow that extend throughout the blue sky? I am enchanted with something I am *looking at and seeing through my eyes*, not something I am nonsensuously intuiting. The beauty at which I am looking is not something different from the glowing colors of the sunset that extend through the blue sky. Rather, it *is* they. There is no distinction here between neutral and sensuous features of the sunset (its colors) and a nonsensuous value-property of beauty. If we are to speak of a nonsensuous beauty in connection with the sunset, we must refer to the universal concept of "Beauty" of which the sunset is an instance. The colorful sunset is *a beauty*, an instance of the universal, "Beauty," but whereas the universal is nonsensuous, this instance is something visually sensed. Other instances of "Beauty," e.g., the intellectual beauty of formally correct and symmetrical mathematical equations, may be nonsensuous and be apprehended in a nonsensuous awareness, but the present instance of beauty is a sensuous instance. The beauty, then, in the present instance, is not one feature of the sunset among many other neutrally appearing features; rather, all the features I visually apprehend are constituents of this beauty.

In the case of other kinds of supposed value-facts, such as the moral value-fact of cruelty, the analysis is different. For Scheler, in being outraged at a person's cruel action, I am intuiting a value-fact of *cruelty* that attaches to the person's action. This value-fact of cruelty is neither the action itself nor a normative phenomenon comprising the ought-not-to-be-done of the action; it is a third thing, distinct from the action and the ought-not-to-be-done; it is an indefinable and simple value-quality that appears in the outraged intuition.

However, I believe that no such value-fact of cruelty appears. In my outraged intuition, I am intuitively apprehending two distinguishable aspects, the person's *action* and the action's attribute or feature of *ought-not-to-be-done*. The action or behavior of the person is to be understood in the wide sense as the complex consisting of the person's deliberate, needless, and enjoyable infliction of pain upon another person; in apprehending this complex, I intuitively realize that it ought not to be done. This action *qua* ought-not-to-be-done *is* the concrete phenomenon of cruelty. There is no third phenomenal aspect here, a simple and indefinable value-quality of "cruelty" that is distinguishable from both the action and its feature of ought-not-be-done. It is not as if there were several neutral aspects or features appearing to me and one value-fact of cruelty; all the features of the person's behavior that are apprehended in my outraged intuition are constitutive aspects of an importance of cruelty, viz., all the features of his action including the ought-not-to-be-done of this action.

Despite the differences between Scheler's and Moore's theories of the "feeling of values," they share a common presupposition to the effect that the world is divided into *value components* and *neutral components*, and that it belongs to the "feeling of values" to apprehend the value components of the world and to the other modes of awareness, such as sense-perception or thinking, to apprehend the neutral components. This dichotomizing of the world into value/neutral components and of human beings into feeling/nonfeeling aspects belongs to the traditional rationalistic assumption that human nature divides into a higher rational faculty and lower irrational faculties, one of which is feeling, whose function is to serve reason. This presupposition is only partly overcome if, with Scheler, one reverses the traditional evaluation of reason as the highest faculty and feeling as a lower faculty, and asserts that feeling is really the superior or predominant element in man. To say with Scheler that feeling or love is the primary aspect of man, so that man "is an *ens amans* before he is an *ens cogitans* or an *ens volens*,"[12] is still to remain within this dichotomization. One must, rather, overcome this dichotomization altogether and recognize that *all* of our modes of awareness are *feeling-awarenesses* and that *everything* we apprehend in the world is an *importance*.

An elucidation of this unitary nature of man and the world will be further developed in the ensuing sections, but first I would like to state how my usage of the word "importance" differs from the technical usage of it by two other philosophers, Alfred N. Whitehead and Von Hildebrand. These two thinkers use the word "importance" in a dichotomizing manner that is somewhat similar to Moore's and Scheler's usuage of the term "value."

In chapter 1 of *Modes of Thought* (1938), Whitehead argues that the concrete world consists of factual phenomena of nature, which are studied by the physical sciences, and the importances of these facts, these importances being grouped under the headings of "morality, logic, religion, art."[13] In contrast to this usage of the word "importance," I use it to refer to every phenomenon in the world, those of physical nature as well as the phenomena of morality, logic, art, etc.

Von Hildebrand's usage of this word is similarly dichotomizing. Although Von Hildebrand's ethics was influenced by Scheler's, he did not adopt Scheler's conception of values as value-facts, but conceived values, the importances-in-themselves, to be properties of things which characterized them as things that ought to be. In chapter 3 of his *Ethics* he writes:

> . . . let us suppose that we witness a generous action, a man's forgiveness of a grave injury. This again strikes us as distinguishable from the neutral activity of a man dressing himself or lighting a cigarette. Indeed, the act of generous forgiveness shines forth with the mark of importance, with the mark of something noble and precious. It moves us and engenders our ad-

miration. We are not only aware that this act occurs, but that it is *better* that it occurs, *better* that the man acted in this way rather than in another. We are conscious that this act is something which *ought* to *be*, something *important*.[14]

I can agree with Von Hildebrand that an act which ought to be is something important, but I must allow (as I did with Moore) that it is only one of the numerous ways in which things can be important. For example, if a man is observed to be lighting a cigarette — to take Von Hildebrand's own example — he appears to me to be important at least in that he is engaging in a *noteworthy* action. It is true that Von Hildebrand distinguishes two other types of importance, the subjectively satisfying and the objective good for a person, and he asserts that every being has a property of being important, but he nevertheless distinguishes these importance-properties of things from their neutral properties. He states, for instance, that material things have a *dignity qua* material things, but like Whitehead he distinguishes such properties from the supposedly neutral properties of *weight* and *extension*.[15]

By way of concluding this section, I shall briefly indicate that some form of the feeling/nonfeeling and importance/neutral dichotomies is retained even by the existentialists, despite their rejection of many of the traditional dichotomies. For example, they appear in Heidegger's idea that ways of "mattering" are only some of the determinations that can be possessed by beings within the world — to be distinguished, for instance, from such present-at-hand determinations as extension — and in his distinction of moods or *Befindlichkeit* from understanding and discourse. Sartre distinguishes the magical categories revealed in emotional consciousness from the rational-instrumental categories disclosed in rational consciousness. Nevertheless, Sartre and especially Heidegger should be credited with the express recognition that felt meanings, magical categories and ways of "mattering," are not essentially ethical or axiological phenomena.[16]

II. 12. *The Language of Importances*

In the last section I elucidated in a general way the thesis that all awarenesses are feeling-awarenesses and that all apparent things in respect of all their apparent features are importances. This thesis can be substantiated in a more specific way if the particular types of awarenesses and things ordinarily distinguished from feeling-awarenesses and felt things, e.g., perceiving and perceived things, thinkings and thought-about things, are shown to be types of feeling-awarenesses and felt things. But it is not possible to comprehend how these phenomena can be described as feelings and importances unless one has achieved an appropriate understanding of the language that is used in these descriptions. These descriptions must be preceded by an elucidation of language in its nature as a *language of felt importances*.

Words are not neutral entities, but importances, and their way of being important is to *elicit appreciations of importances other than themselves*. The importance of words is appreciated when this importance elicits a feeling-awareness of the important state of affairs for which the words are words. The sentence, "the sun is shining," is appreciated in its linguistic importance when it elicits an appreciation of the important state of affairs of *the sun's shining*. This is the *signifying* importance of words, although they also possess importances relative to their sonority and rhythms, which are especially appreciated in poetry reading.

There is one facet of this signifying importance of words that is especially pertinent to the words I shall be using in describing the specific types of feeling-awarenesses and apprehended importances in the following sections. Words can be used to elicit importance-appreciations in a manner that varies between the two extremes of *evocativeness, suggestiveness*, and *intimativeness* on the one hand, and *exactness* and *explicitness* on the other. This distinction was touched upon in the fifth section of the Introduction in connection with the appreciative levels of metaphysical knowing, but it can be discussed in a more general way here. It can be noted that some words are typically or frequently used to elicit importance-appreciations in a predominantly evocative and suggestive manner, and other words are typically used to elicit importance-appreciations in a manner that is more exact and explicit. Many words used in metaphorical ways, as well as words used literally, such as "bad," "beautiful," "dangerous," "astounding," "immense," "mysterious," etc., are often used in an evocative manner, whereas words in their literal employment like "blue," "1,000 feet long," "elliptical," "predicate," "subtract," "saucer," "two-legged," etc., are usually used to elicit importance-appreciations that are more precise and explicit.

Now the point I wish to make about these two roughly distinguishable classes of words is that their members can be and often are used to elicit appreciations of the *very same things*, but are used to do so with different degrees of evocativeness and exactness. In these cases, evocative words are not used to refer to *different features* of these things than the exact words are used to refer to, but are used to refer in a more vague and evocative way to the *same features*. Three examples will illustrate these complementary manners of eliciting importance-appreciations.

While standing in an open doorway, I can exclaim, "It is a beautiful day today!" The linguistic importance this sentence is intended to have in this particular situation and context, and through being uttered in an enthusiastic and enchanted tone of voice, is to evocatively make manifest to the listeners the important state of affairs, *the beautiful day*, as it appears to my enchanted intuitive feeling. Another person may agree with me that the day is beautiful, and articulate this important state of affairs in a more explicit and exact way: "Yes, you are right! The sun is shining in a cloudless blue sky, and a warm breeze is blowing." In this situation and context, the sentences "It is a beautiful day today!" and "The sun is shining, etc.," are not understood as referring to different things or to different features of the same thing. They are both understood as referring to *the day*, and to the *same features* of the day. The term, "beautiful," is not used to refer to some value-property of the day that is different and other than the day's neutral and factual properties of being warm, breezy, cloudless, and sunny. Rather, the day's being "beautiful" is here understood to mean that the day has the features of being warm, sunny, etc. But it is understood to mean these features in an evocative and suggestive way, and to elicit an appreciation of these features as they appear in a holistic and vague way to an enchanted intuitive feeling. The second sentence, "The sun is shining, etc.," is understood to be different than the first in that it is intended to elicit an appreciation of these features as they appear in a manner that is more precisely and explicitly differentiating. The difference lies not in the things and features referred to, but in the way of referring to them.

This can be illustrated by another example. In a certain situation, I can say, "Compared with distances between places on the earth, the distance of the earth to the moon is *immense!*" Here I intend to evoke in the listener an appreciation of this distance as it appears in a relatively vague but awestruck awareness. I may continue and describe this distance in a more exact and less evocative manner: "The distance from the earth to the moon is not like that between New York and Paris, but is more than fifty times such distances." In the present context, the second sentence is not meant to describe a *different distance* than the first sentence, but the *very same distance*. The second sentence differs from the first in that it describes more exactly the nature of the distance ("it is more than fifty times . . .") instead of indefinitely and evocatively suggesting it ("it is immense").

For our final example, we can observe that in a certain context the sentence, "The nation is still in chains," may be used as a suggestive and evocative way of saying what can be said more precisely and explicitly in the sentence beginning with "The nation is still being despotically ruled by a dictator, who is oppressing the citizens in the following ways. . . ." "In chains" is here intended to be a metaphorical evocation of the same state of affairs the latter sentence describes in a literal and detailed manner.

In certain cases, the same words that are used in an evocative way in one context can be used in an exact way in another context, and vice versa. A word like "downcast" when used to describe a person is frequently used inexactly and suggestively, e.g., it suggests that a person has depressed feelings, a bowed head, is morose and sullen, has certain pessimistic beliefs, etc. But when used to describe the feeling-flow of sadness, it is used to describe exactly a direction in which the sad feeling-sensation and feeling-tonality flows.

The example of feeling-flows also manifests the fact that metaphors in some cases can function as exact linguistic articulations of things, and are not always replaceable by more exact literal articulations. Indeed, in regard to feeling-flows there are no literal articulations; there are only more or less exact metaphorical articulations.

Exact and explicit articulations of some phenomena often seem vague and inexact relative to the exact and explicit articulations of other phenomena. This is due to some phenomena having a less complex, structurally articulated, and exactly determinate nature than other phenomena. Exact descriptions of feeling-flows seem vague relative to exact descriptions of automobiles, for feeling-flows have but a manner and direction of flowing, whereas automobiles have a manifold of parts each of which is classifiable, its size and shape determinable, its function specifiable, etc.

This discussion of the exact and evocative ways of linguistically articulating importances enables the provisional characterization of importances offered in the last section to be expanded upon. I there said that an importance is whatever is a source of a feeling-flow. To this characteristic there can be added the second characteristic of being *evocatively and exactly describable*. Something is an importance if it is a source of a feeling-flow and if there are possible evocative and exact descriptions of it. Since I am maintaining that every phenomenon is an importance, this means that every phenomenon is describable in both evocative and exact ways.

It is pertinent at this juncture to raise some questions concerning the linguistic coherency and informativeness of my claim that "every phenomenon is an importance" and has the two characteristics of being a flow-source and being evocatively and exactly describable. For does not this claim (and the associated claim that every awareness is a "feeling" in the sense of a feeling-awareness) involve using the words "importance" and "feeling" in ways that *violate ordinary usage*? Words like "importance" and "feeling" are normally used in a restricted sense, to refer to only *some* phenomena and *some* awarenesses. In being used in an extra-ordinary and unrestricted way, do not these words lose whatever sense they ordinarily have, and thereby become senseless? And if they are able to be given any sense at all, must not this be through making them synonyms of words that are ordinarily used in a similarly unrestricted sense, words like "phenomenon" and "awareness"? And in this case, would not my thesis that "every phenomenon is an importance" and "every awareness a feeling" become an uninformative tautology that does no more than pointlessly require us to learn new uses of "importance" and "feeling"?

Two things need to be considered here: the first is whether violation of ordinary usage leads to nonsensical verbiage, and the second is whether the only possible sense I can give to "importance" and "feeling" in my extra-ordinary usage of them makes the thesis I am propounding uninformative and pointless.

The usage of words in any given culture is in large part an expression of the underlying spiritual-historical attitudes of that culture. Most cultures hitherto and at present are dominated by the spiritual-historical attitudes characteristic of the epochs of rational meaning or meaninglessness. The usage of words in our culture in particular is largely an expression of rational-spiritual attitudes.

If this is the case, then it cannot be, as some ordinary language philosophers claim, that metaphysical problems and attitudes arise only if language is used in an extra-ordinary way. To assume that the only coherent attitude to the world is the one embodied in the ordinary language of some culture is not to eschew metaphysics but to promote one kind of metaphysics, usually a *rational* metaphysics. This assumption can be shown to be false by actually using words in an extra-ordinary way (particularly in a way *not* expressive of a rational-spiritual attitude) and by finding in such usage that the words *do* make sense and are capable of making manifest the world. A precondition of finding that words used in this way do make sense is that there be an understandable transition from the ordinary usage to the extra-ordinary usage. This transition can be of several types, one of which I will illustrate in the following in regard to the extra-ordinary usage of the word "importance."

In saying that something important is a source of sensuous feeling and is describable in evocative language, I am keeping within the limits of the ordinary usage of this term. I am departing from ordinary usage in two respects, one of them being in the range of application I give to this term, extending it from some phenomena to all phenomena. The transition from the application of it to some phenomena to the application of it to all phenomena is made by showing that the relevant characteristics which belong to the phenomena in the restricted range—the characteristics of being a source of sensuous feeling and of being evocatively describable—also belong to all other phenomena. This "showing" is achieved by actually describing the phenomena in the unrestricted range in evocative language and by linguistically articulating them as sources of sensuous feelings. Through finding that these linguistic articulations do in fact refer to discoverable characteristics of these phenomena, we learn that the extended usage of the term "importance" does make sense and is justified in that it conveys a knowledge of the world that is otherwise unconveyable.

The second departure from ordinary usage lies in extending the connection between "importances" and "exact describability." In ordinary usage, some but not all "importances" (in the sense of evocatively describable sources of sensuous feeling) are regarded as exactly describable, and some but not all exact descriptions are regarded as ways of making explicit "importances."[17] My extended use of "importance" to refer to whatever is exactly describable is justifiable through showing that all evocatively describable sources of sensuous feeling are also exactly describable, and that exact descriptions of all kinds are ways of making explicit evocatively describable sources of sensuous feeling. This "showing" is accomplished by exactly describing each evocatively describable source of sensuous feeling, by describing evocatively and as a source of sensuous feeling each thing that is exactly describable, and through discovering that there are referents of these descriptions.

That every awareness is a "feeling" in the sense of a feeling-awareness can be shown correlatively, by describing each awareness as an awareness of "importances" in the above sense.

By extending the usage of the words "importance" and "feeling" in these ways, I am not making them synonyms of words that in ordinary language have a similarly unrestricted range of application, viz., "phenomenon" and "awareness." For "phenomenon" is used (at least in one of its ordinary senses)[18] to refer to an appearance or something that appears, and "importance" in my extended usage means something more than this, that an appearance or something that appears *also* is a source of a feeling-flow and is describable in evocative and exact language. "Feeling" in the sense of feeling-awareness correspondingly means something more than "awareness," for it adds to the latter notion the idea that the awareness is *of* something that is a source of a feeling-flow and is evocatively and exactly describable. Thus the alteration in the usage of these terms is an informative alteration; it enables us to understand that certain things possess certain characteristics that on the basis of our ordinary linguistic habits we do not assume them to possess.

The above remarks imply that the ordinary usage of these terms to refer to a restricted range of phenomena and awarenesses embodies an erroneous world-view, the view that some phenomena are not importances and that some awarenesses are not feeling-awarenesses. It will be demonstrated in Section 14 of this chapter that this erroneous dichotomization of the world into important/neutral phenomena, and of human nature into feeling-awarenesses and other kinds, has its roots in a rational-spiritual perspective on reality.

In the first section of this chapter I endeavored to justify my extended usage of the term "importance" and "feeling" by veridically describing as importances and feeling-awarenesses selected examples of things that are ordinarily not called "importances" and "feelings." In the following section, I will justify this usage in a more systematic way, by veridically describing as importances and feeling-awarenesses some of the *major types* of things that are customarily distinguished from importances and feeling-awarenesses. The discussion of the evocative and exact "language of importances" in the present section has prepared us for this task, for we shall find that the types of things customarily distinguished from importances and feeling-awarenesses *are* importances and feeling-awarenesses that have been mistakenly identified with their nature as it is describable solely in an exact and explicit language.

II. 13. *Perceiving and Thinking as Feeling-Awarenesses, and Perceived and Thought-About Things as Importances*

Human beings can be evocatively described as *appreciative world-parts*, and the world as a *whole of importances*. More exactly described, humans are world-parts that are appreciative in different modes of appreciation; they perceive, think, imagine, will, etc. And the world is more exactly described as a whole composed of importances that are perceptible, thinkable, imaginable, etc. It is in this fashion that feeling (appreciation) and importance can be said to constitute the nature of humans and the world.

This view conflicts with the traditional view that feeling and felt phenomena constitute only a part of man and the world, and that the above-mentioned phenomena of perception, thought, imagination, etc., are not phenomena of feeling. In this section I will illustrate the manner in which this traditional view can be shown to be false by a description of the phenomena of *perception* and *thought* as feeling-awarenesses and importances.

II. 13.i. *Perceiving as a Feeling-Awareness, and Perceived Things as Importances*

Taken in its broadest scope, what we apprehend through our senses is a holistic and unitary impression of our surrounding environment, an impression describable in such phrases as "It is a beautiful day," "The forest is gloomy," and "This room is filthy." These phenomena of beautifulness, gloominess, filthiness, etc., can be called *panoramic hues* of our environment; they are the ways in which our surroundings perceptually appear to be important *as a whole*. These vague and unitary impressions of the environment appear articulated into this and that hued region and into this and that hued thing within a region. Within the *filthy room* there

appears the *cluttered floor*, the *smudgy walls*, and on the cluttered floor
I see a *greasy plate*, a *crumpled rag*, and a *broken and dusty bottle*. The
greasy plate is implicitly seen to be round in shape, to be white in color
with brown streaks on it, and to be about ten inches in diameter.

It is only the last-mentioned phenomena, the shape, color, and size
of the plate, that would be described as perceived phenomena in the traditional theories of perception, and the various hues, filthiness, clutteredness,
and greasiness, would be ignored or not recognized. However, what we
perceive are in the first instance hued phenomena, and the colors, shapes,
and sizes implicitly appear as the exactly determinable forms of these hues.
"Being white with four brown streaks across it" is an exact way of describing an aspect of the plate's hue of greasiness.

Consider in addition the experience of hearing. Is this a sensing of
neutral sense-qualities, or an apprehending of a neutral material thing
that emits these sense-qualities? In no case is it such; rather, I hear the
eerie creaking of the gate, the *lovely singing of the birds*, the *mournful
droning of the foghorn*. I hear *important things*, and their emitted sounds
are *the ways in which they appear to be important*. The auditory hue of
eeriness can be exactly analysed into a certain pitch, timbre, and intensity, but these exactly determinable characteristics are not what explicitly
appear to me and what I notice when I hear the gate. Implicit in this
eeriness are these precisely determinable structural articulations, but what
is explicitly manifest is the unitary and holistic impression of eeriness that
is formed by these different structural aspects.

When I am trying on a new pair of tight-fitting shoes, I feel the
shoes to be *uncomfortable*; I do not feel a certain degree of pressure and
hardness located at such and such places on my feet, although these
phenomena implicitly appear as the exact structural constitution of the
tactile hue of uncomfortableness.

And so it is with the other modes of perceiving and perceived things.
The problem with the traditional theories of perception is that they describe
perceptual phenomena only in an exact and explicit language, and thereby
neglect the primary perceptual phenomena that are describable in a more
evocative and suggestive language. The *language of hues* (drab, eerie, uncomfortable) aims to evoke and suggest perceived phenomena as they focally appear in a holistic and unitary way, whereas the traditional *language
of sense-qualities* (red, green, pitch, timbre, round, ten inches) aims to
make explicit the exactly determinable constitution of these hues, a constitution that appears in a more marginal and tacit way. Both languages
must be used to describe what we perceive, for both are necessary to describe
what focally and unfocally appears in our perceivings.

It is not to be thought that the implicitly perceived sense-qualities
are in themselves *neutral* phenomena. It belongs to their nature to be

aspects of perceived importances (hues), and as such they are essentially *nonneutral* phenomena. That they are nonneutral phenomena can also be *explicitly* confirmed, for it is possible in exceptional cases to focus on these aspects and allow them to become the primary phenomena of perception. In perceiving a nobly and magnificently hued building, I can adopt the somewhat unnatural attitude of trying to focus solely on the building's white color, which is one of the exactly specifiable aspects of the building's noble and magnificent hue. This color is not apprehended as something that in itself is a neutral sense-quality; not only is it perceptually noteworthy, but it is a kind of color-importance in and by itself. Whiteness as a color-importance is describable in such terms as "pure, undefiled, noble, etc."; as such a color-importance, it contributes to the building's overall hue of being noble and magnificent. Other colors are color-importances of a different kind; red is violent and disturbing, green is restful, dark gray is somber, and so on. These colors when focally appreciated are sources of feeling-flows of corresponding types.

Examples such as these reveal that colors (and other exactly determinable aspects of hues) are not only *aspects* of hues but *are themselves hues*. Their apparent nature is only incompletely captured in the exact sense-quality language, and must also be described in an evocative hue language (pure, violent, restful, etc.).

The above descriptions of perceived importances remain incomplete, for hues are only one of the two basic types of perceived importances. Hues are features of the *concrete things* we perceive. These concrete things are not themselves hues but *configured importances*. A hue is usually appreciated as an *important display* of the whole or part of a configured importance, such that in most cases of perceptual appreciation there is an appreciation of a hue importance and a configured importance. For instance, the configured importance of the *suspiciously opening gate* displays itself to be eerily creaking, and it is to the suspiciously opening gate as manifested by this auditory hue that I affectively respond by fearfully cringing backward.

Hues are *display-features* of configured importances, specifically, relational display features, for configured importances have display-features only insofar as they are relational terms of perceptually appreciating awarenesses. Display-features are in their essential nature displays *to* an appreciative world-part.

The nature of these configured importances and their display-features can be made explicit through describing a particular case of perceptual appreciation. I am sitting across from the magnificently hued building, gazing upon its colored surface as the sun sets. The noble white color-hue of the building's stately surface gradually vanishes and is gradually replaced by a color-hue of distinguished gray, which in its turn is replaced by a somber dark gray. As I appreciate the progressive succession of color-hues, I do not intuitively feel that the building is successively acquiring new surfaces, but that the *same surface* of the building is displaying itself to me as being *differently hued*, first displaying itself to me as nobly white, subsequently as a distinguished gray, and finally a somber gray. And this is precisely how I affectively respond to the stately surface: I feel a quiet admiration *of* the stately surface *for* displaying itself to me as being nobly white, distinguished gray, and somber gray.[19] The stately surface that displays itself to be so hued is a part of the whole configured importance, *the grand building*.

The same stately surface of the grand building can display itself as being *analogously* hued to several different percepients, but the converse can also occur. The surface can display itself to several people as being a noble white, but to one person (who has jaundice or who has taken santonin) as being a refined yellow. This is a sign of the fact that the stately surface is not identical with any one of the hues it displays itself as being, but rather possesses these hues as relational features it acquires in relation to this or that appreciator. In relation to me, the stately surface "is" nobly white (i.e., is-displaying-itself-to-be nobly white), but in relation to the person who has taken santonin, the stately surface "is" a refined yellow (i.e., is-displaying-itself-to-be a refined yellow).

Other examples of configured-importance features besides stately and sturdy surfaces are grotesquely angular shapes, gently curving shapes, gigantic sizes, dwarfed sizes, jerky motions, graceful motions, etc. Each type of configured-importance feature displays itself to be hued in a distinctive fashion. I have already indicated, for instance, that surfaces of configured importances visually display themselves to be color-hued. Another example is that shapes of configured importances display themselves to be shapely hued; e.g., harmonious round shapes of configured importances display themselves to be harmoniously roundly hued when visually appreciated from above, and display themselves to be inharmoniously elliptically hued when visually appreciated obliquely, from one side. In regard to the shapes and sizes of configured importances, we usually take account, on the basis of past appreciations, of the perspectival nature of their displays, and thus appreciatively recognize (for instance) that a shape of a configured importance which displays itself as being inharmoniously elliptically hued when viewed from the side is not an inharmonious elliptical shape but a harmonious round shape.

At the basis of some perceptual illusions is the fact that a configured importance displays itself as being hued in a fashion analogous to the fashion in which other configured importances display themselves to be hued. A weirdly shaped tree at dusk may display itself to be hued in a fashion analogous to that in which a motionless body of a person would display itself to be hued, and this may result in the hue displayed by the weirdly shaped tree being "misappreciated" as a hue displayed by a motionless human body. Further appreciations can allow the weirdly shaped tree to display itself as hued in a recognizably distinct fashion; these hue-displays will occur when I approach the tree more closely or touch it.

Configured importances that display themselves are parts of the whole of a *surrounding configured importance*. A surrounding configured importance is what displays itself to be panoramically hued; it is a city block and sky that display themselves to be a drab panorama or a lake and sky that display themselves to be a calm and serene panorama. Any given configured importance within the surrounding one is appreciated at least tacitly as a part of the whole surrounding importance. Just as hues are articulated into panoramic hues, regional hues, thing hues and sense-quality hues, so the configured importances that display themselves to be hued in these fashions are correspondingly articulated into surrounding configured importances, regional configured importances, thingly configured importances, and configured-importance features.

Some thingly parts of this surrounding configured importance uniquely stand out in that they embody *flowing importances*; it is as flowing importances that other *egos that feel* are encountered in the felt world. Whereas clouds and stones flow only extrinsically in that their flowings are not felt by them but only by somebody who is perceptually appreciating them and thereby animating them with tonal-flows, other egos that feel also flow intrinsically in that they have and experience their own flowings, flowings that are different from and nondependent upon the tonal-flows with which their appreciators animate them. I encounter other feeling egos as importances that intrinsically flow against me in a violently attacking manner, or that flow towards me in a gently binding manner, or that flow backwards and away from me in a fearfully cringing manner, or alternatively, do not flow towards or away from me but towards or away from somebody or something else they find to be more important than myself. When they flow towards or away from me, and I towards or away from them, a reciprocal and mutually adjusted flowing is instituted, even if this "mutual adjustment" takes the form of two violently attacking flows that clash head on.[20]

Configured importances, whether they embody flowing importances or not, are some of the felt realities that have been ignored or denuded in the usual rationalist world-views. Whereas hues have traditionally been neglected or misconceived as neutral and exactly determinate sense-qualities, configured importances and their features have been ignored or misrepresented as neutral and exactly determinate "extended substances" or "material things" and their "primary qualities." Precisely how configured importances have been maligned by being pictured as "material things with their primary qualities" can be exposed if we examine the most frequent way in which rationalist systems have distinguished between sense-qualities and material things with their primary qualities. Although this distinction is as old as Democritus[21] and Aristotle,[22] its peculiarly modern form did not arise until the seventeenth century.

The modern theory is sometimes thought to arise in John Locke's *An Essay Concerning Human Understanding*, in the discussion of "primary qualities," "secondary qualities," and "ideas" in the mind,[23] but Locke's theory at bottom is no more than a modification and terminological transposition of the theory that can be found in the works of Descartes[24] and Thomas Hobbes.[25] But it is not Descartes or Hobbes who first stated the modern theory of this distinction: rather, both adopted this distinction from the writings of Galileo, specifically, from Galileo's *The Assayer* (1623). Galileo's theory of "physical objects" and their distinction from "sensations" embodies two main misinterpretations which decisively influenced the course of subsequent philosophical and scientific thinking.

The first of Galileo's misinterpretations is that the whole composed of all configured importances, the whole that Galileo calls "the universe," is mathematical in nature:

> Philosophy [*La filosofia*] is written in this grand book which is continually open to our gaze (I am talking of the universe), but the book cannot be comprehended unless one first learns to comprehend the language and read the letters in which it is written. It is written in the language of mathematics [*Egli è scritto in lingua matematica*], and its letters are triangles, circles and other geometrical figures, without which it is impossible to understand a single word of it; without these, one wanders about in a dark labyrinth [*un obscura laberinto*].[26]

The second misinterpretation is that hue-features in terms of which configured importances display themselves are not features of configured importances, but of our perceiving:

> I think that tastes, ordors, colors, etc., are nothing more than mere names [*puri nomi*] so far as the object in which we place them is concerned, and that they reside only in our perceiving.[27]

Galileo's theory amounts to the postulate that configured importances are not in fact "importances" at all but neutral objects whose only features are precisely determinable mathematical features. But the concept of such "objects" is in truth a theoretical construct that has no knowable referents. In order to establish that a concept signifies something, rather than is empty and referenceless, the thing putatively signified by the concept must be discovered. The relevant avenue of discovery for Galileo's conceived "material objects" is perception. But what is discoverable through perception possesses the opposite features to those possessed by Galileo's "objects."

To begin with, the configured importances we perceptually appreciate do not have mathematical features. Consider for example that the geometrical features Galileo mentions, triangularity, circularity, etc., do not inhere in configured importances. A circle geometrically conceived (in Euclidian geometry) is 360°, such that the ratio of its circumference to its diameter is π, the area is πr^2, and so on. Anything deviating from this definition of a circle by definition is not a circle. Now no configured importance of which we know possesses this geometrical circularity. The concepts of geometry (Euclidian or non-Euclidian) are inapplicable to the realities discoverable in the world.

However, such words as "circular," "elliptical," and "straight," can be used in a nonmathematical sense to refer to configured-importance features. Used in this way, these terms, like yellow, hot, or drab, are definable in an ostensive way only, and are not mathematically definable. The configured-importance sense of "circular" can be defined by pointing to such configured-importance features as the *harmonious circularity* of a piece of pottery. This harmonious circularity is not a "circularity" in the geometrical sense, for it does not have an area whose measurement is πr^2 or a ratio of circumference to diameter of π. An attempt to measure its area will discover an area that is slightly more or less than πr^2; it may approximate πr^2, but it will not *be* πr^2. Now something whose area is not πr^2 is not a "circle" in the geometrical sense; that is an analytic truth. It is a "circle" in some other sense, the nongeometrical, configured-importance sense. "Circles" in this sense are discovered within the world.

Every configured-importance feature that is *in fact* discovered is not an exact geometrical circle, sphere, or straight line. But *could* we discover such geometrical features to belong to innerworldly things? Note that something which has a ratio of diameter to circumference of π is *in principle* undiscoverable, for its discovery would require the impossible task of completing an infinite series of measurements. Pi is an irrational number, 3.14159265358979332384626433832795028841971 . . . *ad infinitum*, and as such no innerworldly thing could ever be measured as having this number.[28] This shows that we not only *do not* know geometrical concepts to have instances, but *cannot* know if they do.

The "gap" between the mathematical conception of things in the sciences and the intrinsically nonmathematical nature of discoverable reality does not prevent scientists from believing in the referentiality of their conceptions. This is due to the fact that scientific theories are *constructed* through using terms like "circularity" or "straightness" in their mathematical and neutral senses, but they are *verified* through substituting the nonmathematical and important senses of these terms. The perceptual appreciation of the harmonious circularity or inharmonious ellipticity of configured importances is allowed to "verify" a scientific theory that represents the said configured importances as neutral and mathematically determined objects that are "circular" or "elliptical" in a mathematical sense. For example the second law of motion as stated in Book 1 of Isaac Newton's *Mathematical Principles of Natural Philosophy* reads, "The change of motion is proportional to the motive force impressed and is made in the direction of the right line in which that force is impressed." This law is verified by substituting the configured-importance sense of "right line" for the geometrical sense.

It is through making this substitution that we can say that the sciences are "true" and do refer to the discoverable world. However, if it is forgotten that the sciences are verified by means of such conceptual substitutions, or if the matter is not sufficiently reflected upon, the mistaken belief could well arise that things *really are* neutral and geometrically exact because they are represented as such in the sciences. More about this will be said in the next subsection.

The second major misinterpretation of configured importances that Galileo handed down to modern thought is that hues are not features of configured importances but of the perceivings of these importances. Galileo had in mind specifically the exactly analysable hues that are relative to one type of sense perception (colors, tastes, odors, etc.), but his misinterpretation of them was later extended (by Descartes, Locke, et al.) to the exactly analysable hues that are common to more than one type of sense perception, the "common sensibles" (shape-hues, size-hues, etc.). Of the former kind of exactly analysable hues, Galileo wrote, "they reside only in our perceiving." Such a belief, however, is falsified by what is disclosed in our perceptual appreciations of configured importances. *My perceiving* of the building is not nobly white; rather, *the building* is nobly white. The hue of noble whiteness inheres in the building, not in my ego or awareness. The real state of affairs that Galileo had in mind but misinterpreted is that hues are relational features of configured importances, specifically, relational features that configured importances have insofar as they are being perceptually appreciated. Hues are display-features of configured importances: configured importances display themselves to perceptual appreciators *as being hued*.

Galileo presupposed that configured importances are able to exist without displaying themselves to perceptual appreciators. Whether and how this is really possible Galileo did not demonstrate. In order to demonstrate this, it must be shown first of all that the world is independent in some sense of its appreciative parts. This can be made manifest only if the importances of *existence* and *appearance* are first clarified, and indicated to be such that the importance of existence is independent of the importance of appearance. This task is reserved for the three chapters of Part 2, and I will refrain from discussing this complex issue until then.

At this point, the results of the explications in this subsection can be summarized and some conclusions may be drawn. The aim has been to show that perceived things are evocatively and exactly describable sources of feeling-flows, and that perceiving awarenesses consequently *are* feeling-awarenesses, i.e., awarenesses-of-importances. This thesis must not be confused with another theory propounded by many, viz., that *every* act of perception is *accompanied by* a feeling-awareness, and that every perceived object has *besides its perceived features* an affective feature, an affective meaning that is the object of this feeling-awareness. To generalize this by saying that every act of presentation (*Vorstellung*) serves as a foundation for or is conjoined with a feeling-act, or that every concrete act of consciousness includes an affective awareness, or that every understanding has its mood, or something of this sort, is to propound precisely the view *against which* my descriptions are directed, the view that feeling-awarenesses are not *identical with* every awareness but *coexist with* non-feeling-awarenesses. The thesis I am developing is that *there are no* nonfeeling-awarenesses with which feeling-awarenesses do or do not co-exist, and that *there are no* features that phenomena possess besides their felt features. There are *only* feeling-awarenesses and felt features.

But this does not mean I am claiming that there exist only "feeling-acts," "emotional consciousnesses," or "moods" in the sense conceived by one of these philosophers—a claim that is palpably false. Rather, I am claiming that there exist only "feeling-awarenesses" in the sense of awarenesses of exactly and evocatively describable sources of feeling-tonalities that flow in a certain direction and manner.

Moreover, I am not asserting that there exist only "felt features" in the sense understood by these philosophers, as values, affective meanings, ways of "mattering," magical categories, or whatever; instead, I am proposing that there exist only "felt features" in the above specified sense of *important* features.

II. 13.ii. Thinking as a Feeling-Awareness, and Thought-About Things as Importances

Thinking is another type of awareness customarily distinguished from feeling, and that is supposedly an awareness of neutral phenomena. However, a description of what appears in thinking-awarenesses will show that in every case thinking is an awareness of one of two basic types of thought-about importances. The first type is *signified importances*, the configured importances, flowing importances, global importances, etc., that my thoughts signify. Two of the principal ways of thinking about these importances are afterglowing thinking, in which I think about a global or mundane importance as it has explicitly appeared in a prior intuitive feeling, and concentrative thinking, wherein I think about the implicitly intuited content of these importances. Since both afterglowing and concentrative thinking are awarenesses of signified importances, they are feelings, thinking-feelings, and have the typological range of feelings. Afterglowing thinkings are feelings of the same type as the intuitive feelings of which they are the afterglows; they are enchantments, sadnesses, dreads, and the like. Concentrative feelings, on the other hand, are of one type, concentrative interest. This difference in the typological range of the afterglowing and concentrative feelings is due to the difference in the direction of their attentional appreciation; the afterglowing thinkings respond to the important features of a thing as they explicitly appeared in the intuitions, wherein they appeared as the thing's *beautifulness, gloominess* or *ominousness*; concentrative thinkings, on the other hand, respond to the *fascinatingly interesting* content of the features that had been implicitly intuited. This content is the exact and detailed nature of the features, the features as they exactly are. The features of a thing as they exactly are are ways in which the thing is interesting-to-be-made-explicit-in-concentrative-thinking, and when these ways explicitly appear, they are the source of a concentrated feeling-flow.

The kinds of signified importance appreciated in these afterglowing and concentrative thinkings can also be appreciated in analogous types of thinking. The evocative descriptions developed in somebody else's afterglowing thinking and communicated to me orally or in writing can evoke in me an appreciative and glowing awareness of the described importance; such an awareness may be called (to retain the metaphorical association with afterglowing thinking) an *ignited thinking*. Likewise, another author's or speaker's exact descriptions of a fascinating implicit content can elicit in me a feeling of concentrative interest in that content, although this concentrative interest will not be an original explication of that content, but a nonoriginative explicit awareness of it—a "learning" about this content as it was originally made explicit by another.

Thinking-feelings are not only appreciations of signified importances, but also of *important significations*, important thoughts. These are the second basic kind of thought-about importances. Significations are "thought-about phenomena" in a derivative sense of this phrase; in the natural sense of the phrase, what I think about are not thoughts but what these thoughts are of, the signified phenomena. But inasmuch as thinking about these phenomena involves having thoughts of them, the thoughts may be called (in a derivative sense) "thought-about phenomena."[29] Significations are important in that they are *illuminatingly true* or *misleadingly false, strikingly original* or *monotonously repetitious, agreeably easy* or *dismayingly difficult to comprehend*, and so on. These features of significations are not usually attentionally appreciated, for usually my attention is directed upon the phenomena they purportedly signify, but in exceptional cases

I can turn my attention back to the significations and attentionally appreciate one or more of their important features.

Note that the illuminatingly true is only one of the ways in which thoughts are important. This suggests that the view that *truth* is what moves us to think and keep thinking in each case is false. It is not truth but some member of the class of *thought-about importances*, the class of important significations and signified importances, that inspires us to think in each case, although undeniably in some cases truth is the member of this class that inspires the thinking. That it is some thought-about importance and not specifically truth that always incites and sustains thinking is evinced by instances wherein we continue to thoughtfully linger over something profoundly interesting long after its truth has been determined and there is no expectation of arriving at further truths, and by instances wherein we deliberately think of false thoughts in order to appreciate their nobility and sublimity (perhaps a philosopher of empiricist persuasions may read Plotinus or Spinoza or Schelling in this spirit).

If it is the case that thinkings in each case are awarenesses of importances, is it also the case that they are importances themselves? That they are is made evident by the fact that in each case in which a thinking appears, whether attentionally in reflexion or marginally in unreflexive experience, the thinking is a source of a new feeling-flow or at least of a slight alteration in the feeling-flow already experienced. In fact, all feeling-awarenesses and sensuous feelings are importances, for they do not appear without occasioning at least a peripheral modification in the feeling-flow being experienced. Since feeling-flows are aspects of the sensuous feelings, this means that sensuous feelings simply by virtue of being felt are at least slightly restructured or retinged — a sign that what a person is feeling is indeed important to that person.

If each and every thinking is an appreciation of importance, whether this importance be a signification or something signified, this suggests that the description and results of the thinking practiced by the philosophers, scientists, and mathematicians in the epochs of rational meaning and meaninglessness are seriously problematic in that they are based on a denial of the real nature of thinking and thought-about phenomena. This denial as it is expressed in philosophical thinking shall be discussed in the following section, where the origin of this denial in an epistemically unsound rational perspective on the world will be the theme of my investigations. At present I shall confine myself to saying a few words about this denial as it appears in mathematics and the sciences.

Significations formed in afterglowing and concentrative thinking-feelings are significations *of* explicitly or implicitly felt importances. Significations formed in afterglowing and concentrative mathematical thinking-feelings signify *mathematical importances* that originally and holistically appear in intuitive ideative feelings.[30] An example of such an ideative feeling is the astonished insight that the set of all algebraic numbers has the paradoxical feature of containing as many members as its subset of all rational integers. This feature is paradoxical by virtue of being contrary to the nature of finite sets with which we are ordinarily acquainted, finite sets being such that they necessarily contain more members than any one of their proper subsets. The paradoxically important feature of the set of all algebraic numbers appears originally in a holistic way in the astonished insight, and is subsequently explicated in afterglowing and concentrative thinking-feelings. It is in the concentrative thinking-feelings that the mathematical formulas are developed which explicate in detail the paradoxical importance.

This exemplifies the concrete nature of mathematical thinking-feelings and theory formation. But this nature is denied in the conceptual expression of mathematical theories in treatises on the subject. The mathematicians abstract from the intuitively felt holistic importance of the mathematical states of affairs, eliminate all evocative descriptions of these states of affairs, and identify the states of affairs with their exactly analyzed nature. The intuitively felt holistic nature of the importance as (for instance) "the paradoxical" is eliminated, and the importance is identified with its implicit content as this implicit content has been made fully explicit in the concentrative feelings. But this denial extends even further: the numbers, equations, and principles are tacitly conceived as phenomena that are neutral in themselves, unrelated to feeling, so that even the fascinatingly interesting nature of their implicit content is denied expression.

This means that in the strict sense the theoretical expressions in mathematical treatises are not expressions of mathematical states of affairs as they really are. This is not because the mathematical computations are erroneous but because no numbers or equations are discernable in intuition or thought that *are* just as they are purported to be in the mathematical treatises. Mathematical states of affairs are discoverable only as paradoxical, etc., holistic importances whose implicit nature is interesting-to-be-made-explicit.

The problems are more complicated in the sciences, especially the physical sciences, where neutral mathematical formulae are used to putatively "refer" to features of configured importances. The problem with this mathematical conception of configured importances was discussed in the last subsection; here the scientific "neutralization" of configured importances can be discussed.

Configured importances, whether they be superclusters of galaxies or hadrons and leptons (to use their "scientific" names), are conceived in the physical sciences as neutral things possessing exactly determinate features. But this theoretical representation of things in the scientific treatises is not in accordance with the "data" the scientists rely upon to confirm these theoretical representations. For the "data" are perceptually appreciated configured importances. Usually the things the theories are purportedly about do not directly display themselves in the confirming perceiving-feelings, but do so indirectly. For example, photographs of galactic clusters, and of atomic particle interactions in cloud chambers or particle accelerators, are indirect ways in which the clusters or interactions display themselves. It is in perceptually appreciating that which indirectly displays itself in these photographs that we obtain the decisive element of the "empirical evidence" that the relevant scientific concepts signify something and are not mere conceptual constructions. What appears in these confirming appreciations are configured importances possessing such important features and relations as being *immensely distant from us*, being *majestically spirally shaped*, or being *tremendously small and terrifically swift*. In these indirect self-displays, the configured importances reveal their holistic nature, which is describable in evocative terms. For instance, a cluster of galaxies displays itself as a *gargantuan configured importance* which is at an *exceedingly immense distance from us*. Such a holistic importance is purely appreciated in an awestruck perceiving-feeling. The immensely distant and gargantuan importance, as indirectly displayed in the photograph, emanates an awesome tonal-flow that towers up and over me from within the sensuously felt interior of the photograph and transfixes me so that I shudder back from it in awestruck appreciation. This immensely distant gargantuan importance is explicated in evocative significations in the afterglow of the awestruck perceiving-feeling. In these significations, the "empirical evidence" is described just as it was explicitly intuitively felt in the confirming appreciation. But in astronomical theory, this important holistic nature of the cluster of galaxies is abstracted from, and the "empirical evidence" is conceptually reconstructed in terms of supposedly neutral mathematical determinations. Not only are the evocative explications eliminated, but the exact explications of the holistic importance in terms of configured-importance sizes, shapes, and distance relations are neglected in favor of mathematical and neutralizing conceptual substitutes. In its pursuit of perfect conceptual exactitude, astronomical theory loses its reference to the empirically discoverable realm of imperfectly exact and holistic configured importances.

In order to avoid some of the possible misunderstandings to which the above analysis of scientific thinking is subject, the following clarification is in order. My analysis is not to be understood as espousing one of the "philosophies of science" that have been developed in this and the last century, phenomenalism, operationalism, and scientific realism.

The first philosopher to develop thematically a phenomenalist or operationalist theory of science is Ernst Mach;[31] subsequent thinkers who expounded one or the other of these two philosophies of science include Henri Poincaré, Pierre Duhem, Russell (in his phenomenalist period from 1914 to 1924), Percy Williams Bridgman, Carnap (in 1928), Herbert Dingle, Gustav Bergmann, Karl Pearson, and Stephen Toulmin. The difference between my account of science and these phenomenalist and operationalist theories appears in my affirmation that there *exist* configured importances that are gargantuan and immensely distant from us, or that are tremendously small and terrifically swift. These importances indirectly display themselves to us in photographs (for example). They are neither "neutral constructions out of neutral sense data" nor "neutral constructions out of directly observed neutral material objects." Nor are they even important constructions out of hues or directly displayed configured importances. They are not *constructions* (theoretical fictions, mere explanatory devices) at all, but *existing innerworldly importances* that we discover upon the occasion of their indirectly displaying themselves in our perceiving-feelings. My discussion of the manner in which configured importances exist in VI.38 will make it more clear how my conceptions of these importances differ from any phenomenalism or operationalism.[32]

It would be a mistake, however, to conclude that since I am not a phenomenalist or operationalist I am therefore a "scientific realist." It is arguable that scientific realism as an expressly formulated philosophy of science first appeared in the preface to Christian Huygens's *Treatise on Light* (1690); contemporary versions of this philosophy have been formulated by Karl Popper, Hempel, Wilfred Sellars, Russell (in his later period), William Kneale, Lewis White Beck, and Grover Maxwell. My account of science differs from theirs in that I hold that scientific concepts *as* scientific concepts do not refer. It is the conceptions-of-importances into which the scientific concepts are translatable that refer. This does not mean that I believe there to be no difference between a "substantiated" scientific theory and an "unsubstantiated" one. It is true that both substantiated and unsubstantiated scientific theories are referenceless, but they differ in that the decisive conceptual constituents of the substantiated theories are translatable into conceptions-of-importances that are referential, whereas the decisive concepts of the unsubstantiated theories are not so translatable. It is not probable that the conceptions-of-importances into which Georg Ernest Stahl's conception of "phlogiston" is translatable refer, but it is probable that the conceptions-of-importances into which current atomic theories of combustion are translatable refer.

The above remarks are not sufficient to constitute a "philosophy of science" — as certainly many problematic issues have been left undiscussed — but they are sufficient for my purposes of establishing that the *important* nature of reality is not taken into account in scientific thinking. This may seem like an innocuous and conventionally acceptable statement until one remembers that in this chapter I am presenting evidence that reality has *no other nature* than its important one.

My analysis of mathematics and science has aimed to show that the conception of thought-about phenomena that is operative in these disciplines exemplifies at bottom the same problem we found in the usual theories of perceptual phenomena, namely the tendency to conceive phenomena as neutral things that are apprehended in awarenesses different in kind than feeling-awarenesses. The importance/neutral dichotomy, with the attendant belief that the world "as it really is" is neutral and is apprehended in nonfeeling awarenesses, is characteristic of most contemporary outlooks upon the world.

We can begin to understand the epistemological origin of this view of reality if we have recourse to the distinction between evocative and exact descriptions made in the previous section, "The Language of Importances." Each phenomenon is both evocatively and exactly describable, such that it can concretely and completely be made manifest only if both of these descriptions are used. However, due to certain spiritual-theoretical motivations (to be discussed in the following section), one may be led to divorce these two ways of describing phenomena and to identify a selected group of phenomena with their nature as it is exactly and explicitly describable. In such a case, the exact conceptions of these phenomena are not understood to be ways of analyzing and making precise the evocatively and holistically describable nature of the phenomena, but are interpreted as complete conceptions of phenomena that concretely exist with a nature that is solely exactly analyzable. These phenomena that are solely exactly analyzable are then conceived as phenomena that in themselves are neutral and unrelated to feeling.

In several areas, a further step away from reality is taken. The exact conceptions derived from the phenomena themselves are found not to be "exact" enough, and this leads to the construction of perfectly exact concepts that can function in place of the former conceptions. Perfectly exact concepts, generated in *a priori* thinking (e.g., in *a priori* mathematical thinking), are substituted for the "merely" empirically exact concepts. But in this substitution, the substituted perfectly exact concepts were believed to possess an empirical reference, to refer to concrete things that really exist. In this way, the world is "reconstructed," as it were, to accord with the concepts of *a priori* thinking. But in truth what occurs is that thinkers find themselves faced with an exact-neutral world picture that refers to nothing at all.[33]

What motivated thinkers to believe in the referentiality of these theoretical constructions? This belief is an expression of rationalist spirituality, and is based upon the spiritual presuppositions that guided the epochs of rational meaning and meaninglessness. It is the *rational-spiritual perspec-*

tive that lies at the origin of the importance/neutral dichotomy and that leads to the belief in the referentiality of the exact-neutral reconstruction of reality. This perspective is explicitly developed and expressed in rationalist philosophy, and it is to this philosophy in its ultimate roots that we must turn if the importance/neutral dichotomy is to be traced to its origin.[34]

II. 14. The Origin of the Importance/Neutral Dichotomy in the Degeneration of Feeling to Reasoning

The dichotomization of the world into neutral and important aspects expressly originates in philosophical thinking as an essential element of its construction of a rational-metaphysical theory of the world. It is the task of this section to show how this dichotomy, and the attendant rational perspective on the world, result from certain feelings "degenerating" by withdrawing from reality and denying the basic conditions of truth.

The analysis of this degeneration is motivated by the following questions. If humans in essence are appreciative and extrarational beings, then how could the exact-neutral and rationalist view of the world ever have come about? How is it that *feelings themselves* (for all human awarenesses are feeling-awarenesses) could *denigrate* feelings and importances, and construct a view of man as the "rational animal" and a view of the world as a solely exactly determinable network of causal and teleological reasons and consequences? How is it that the world *as a whole of importances* is disregarded and is instead "reconstructed" in *a priori* thinking as a series of causes and effects and means and ends that are effects of an uncaused cause and are means to an ultimate end?

The nature and invalidity of this rational-metaphysical world-view was discussed in a historical context in the Introduction. In this section, I am going to trace the epistemological rather than historical genealogy of this rationalist metaphysics. This means analyzing the *epistemic degeneration* of certain feelings, their "fall" from their proper and sound epistemic functioning to an improper and unsound one. This analysis will be regressive; given the fact that these feelings have epistemically degenerated, what are the origins, motives, and stages of this degeneration?

This regressive analysis has two assumptions that I am endeavoring to substantiate in this treatise: (1) humans are appreciative beings, and the world is a whole of importances; and (2) the metaphysics of reason is untenable. If these two assumptions are true, then how can we epistemologically account for the emergence of a rationalist spirituality?

Due to the unfamiliarity of the terrain to be traversed in the following analysis, the sense and direction of the analysis will appear somewhat obscure at first, but shall gradually become clear as the analysis is brought to a conclusion.

The feelings that degenerate and originate the rational-metaphysical perspective are philosophically concentrative feelings. In their nondegenerate nature, these concentrative thinkings are second-order reappreciations of the intuitively felt world. While the first-order reappreciations, the afterglows, form evocative significations that capture the intuitively felt importances as they explicitly and holistically appeared, the concentrative feelings form exact significations that capture the precisely analyzable content of these importances that implicitly appeared. In this way, the concentrative thinking-feelings exist in harmony with the intuitive feelings and the afterglowing thinking-feelings; all three cooperate in a methodological sense in making manifest the truth about the world. The concentrative feelings, however, are not fastened unfreely and without alternatives to this cooperation. Concentrative feeling possesses a freedom and creative power, and is able if it wishes to deny its dependency upon the two lower levels of methodological feeling and attempt to become, to the degree that it can, an independent and self-sufficient source of truth about the world. The desire for such independency is an everpresent possibility inherent in concentrative thinking; this thinking can become "infatuated" with itself and its explications, and through this infatuation can be led to believe that only "exact thinking" and "exact significations" are capable of making manifest the truth about the world. With this conviction, concentrative thinking is moved to "purify" its conceptual contents from the contributions of evocative thinking; the vague and evocative significations that capture the holistic importance of intuitively felt phenomena are eliminated, and only exact significations are retained. The conviction is developed that the world as it really is, is solely exactly determinate in nature and that significations are untrue and inadequate to the extent that they are "inexact."

It is in this conceptual "reconstruction" of the world as solely exactly determinate that the importance/neutral dichotomy first arises. Two senses of this dichotomy are developed, one being based upon the other.

In the first and more fundamental sense of the dichotomy, the nature of things as it is holistically manifest in intuitive feeling and is evocatively described in afterglowing thinking is dichotomized from the nature of things as it is exactly manifest in concentrative thinking, such that the nature as it holistically appears is interpreted as unreal, as a "mere semblance," and the nature as it appears in an exactly analyzed way in concentrative thinking is interpreted as the sole and complete "reality" of things. Intuitive feelings are interpreted to be "confused apprehensions" of the exactly determinate nature of things, such that what is *explicitly* felt in intuitive feeling, the nature as it holistically appears, is degraded to the status of a confused and misleading appearance of what is *implicitly* felt in the intuitive feeling, the nature as it is exactly analyzable.

In this sense of the dichotomy, importance has the sense of the nature of things as it is explicitly intuitively felt and is evocatively describable, and "neutral" has the sense of the nature of things as it is implicitly intuitively felt and as it is explicitly and exactly knowable in concentrative thinking.

This sense of the dichotomy sets the stage for the development of a second sense of the dichotomy, which is conceived to obtain within one half of the first dichotomy, the exactly determinable half. The exactly determinate features of things are divided into factual features (such as size and mass) and valuable features (the good and the evil). This neutral/importance dichotomy in the sense of a fact/value dichotomy originates in a further degeneration of the concentrative feelings beyond the point described above. This further degeneration is the decline into the full-blown "rationalist perspective" on the world, and can be outlined in some of its main stages as follows.

The step of identifying realities with the exactly determinable contents that are implicitly manifest in intuitive feeling is not sufficient to satisfy the degenerated thinking-feeling's desire for maximum autonomy and self-sufficiency. For this identification entails that the degenerated thinking-feelings are still dependent in an essential way upon the intuitive feelings for their knowledge of realities. This dependency consists in the fact that the significations formed by the degenerated concentrative feelings are still understood to be significations of something that is manifest in intuitive feeling, namely the exactly determinate nature of things that is implicitly but not explicitly felt in intuitive feelings. The degenerated concentrative feelings desire to be able to formulate true significations that do not depend for their truth upon being related to something that is manifest in intuitive feelings, significations whose truth can be established by "pure thinking" alone.

The condition for this desire to emerge is that the degenerated feelings become blind to the criterion of the truth of the significations they form. This criterion is implied in the nature of the truth of significations. The nature of significational truth is *signifying something*; that is, a signification is true in that it signifies something. This implies that the criterion of the truth of a signification is *the discovery of the thing* purportedly signified by the signification. A signification is verified as true if the thing it purportedly signifies is discovered. In order to discover the signified something, one must go beyond a mere concentration upon the signification itself, for in such concentration one can only discover that there exists a signification being concentrated upon. To find the signified, one must leave the realm of concentrated-upon significations and have recourse to what is manifest in intuitive feeling, where one will find (if the signification is true) that which the signification signifies.

The becoming blind of the degenerated concentrative feelings to this criterion of truth is a result of their "infatuation" with the exact significations they form; these feelings close themselves off from intuitive and afterglowing feelings, and endeavor to shut themselves up in a "passionless" realm of pure thought. We find here the opposite state of affairs than that traditionally held responsible for a blindness to the truth. For it is not through succumbing to "passion" (taken here to mean intuitive feelings and their afterglows) that blinds one to the truth, but through succumbing to "passionlessness."

Through succumbing to "passionlessness," the degenerated concentrative thinkings come to believe that significations can be formed whose truth is verifiable by pure thinking. It is believed that such significations can be formed if some principles can be constructed that putatively sanction such formations. These principles would seemingly justify a thinking that, although beginning with a reference to intuitive feeling, is able to continue independently of this reference; specifically, these principles would seem to justify an inference *from* a true signification of an intuitively felt reality *to* a true signification of an unintuited reality. This inference would be justifiable if it could be "known *a priori*" that each intuitively felt reality is a term of certain kinds of relations to other realities, such that if these other realities are not themselves given in intuitive feeling, their existence can nevertheless be inferred from the existence of the intuitively felt reality.

These supposedly "*a priori*" principles are constructed from materials that are originally manifest in intuitive feeling. These intuitional materials are kinds of intuitively felt relations susceptible to being conceptually fashioned as relations which can be "known *a priori*" to connect intuitively felt realities with other putative realities that are not intuitively felt. There are two basic kinds of felt relations that meet these conditions.

Relations of the first kind are explicitly manifest in intuitive feeling as relations of *enhancement* and *detraction* between importances. One intuited phenomenon is felt to enhance or detract from the importance of some other phenomenon. A man cutting a limb from a beautifully blossoming tree, or a flash of lightning doing the same, is felt to detract from the beautiful tree's importance. A blazing fire that heats up a portion of mutton is felt to enhance the mutton's importance in that it adds to the mutton the positively important feature of being cooked to a tasty and nutritious state. And again, the bountiful sun is intuitively felt to enhance the importance of a stone by generously bestowing upon it an agreeable warmth.

These are some of the examples of enhancing and detracting relations that are intuitively felt to obtain among importances. "Enhancing" and "detracting" are evocative significations that capture these relations as they explicitly and holistically appear in intuitive feeling. The degenerated concentrative feelings do not build upon but eliminate these evocative significations, replacing them with exact significations that explicate the precisely determinable nature of these relations that is implicitly manifest in intuitive feeling. The precisely determinable nature of the intuitively felt relations is regarded as the *sole* and *complete* nature of the relations, and is given the name "causal relations." The concept of "cause," which in truth is an exact way of making explicit the intuitively felt *enhancing* and *detracting importances*, is interpreted as referring to a reality that is solely and completely exactly determinable, and the concept of an "effect," which is in truth a way of exactly explicating the *enhanced* and *detracted-from importances*, is interpreted analogously. These concepts are then employed in the formulation of a supposedly *a priori* "principle of causality," that "each thing in the world is an effect of a cause" (or "each thing in the world has a causal explanation"). This principle is believed to enable the degenerated thinking-feelings to transcend intuitively felt realities, in that it allows each intuitively felt reality to be regarded as an effect of some cause, such that in cases where no cause is manifest ("confusedly") in any intuitive feelings, the thinking-feelings are permitted to infer the existence of a cause.

In order for the inferred causes to be "knowable" in a determinate way, the basic principle of causality must be expanded upon to include such subsidiary principles as "effects resemble their causes," "effects cannot be more perfect than their causes," and numerous others. And in order for the degenerated thinking-feeling to be able to infer more than one unintuited cause for a given intuitively felt reality, a principle that seems to warrant inferences to completed causal series is formulated. It is supposed that each thing in the world not only has a causal explanation, but a *complete* causal explanation. Any given unintuited cause is assumed to be an effect of a more remote unintuited cause, and this of a still more remote unintuited cause, and so on until the series is completed.

It is in the principles concerning completed causal series that the degenerated thinking-feelings allow themselves to obtain a special kind of "metaphysical knowledge" that is intuition-transcendent and unique to themselves. Since these degenerated feelings aspire to be the sole arbitrators of the truth, this putative metaphysical knowledge is believed to be the only kind of metaphysical knowledge. The knowledge in question concerns the ultimate terminus of the causal series. By following in "pure thought" the chain of unintuited causes and effects to its completion, the degenerated thinking-feelings arrive at a concept of an uncaused first cause of the entire causal series. There are essentially two principles that supposedly warrant this inferential knowledge of a first cause. The first is that a temporally regressive series of causes and effects cannot be infinite, but must terminate in a first cause, and the second is that a series of causes and effects that exist simultaneously cannot be infinite but must terminate in a first cause that ultimately sustains the other causes in existence. If both principles are employed, the first cause of both of these series is interpreted to be the same existent, and this existent is represented as the "meaning" of the world, in the sense of the *causal reason* that explains it.

Further principles and conceptions, such as that of an existent whose essence is to exist, are formed in order to complete this conception of a causal reason for the world. But the principles and concepts that are based upon or directly associated with the principle of causality are not sufficient to allow the degenerated concentrative feelings to believe they can attain a complete intuition-transcending explanative knowledge of the world. A further basic principle also needs to be constructed. This is indicated by the fact that a recourse to the principle of causality raises but leaves unanswered a fundamental kind of explanative question: Why does this thing cause that thing? This question ultimately has the form: Why does the first cause cause the world? A reason that explains why causes operate is needed. Such a reason must be a term of a relation that is of such a nature that it explains the existence of the causal relation.

As with the case of the causal relation, the construction of the concept of this second kind of explanative relation operates with materials selected from the phenomena of intuitive feeling. The suitable intuitional materials are relations which explicitly and holistically appear in intuitive feelings as *magnetizing relations*. These relations have as one of their terms *magnetizing importances*, these being felt meanings that beckon or draw us towards themselves. Sometimes we are beckoned towards two or more such importances, but only one may end up drawing us towards itself. In such a case, the magnetizing importance emits felt lines of attraction that induce our body and surrounding phenomena to gravitate towards the magnetizing importance, and to thereby acquire a gravitated importance. *Gravitated importances* are the other terms of the magnetizing relation. An example illustrates how these relational terms are manifest in intuitive feeling. The magnetizing importance that manifests itself in intuitive feeling as the endangered-neighbor-who-is-screaming-for-help-and-who-needs-to-be-rescued emits lines of attraction that induce surrounding phenomena to become important in a gravitated way. The floor becomes gravitated towards this magnetizing importance through becoming important-to-be-hurried-over-to-the-rescue; the rope and knife become gravitated through becoming important-to-be-grabbed-as-I-hurry-past-towards-the-rescue; and my body becomes important-to-hurry-over-the-floor-and-towards-the-knife-and-rope-on-the-way-to-the-rescue.

Magnetizing relations can also be intuitively felt to be dormant in cases when a magnetizing importance is not currently emitting lines of attraction. Things are then felt to be disposed to be attracted by certain types of magnetizing importances. The ax that is lying besides me has the disposition of being magnetizable by such types of importances as the warming-firewood-needing-to-be-chopped.

The nature of these phenomena as it is explicitly and holistically felt is disregarded by the degenerated concentrative feelings, and their nature as it implicitly appears and is exactly determinable is interpreted as their sole and real nature. This exactly determinable nature is conceptualized in categories of putatively complete realities, called "purposes" (or "ends"), "means," and "teleological relationships." Magnetizing importances are exactly analysed and completely identified with their implicit nature as *purposes*, gravitated importances as *means* to these purposes, and magnetizing relations as *teleological relations*.

These conceptual constructions enable the degenerated feelings to construct a supposedly "*a priori*" principle of teleology, that "each thing in the world is a means to an end" (or "each thing in the world has a teleological explanation"). Realities that are "confusedly" manifest in intuitive feeling can be interpreted as means to some end, such that if the end or the teleological relationship that the felt reality has to this end is not itself manifest in intuitive feeling, its existence can be inferred by an intuition-transcending thinking. The scope and content of such inferences are increased through the construction of subsidiary teleological principles, such as the principle which states that "things of an inferior type (e.g., plants) are a means to the existence and well-functioning of things of a superior type (e.g., animals)," and the principle of *complete* teleological explanation, which asserts that "the series of means and ends culminates in an unconditioned end." These principles, combined with related principles, are believed to enable the degenerated concentrative feelings to reason *a priori* to the concrete nature of the unconditioned end, which is the final purpose of the world's nature—this purpose being the contemplation of the causal reason for the world.

The teleological relation of a means to an end is such that it is able to provide the explanation of the causal relation desired by the degenerated thinking-feelings. The reason a certain effect is brought about is because that effect is a means to the attainment of some purpose, and the reason the purpose is attained is that the purpose either is a means to the unconditioned purpose or is itself the unconditioned purpose. It is the unconditioned purpose that provides the final reason for every conditioned purpose and for every effect. The unconditioned purpose also explains why the world-whole itself is caused; it is in order to attain the unconditioned purpose that the first cause causes the world.[35]

A purpose, since it is the reason for the existence of the means to that purpose, can be termed a "teleological reason." Means, correlatively, can be termed "teleological consequences," i.e., consequences of a teleological reason. A means exists *because* or *for the reason that* it is required to attain a certain purpose.

That which brings a means into existence is a cause. Every means is an effect of a cause and hence is not only a teleological consequence but also a "causal consequence," i.e., a consequence of a causal reason.

Since in this fashion purposes and causes are both *reasons* for things, and means and effects are both *consequences* of reasons, the principle of causality and the principle of teleology can be united under a more general principle, which states that "each thing in the world is a consequence of reasons that sufficiently explain it." This is the principle of sufficient reason, which is the most general and fundamental principle of degenerated and intuition-transcending thinking.

The principle of sufficient reason, in order to provide a complete guidance to the degenerated thinking-feelings, must be expanded to apply to the significations formed by these thinking-feelings as well as to the realities putatively signified by these significations. The signified realities are interconnected as reasons and consequences in the causal and telic sense, and the significations themselves must be conceived to be correspondingly interconnected as reason and consequence, but in a different sense of "reason" and "consequence." This is a *logical* sense, where some significations are "logical reasons" (premises) for other significations, the "logical consequences" (conclusions) of these reasons. The putatively signified reasons and consequences comprise the subject-matter or material of the degenerated thinking, and the signifying reasons and consequences comprise the method and form of this thinking. "Reasoning" accordingly has two senses. In its material sense it is a thinking about causal reasons and their consequences or telic reasons and their consequences; reasoning in this sense is named "causal reasoning" or "teleological reasoning." Reasoning in its formal sense is the logical manner of forming significations about causal and telic reasons and consequences; "reasoning" in this sense means inferring conclusions from premises.

Reasoning in these two senses operates in reference to two corresponding senses of "Why?" and "Because . . . " The material Why? asks about a causal or telic reason for the existence or nature of a thing and is answered, "Because of this cause of which the thing is an effect" or "Because of this purpose to which the thing is a means." The formal "Why?" asks about the logical reasons for the truth of a proposition and is answered, "Because of these premises from which the proposition is inferred" or "Because (as a self-evident proposition) it contains the reason for its truth within itself."

These material and formal senses of why/because and reason/consequence are believed to parallel each other in the two orders of the signified and the signifying. Logical reasons are conceived to be significations of realities that are causal or telic reasons, and logical consequences are conceived as significations of realities that are causal or telic consequences. Every effect can be signified in a proposition that is a conclusion of premises at least one of which signifies the causal condition of the effect, and every means can be signified in a proposition that is a conclusion of premises at least one of which signifies the purpose to which the means is a means.[36]

By means of this parallel ordering of formal and material reasons and consequences, degenerated thinking believes itself able to obtain in principle an inferential knowledge of the unconditioned cause and purpose of intuitively felt realities. This knowledge is supposed to be obtainable through backward inference; that is, given a true proposition, it is supposed to be possible to construct premises from which this proposition can be deduced. This chain of backward inferences is assumed to begin with the realities that are "confusedly" manifest in intuitive feeling. These realities are conceptually interpreted as a means or effect; a proposition is formed about the means or effect, and is assumed to be a logical consequence of other propositions asserting the purpose or cause that explains the means or effect. These latter propositions can then be formed, and they can in their turn be represented as logical consequences of still further propositions. This is possible because the propositions asserting the purpose or cause of the original "confusedly" intuited means or effect are reinterpretable (according to the principle of sufficient reason) as propositions about purposes that are themselves means to some further purpose, or causes that are themselves effects of further causes. These further purposes and causes are then backwardly inferred, and the inference chain continues until the final purpose and first cause are reached. The propositions asserting this final purpose and first cause will be the first premises of all knowledge, the unconditioned logical reasons of which every other logical reason is a direct or indirect consequence.

This parallel ordering of logical and causal/telic reasons and consequences in an explanatory chain that terminates in the unconditioned is presupposed as obtainable in principle by the degenerated thinking-feelings, even though in empirical fact these thinking-feelings may not be able to obtain a complete knowledge of it. The chain of inferences may be too great or complicated to be constructed *in toto*. Accordingly, a knowledge of the existence of this chain, and especially of the unconditioned causal and telic reasons that stand at its termination, is allowed to be obtainable even if a knowledge of the entire chain is not attainable. It is allowed that some arguments can directly lead to a knowledge of the unconditioned, without the chain of conditions needing to be backwardly traversed *in toto*. One of these arguments was referred to above, viz., "There exists a causal chain; a causal chain cannot be infinite; therefore, there is a first cause." It also can be allowed that the premises asserting the unconditioned causal or telic reasons are not only unconditioned logical reasons, but also are logical reasons that are self-evident to us and accordingly can be immediately and noninferentially known

It is in such a manner that we see the unfolding of the "rational perspective" on the world. It is in relation to the full unfolding of this perspective that we are able to comprehend the origin of the neutral/importance dichotomy in the second sense indicated above, the sense of the fact/value dichotomy. Importances in the sense of values are defined in terms of the concepts of reason and consequence.

The concept of a teleological reason plays the leading role in this definition of value. Every purpose is conceived to be (identically) a real or apparent good. A real good is regarded as a purpose that either is or is a means to the unconditioned purpose, and a real good is knowable in principle in that a proposition asserting it either is or is a logical consequence of a proposition asserting the unconditioned purpose. A merely apparent good is a real evil; it is a purpose that in reality is not a means but an obstacle to the attainment of the unconditioned purpose.

The concept of a teleological consequence (means) is also essential to the definition of value. Teleological consequences are good or evil indirectly, depending upon whether they are consequences of good or evil telic reasons. Ultimately, all good telic reasons but the unconditioned telic reason are good because they are immediate or mediate consequences of the unconditioned telic reason; the unconditioned telic reason is unconditionally good, i.e., is good in itself.

Telic reasons and consequences are related to causal reasons and consequences as their explanations, and through this explanative relation determine the causal reasons and consequences to be good or evil. A cause produces an effect because the effect either is or is a means to a purpose. A causal activity is good if its effect either is or is a means to the unconditioned purpose, and is evil if its effect is an obstacle to this purpose.

The goodness of a causal activity is determined by its essential, not accidental, effect. The essential effect of one animal eating another is the nourishment of the eater (which is good), and the accidental effect is the death of the eaten animal (which is evil). Consequently, the causal activity of eating the animal is good. This means that evils arise in the world not only as merely apparent good purposes but also as accidental effects of the attainment of really good purposes.

It is in such fashions that telic and causal reasons and consequences are believed to comprise the good and evil properties of things. These properties coexist with factual properties. Things not only have the properties of being purposes and means to purposes, and of being causes and effects, but also such properties as being round, white, four feet in diameter, etc. Factual properties, in other words, are those properties *other than* the ones that enable things to be reasoned about in intuition-transcending explanative thinking.

The identification of causal and telic properties with "important properties" and the other properties with "neutral properties" is based upon what seems "important" and "unimportant" to the degenerated feelings. What seems "important" to these feelings are the features of things that purportedly enable them to be reasoned about in an intuition-transcending thinking. What seems "neutral" to these feelings are the features of things that are not purported to be the bases of such thinking. "To be important" is to be a reason or consequence, i.e., to be something that supposedly can satisfy the need of the degenerated concentrative feelings to transcend intuitive feelings and engage in an autonomous determination of the truth.

The origins of this distinction can be understood in a more fundamental sense if the concepts of value and fact are traced back to the intuitional materials from which they were constructed. The world as it is intuitively felt manifests a number of different kinds of important features, of which the relational features involved in enhancing/detracting and magnetizing relations are only some. Many of these important features served as materials for the conceptual constructions of the exactly determined properties that were attributed to things in the rationalist world-picture. Some of these important features, the above-mentioned ones, were used as materials for constructing concepts of value-properties, and other of the important features, such as many configured-importance features, were used as materials for constructing concepts of factual properties. The idea of being "important" in some sense was retained only in regard to the features that could be conceptually reconstructed in ways that suited the intuition-transcending needs of the degenerate concentrative feelings. All important features but the relational features involved in the enhancing/detracting and magnetizing relations were stripped of any vestige of their importance and regarded as "neutral properties."

The sense in which these degenerate feelings regard values as "important phenomena" and facts as "neutral phenomena" can be clarified in terms of the ordinary sense of "important" and "neutral" discussed in Section 12 of this chapter, "The Language of Importances." In the ordinary sense, something is important if it elicits sensuous feelings and is evocatively describable, and something is neutral if it does not elicit sensuous feelings and is only exactly describable. The importance/neutral dichotomy in the second philosophical sense, the value/fact dichotomy, involves one aspect of this ordinary sense of the dichotomy: the idea that important phenomena elicit sensuous feelings and neutral phenomena do not. This idea appears in the theory that good properties of things cause pleasurable feeling-sensations and evil properties cause painful feeling-sensations, whereas factual properties do not cause feeling-sensations.

The other aspect of the ordinary sense of the dichotomy, that something important is evocatively describable and something neutral only exactly describable, is involved in the first philosophical sense of the dichotomy. In this sense, an importance is regarded as the holistic and evocatively describable appearance of a thing, and something neutral is regarded as the exact nature of a thing that explicitly appears in concentrative thinking.

The above analyses concern the basis of the fact/value dichotomy that was conceived in the metaphysical theory of rational meaning. In order to illustrate the form this dichotomy takes in the metaphysical theory of rational meaninglessness, the outline of the degeneration of the concentrative feelings must be developed further.

So far I have described two main stages of the degeneration of the concentrative feelings, the elimination of evocative significations, and the practice of intuition-transcending thinking. A third stage evolves from the first two, the stage of self-criticism. The emergence of this stage is motivated by the desire for conceptual exactness that gave rise to the first stage, except now this desire does not lead the concentrative thinking-feelings to "purify" their concepts from evocative elements (which has already been achieved), but to reexamine the concepts formed in the second stage to determine if they are as exact and logically rigorous as possible. Such a reexamination leads to the discovery that the theory formed in the second stage is not rigorous enough and that the degenerated feelings, due to the pressure of their desire to transcend intuitive feelings and engage in an autonomous determination of the truth about the world, developed many ill-formed concepts, propositions, and arguments. The faulty theoretical formations include such basic notions as the idea that there must be a first cause of the world, the idea that this cause is a necessary existent, and that each thing in the world is a means to a purpose and ultimately to an unconditioned purpose.

The devastating nature of these self-criticisms leads the concentrative feelings to question the very legitimacy of the desire to transcend intuitive feeling, and this questioning enables these feelings to recover in part from their "blindness" to the criterion of truth, the criterion which asserts that significations are verifiable only through signifying something that is discoverable in intuitive feeling.

We find in this "regaining of sight" a *partial regeneration* of the degenerated concentrative feelings. They regenerate to the extent that they recognize their dependency upon intuitive feelings for their determination of the truth. But this regeneration is only partial, for these feelings have not become wholly awakened to the criterion of truth, and they still retain a number of false or unverifiable concepts formed by the intuition-transcending concentrative feelings.

The awakening to the criterion of truth is only partial in that the "intuitive feelings" the concentrative feelings are recognized to be dependent upon are "intuitive feelings" in the truncated version conceived in the first stage of degeneration. In this stage, the holistic and evocatively describable nature of the phenomenon that explicitly appears in intuitive feeling is regarded as a confused manifestation of the thing's exact nature that implicitly appears, such that this exact nature is regarded as what the thing "really" is. Significations are regarded as verifiable insofar as they signify this exact nature of the intuitively felt thing. This belief about verifiability is tantamount to retaining the importance/neutral dichotomy in the first sense.

The second respect in which these critical degenerate feelings fail to regenerate completely concerns the retention of essential elements of the fact/value dichotomy. For instance, values are still held to be related to sensuous feelings, and facts to lack such a relation. The retention of this and other elements of the fact/value dichotomy is accompanied by a rejection of the elements that provided for a rationally meaningful world-view. The idea that there is an unconditioned and absolute value that is knowable in intuition-transcending thinking is rejected, and values are conceived in a relativistic and anthropocentric manner. The world or nature is regarded as intrinsically valueless, as a nonteleological realm of neutral facts. "Importances" in the sense of "values" are regarded as "projected upon" the realm of neutral facts in a logically unjustifiable way by human beings.

This nihilistic version of the importance/neutral dichotomy in the second sense is a result of the *merely partial* regeneration of the degenerated feelings. They retain *some* elements of the wholly degenerated feelings, the concepts of fact and value and of causal and telic reasons and consequences, and at the same time become *somewhat* reintegrated with intuitive feelings by denying the possibility of an intuition-transcending knowledge of an unconditioned value and of unconditioned reasons in general. These partly regenerated feelings can overcome their nihilism *either* in a deceptive manner by slipping back into the completely deluded beliefs of the wholly degenerated feelings, *or* in a veridical manner by completely regenerating.

The complete regeneration of these feelings amounts to their adoption of the metaphysical perspective of feeling. This regeneration involves abandoning all senses of the importance/neutral dichotomy.

To abandon the first philosophical sense of this dichotomy is to recognize that each intuited reality is veridically describable in both evocative and exact ways. To abandon the second sense of the dichotomy is to recognize that each intuited reality is a source of sensuous feeling.

With regard to the degenerately formed significations of *facts, values, causes, effects, purposes,* and *means,* this means that such significations are to be recognized as unverifiable. They do not signify any reality that can be discovered in intuitive feeling. For they are significations of realities that are solely exactly determinable, and no such realities are discoverable. Moreover, the concept of a fact is additionally problematic in that it is the concept of something that is not the source of a sensuous feeling, and such neutral things are undiscoverable. What are discoverable are not facts and values, and causal and telic reasons and consequences, but *importances* in the nondegenerate sense.

Nevertheless, if we are willing to use the terms "fact, value, cause, effect, purpose, and means" in new and nontraditional senses, it is possible to allow that such terms have a reference. They can be used to express ways of making explicit such holistically felt and evocatively describable importances as magnetizing importances, enhancing and detracting importances, and configured importances. The significations of value, cause, etc., are verifiable only insofar as they signify the implicitly intuitively felt nature of an importance that explicitly appears in a holistic and evocatively describable way.

If the terms "fact" and "value" are used in this way, it can be seen that the fact/value dichotomy is not between neutral phenomena and important phenomena, but between two types of importances in respect of their implicitly felt nature. Certain magnetizing importances, for instance, differ from certain configured importances in that the former implicitly manifest aspects like fairness or generosity, whereas the latter implicitly manifest only such aspects as circularity or ellipticity.

The complete regeneration of the concentrative feelings not only involves appreciating world-parts as importances in the non-degenerate sense, but also appreciating the world-whole in this way. The critical degenerate feelings regard the world-whole as a *brute fact,* as an intrinsically neutral whole that cannot be known to be created for the sake of realizing value. The world-whole's purposelessness and valuelessness, however, is in truth an implicitly felt aspect of *a way in which the world-whole is important,* its *futility* and *emptiness,* an importance that is the source of a feeling-flow of hopelessly-sunken-to-the-bottom-of-the-world.[37] This importance, moreover, is only *one* of the many important features of the world-whole, along with other such features as fulfillment, supremacy, immensity, harmoniousness, etc.

This reference to the spiritual regeneration of the feelings that concentrate on the world-whole brings to a conclusion my outline of the motives and stages of the epistemic degeneration of the philosophically concentrative feelings. This outline has made manifest that the rationalist view of the world and the attendant important/neutral dichotomy do not arise from a "faculty" in man distinct from and superior to his feelings, a putative "rational faculty" that knows the world in intuition-transcending thinking, but instead arise as an expression of *one type of feeling*, an epistemically degenerate type. The concentrative feelings through denying their real nature and disassociating themselves from the intuitive and afterglowing feelings falsify the world and set the stage for a crippling nihilism. Regeneration can only come through reintegrating themselves with the intuitive feelings and their afterglows so as to cooperate in unfolding an epistemically sound view of the world as a meaningful whole.

In the immediately preceding pages, I have discussed the *predominant* form of the degeneration of feeling that is manifest in the epoch of rational meaninglessness. A word here can be added about a very different form this degeneration sometimes acquires. This form appears in a *reversal* of the relative epistemic positions assumed by the concentrative and evocative thinking-feelings during the epoch of rational meaning. The evocative thinking-feelings revenge themselves, as it were, against the concentrative feelings by asserting their own epistemic superiority, and divorce themselves from the concentrative explications of that which is evocatively thought. "Poetic thinking" or the like is heralded as the arbitrator of the deepest truths about the world, truths that are completely disclosed by this thinking, such that these truths cannot be further developed by exact thinking, and are distorted or destroyed by such attempts at development. Exact thinking is misrepresented or is represented merely as "calculative thinking" (or alternatively, as "logocentrism"), and *merely* vague notions are put forth concerning presence, the ontological difference, traces, *différance*, totality, infinity, the face, and the like. This degeneration involves a denial of or blindness to an epistemological principle the descriptions in this treatise are devoted to establishing: that every evocatively describable phenomenon has an implicit content that can be made explicit in precise concepts, and can be done so without impairing or destroying but instead by *harmonizing with* the evocative explications. The degeneration of the evocative feelings, far from healing the traditional spiritual division in human beings between their evocative and exact awarenesses, *retains* it — but in a reverse form.

Much more could be said about this degeneration of the evocative feelings, but I shall not pursue this matter here, inasmuch as I am concerned with analysing the predominant form in which the degeneration of feeling has assumed in the epoch of reason — the degeneration of the concentrative feelings.

The analysis of the origin of the rational perspective on the world in the degeneration of concentrative feelings presented in this section further brings to completion the task set for ourselves in the introduction to Part 1. It was indicated in these introductory remarks that the nihilism in which we are currently enveloped can be transcended if we come to realize that the discoverable world is not a network of causal and telic reasons and consequences that are themselves ultimately for no reason, but is instead a whole of important sources of tonal-flows. In Chapter 1, I made it manifest that the world as sensuously felt is not a world of causal reasons that explain our feeling-sensations of pleasure or pain, but is composed of feeling-tonalities that flow in a certain direction and manner. In the present chapter it has been shown that the exactly determinate "causal reasons" conceived in the traditional theory of the sensuously felt world are in truth mere constructs created by degenerated feelings. What is connected to our sensuous feelings are not "causal reasons" but *importances*. Each phenomenon in the world is an importance in that it is a source of flowing tonalities and in that it is evocatively and exactly describable. It is *as such* that the world is discoverable.

Most of the descriptions in this chapter, however, have elucidated the important nature of the world in reference to important *parts* of the world-whole, such as hue-displaying configured importances, magnetizing importances, flowing importances, and the like. The important *features* of the world-whole have not received sufficient attention. It is the explication of these features that is especially crucial to spiritual regeneration, for this explication directly confutes the nihilistic belief that the world *as a whole* has no knowable meaning. The next chapter is devoted exclusively to these global meanings and the feeling-awarenesses in which they are revealed.

CHAPTER III

Global Feeling-Awarenesses and Global Importances

The aim of Part One of this treatise is to examine the nature of feelings and the world as felt, with special attention to global feelings and the felt features that belong to the world in its wholeness. I have maintained that the I's feelings are feeling-sensations and feeling-awarenesses, and that the features of the world as felt are feeling-tonalities and their important sources. In Chapter 1, I examined the purely sensuous aspect of these phenomena, the feeling-sensations of the I and the feeling-tonalities of the world. In Chapter 2, I described the other aspect, the I's feeling-awarenesses and the importances of the world apprehended in these feeling-awarenesses. But the descriptions in the latter chapter were incomplete; I described primarily the mundane feeling-awarenesses and importances, without thematically investigating their global modalities. This deficiency is remedied in the present chapter, the subject of which is the *global feeling-awarenesses* and the *global importances* which are appreciated in these feeling-awarenesses.

My interest in particular is in the *intuitive* global feeling-awarenesses, and the global importances as they appear in these feeling-awarenesses, for it is these phenomena that form the basis and reference point of the nonintuitive and reappreciative feeling-awarenesses of the world-whole's importances. These intuitive feeling-awarenesses are the *global moody intuitions* and the *global affective intuitions*. The moody phenomena are described in Division A of this chapter, the affective phenomena in Division B.

Division A:
GLOBAL MOODS AND GLOBAL IMPORTANCES AS THEY ARE MOODILY APPRECIATED

III. 15. Preliminary Characterization of Moods and Their Difference from Affects

Moods, like affects, have a multiform nature. I am interested in describing their globally intuitive nature, but this requires that we first gain some idea of the nature of moods in general. This can be achieved by briefly contrasting the general nature of moods with that of affects, and by reviewing in a summary way the historical development of the distinction between moods and affects.

A principle difference between moods and affects concerns their *origination*. Affects are consciously directed responses to the importance that elicits them, whether this eliciting importance be a part of the world or the whole of the world. But moods are not conscious responses to the phenomena that originate them; moods are diffuse feelings about everything in general, even though this felt "everything in general" is not necessarily, and does not appear as, what brought on the mood in the first place.

Compare the mood of melancholy with the affect of grief. Melancholy "comes over me" as a generalized feeling about the world, without my apprehending anything that gave rise to the melancholy. But the affect of grief arises as a response to the important event that elicited it, such as the death of a beloved.

This difference between the relation of moods and affects to their origination has been explicitly noted by some of the phenomenological philosophers in this century, but it has been implicitly recognized as far back as the fourth century B.C. We know that Aristotle was aware of affects and their responsive relation to their originating phenomena, for his classifications of feelings in Book 2 of *Rhetoric* concern the feelings that involve a conscious relation to their causes. "Pity," Aristotle writes, "is definable as a feeling of pain caused by the sight of a destructive or painful evil that happens to a person who does not deserve it."[1] Here the "sight of some evil" may be understood as Aristotle's conception of the *affective awareness of an importance* that belongs to the concrete feeling of pity. In Book 1 of *On the Soul* Aristotle makes a remark that seems to indicate he also recognized the phenomena of moods; he writes that "men sometimes are overcome by a feeling of fear without anything threatening having occurred."[2] This remark evinces a recognition of the mood of fear or anxiety, which comes over one without being felt as a response to any threat that instigates it.

The same implicit and brief recognition of moods also appears in Descartes's *Passions of the Soul*, which, like Book 2 of Aristotle's *Rhetoric*, is a classification of affects. Descartes remarks in passing that sometimes "we feel sad or joyous without being able to give a reason,"[3] although at other times the sadness or joy is experienced (in an affective awareness) as an effect of an evil or good object of the senses.[4]

The recognition of the difference between moods and affects is expressed in some of the works of twentieth-century analytic philosophers, e.g., in Russell's *An Outline of Philosophy*,[5] but it is the phenomenological philosophers who explain this distinction in an explicit and systematic way. This distinction is merely incipient in Husserl's writings,[6] but in Scheler's writings it is expressly made. Scheler points out that affects are responses to a valuable phenomenon which is grasped as their motivating object, whereas moods possess no such directedness to a motivating object. An affect of joy, for example, is a response to the presence of some good, such as the return of one's beloved after a long absence, whereas a mood of cheerfulness is not directed towards anything that is comprehended as the motive for the cheerfulness. Thus it is possible to wonder in moods: "Why am I in this or that mood [*Stimmung*] today? What is it that makes me melancholy or cheerful?"[7] I can form hypotheses about the motive for my mood, but the mood itself does not refer to its motive.

Von Hildebrand developed Scheler's distinction between moods and affects in chapter 17 of *Ethics* by maintaining that moods are unintentional experiences, whereas affects are intentional. Moods or states, "such as being tired, being in a bad humor, being irritated, and so forth, have no conscious relation with an object."[8] They do not intentionally refer to an object, like affects (the intentional object of affects being their motive), but are subjective states of mind that do not refer beyond themselves.

A new way of looking at moods developed out of Heidegger's analyses of findedness (*Befindlichkeit*) in *Being and Time*. By "findedness," whose ontic manifestations are "moods" (*Stimmungen*), Heidegger did not mean "moods" in the sense of a class of feelings distinguishable from other classes of feelings (such as affects), but feelings in general. Nevertheless his analyses prove applicable to "moods" in the narrower sense as a specific class of feelings. This holds true in particular for his distinction of anxiety from fear. Although Heidegger himself does not say this, anxiety can be understood as a mood (in the narrower sense) and fear as an affect. Fear is a fear of a definite being within the world (e.g., another *Dasein*), whereas anxiety is not about this or that being within the world, but about Being-in-the-world as a whole.[9]

Strasser, strongly influenced by Otto Bollnow, who was himself influenced by Heidegger,[10] developed these ideas of Heidegger and attempted to synthesize them with some of Scheler's and Von Hildebrand's insights. While maintaining the thesis of Scheler and Von Hildebrand that affects refer to their motives whereas moods do not, he rejects the thesis that moods are purely "subjective states of mind" that do not refer to the world, and replaces it with the Heideggerian idea that moods disclose Being-in-the-world as a whole.[11] Strasser acknowledges that moods do not have an intentional consciousness of an object, but asserts that they nevertheless have a preintentional and nonobjectifying awareness of the world as a whole:

> A mood is not "purely subjective"; it is transubjective and transobjective as well. It precedes the subject-object dichotomy which our knowing, evaluating, striving, intending, and opining consciousness usually always produces. A mood is a feeling of the All.[12]
>
> To show this phenomenologically is not difficult. If I am in an elevated mood, *all* appears to me "in a rosy light"; if I am depressed, then I see *all* "gray on gray."[13]

With this theory of Strasser, which is repeated in its general outlines by Paul Ricoeur,[14] we have a recognition of the *global* character of moods. This global character was expressed in a succinct way by Robert Solomon, who said that moods "attend to the world as a whole, typically without focusing on any particular object or situation."[15] Now it is not encumbent upon us to accept the details of these conceptions of the global character of moods, or of these conceptions of the nature of the world-whole revealed in moods, but we can accept the general tendency of these conceptions and use it as a point of departure of our own investigations into the moody intuitions of the important world-whole. Following the ensuing three sections on moods, affects will be examined in order to show that they are also capable of being global in nature, although in a different way than moods.

III. 16. *The Constant Global Characters of Moods*

In every mood there is an awareness of the world-whole, and to this awareness there belongs several distinguishable characteristics, which I shall call the *constant global characters of moods*. In each mood there also lies a potential to achieve a special kind of awareness of the world-whole, a contemplative awareness, but this potential is seldom realized. To this occasionally experienced contemplative awareness there belongs the *exceptional global characters* of moods. In this section, the constant global characters are discussed; the exceptional characters are the subject of the next section. In the third section I elucidate a metaphysical problem that is posed by these constant and exceptional global characters of moods but which is insoluble on the basis of these moody characters alone. The recognition of this problem will serve as an impetus to proceed to an explication of global affects, wherein this problem finds its resolution.

The constant global characters can be described from a fourfold point of view, relative to: (i) the moody awareness of the deep and broad world-emanation of the moody tonalities, (ii) the intuitive character of the moody awareness of the important world-whole, (iii) the unfocused character of this awareness, and (iv) the extralogical character of this awareness. A description of these characters will show that we are not trapped in mundanity, aware only of a small part of the world, but are in our moods constantly opened up to the world as a whole, and to a meaning of the world as a whole. It is by virtue of our moody feelings, and not by virtue of *a priori* "rational thinking," that all of us are in daily contact with metaphysical meanings, and thereby are metaphysical beings in our innermost nature. In rational metaphysics, it is usually assumed that we can intuit only this or that part of the world and that to apprehend the world-whole we must engage in intuition-transcending thinking. But a metaphysical perspective that is epistemically sound and integrated with intuitive feeling is based on a recognition that we *do* have intuitive access to the world-whole, a regular and daily access in our moods, and hence that it is neither necessary nor permissible to transcend intuition in order to obtain a metaphysical knowledge. A metaphysical theory can be developed through describing what appears in these daily moody intuitions.

III. 16.i. The Moody Awareness of the Deep and Broad World-Emanation of the Moody Tonalities

The global awareness that belongs to every mood is an awareness of concrete moody features of the world-whole, i.e., of moody tonal-flows that have a deep and broad world-emanation, and of the global importances that are the sources of these tonal-flows.

We know from Chapter 1 that feeling-tonalities have a deep world-emanation if they flow from the *interior* of the world, from behind its sensible surface. They have a deep and broad world-emanation if they flow from the *whole interior* of the world, the world as a whole that lies behind the entire sensible surface of my surroundings. The sources from which the moody tonalities flow lie within this global interior; these sources are the important features of the world-whole.

The different ways in which the world-whole is important are experienced as correlating with the different types of moody tonalities, so that each type of global importance is the source of a corresponding type of moody tonality. As a moody tonality of anxiously suspended quavering begins to permeate everything in my surroundings, I begin to apprehend the world-whole as *ominously* important, and I feel this global ominousness to be the source from which the anxious tonality is flowing. Likewise, an upwardly radiated euphoric tonality has its source in the global importance of *fulfillment*, and the hopelessly sunken tonality of depression flows from the *emptiness* of the world-whole.

The moody tonalities are different from the global importances in that, among other things, they are *sensuous feelings*, whereas the importances are neither sensuous nor feelings. The moody tonalities have a pleasurable or painful quality, and flow in a certain direction and manner, but the importances have none of these characteristics. The importances are rather features of the world-whole that are the *sources* of the sensuous and qualitatively flowing moody tonalities. The importances are *that which is appreciated* in moods, whereas the tonalities are constituents of the moody appreciation.

The nature of the moody tonalities has largely been described in the discussion of the broad and deep world-emanations in Chapter 1, but their important sources have not yet been investigated. Accordingly, the following three subsections shall be concerned with the moody awareness of these importances.

III. 16.ii. The Intuitive Character of the Moody Awareness of the Important World-Whole

The moody awareness of the important world-whole is intuitive in that it is immediate or direct; it is not mediated by words, concepts, or images. The words "world as a whole," "empty," or "harmonious" are not present to my awareness. I apprehend the world-whole wordlessly, in an inner silence. And I do not have a concept of the world-whole; I am not holding before my intellect a concept that signifies or refers to the world-whole. Nor do I have before my mind an image that symbolizes the whole. Rather, the whole is directly apprehended; what is before me is the world-whole itself, not some mental representation of it.[16]

But if the moody awareness is to be called "intuitive," this cannot be meant in the traditional sense of a *unidirectional* apprehension that singles out one phenomenon among others. With Henri Bergson, for example, one beholds the duration of the self; with Husserl, one is intentionally directed upon an *eidos*. The moody awareness by contrast is *omnidirectional*; I feel the presence of a phenomenon everywhere, without having to turn my awareness in this or that direction in order to apprehend it. The omnipresence of a world-importance pervades the field of my awareness, extending ominously or mysteriously or monotonously everywhere I turn.

In most moods, the omnidirectional intuition is a marginal *intuitive sensing* of the world-importance. The important whole does not appear in the foreground of my awareness but in the background; its presence is vaguely sensed on the horizon of the phenomena of which I have an attentional awareness. For example, I can read a book while in a depressed mood. Here I am attending to what I am reading, but at the same time I have a marginal awareness of a depressing world. On the horizon of my concentration upon the subject matter of the book, I have a dim sense of the futile and empty importance of everything.

The horizonal character of the moody awareness means that the mood opens up a space in the foreground of my awareness for a concern with specific activities or existents within the world. I can engage in vocational activities, interpersonal relations, etc., or I can let my attention wander, and daydream. It is by virtue of the horizonal character of the appearance of the whole of the world that the foreground of my awareness is relegated to an occupation with this or that part of the world.

The moody awareness contrasts quite sharply in this respect with the awareness usually characteristic of affects. This affective awareness does not open up any attentional space for me, but occupies all my attentional space. In the affects of rage, terror, and joy, my attention is completely absorbed in being aware of the phenomenon I am raging at or am terrified of. It is obvious that I cannot read a book while undergoing a terrified affective response to an armed robber.

While in most moods the omnidirectional intuition is a horizonal sensing, in some moods it is a *foreground contemplating*. The potential to achieve such a contemplative awareness is possessed by all moods, but only occasionally is it realized. Due to the complex and exceptional nature of this contemplative awareness, I shall devote a separate section to it (*III.17*).

III. 16.iii. The Unfocused Character of the Moody Awareness of the Important World-Whole

The moody awareness is not focused but is relatively indefinite and indeterminate. This character of the moody awareness can only be understood if it is clearly distinguished from the usual horizonal character of the awareness. That to have an unfocused awareness is not the same thing as to have a horizonal awareness is shown by the fact that it is possible to have an unfocused foreground awareness. This is not only possible in moods, but also in such holistic bodily feelings as delirium, drunkenness, and exhaustion; in such feelings I am not experiencing a focused act of attention but a diffuse awareness that does not apprehend definite phenomena which have finely articulated structures or sharply defined boundaries.

It is such indeterminacy that belongs to the moody awareness of the important world-whole. In the following, I will consider first what it means to have an unfocused awareness of the *world-whole*, and then what it means to have such an awareness of an *importance* of the world-whole.

It may be asked, "Of the many different kinds of wholes-of-parts, what kind of whole-of-parts is the world apprehended as in the moody awareness?" But such a question cannot be answered without falsifying the moody awareness, for it would be to make definite and determinate what is indeterminately given in the mood itself. Inasmuch as this awareness is unfocused, all that can be affirmed of it is this: it is not an enumerating or collecting awareness of the world; it does not single out each and every individual in the world and combine or add them together into a totality. Rather, it is an awareness of something unitary. The "whole" of the world appears as a unit, a one, but not as a simple one; it manifests itself as a one-of-many, as a single whole composed of multiple parts. Some of these parts individually appear, such as this table or that tree, but most appear in the almost wholly indiscriminate form of "that which composes the world." Moreover, this awareness is too unfocused to even articulate this whole into basic sections (e.g., "nature," "society") or types of constituents (e.g., "animate things," "inanimate things").

Analogous remarks can be made about the unfocused awareness of the importance of the world-whole. The world-whole appears to be important in some way, but there is no determinate aspect of the whole that appears to have this importance. Not only do I mean that no *part* of the world-whole, e.g., this person or that region of nature, is given as what has this importance, but also that no determinate character that the world possesses in its nature *as a whole* is given as having the importance. In serenity, for example, I am aware of a good and harmonious world-whole. But I am not aware of any specific way in which the world-whole is good and harmonious. If somebody asked a serene person, "In respect of what is the world good and harmonious?" or "What is it about the world that leads you to believe it is good and harmonious?" the serene person would not be able to answer. The good and harmonious nature of the world-whole does not appear to be structurally articulated. It is not the case, for example, that the world-whole appears harmonious *in that* it is a teleologically ordered network of means and ends, or *in that* everything is an expression of an *élan vital*, or *in that* everything is a manifestation of Brahman. Rather, the world-whole appears harmonious *in no determinate way*. The unfocused awareness of the serene mood can be explicated no more exactly than by saying that it is an awareness of "a good and harmonious whole."

III. 16.iv. The Extralogical Character of the Moody Awareness of the Important World-Whole

The unfocused omnidirectional intuition of the important world-whole unfolds on an extralogical level. What the mood is aware of cannot be derived from *a priori* logical principles or justified by logical arguments. This means not only that the moody awareness does not engage in deductive or inductive methods of thinking, but also that the results of these logical methods have no necessary bearing or effect upon the moody awareness.

To begin with, consider the irrelevance of syllogistic demonstrations to the moody intuition that the world-whole is important in some way. The endeavor to logically justify the mood of serenity, for example, by arguing that the world can be demonstrated to be good and harmonious, is essentially irrelevant to the serene intuition of this goodness and harmony. One could argue with Aquinas that the proposition that "the being of everything is good" can be deduced from the premises that "what is desirable is good" and "everything desires its own being."[17] But such a deduction has no essential bearing upon the serene intuition of goodness. The serene intuition is not aware of this demonstration of the world's goodness, is not based upon this demonstration, and senses no need for such a logical justification. A person could be completely ignorant of this demonstration and all similar demonstrations, and still feel assured in his serenity that everything is good. Moreover, a person could even be aware that this demonstration and all similar demonstrations have been shown to be invalid, and remain unaffected in his serenity.

But the failure of all attempts to demonstrate syllogistically that the world-whole is good is not all that is irrelevant to serenity. It could even be successfully argued on inductive grounds that the world-whole is not good and harmonious, but malevolent and strife-ridden, and this would still leave the serene intuition unaffected. An inductive argument might conclude that the empirical evidence indicates that the world exhibits a vicious struggle of part against part, that it is a chaos of conflicting elements, or a "swarming confusion" of particles/waves of energy. But such inductive arguments would not exclude a mood of serenity, for this mood is not an intuition of these inductive generalizations, and it is not based upon these generalizations. It is possible, for instance, that a Darwin or Heisenberg would be no less capable of a serene mood than thinkers who come to fundamentally different conclusions about the world, e.g., an Aristotle or Ptolemy. A Darwin or Heisenberg could very well conduct his studies in an "unaccountable serenity"; he could have an intuitive sense that "everything is good and harmonious at bottom," without attempting to articulate or explain this intuition to himself and without attempting to relate this intuition to the results of his scientific investigations. The "eyes" through which he looks upon the world in his moods are different from the "eyes" through which he looks in his scientific cognitions.

The above-mentioned differences between the moody awareness and the logical modes of awareness can be summed up by saying that the moody awareness is *noninferential*; it is not involved in, and is not based upon, inferring conclusions from deductive or inductive premises. The moody awareness apprehends that the world-whole is important, and that it is important in this or that way, without grasping any ground for this apprehension and without sensing any need or requirement for such a ground.

These remarks on the extralogical character of the moody awareness conclude the discussion of the constant global characters of moods. The exceptional characters are discussed in the next section.

III. 17. *The Exceptional Global Characters of Moods*

What is it to achieve a foreground awareness of the world-whole? Do I become completely oblivious of this or that part and grasp instead a distinctionless unity? (How could such a pure undifferentiated unity be the world-*whole*, i.e., a whole-*of-parts?*) Or do I remain marginally aware of the individual nature of some parts and achieve a foreground awareness of the whole they help to compose?

It appears that the latter is the case. The first possibility may be an experienceable awareness, but it is not the global awareness experienced in moods.[18] The foreground moody awareness of the whole I call a *metaphysical* or *global contemplation*. In it a feeling-tonality of the world-whole comes to a foreground appearance (cf. III.17.i.), as well as a global importance (cf. (III.17.ii); contemplation is different, however, from a foreground moody mulling (cf. III.17.iii).

III. 17.i. Realizing the Potential for Contemplating a Feeling-Tonality of the World-Whole

An essential factor that is involved in realizing the potential for global contemplation is "getting in touch" with the moody feeling. Usually the moody feeling is consigned to the periphery of my experience, pushed aside, as it were, by the urgency of my mundane strivings or the intensity of my affective responses to this or that world-part. In order to "get in touch" with the moody feeling, I must relax my concern with the mundane importance that is the source of the striving or affect, and let myself flow primarily with the moody feeling that has its source in the whole.

Consider that in a bored mood I am frequently attentionally engaged in some vocational activity or in some attempt to divert myself from the boredom. But the possibility is always before me of terminating my resistance to my boredom, of abandoning or relaxing my strivings to do this or that, and of "giving in" to my bored orientation to the whole. This process of "giving in" is not, however, a turning of my awareness back towards my ego and of directing my apprehension upon the feeling-sensation of boredom that adheres to my ego. In such a case, I would achieve a foreground awareness only of one part of the world, namely my ego and its feeling-sensation. To bring the boring world-whole into the foreground of my awareness, I must unfocus my awareness and let my awareness become pervaded by the feeling-tonality of the world. I let myself sink into the gray haze of the boring world-whole. A vast fog of boredom seems to emanate from a source deep within the global interior; it drifts listlessly from everywhere, muffling and enshrouding everything. My awareness comes to an unfocused rest in this great stagnancy of the whole.

In this process of opening up contemplatively to the moody tonality of the world-whole, I do not close my eyes or otherwise become oblivious to my perceptual surroundings. Rather, my surroundings appear as the part of the world in which the feeling-tonality of the whole is able to be sensuously apprehended. The boring and stagnant tonality of the whole seems to imbue the perceptual phenomena in my surroundings: the landscape, the sky, and everything else within my view seems to be dull and lifeless. The boring stagnancy of the whole seems to penetrate through this landscape and sky and acquire here a sensuous embodiment for me. But my awareness is not confined to what I perceive; I apprehend my surroundings as only one part in the vastness of the boring whole.

If I cease my strivings in order to "give in" to the boredom, I will no longer experience (even marginally) a feeling of striving, but I will marginally experience some type of mundane feeling. This is necessary, for I am still *aware* of individual world-parts, this sky, those trees. I am marginally experiencing a perceptual appreciation of the panoramically hued environment, e.g., a somber landscape. This somber panorama marginally emanates a tonal-flow that adds a dark tinge to the dulled flow of the boredom.

In order to engage in global contemplation, it is not always necessary to cease my strivings and to experience on the mundane level nothing more than a marginal perceptual appreciation of my panoramically hued surroundings. I can "let myself go" and drift into the vast monotonous whole as I absently engage in some routine chore, like washing the dinner dishes. In such a case, the global dullness is coexperienced with a marginally felt *physical effort.*[19]

III. 17.ii. Realizing the Potential for Contemplating an Importance of the World-Whole

The contemplative opening up to the moody feeling-tonality of the world-whole is at the same time a realization of a foreground contemplation of the importance of the world-whole. This contemplation is realized through allowing the important whole to emerge from the horizon and swell into the foreground, so as to overwhelm apparentially the mundanely important things that once occupied the foreground. An omnidirectional intuiting displaces the unidirectional intuiting as the center of my experiencing. I open myself primarily to that which is omnipresent. This means neither that I am lost in a distinctionless simplicity nor that I am singling out each thing that exists, but rather that I am directed to the one omni-apparent whole of which each thing partakes. I am singling out a few world-parts, but they are being appreciated primarily in regard to their feature of *partaking of* the omnipresent whole. The mundane importance that these parts have relative to their individual nature (as this or that configured importance, magnetizing importance, intrinsically flowing importance, enhancing or detracting importance), appears only marginally and is overshadowed by the metaphysical importance these parts have in their common aspect as participants in the important world-whole.

In euphoric contemplation, there is a diffuse intuitive feeling that the world is a *fulfilled* whole. As this fulfilled whole emerges into the foreground, I begin to appreciate the parts around me primarily as *ful-*

filled parts of this whole. Each part has this importance, not through being this person or that tree, but simply through being *a part* of the fulfilled whole.

Although both the fulfilled whole and its fulfilled parts that are around me appear in the contemplated foreground, my contemplative awareness is more oriented to *the whole*. This whole shines into me from before me and all around me as the boundlessly appreciable. It is comprised of every innerworldly importance that exists; there is no importance that falls outside of it. I am experientially deepened and broadened into a feeling of *maximal importance*, a feeling of an importance that is *more important* than any other importance. Every other importance is but a part of the maximal importance, and is only partly as important as the maximal importance.

This contemplative feeling of maximal importance is made fully explicit in the moodily reappreciative thinking-feelings in the following way. Each and every thing that appears in a feeling-awareness is an importance. In globally contemplative feeling-awarenesses, all the things in the world in some sense appear, although most of them appear in an indeterminate way and are not individually singled out. Most of them appear vaguely as belonging to the indiscriminate mass of "all the other things beyond the ones I am currently singling out in my perceiving or striving." Nevertheless, they do appear in some way, and in so appearing they appear (as do all appearing things) as importances. It is realized in the reappreciative thinking that a whole composed of anything less than all the parts of the world does not include some importances. Accordingly, a whole that includes both the importances of this lesser whole and the importances this lesser whole does not include, is a whole of more importances than the lesser whole. And this means the greatest whole there is, the world-whole, is the whole that includes the *most importances* within itself. In this sense there is *more importance* belonging to this whole than to any whole that is a part of the world. And this is what it means to say that the world-whole is the most important whole that exists.

It is possible to perform an imaginative exercise in the reappreciative awareness that illustrates and further substantiates this sense that the world-whole is the most important importance. I can begin by imagining some mundane whole, such as myself, and comparing it with a whole that includes myself and some other things, e.g., members of my family. It is imaginatively and noninferentially felt that the whole composed of myself and other members of my family is a more important whole than the whole represented by myself alone. If this were not the case, I would have to feel that the other family members are absolutely unimportant and that they cannot add any further importance whatsoever. But in apprehending them, I feel that they *are* important, and hence that they add to my importance. I can further imaginatively compare the whole composed of my family members and myself with the whole of humanity. It is felt that my family, myself, and all other human beings comprise a more important whole than that comprised by myself and my family alone. I can then add all other living and nonliving things to the whole of humanity and imaginatively feel that this larger whole is even more important than the whole of humanity.

But most significant of all is the last stage in this imaginative experiment. I can imagine the whole of all that exists except for one thing that is relatively unimportant, e.g., a pebble on a beach. Does the addition of this pebble make an even more important whole? The pebble is relatively unimportant, but it is not absolutely unimportant: it is noteworthy (it is worthy at least of being examined to see how important it is), substantial, smooth, shiny, and it is something that exists. I can appreciate it in a perceiving-feeling as a hue-displaying configured importance. It is a source of feeling-flows, perhaps of enchantment with its smooth and shiny surface or perhaps only of inertial indifference.[20] It is both evocatively describable (shiny, etc.) and exactly describable (reflects light, etc.). I see that it is important, and thus that the whole that includes the pebble, and which is the whole of *everything*, is more important than the whole of everything but the pebble. In this way it is imaginatively realized that the world-whole is more important than any mundane whole, no matter how large the mundane whole may be.

Despite this fact, most people devote most or all of their time to appreciating in a foreground way some mundane whole, such as themselves, their families, their fellow workers and workplaces, and their friends and recreational entertainments. Humans for the most part spend their lives appreciating, without realizing this explicitly, importances other than the most important importance. They do not realize this explicitly because they fail to realize their potential for global contemplation that belongs to their moods. This failure is due to the *declination into mundanity* that holds sway throughout virtually all human existence, the perpetual *narrowing* or *making shallow* of one's appreciative openness, so that one becomes receptive to the importance of *this thing* or *that thing* but not of *everything*. The deep and broad reception of the absolute totality of importance is usually or always confined to the horizon of one's experience, displaced by the magnetizing importances, configured importances, and intrinsically flowing importances that emanate mundane striving or affective flows. The metaphysical nature that belongs to all humans remains for the most part horizonal and undeveloped.

III. 17.iii. Global Contemplation Distinguished from Moody Mulling

Global contemplation is somewhat similar to, but is not to be confused with, another attitude that can also be adopted in moods, a mulling over mundane concerns. Moody mulling is similar to global contemplation in that it involves letting myself go from my mundane strivings and affects and "giving in" to the sensuous moody feeling and awareness of importance. But the moody feeling and awareness of importance are not allowed to hold sway in their pure state, as a feeling and awareness of importance that are oriented to the world-whole. Rather, they are diverted towards specific individual phenomena that are singled out on the basis of mundane concerns. Moreover, whereas the global contemplation is intuitive, the mulling is nonintuitive, involving thinking about or imagining this or that world-part. I begin mulling over these phenomena in the light of my moody feeling and sense of importance: I become involved in moody thoughts, in reliving certain scenes in my memory, and in daydreaming. In a depressed mood, for instance, I cease my strivings and "give in" to my downcast feeling and to my sense of futility and emptiness; but instead of contemplating the world-whole in this light, I begin mulling over mundane matters. I have depressed thoughts that "I will never be successful in my career as a doctor," that "my friends don't really like me," that "I will never be able to pay off all my debts," and so forth. What I appreciate as futile are the specific activities and phenomena that belong to the sphere of my mundane concerns. I am not letting myself "give in" to the pure moody sense that *everything* is futile and empty instead of just my career and financial state. By mulling over the futility of this or that mundane concern, I keep the futility of everything at bay, relegated to the horizon of my awareness.

This differentiation of mundane mulling from global contemplation concludes the description of the exceptional global character of moods. In the next section we shall encounter the metaphysical problem that is posed by the constant and exceptional global characters of moods.

III. 18. *The Metaphysical Problem Posed by the Moody Awarenesses*

There lies dormant in moody intuitions a metaphysical problem whose implications seem to cast into doubt the veridical character of the moody awarenesses, and which appears to be insoluble on the basis of the metaphysical data provided by moods alone. This is the problem of *the seemingly clashing ways in which the world-whole is felt to be important*. This problem arises in moods themselves, and on the basis of the phenomena manifested in the moods themselves, and is not a problem imported into moods from the outside. It is originally experienced in the *reappreciative moody thinking* that arises in the afterglow of certain mood changes. It is recognized that the way in which the world-whole appears to be important in one mood clashes with the way it appears to be important in another mood, and that there is no basis or criterion in the moody intuitions themselves for deciding which of these clashing appearances is the veridical one.

Consider the following mood changes. I may begin by feeling depressed, and in this depression the world-whole intuitively appears to me to be empty and futile. But then my depression lifts and I begin to feel serene or even euphoric, and the world-whole appears to be harmonious or fulfilled. As this latter mood comes over me, I form the tacit judgement that the world-whole is not really futile and empty after all, but had merely seemed to be empty due to my depression. In the new mood, let us say it is a euphoric one, I feel that the world-whole is really fulfilled and that it really deserves a euphoric appreciation rather than a depressed one.

Now the problematical character of this "see-saw" among mutually cancelling world-views is not recognized in these moody intuitions themselves, for in each mood it is unthematically and intuitively felt to be the case that the world-whole *is* the way it appears to be in that mood, and the previous clashing appearances exhibited by the world-whole are tacitly discounted as deceptive appearances. It is not until a moody thinking has ensued wherein I no longer *live in*, but *reflect upon*, my moody intuitions that I can recognize the problematic nature of these changing world-views. In the afterglow of one of these mood changes, I can turn back upon and compare the incompatible feelings of intuitive givenness; in this reflective comparison I can recognize that the givenness which is felt in the mood whose afterglow I am experiencing is *no different in character* than the givenness felt in the incompatible mood I had earlier experienced. In both cases, there is a *feeling of the intuitive presence of a certain global importance*, and since there is no other internal mark that could serve to distinguish on an epistemic level one of the moody intuitions from the other, the reflection upon these intuitions is led to the conclusion that the purported metaphysical data provided by these intuitions are *unreliable and incoherent when considered in terms of themselves alone.*

Stated in a more explicit way, this conclusion has the following form: if the world-whole is thought to really have the features it appears to have in the moody intuitions, then it is thought to really have features it cannot possibly have; for the world-whole cannot possess features that cancel each other out. Moods must be deluded experiences of the world-whole.

This is the conclusion to which moody thinking is led *insofar as the moody intuitions are considered by themselves alone.* However, if new and additional data can be obtained about the importances revealed in moods, data that show these importances to be *mutually compatible*, then this conclusion can be avoided. If such data could be obtained, then one of two possible ways of avoiding this conclusion would present itself. First, it might appear that the newly understood structural aspects of the importances indicate that some of them are real importances of the world-whole, whereas other ones, the ones clashing with these, are not real importances of the world-whole but merely deceptively seem to be so in certain moods. For example, if we learned more about the nature of the world-whole's fulfillment and emptiness, we might find ourselves in a position to know that the world-whole really is fulfilled, and really is not empty, although it deceptively seems to be empty in the deluded mood of depression.

The other possibility is that the world-whole really has *all* the ways of being important it appears to have in moods, but it has them *in different and nonclashing respects*. Thus we would no longer describe the fulfillment and emptiness of the world-whole in the brief sentences "The world-whole (as such and without qualification) is fulfilled" and "The world-whole (as such and without qualification) is empty," but would add further qualifications: "The world-whole *in this respect* is fulfilled," but "The world-whole *in this other respect* is empty."

Now it is known to the moody thinking that we experience *global affective intuitions* as well as global moody intuitions, and it can be recognized in this moody thinking that these affective intuitions are able to provide the further data about the world-whole's importances which are required in order to solve the problem posed by the moody appearances of these importances. The solution to this problem, as we shall see in Division B of this chapter, is the second of the two above-mentioned ones, viz., the world-whole really has all the importances it appears to have in moods, but it has them in different and nonclashing respects.

DIVISION B:
GLOBAL AFFECTS AND GLOBAL IMPORTANCES AS THEY ARE AFFECTIVELY APPRECIATED

III. 19. Preliminary Descriptions: Similarities and Differences between Global Affects and Moods

The aim of this division is to show how the metaphysical problem posed by moods can be solved by an explication of global affective intuitions. This will be done by comparing moods and affects and indicating how the unique metaphysical characteristics possessed by affects enable them to reveal the respects in which the different global importances are mutually compatible.

Global affects and moods are similar in that they are awarenesses of the important world-whole and of sensuous feelings that have their source in this whole. The quality and flow of their sensuous feelings are parallel in type: just as there is a mood of *depression* that has a downward and sunken feeling-flow, so there is an affect of *despair* that has a parallel feeling-flow; the affect of *joy* corresponds to the mood of *euphoria*, the affect of *dread* to the mood of *anxiety*, and so on.[21]

One of the differences between global affects and moods was stated at the beginning of III.15: global affects are consciously directed responses to the global importance that elicited them, whereas moods, although aware of a global importance, do not apprehend this importance as that which brought on the mood in the first place. Rather, in moods the originator of the moody feeling is not given. I feel anxious or serene, but do not know from what. In the following, this difference will be specified in terms of different *nontypological flow-characters* and *awareness-characters* of moods and affects.

The affective flow is experienced to have the character of being "made to flow" by the important world-whole: it is experienced as *emanated from and by* the important world-whole. But the moody flow is not experienced to be *emanated by* the whole. This does not mean that the moody feeling-flow lacks a directional source; it means only that the moody "flowing from" the whole is not a flowing that is engendered by the whole. The moody feeling-flow is *emanated from* the whole, but not *emanated by* it. The "from" in the phrase "emanated from" has only a directional sense; the world-whole as the global interior is the "place from which" or the "directional source" from which the moody flow flows, but is not also the engendering power that *makes* the moody flow emanate from this directional source.

The engendering relation experienced in affects is a type of enhancing or detracting relation. Affective flows in respect of their feeling-sensations are important features of the I that feels, and their being engendered *by* a global importance is a way in which the importance of the I that feels is enhanced or detracted from.

The concept of "causing" is a way of exactly conceiving what implicitly appears in an intuitively felt enhancing or detracting. Accordingly, the engendering of an affective flow by a global importance can be said to be a "causing" of this flow.

Although engendering features are exactly determinable as causal features, source-features are not. To be a source from which a feeling flows is not by that fact to be a "cause" of the flow.

The world as it is felt, then, cannot (if only for this one consideration) be essentially characterized as a world of "experienced causes of feeling." For "felt causes" only manifest themselves in the world as it is affectively felt and not in the world as it is moodily felt.[22] The world as felt is essentially characterized in a way that pertains to both moods and affects, as a world of "experienced *sources* of feeling."

The above-described differences in the flow-character of moods and affects are mirrored by differences in their awareness-characters.

Moody intuitions are not captivated by the important whole. Consider, to begin with, the moods in which the potentiality for global contemplation is not being realized and which are engaged only in a horizonal *intuitive sensing* of the whole. In these cases, the important whole appears so uncaptivating that it leaves my attention free to concern itself with some other matter, with some world-part that is mundanely important.

Moody *contemplations* likewise are uncaptivated: they originate in my free choice to turn towards the already horizonally felt whole and to allow this whole to emerge into a foreground appearance. The whole does not capture my attention and hold it upon itself; I turn towards it and hold my attention upon it.

Contrast this voluntary origin of the contemplation with the involuntary origin of the affective *captivation*. In affects, an important feature of the world-whole spontaneously irrupts into appearance, without my first having decided to turn my attention towards that feature. It captivates me: a single spellbinding presence occupies and rivets my attention. This irruption may be occasioned by some event in my surroundings or by some train of thought or imagery, but this occasioning is not something planned or chosen. I look out my window and see a gloriously red sky; suddenly there emerges into presence the joyous *fulfillment* of the whole. Or I resolve some turmoil about my career or family, and the resolution occasions an expansion of awareness of such a sort that the *harmoniousness* of the world suddenly rises into appearance and bathes me in a global peacefulness.

In some cases, an irruption into affective omnipresence may not appear to be occasioned by anything; without warning, and without apparent connection to anything, the *emptiness* and *futility* of everything washes over me and casts me into the hopelessly sunken abyss of despair. Or I wake up in the middle of the night, startled at the *miracle* of the world.

Obviously these captivating importances cannot break forth into the consciousness of one who is closed off from the whole and who is completely and constantly absorbed in mundane importances. The whole cannot show itself to somebody who lacks the capacity or desire to appreciate anything but his family and friends, his career, his television set, and his next meal. A person must be globally receptive and open. These last remarks point to another way in which the origination of global affects differs from that of moods. Moods are originated regularly in everybody (although usually in a horizonal way), whereas global affects are only occasionally originated in some people.

The rarity of the experience of global affects is due to three things. One of them, already indicated above, is the *mundanity* of most people's concerns and capacities. This mundanity can be further described, following which the other two factors will be discussed.

Spirituality, the desire and capacity to know and appreciate meanings of the world as a whole, is not possessed by all people, and those who do possess it have it in different degrees. Relative to spiritual or global desires, four cases can be distinguished.

A person's predominant desire may be to know and appreciate global meanings; this person is maximally receptive to being captivated by global importances and he experiences global affects more often than mundane affects. This is the rarest type of person.

More common is the person whose global desires are secondary to his mundane desires for family intimacy, career success, friends, etc. This person may infrequently experience global affects, perhaps on occasions of great mundane crises or successes, but is usually closed off from them; they do not form the focus of the feelings of importance that govern his life.

A third case is a person who is bereft of global desires. His affective life is wholly absorbed by the mundane, and he feels no need for anything greater or more important than the objects of his mundane desires.

A fourth case concerns those people to whom global matters are neither something desired nor something to which they are indifferent, but are something to which they feel an aversion. In some cases, this aversion is based on a fear of global reality as something unfamiliar, as something that threatens the "reality"of their familiar mundane sphere. Such persons suppress any foreground global awareness, so that even their fear of global reality remains suppressed. In other instances of aversion to metaphysical importances, the aversion takes the form of scorn and contempt of the persons who affectively experience these importances. Persons who are wholly absorbed in mundanities, and yet who pride themselves on being "wise" and "intellectually superior," cannot allow that other people have a more fundamental experience of reality than they themselves do. In order to preserve their sense of superiority, they go out of their way to heap ridicule upon globally sensitive persons and to assert that such persons are "sick" or "deluded." All that can be "known" to be real, they passionately avow, are mundanities of the type in which they themselves are absorbed.

It is not only lack of desire but also lack of capacity that prevents many people from being receptive to global affects. It is clear that different people have different capacities to intuit or comprehend different things; e.g., some people have better eyesight than others, are more aesthetically sensitive, or are more able to comprehend mathematical theories, etc. Analogously, some people have a greater capacity to focus intuitively upon the world-whole. Just as an unintelligent person cannot intellectually grasp a complicated argument or a tone-deaf person cannot auditorily grasp a difference between two tones, so a globally insensitive person cannot intuitively grasp *the whole*. Globally insensitive persons who pride themselves on being "intellectually superior" frequently adopt the above-described attitude of scornful aversion to sensitive persons and to claims about global intuitions; their implicit belief is, "if *I*, a wise person, do not or cannot experience these intuitions, then they cannot be *veridical* intuitions!"

The second major cluster of factors besides the lack of global desire or capacity concerns the kind of spirituality people possess. Most people who are spiritually desirous and capable have a rational spirituality, and this means their spiritual affective life is directed towards the presence or absence of God (or absolute goodness) rather than the importance features of the world-whole. They experience mystical affects, or contrary affects like Godless desolation, nausea, or *angst*, but not *global affects* in the sense pertinent to the metaphysics of feeling. (Global affects are distinguished from mystical and other seemingly spiritual affects in III. 21.)

A third factor concerns people who are both desirous and capable of experiencing global affects but do not believe these affects are veridical. This sceptical attitude closes them off from the omnipresent global importances that they would otherwise be captivated by. One of the tasks of the metaphysics of feeling is to show that global affective intuitions *are* veridical and that such scepticism is unwarranted. The veridicality of global affects is not a "premise" of the metaphysics of feeling, or something to be "taken on faith," but is something to be *established* by the metaphysics of feeling. This establishment begins in the next section.

III. 20. The Difference between Global Affects and Moods That Enables the Global Affects to Resolve the Metaphysical Problem Posed by Moods

III. 20.i. Affective Intuitions Are More Focused than Moody Intuitions

The differences in the way moods and global affects are originated point to the third and crucial difference between these feelings, crucial in the sense that this difference is what enables global affects to resolve the metaphysical problem posed by moods. This third difference is what accounts for the first two differences, namely, why global importances *engender* the affective flows but not the moody flows and why these importances *captivate* the affective awarenesses but not the moody awarenesses. The explanation is that some aspects of these importances, the aspects which are flow-engendering and captivating, appear in affects but not in moods. More of the global importances, that is, more of their structural constitution, comes to appearance in the affects, and these constitutive aspects of the importances are such that when they come to an intuitive appearance they engender a feeling-flow and captivate one's attention. The global affect of tedium, for example, is more focused than its parallel mood of boredom. [23] Both are feeling-awarenesses of the global importance of monotonousness, but in the boredom, this monotonousness appears in a vague and unarticulated way, such that the monotonousness as it is manifest in the boredom cannot be analyzed into further elements or aspects that make it up. In the affect of tedium, on the other hand, the world-whole appears to be monotonous *in that* there are no interesting sequences unfolding in the world *qua* whole. Every moment, every hour, every day, the world in its wholeness is "just there," always the same, enduring inertly. All processes—interpersonal, physical, ideational, and the like—are or are features of this or that part of the world and are not features of the whole of the world. In this sense, the monotonousness comes to appearance in the tedium *as* articulated into structural aspects; it appears *as* the enduring unchanged of the processless "being a whole" of the whole. It is this determinate constitution of the monotonousness that captivates me, binds in a wearying way my affective awareness, and "makes me flow" backwards in a dulled manner. [24]

This difference gives rise to a different understanding of the *language* used in describing the importance as it appears in the boredom and global tedium. Relative to boredom, the sentence, "The world-whole is monotonous," is an *exact* explication of what appears in the bored intuition. But this same sentence understood as applying to what appears in global tedium is *inexact* and *suggestive*, the exact explication being "The world's physically, interpersonally and ideationally processless character of 'being a whole' endures unchanged."

In order to find an explication of the world-whole as it appears in the bored mood that, relative to this appearance, is inexact and suggestive, one must turn to such phrases as "all is gray upon gray" or "everything is muffled by a cosmic fog." (And these phrases would be even more inexact and suggestive than "the world-whole is monotonous" relative to the *tedious* appearance of the world-whole.)

The terms for the different global importances, *monotonousness, fulfillment, emptiness, supremacy, immensity, closeness, miraculousness, ominousness,* etc., may be understood as exact terms insofar as they are used to describe the appearance of these importances in moods, but as inexact and suggestive terms when employed to explicate their appearance in global affects. [25]

At this point we may raise the question, How does this difference in the determinateness of the appearance of global importances in moods and affects provide a means of solving the metaphysical problem posed by moods? It will be recalled that at the end of Division A of this chapter

I indicated that the affective intuitions enable us to understand how the importances belong to the world-whole in different and compatible respects. The determinacy of the affective appearance of the importances is such that the unique respect in which each importance belongs to the world-whole comes to appearance in the affective intuition of the importance itself. Because of this, it can be understood how the different ways in which the world-whole is important are compatible with one another, for each importance affectively appears as belonging to the world-whole *in a different respect.*

This can be illustrated by the global affects of tedium and awe and their corresponding moods. In ordinary language there is no word commonly used to designate the mood that parallels the affect of awe, so I shall decide somewhat arbitrarily to use the word "amazement" for this purpose. [26] The moods of boredom and amazement seem to disclose incompatible features of the world-whole, for it seems that the world-whole cannot without qualification be both *boring* and *amazing.* It seems that the world-whole must have either the importance of monotonousness and dullness or the importance of stupendousness and immensity.

But this seeming incompatibility is resolved once the determinate nature of these importances becomes disclosed. In tedium, it becomes manifest that the world-whole is dull and monotonous *in respect of the enduring unchanged of its processless nature;* in awe, it becomes apparent that the world-whole is stupendous and immense *in respect of its character as the greatest whole there is,* as a whole that is so great it indefinitely surpasses my capacity to single out in thought or imagination each and every one of its parts. It is recognized, in a reappreciative thinking that reflects upon and compares these two determinately appearing importances, that they belong to the world-whole in different and compatible respects. The world-whole is not immense *in that* it endures processlessly, but *in that* it is the greatest whole there is; it is not monotonous *in that* it is the greatest whole there is, but *in that* it endures processlessly. It is manifest, moreover, that the world's feature of being the greatest whole there is, is compatible with its feature of being a processless whole that endures unchanged.

It appears, then, that in global tedium I am aware of a different importance of the world-whole than I am aware of in awe. It is not as if in passing from tedium to awe I tacitly "change my mind" about how the world-whole is important (as I may seem to do in passing from boredom to amazement); rather, I change *the direction of my attention,* so that I turn towards a different feature of the whole.

The *complete* resolution of the problem of the seeming incompatibility of the global importances is accomplished through describing the affectively disclosed determinate nature of each global importance, and showing how these determinately disclosed importances are mutually compatible. This task is largely accomplished in Part 2, where the determinate nature of the various global importances is the major theme of my descriptions.

It can be pointed out here that the disclosure of this compatibility dissolves the basis for doubting the veridicality of global intuitive feelings. If global intuitive feelings clash with one another, then it is questionable if they are veridical. But if they are mutually agreeing, and no other veridical intuition clashes with them, then there is no justifiable basis to doubt their veridicality. If they seem in all respects to be veridical, then they *are* veridical.

This last remark introduces in a summary way the following detailed criticism of scepticism about global affects. I will show that any basis for doubting the veridicality of global affective intuitions is also a basis for doubting all intuitions, and that all intuitions cannot be coherently doubted.

III. 20.ii. *The Veridicality of Global Affective Intuitions*

That global affective intuitions are veridical can be shown if the nature and criteria of intuitional truth are made fully explicit. The nature and criteria of intuitional truth differ from the nature and criterion of significational truth; a signification is true if it signifies an importance, and the criterion for determining its truth is the intuitive discovery of the importance that the signification purportedly signifies.[27] Intuitive feelings, since they are not significations, possess a truth that has a radically different nature and set of criteria.

The nature of intuitional truth is manifested in intuitive feelings wherein the putatively intuited importance *is* and *is as it is intuitively felt to be*. In all intuitions, there intuitively seems to be an important state of affairs, and if there really is an important state of affairs, and if it really is just as it intuitively seems to be, then the intuition is veridical. The intuition is nonveridical if there intuitively seems to be an important state of affairs that *is not* or *is not as it intuitively seems to be*.

The criteria for determining the veridicality or nonveridicality of intuitive feelings become apparent once it is noted that in the strict sense of "intuition" only *veridical* awarenesses can be intuitions. For an *intuition* by its very nature is an immediate apprehension of something *as it really is*. A nonveridical awareness cannot, strictly speaking, *be* an intuition, but can (in some cases at least) *deceptively seem to be* an intuition. Such feeling-awarenesses are *delusory intuitions*. Real intuitions and delusory intuitions are analogous in that they both seem to be (real) intuitions, such that in this respect there is no experienced difference between the two. There cannot be an experienced difference in this respect, for if there were, a delusory intuition would not *be* a delusory intuition, i.e., it would not deceptively *seem to be* a real intuition.

This observation enables us to understand that there are two criteria for determining whether or not a seeming intuition is a real or delusory intuition. First, there is the *intrinsic criterion,* how the feeling-awareness *seems* to the person who is experiencing it. If the feeling-awareness *seems to be* a real intuition, then (according to this criterion alone) it *is* a real intuition. The second criterion is *extrinsic:* if there are extrinsic grounds for believing that the supposedly intuited importance does not exist, or does not have the features it was supposedly intuited as having, then the intrinsic ground, how the feeling-awareness seemed to the person who experienced it, is overridden, and the seeming intuition is determined to be delusory. But if there are no such extrinsic grounds, then the intrinsic ground is sufficient to determine the seeming intuition *to be* a real intuition.

Since real and delusory intuitions both meet the intrinsic criterion, since they both *seem to be* intuitions, it is only by reference to extrinsic grounds that they can be distinguished. Delusory intuitions are seeming intuitions the intrinsic grounds of which are overridden by extrinsic grounds, and real intuitions are seeming intuitions the intrinsic grounds of which are not overridden.

Since I shall maintain that we are justified in believing many global affects to be real intuitions, in that they are seeming intuitions whose intrinsic grounds are not overridden by any known extrinsic grounds, it is crucial to establish firmly that intrinsic grounds *are* sufficient (in the absence of overriding extrinsic grounds) to determine seeming intuitions to be real intuitions.

The intrinsic criterion for intuitional truth is an instance of the more general principle of intrinsically grounded belief, which states that "if something seems to be the case, then (in the absence of extrinsic grounds for believing otherwise) the very fact that it *seems to be* the case is a ground for believing that it *is* the case." This principle is equivalent but not identical to the principle of veridical seeming, which states that "all seemings are intrinsically veridical seemings; that is, in the absence of overriding extrinsic grounds, seemings are veridical." If the principle of veridical seeming is true, the principle of internally grounded belief is true, and if this latter principle is true, so is the principle asserting the intrinsic criterion of intuitional truth. It will suffice, then, to show in the following that the principle of veridical seeming is true.

That the principle of veridical seeming is true can be made manifest by describing what appears in a certain type of affect, an *absolutely epistemically confused affect.* This affect is an affective believing in the truth of a sceptical principle, a principle that is tantamount to a denial of the principle of veridical seeming. This sceptical principle is that "all seemings to be are intrinsically deceptive; they do not have an intrinsic ground of veridicality but of nonveridicality." This principle *seems true* to the absolutely confused person. It can seem true to him because he is too confused to recognize that if this principle does seem to him to be true, then it *is* false. There are two possibilities in regard to this seeming to be true. Either the principle's seeming to be true is a deceptive seeming and the principle is false, or the principle's seeming to be true is a veridical seeming, *in which case the principle also is false.* Consider this second possibility. If the seeming to be true is a veridical seeming, then the principle *is* true, and *all* seemings, including this one, are deceptive. Thus if this seeming to be true is a veridical seeming, it also is a deceptive seeming. And this means it cannot be a veridical seeming, for a veridical seeming whose very veridicality implies its nonveridicality *is nonveridical.* The sceptical principle, then, cannot veridically seem to be true, and this implies that its denial, the principal of veridical seeming, is true.

It might be believed that the denial of the principle of veridical seeming can be attempted in another way, a way that *is* coherent. Instead of asserting that all seemings *are* intrinsically deceptive, it could be asserted that all seemings *could be* intrinsically deceptive. More exactly, it is believed that "all seemings may be intrinsically deceptive or may be intrinsically veridical, and there is no presumption in favor of either possibility."

But this second sceptical principle also cannot veridically seem to be true, and can only seem to be true in an absolutely epistemically confused affective believing. For if all seemings could be intrinsically deceptive, then it is a possibly true belief that all seemings are intrinsically deceptive. That is to say, it is possible that there is a veridical seeming that all seemings are intrinsically deceptive. But it is not possible that there could be such a veridical seeming, for if all seemings are intrinsically deceptive, this seeming also is deceptive.

Since it is not possible or actual that all seemings are intrinsically deceptive, all seemings are intrinsically veridical. [28]

This applies to seeming intuitions. All feeling-awarenesses that seem to be intuitions *are* (in the absence of overriding extrinsic grounds) veridical seemings; that is, they are what they seem to be, intuitions.

In regard to seeming affective intuitions of the important world-whole, this means that if they are not overridden by extrinsic grounds, then their intrinsic claim to veridicality is unimpeached. The only possible source of extrinsic grounds capable of overriding seeming global affective intuitions would be veridical mundane intuitions that clash with the seeming global intuitions (for apart from intuitions of the whole of the world, the only other intuitions are of some part of the world). For example, if there were a seeming global intuition of the world-whole as being temporally finite, and if there were veridical mundane intuitions of world-parts that were temporally infinite, these latter intuitions would clash with and override the seeming global intuition. One of the aims of my descriptions in Part 2 is to make it manifest that there are many seeming global intuitions which are not overridden by mundane intuitions, and hence that there is no justifiable basis for doubting the veridicality of all global affects.

III. 21. Global Affects Distinguished from Mystical Affects, Existential Affects, Essential Affects, and Nature Affects

If the subject of my descriptions in Part 2 is to be the particular types of global affects, then it is necessary to first achieve a more precise idea of the general nature of these affects. In the preceding sections, I offered a positive account of their general nature. But equally significant is a negative account, that is, a determination of what these affects *are not*. This is of especial significance in a metaphysics of feeling, as there are several different types of affects that have frequently been thought to be "meta-physical" or "spiritual" in some sense, but which are fundamentally different from what I have described as metaphysical affects, the affective intuitions of the felt meanings of the world-whole. Four such seemingly metaphysical affects are the mystical, existential, essential, and nature affects. In the following four subsections, I shall elucidate these four affects and indicate how they differ from global affects.

III. 21.i. Mystical Affects Distinguished from Global Affects

It is clear from the contemporary literature on mysticism that there is no universally accepted definition of a "mystical experience" or a "mystical affect." It remains true nevertheless that mystical affects are *usually* (but not always) considered to be *seeming intuitions of God*, the unconditioned cause of the world, and in accordance with this predominant viewpoint I shall use the phrase "mystical affects" to refer to these seeming intuitions.

An elucidation of the nature of the mystical affect can be achieved by way of substantiating the above claim that the mystical affect is "usually considered" to be a seeming intuition of the uncaused cause of the world. I will show that in most mystical traditions, the Hindu, Neoplatonic, Christian, and Islamic, the mystics within that tradition predominantly conceive of their mystical experiences as intuitions of the unconditioned cause of the world. This will prepare the way for a sharp distinction between the mystical and global affects.

The earliest expressions of mysticism appear in the Hindu scriptures, particularly in the *Upanishads*. In these writings the mystical affect is predominantly considered to be a "union with the Lord [*Isá*] of the world,"[29] this Lord being *Brahman*, who is also identical with the Self, *Ātman*. The nature of this union is characterized in the *Brhadāraṇyaka Upanishad* as follows: "He who has discovered and become aware of his Self [*ātmā*] and entered into this impenetrable dwelling, he is the cause of everything, the cause of the whole world, in fact, he is the whole world."[30] The apparent paradox that is created by this statement that in mystical union one has achieved identity with the cause of the world and with the world itself is dispelled once the pantheistic basis of the Hindu doctrine is understood. *Brahman*, the cause of the world, is also the real nature of each and every thing in the world. "This whole world is *Brahman*."[31] The world *qua* caused by Brahman is *maya*, illusion, whereas the world as it *really is*, is Brahman himself. It is written in the *Śvetāśvatara Upanishad* that "*Brahman* is the illusion-maker [*māyin*], who created this whole world as an illusion [*maya*] in which the human soul is bound."[32] The human soul is released through recognizing that the world as caused is an illusion and through being united in mystical contemplation with the cause of this illusion.

This understanding of the mystical experience is shared by Sankara, the most well-known and influential Hindu philosophical mystic. Sankara held that Brahman is the cause of the world and that in this sense "*Brahman* is other than the world. [But] there exists nothing that is not [in reality] *Brahman*. If something other than *Brahman* appears to exist, it is unreal, like a mirage."[33] In mystical intuition one "sees the world as the non-dual *Brahman*,"[34] i.e., one sees the world as it *really* is.

The pantheistic element in Hindu mysticism is less present in Neoplatonic mysticism and in the Christian mysticism that stemmed from the Neoplatonic mysticism. The principal Neoplatonic mystics include Plotinus, Porphyry, Iamblichus and Proclus. They conceived of the mystical affect as an intuition of the One (*to hen*), which is the first reason of the world, although they conceived this intuition and the One in somewhat different ways. According to Plotinus, " . . . the One causes all things,"[35] and when the soul engages in its potentiality to not know (*to me noein*)[36] it can ascend to and become united with this cause: "He becomes absorbed in the Supreme, at one with it, like a center coincident with another center."[37]

The Neoplatonic doctrine influenced the early Christian mystic Dionysius the Areopagite, who proclaimed "the necessity of being united with and praising Him Who is the Cause of all and above all."[38] The conception of the mystical affect as being of the first reason can also be found in the writings of the later Christian mystics, John Tauler, Henry Suso, John Ruysbroeck, St. Teresa, St. John of the Cross, Jakob Boehme, and numerous others, but a brief consideration of the writings of Meister Eckhart, frequently considered to be the most significant of the Christian mystics, should suffice.

In one of his earlier sermons, Eckhart asserts that "our whole perfection and blessing depends on our stepping across or beyond the estate of creaturehood, time, and Being and on getting at last to the Cause that has no cause."[39] In a later sermon he writes of the mystical union in which "I was my own first cause as well as the first cause of everything else."[40] But with Eckhart it cannot be said without qualification that the mystical affect is an experienced unification with the uncaused Cause. Eckhart distinguishes God (*Gott*) from the Godhead (*Gottheit*) and attributes the characteristic of being the cause of the world to the former. The deepest mystical union, however, is not with God but with the Godhead. Of the distinction between God and the Godhead, Eckhart writes, " . . . creatures speak of God — but why do they not mention the Godhead? Because there is only unity in the Godhead and there is nothing to talk about. God acts. The Godhead does not."[41] The union with the Godhead involves going beyond God: "When I return to the core, the soil, the river, the source which is the Godhead, no one will ask me whence I came or where I have been. No one will have missed me — for even God passes away!"[42] Accordingly, to be united with the Godhead is to be united with *that which* is the cause of the world (for the Godhead is the Godhead *of* God), but it is not to be united with it *qua* cause of the world, i.e., *qua* having the distinction of being the cause of the world, but *qua* distinctionless unity.[43]

Islamic mysticism is based on seeming intuitions of *Allah*, the uncaused cause of the world. The Islamic mystics, the Sufis, flourished from A.D. 800 to 1400 and included such figures as Ziyad B. al-Arabi, Al-Bistami, Al-Ghazali, Attar, Ibn al-Arabi, and Rumi. Ziyad B. al-Arabi characterized the mystic's intuition as a "vision given to him by his Creator";[44] Ibn al-Arabi wrote that in the mystical experience "the mystic is one with the Divine,"[45] i.e., with "He [who] called into being the things that are";[46] and Al-Ghazali maintained that in mystical union (*faniya*) one had "passed away from everything" but "the Creator."[47]

Many of the Sufis exhibited a tendency different from that of the Christian mystics but similar to that of the Hindu mystics, namely, to conceive of the mystical union as an *identity* with the first reason of the world.[48] Ibn al-Arabi maintained that when the mystical union came upon you, "you will understand that you are no other than God."[49] He continued:

> Thus, instead of his [the mystic's] own essence, there is the essence of God and in place of his own qualities, there are the attributes of God. He who knows himself sees his whole existence to be the Divine existence, but does not realize that any change has taken place in his own nature or qualities. For when you know yourself, your "I-ness" vanishes and you know that you and God are one and the same.[50]

Contrast this with St. John of the Cross's conception of the union, which

according to him was not a union of identity but a "union of likeness."[51]
In *The Ascent of Mount Carmel* (1579-85) he wrote:

> A man must strip himself of all creatures and of his actions and abilities
> (of his understanding, taste, and feeling) so that when everything unlike
> and unconformed to God is cast out, his soul may receive the likeness of
> God, since nothing contrary to the will of God will be left in him, and thus
> he will be transformed in God. . . . Yet truly, its [the soul's] being (even
> though transformed) is naturally as distinct from God's as it was before . . .[52]

Besides the Hindu, Neoplatonic, Christian, and Islamic mystical
traditions, the Jewish and Taoist mystical traditions also were based on
a conception of the mystical affect as relating to the first reason of the
world.[53] But it should not go without mention that the major exception
to these six mystical traditions is Theravada Buddhism. The experience
of enlightenment (*anuttara-samyak-sambodhi*) was conceived as an experience of *Nirvana*, and *Nirvana*, although eternal and uncaused,[54] was
not held to be the first reason of the world of change (*samsara*).[55]

Nevertheless, Mahayana Buddhism, which developed from Theravada Buddhism, did display a predominant tendency to describe the mystical experience as an intuition of the world's first reason, often called *tathatā*
(Suchness), which is an uncaused and eternal Mind. Asvaghosha
endeavored to summarize the essentials of Mahayana Buddhism in his
Awakening of Faith in the Mahayana. He wrote that "*samsara* [the world
of change] has its ground or reason in *Tathāgata-garbha* [the womb of
Suchness],"[56] which is the uncaused and eternal Mind as it exists imma-
nently in man. *Samsara* arises out of *tathatā* through ignorance, and the
mystical experience consists in returning to identity with *tathatā*, the uncaused and eternal Mind.

Zen Buddhism, one of the branches of Mahayana Buddhism, also
manifested a central tendency to conceive of *satori*, enlightenment, as an
intuition of the first reason of the world, which is frequently called *śūnyatā* (Emptiness) and *tathatā* (Suchness).[57]

The above represents a brief attempt to substantiate my claim that
the predominant way in which the so-called "mystics" have understood
the mystical affect is as an intuition of the first reason of the world. A
further substantiation appears in the fact that virtually every philosopher
of mysticism, including W.R. Inge,[58] Evelyn Underhill,[59] Rufus Jones,[60]
Rudolph Otto,[61] Walter T. Stace,[62] and R. C. Zaehner,[63] has espoused
the idea that all or at least the highest kind of mystical experiences are
of the world's first reason.[64]

The mystical writings and the philosophies of mysticism to which
I referred reveal that the mystical affect is to be understood primarily as
a mode of affective experiencing that belongs with and is complementary

to the metaphysics of rational meaning. The mystical affect is the supreme metaphysical affect, where "metaphysics" has the sense of rational metaphysics, i.e., the theory that the world has a reason that explains its existence and nature. This affect is the nonlogical way of apprehending the first reason of the world, whereas the inferential reasoning practiced by the metaphysicians (and by the mystics who are also metaphysicians, such as Śaṅkara, Plotinus, Dionysius, and Al-Ghazali) is the logical way of comprehending the first reason.[65]

In many of the writings of the mystics and the philosophers of mysticism, these two ways of apprehending the first reason are conceived to be based upon two different aspects or ways of appearing of the first reason, the logical and the nonlogical. The most incisive development of this conception can be found in Otto's *The Holy, Eastern and Western Mysticism,* and *Religious Essays.* In *The Holy,* Otto states that a distinction should be made between the logical attributes of God and the nonlogical subject of these attributes, which is the object of mystical intuition.[66] The attribute of being the creator or cause of the world is one of God's logical attributes, and this attribute is not intuited as such in mystical experience.[67] However, there is a mystical intuition of a parallel nonlogical aspect of God, His "overpoweringness" or *majestas,* and a consequent feeling of one's own stature as a creature (which is to be distinguished from the intellectual recognition of the fact that one is created by God).[68]

At this point we are in a position to raise the crucial questions of this subsection, viz., is the nonlogical and mystical affective experience of the world's first reason a *global affect*? and is the mystical affect an affect that can be known to be veridical?

With regard to the first issue, it will be recalled that a global affect has been characterized as a captivated intuition of a *feature* of the world-whole. But God, the focus of the mystical affect, is not a feature of the world-whole; rather, He is a relational term that is related to the world-whole through the relation of *causation* (taken in the wide sense, to include emanation, manifestation, grounding, illusion-making, etc.). The world-whole, through being the other term of this relation, acquires the relational feature of *being the effect of God*. To be a global affect, the mystical affect would have to be a captivated intuition of this relational feature of the world-whole. However, it is clear from the above accounts of the mystical affect that in this affect one is absorbed *in God*, not in *the world-whole qua* effect of God. Ruysbroeck writes that in the mystical affect one "feels nothing but the unity [of God],"[69] such that all "creaturely distinctions" belonging to the world have ceased to appear. The mystical affect, then, cannot be understood as an intuition of a feature of the world-whole and thus cannot be called a global affect.

If the mystical affect is not a *global* affect, is it then a *mundane* affect? A mundane affect is a feeling-awareness of a part of the world-whole. But is God, if He exists, *a part* of the world-whole?

In the traditional use of the term "the world" or "the world-whole," both by the mystics and by the metaphysicians of rational meaning, "the world" refers to *the whole of created being*, and as such is distinguished from the Uncreated Creator, Who existed "beyond" (and/or "behind" or "within") the whole of created being. But no such rational-metaphysical definition of "the world-whole" can form the starting point of a metaphysics of feeling. In this metaphysics, the sense of the expression, "the world-whole," must be derived from *feelings themselves*, specifically from the types of feeling that are reappreciatively articulated *as* "intuitive feelings of the world-whole."[70] These types of feeling, as I have tried to show in this chapter, are *moods* and what I have called *"global affects."* The world-whole as it is revealed in moods is relatively indeterminate in its nature and possesses no such determination as *the whole of created being*. This is obvious, for if the world-whole as revealed in moods were revealed *as* the whole of created being, then it would be impossible to feel a mood unless one believed that God existed. But clearly moods are independent of any such belief. The world-whole as revealed in moods, and in the global affects that are parallel in type to moods, is intuitively felt to be *"the whole composed of myself, these-things-around-me-and-everything-else,"* where the "things" that compose this whole have no such limited sense as *"created things."* Rather, these "things" are "things" in an *unrestricted* sense, inclusive of all possibilities, such as created things, uncreated things, creative created things, and creative uncreated things. God, if He exists, is a creative uncreated thing that creates all other things, and as such He would be one of the "things" that compose the world-whole, albeit by virtue of His creativity He would be *the preeminent thing*. In accordance, then, with this understanding of the expression, "the world-whole," God must be understood as *a part* of the world-whole, and the mystical affect must be understood as a *mundane affect*, although this affect is *the preeminent mundane affect*, inasmuch as it is an awareness of the preeminent part of the world-whole.

It follows from the above considerations that "the world-whole" believed by the mystics to have the relational feature of *being an effect of God* is *the whole of created things*, not "the world-whole" in the unrestricted sense. The whole of created things is, like God, a *part* of "the world-whole" in the unrestricted sense. If God exists, then the two basic parts of "the world-whole" in the unrestricted sense are *God* and *His creatures*. This means that even a captivated intuition of *"the world-whole"* (in the sense of *the whole of created things*) *qua* having the relational feature of being an effect of God is, like the awareness of God, a *"mundane affect"* in the unrestricted sense I have given to this phrase.[71]

The above remarks constitute the first point I wished to make, that the mystical affect is not a *global* awareness. My discussion indicated that the mystical affect is not a "global awareness" either in the restricted or unrestricted sense: it is not a captivated intuition of a feature of the whole of created things, and it is not an intuition of a feature of the whole of myself, these-things-around-me, and everything-else.[72]

The second issue concerns whether the mystical affect can be known to be veridical.[73] Is it the case that there are no knowable extrinsic grounds that count against the seeming mystical intuition's intrinsic claim to veridicality?

One of the factors that prevented people in the epoch of rational meaning from questioning the veridicality of seeming mystical intuitions was their acceptance of an erroneous rational-metaphysical principle, that the series of causes and effects *must* terminate in a first cause. With this prior conviction of the existence of a first cause, it seemed to them evident *a priori* that all considerations extrinsic to the seeming mystical intuition *must* support rather than override this seeming intuition's intrinsic claim to veridicality.

The recognition of the falsity of this principle provides a motive for examining relevant extrinsic factors to determine if they in fact support or override the seeming mystical intuitions. Such an examination reveals that the phenomena most relevant to this determination *count against* the veridicality of the mystical affects. The phenomena in question are seeming intuitions opposite in nature to the mystical affects; they are seeming intuitions of the *nonexistence* of a first cause.

One such seeming intuition is the affect of *Godless desolation*. In this desolate affect, I seem to intuit the absence of a divine part of the world that causes myself and other world-parts. I seem to intuit a *nothingness* beyond the empirical and natural chain of causes and effects. My intuitive penetration beyond the natural order is met by an absolute emptiness, a darkness and silence devoid of God.

It seems obvious to me in my desolation that it is not the case that I am merely unable to find God; instead, it seems that I am intuitively discovering that there is no God, and that the people who believed they intuited God were deluded. I seem to be directly beholding the nonbeing of God.

According to Richard Swinburne, "there cannot be perceptions of the absence of God."[74] By this he means that the seeming experiences of

God's absence cannot possess the evidentiality possessed by seeming experiences of God's presence. This is based on the principle that:

> . . . how things seem positively to be is evidence of how they are, but how things seem *not* to be is not such evidence. If it seems to me that there is present a table in the room, or statue in the garden, then probably there is. But if it seems to me that there is no table in the room, then that is only reason for supposing that there is not, if there are good grounds for supposing that I have looked everywhere in the room and (having eyes in working order, being able to recognize a table when I see one, etc.) would have seen one if there was one there. An atheist's claim to have had an experience of its seeming to him that there is no God could only be evidence that there was no God if similar restrictions were satisfied. They could not be—for there are no good grounds for supposing that if there is a God, the atheist would have experienced him.[75]

To show that Swinburne is mistaken about the experience of God's absence being nonevidential we can point out that this experience does satisfy "similar restrictions" to those satisfied by the seeming absence of a table in the room. The latter restrictions are "I have looked everywhere in the room" and "(having eyes in working order, being able to recognize a table when I see one, etc.) [I] would have seen one if there was one there." These restrictions can be generalized so we can determine their specific application to the affect of Godless desolation. The first restriction can be generalized to read: "One must direct one's intuition upon the spatial, psychical, ontological, etc., region where the thing in question would be situated and manifest if it existed." The ontological region where God would be situated if He existed is a supernatural region that lies beyond the natural region as the latter's causal ground. The person experiencing the desolate affect does meet this first restriction, for he is intuitively directed beyond nature to nature's possible supernatural ground, but instead of being encountered by the presence of this ground, he is encountered by nothingness.

The second restriction can be generalized as: "One must have the capacity to discern the thing in question." In regard to God, the capacity is to direct oneself intuitively beyond nature and to nature's possible causal ground. This capacity is possessed no less by the desolate person than by the mystic, for both intuitively transcend nature to its possible causal ground. The difference is that in one case the possible ground seems to be actual, and in the other case not.

Since the desolate affect meets these two restrictions, it does possess an evidentiality and as such is on a par in this respect with the mystical affect.[76] In terms of my previous descriptions of the criteria of intuitional truth, this means that both affects possess an intrinsic basis of veridicality.

If there are no factors extrinsic to both of these seeming intuitions that confirm one of them and override the other, then there is no basis for deciding which of these seeming intuitions is the real one. I believe there are no such extrinsic factors, and accordingly that the issue of which seeming intuition is real, and of whether God exists or not, cannot be decided.

The conclusion *based on the available evidence of intuitive feelings* that it cannot be known if God exists or not seems to agree with the outlook of the metaphysics of rational meaninglessness. In fact, however, there is a fundamental difference between this conclusion and the basic thesis of the metaphysics of rational meaninglessness. This difference concerns the notion of metaphysical meaning. In the metaphysics of rational meaninglessness, the issue of metaphysical meaning is essentially tied up with the issue of whether God exists or not. Since the existence of God is unknowable, the existence of metaphysical meaning is likewise held to be unknowable. In the metaphysics of feeling, on the other hand, the issue of God's existence or nonexistence is ultimately *irrelevant* to the question of metaphysical meaning. For metaphysical meanings are here thought to be, not unconditioned reasons that explain other reasons, but important features of the whole of all that exists. God, if He exists, is not an important feature of the whole of all that exists, but is *one part* of this whole, a part that is the causal reason for the other parts. Moreover, it will be shown in Part 2 that the moodily and affectively felt world-whole possesses all of its basic important features, fulfillment, miraculousness, emptiness, etc., *regardless* of whether or not God exists as one of the parts of this whole. The unknowability of the existence of God is not a matter of metaphysical lament, but of metaphysical insignificance — for the unknowability of God's existence does not affect the knowability of the *felt meanings of the world-whole.*

III. 21.ii. Existential Affects Distinguished from Global Affects

Existential affects are about one's own existence; they are about either one's existence as a whole, one's existence in respect of its fundamental structure or characteristic, or one's existence in its very being. Since *my existence* is only one part of the world-whole, these affects are mundane and have no significant place in a metaphysics of feeling.[77] This fact can be illustrated by a brief examination of several examples of existential affects. In the following description of these affects, it must be remembered that the expressions "world-whole," "world-part," "global," and "mundane" are used in the sense established in the metaphysics of feeling, and not in the senses these philosophers give them, as many of these philosophers would deny (correctly) that these existential affects are "mundane" in the different and various senses they give to this and related terms.

According to Sartre, anguish (*angoisse*) is about the very being of the for-itself, its freedom. "Freedom is the being of consciousness" and "it is in anguish that man has the consciousness of his freedom."[78] But since a consciousness or for-itself is only one part of being, coexisting with other for-itselfs and with being-in-itself, the anguished consciousness is a mundane consciousness.

The other major affect Sartre discusses, *nausea*, is also a mundane affect, although it is not an existential affect. Nausea (as it is described in the novel of that title) has a parallel function in Sartre's ontology to anguish; just as anguish is the consciousness of the being of the for-itself, so nausea is the consciousness of the being of the in-itself. Both of these affects relate to one region of being, and neither of them is a global intuition of *the whole* composed by the for-itselfs and the in-itself.

Jaspers describes in his *Philosophy* an "anxiety about my authentic being as existence [*Angst um das eigentliche Sein als Existenz*]."[79] Specifically, it is an "existential anxiety about the possibility of nothingness [*existentielle Angst vor der Moglichkeit des Nichts*],"[80] where the possible nothingness is the nothingness of one's own *Existenz*. This anxiety is not about the possible death of myself *qua Dasein*, but about "guiltily losing my self" *qua Existenz* and of thereby becoming nothing more than a *Dasein*, no longer able to tell if anything matters and "doing things blindly and arbitrarily."[81] But my *Existenz*, however, is not the world-whole, and consequently my existential anxiety is not a global anxiety.

Jaspers also describes a love of and serenity in transcendence, being-in-itself. Love and serenity are not existential affects, but they are not global affects either, for being-in-itself is not that which is wholly identical with being-in-itself and the two manifestations of being-in-itself, subjective and objective being. Being-in-itself is but one part of this whole (although this whole is not a "whole" in the restricted sense in which Jaspers used this term).

It is true that Sören Kierkegaard's *angest*, like Sartre's *angoisse* and Jasper's *angst*, is an existential affect in which I feel anxious before "the nothingness of my free possibilities" in some sense of this phrase, but less noticed as a central existential affect in Kierkegaard's philosophy is *repetition*, which is a rapturous affect. In part 1 of *Repetition*, Kierkegaard describes an aesthetical repetition, in which I come close to being "absolutely content in all imaginable ways"[82] and therein am rapturously directed towards "the whole of [my] existence."[83] The religious repetition he describes in part 2 is, despite its name, not a rapture about God, but about the authentic existence of my self.[84] My true self is regained and unified: "I am again myself, here I have the repetition . . . and existence seems to me more beautiful than ever. . . . This self which another would not pick up from the road I possess again. The discord in my nature is resolved, I am again unified."[85]

Other examples of existential affects include Nietzsche's sadness (*Traurigkeit*) about the purposelessness of one's own existence,[86] Schopenhauer's boredom (*Langeweile*) concerning the worthlessness of one's existence,[87] and Scheler's "spiritual feelings" (*geistigen Gefuhle*), which are about one's personal existence as a whole.[88] In these as in other existential affects, one's awareness is narrow in its focus: instead of taking in the importance of everything whatsoever, one appreciates the importance of the part of everything that one is.

III. 21.iii. Essential Affects Distinguished from Global Affects

An essential affect is an affective feeling about an essence, or universal or the *a priori*. Such phenomena, as I shall show in Part 2, Chapters 5 and 6, are constituents of the world-whole, and consequently an essential affect is mundane.

The explanation of the nature of essential affects can be introduced by a discussion of Heidegger's *angst*. In Division A, section 15 of this chapter, I indicate that Heidegger's *angst*, from one point of view, could be considered as a mood, even though Heidegger himself did not make a distinction between moods and affects. However, it is also possible to consider this *angst*, from another point of view, as an essential affect, and this is how I shall consider it in the following.

It may be wondered why I am considering Heidegger's *angst* as an essential affect, rather than as an existential affect like Sartre's *angoisse* and Jasper's *angst*. The reason is that Heidegger's *angst* is not about *my* existence (in the *ontisch* and *existenzeill* sense), but about existence in its *a priori* structure (existence in the *ontologisch* and *existenzial* sense). More fully, anxiety is about Being-in-the-world-as-such, which is a "necessary *a priori*"[89] structure of *Dasein*. For anxiety "innerworldly beings [*Seiende*] are not 'relevant' at all. Nothing to-hand [*zuhanden*] or at-hand [*vorhanden*] within the world functions as what anxiety is anxious before.[90] [Rather] *anxiety is before Being-in-the-world-as-such* [*In-der-Welt-sein als soches*]."[91] In contrast with this, Jasper's *angst* is about my individually unique *Existenz*, not about some necessary *a priori* structure that would be common to all existences.[92] The same is true for Sartre's *angoisse*, for the freedom I am anguished about is not an essence or *a priori* character for the for-itself, but the particular and unique freedom of my being.[93] The existential affects described by Scheler, Nietzsche, Schopenhauer, and Kierkegaard are also about *my existence* in its uniqueness, rather than about its *a priori* structure.

Heidegger's *angst*, as an essential or *a priori* affect, is mundane. Consider that *angst* is about an ontological or *a priori* whole, Being-in-the-world-as-a-whole (*In-der-Welt-sein als Ganze*).[94] This whole differs from the *a posteriori* and ontical whole, which is the whole of being (*das Seiende im Ganzen*).[95] The ontical whole is disclosed in boredom (for example): "This boredom makes manifest being as a whole [*Diese Langeweile offenbart das Seiende im Ganzen*]."[96] Now we must think in a more fundamental and unrestricted sense than Heidegger, beyond the confines of his absolutized ontological/ontical dichotomy, to recognize that the ontological and ontical wholes *are both parts of the whole composed of the ontological and ontical wholes*. It is this transontological and transontical whole that is the world-whole in the unrestricted sense and is that to which global affects relate. If the whole of the *a priori* and the whole of the *a posteriori* are *parts* of the world-whole in the unrestricted sense, then an anxiety that relates merely to the whole of the *a priori* must be a mundane anxiety.[97]

Most of the affects described in the rational metaphysical tradition that are neither affective feelings about God nor sensible affects about this or that sensible thing are essential affects. Plato's "divine madness" that he describes in the *Symposium* and *Phaedrus* is an affect in which one "intuits Beauty itself" (*Symposium* 211E), i.e., the *eidos* of Beauty, and as such it is an essential or *eidetic* affect. The "feeling of respect" Kant describes is a feeling instigated by a consciousness of the universal and *a priori* moral law[98] and as such is an essential affect. Further examples are the feelings Hegel describes as "related to an absolute universal, to the right, morality, religion, the beautiful, and the true." These feelings "are unmixed with the subject's particularity and are as such elevated to pure forms of the universal in and for itself."[99]

It is true that essences are not "things" in the sense that rocks or people are "things," but they are "things" in *some* sense (i.e., they are not absolutely *nothing*). Since the "things" that appear to compose the whole of myself, these-things-and-everything-else are not restricted to this or that class of things, it is the case that "essence things" as well as particular things are part of the world-whole,[100] and consequently that an affective awareness of "essence things" is different than and more narrow than an affective awareness of the world-whole.

III. 21.iv. Nature Affects Distinguished from Global Affects

The last affects which I shall distinguish from the global affects are *nature affects*. Some philosophers have conceived such affects to be about "the world." Witness Russell's description of a despair before "Nature, omnipotent but blind." "Purposeless," Russell writes, and "void of meaning, is the world which Science presents for our belief."[101] Russell distinguishes this "alien and inhuman world"[102] that evokes despair from "the ideal world,"[103] which is comprised of the human ideals of morality, knowledge, and beauty. Accordingly, the inhuman world of nature is but a part of "the world" in the unrestricted sense that includes both the natural world and the ideal world, and a despair in face of the purposelessness of the natural world is thus a mundane despair.

Even the spatial-physical universe considered in its entirety is but a part of "the world-whole" in the unrestricted sense, and hence the affect of astonishment John Stuart Mill describes in "Nature" is a mundane nature affect:

> One of these feelings is the astonishment, rising into awe, which is inspired (even independent of all religious sentiment) by any of the greater natural phenomena. A hurricane, a mountain precipice, the desert, the ocean either agitated or at rest, the solar system and the great cosmic forces which hold it together, the boundless firmament and to an educated mind any single star excite feelings which make all human enterprises and powers appear so insignificant that to a mind thus occupied it seems insufferable presumption in so puny a creature as man to look critically on things so far above him, or dare to measure himself against the grandeur of the universe.[104]

But this "universe," like Russell's "Nature," does not include the good, the true, or the (artistically) beautiful and thus is not the whole of which *all* things are parts. The grandeur that elicits the astonishment is not a feature of the world-whole, but of the natural part of this whole.

This discussion of nature affects serves to conclude my demarcation of global affects from other types of affects that may seem to be analogous in some way to the global affects. In the examination of each of the authors' definitions of one of these affects, mystical, existential, essential, or natural, I pointed out or implied that the described affect is not about the unrestricted *whole* that is tacitly presupposed but unthought in each thinker's world-view, and consequently that the affects these thinkers described are one and all mundane.

In this chapter I set out to describe the basis of our appreciative metaphysical knowledge, the *intuitive feelings* of the important world-whole. We have an almost constant but usually horizonal intuitive awareness of the world-whole in our moods, but also have the possibility of experiencing a more focused intuition of the whole in the more rarely experienced global affects. It is these latter intuitive feelings that are of central import to a metaphysics of feeling, for in these feelings the felt meanings of the world acquire a determinate appearance. It is these affects that must be examined in detail if we are to acquire a *determinate* appreciative knowledge of the world-whole. The attainment of this knowledge is the aim of Part 2.

PART TWO

The Basic Felt Meanings of the World

*T*he aim of Part 2 is to examine in a relatively comprehensive way the global affects that are parallel in type to our moods, and by this means to uncover the determinate character of the felt meanings of the world. This examination will be relatively but not absolutely comprehensive in that I shall not explicate each and every global affect, but only some of them. Nearly a score of these affects will be discussed, but three in particular will be singled out for the most thorough and exhaustive explications: *rejoicing* in the world-whole's fulfillment, *loving* the world-whole for its closeness, and *revering* the world-whole for its supremacy. Each of the three chapters of Part 2 is devoted to one of these affects, and the other global affects are described by way of comparing and contrasting them with these affects.

Global rejoicing, loving, and revering are selected as the main subjects for investigation because they are fundamental global affects. Every other affective appreciation to be examined is based on one or more of these three affects. This can be elucidated in a brief and preliminary fashion in the present section; the complete explication and demonstration of this thesis will appear in the following chapters.

Rejoicing in the world-whole's *fulfillment-of-happening* is the most fundamental of the metaphysical affects; every other such affect is based on rejoicing, but rejoicing is based on no other global affect. Rejoicing in the happening of the world is absolutely basic in that an affective appreciation of the world's happening belongs to and is an aspect of the affective appreciation of every other way in which the world is important. Correlatively, fulfillment-of-happening is the absolutely basic global importance in that it is an aspect of every other global importance, whereas no other global importance is an aspect of it.

The other global affects I examine are either directly, indirectly, or doubly indirectly based on global rejoicing. Love, marvelling, awe, tedium, and peacefulness are examples of the directly based affects. The indirectly based affects, exemplified by reverence, pride, wonder, and desolation, are directly based on global love; since love is directly based on rejoicing, these affects are indirectly based on rejoicing. The doubly indirectly based affects include dread, humility, and stupefaction; they are directly based upon global reverence, which is itself directly based on global love, which in its turn is directly based on global rejoicing.

Global love and reverence are in this manner fundamental affects like rejoicing; other affects are based upon them. However, unlike rejoicing, they are only relatively fundamental, for love is based on joy, and reverence upon love.

Global love is the affective captivation with the *happening world-whole's apparential closeness to me*, its immediate appearance to me. The immediate appearance of the happening world is a second basic feature of the world after happening. Happening is an aspect of the *happening world-whole's apparential closeness*, and thus the latter importance is based upon the former. And the happening world-whole's apparential closeness is itself an aspect of further more complex importances, and these importances accordingly are based upon it. These latter importances are the ones affectively appreciated in global reverence, pride, wonder, desolation, and others.

The global importance appreciated in reverence is *supremacy,* or more exactly, the *independence of the world-whole's happening from its immediate appearance to me.* This supremacy of the world-whole is in its turn an aspect of even more complex importances, those appreciated in global dread, humility, stupefaction, etc.

In Chapter 4 I examine global rejoicing and some of the affects directly based on rejoicing; in Chapters 5 and 6 I describe global loving and revering and some of the affects they directly support.

The import of Part 2 can be summarily stated. We shall find that fulfillment-of-happening is the meaning of the world-whole's *temporal presence* and *existing*, that the happening world-whole's apparential closeness is the *ultimate felt truth*, and that global supremacy refers to the *human-independent absolute reality*.

CHAPTER IV

The Fulfillment
of the World

*T*he global importance of fulfillment is indeterminately revealed in the mood of euphoria and determinately revealed
in the parallel global affect, rejoicing. Rejoicing reveals *happening* to be
the determinate constitution of the importance of fulfillment. Happening constitutes the intuitively felt global *temporality* (cf. IV.22-23) and the
intuitively felt global *existing* (IV.24-26). The world-whole's fulfillment-
of-happening can be purely appreciated only in an affective rejoicing; other
affects, such as global despair, marvelling, awe, tedium, and peacefulness,
are *impure appreciations* of this importance and are based upon its pure
joyous appreciation (IV.27).

IV. 22. Rejoicing in the World-Whole's Fulfillment-of-Happening

I am sitting on a veranda on a summer afternoon, watching the trees
as they sway gently in the sunlight. My awareness gradually broadens and
deepens, and soon a joy begins to arise in me, a rejoicing in the *fulfillment* of the very world that is composed of myself, these swaying trees,
this blue sky, and the indistinctly manifest "everything else" that extends
beyond all that I am perceiving. In this rejoicing I am experiencing a captivated intuition of the determinately appearing importance of global
fulfillment. What, exactly, is the nature of this intuition, and what is the
determinate character of the world-whole's fulfillment?

The sensuously felt aspect of this joyously appearing world-whole
can be made explicit first. My perceptible surroundings seem to be infused with an upwardly radiated feeling-flow of joy, a joyous feeling-
tonality that has its source, not in the gardens, trees, and sky, but in the
fulfilled global interior that appears to be "far behind" and "far within"
these perceptible phenomena. This fulfilled global interior joyously radiates
everything—including myself—upwards, "on high," to the sensuously felt
"top of the world." By virtue of my being *affected* by the fulfilled whole,
everything is felt to be flowingly elevated to the highest tonal region of
the world.

But my captivated intuition is not directed primarily towards the joyous feeling-tonality that emanates from the fulfilled global interior. The senuous tonality of joy is marginally apprehended; attentionally I am aware of the global interior that is the source of this tonality. In the following, several characteristics of this rejoicing intuition of the global interior will be made explicit.

First, this global interior is intuitively manifest as the world-whole in respect of its feature of fulfillment. The world-whole is intuitively felt to be a plenum, a fullness, a positivity. The intuitive feeling of this fulfillment is something that properly and uniquely belongs to the affect of rejoicing, for this affect is in its essential nature a *feeling-of-fulfillment*. In rejoicing, what I rejoice in is that something *has what it needs to be fulfilled*. This is true for mundane joys as well as global joys. In mundane rejoicing, there is often a feeling that *I myself* possess what I need in order to be fulfilled. For example, I can feel joy upon learning that a woman whom I love loves me in return. Here I feel that I, as a person who needs a loving togetherness with another person in order to be fulfilled as a person, possess this loving togetherness. Mundane rejoicing can also be a rejoicing in the fulfillment of something else. I can feel that the political party espousing the just cause has triumphed—has won the election—and that society is thereby fulfilled in respect of its need for just political leaders.

In order to determine what kind of fulfillment the world-whole is felt to possess in global rejoicing, some further characteristics of the rejoicing intuition must be considered. One of these is the feeling that the rejoiced-in fullfillment is *possessed completely and all at once*, rather than being possessed piecemeal and in stages, with the fulfillment being gradually and successively acquired.[1] If we combine this characteristic of the rejoicing with the above one, global rejoicing can be understood as an intuitive feeling of the world-whole's *being fulfilled completely and all at once*.

A third characteristic is that in rejoicing it is especially true that one is able to "live in the present" and to appreciate the present as a fullness in itself. In normal strivings we are primarily future oriented: the present is appreciated, not as a completeness in itself, but as a means to some future state. Strivings presuppose that the fulfillment of things lies in the future and that only by changing the present state of things can this fulfillment be brought about. In rejoicing, however, the present as such and in itself is appreciated as something that is intrinsically a completeness. Just *to be present* is enough in itself to fulfill.

Global rejoicing, then, can be described as an intuitive feeling of the world-whole *completely and all at once possessing the fulfillment of being present*.

But such a feeling is only possible if the rejoicing intuition is a *simplified* feeling-awareness. Normally, in nonjoyous awarenesses, the world's being present or being in the present is apprehended only in the context of possessing further features or of belonging to a network of relations to various things that are in the present or lie in the future or past. But in global rejoicing, these complexities are stripped away, as it were, and the global being present is allowed to shine forth in its purity.

The nature of this fullness of presence that purely appears can be specified in terms of three characteristics, one concerning its negative nature, one concerning its manner of appearance, and, most significant of all, one concerning its concrete structure as a dynamic phenomenon.

The negative characteristic of this fullness is its *otherness*, its being completely unlike the world-parts with which we are acquainted. The world's fullness of presence is invisible and inaudible, and cannot be touched, tasted or smelled. It is without sensuous and physical form, and is not located within any spatial region. Moreover, it is not an image or concept or act of awareness. In these respects, it is utterly unlike the physical and psychical parts of the world and thus, in relation to them, is *the Other*.

But this otherness of the fullness of presence does not mean it is inapprehensible. Rather, it is *omniapparent*. Instead of being apparent *here* and unapparent *there*, it is everywhere-apparent. It is one and indivisible in terms of the regions of its appearance; no matter where I turn my attention I find it as an undivided omnipresence.

Although other and omniapparent, the world-whole's fullness of presence is not absolutely static and inert. Rather—and this is the third and principal characteristic of this fullness, its concrete dynamic character— this fullness is a *happening*; in fact, it is *the very happening of the world-whole itself*. The world-whole's fullness breaks forth into fullness from an emptiness and into an emptiness. The world-whole's fulfillment appears to be renewed again and again, as each new fullness arises from and vanishes into the emptiness. Each fullness has been an emptiness and will be one; the emptiness that each arisen fullness has been is a happening-not-yet, and the emptiness that each will be is a happening-no-longer. The happenings-not-yet and -no-longer are internally characterized as lacks or emptinesses of happening: happening is the fullness of which they are deprived in the mode of the *not yet* and *no longer*.[2]

These happenings are not "happenings" in the ordinary sense of events or changing things in time, for they are changing temporal intervals themselves. Specifically, they are the intervals which are acquiring and losing the feature of presentness.

While intervals successively pass by, in that they consecutively acquire and then lose the feature of presentness, the presentness that inheres in these intervals does not itself pass by. Presentness remains identically presentness at each different moment of time, the only sort of change it undergoes being one of successively inhering in the different intervals. Presentness is like a constantly shining light, holding all in which it inheres out of the darkness of the no-longer, the not-yet, and the never.

The world-whole *is present* through occupying an interval that is present. And the world-whole *is happening* through occupying an interval that is (identically) a happening, i.e., an interval which is involved in the change of acquiring and losing presentness. Since the presentness of the world-whole is that of an interval occupied by the world-whole, the fulfillment or fullness-of-presence possessed by the world-whole concretely understood is *the present interval* it occupies, *the happening*, and not the feature of presentness considered by itself, in abstraction from the interval in which it inheres.

The world-whole endures in that it successively occupies different present intervals. Because it endures, the world-whole remains in a constant state of fulfillment: the present intervals pass by and become emptinesses, but the presentness that shines through these intervals continues to fill the world that occupies them with its light.

It is this constant state of fulfillment that I am joyously feeling. I rejoice that the whole composed of myself and these swaying trees and this blue sky and everything else is *renewed again and again* by occupying the successive happenings. I rejoice that this whole *goes on*! and *on*! and *on*! and does not *come to an end* and vanish into the emptiness of the past, the emptiness of happening-no-longer. I also rejoice that it *is arriving* in the present from the vast emptiness of the future, and that this whole thereby does not possess exclusively the privational feature of happening-not-yet. I celebrate the dynamic going on / arriving of the whole from the emptiness and into the fullness.

But it is not disclosed in the rejoicing intuition whether the world-whole occupies *every* happening, including all those not being joyously intuited. The world-whole may have begun or may end at some time in the distant past or future, such that prior to and after the duration of the world the happenings are unoccupied and make up a pure time unfolding by itself.[3] Furthermore, it is not disclosed whether time itself is infinite or finite; time itself may have begun and may end with the beginning and end of the world, if the world begins and ends.[4]

I rejoice that the world-whole *currently* is fulfilled, not that it always has been and will be, and I rejoice that *this* and *this* and *this* present interval is occupied by the whole, not that an infinite number of intervals of the same length have and will be occupied.

It is also not disclosed in the rejoicing intuition whether time is composed of simple instants as well as intervals. The happening that explicitly and holistically appears in the joyous intuition is an interval or length of time that implicitly appears to be composed of a briefer happening and a corresponding brief happening-no-longer and happening-not-yet that are immediately contiguous with the briefer happening. This briefer happening implicitly appears to be similarly composed, and so on until the bounds of intuitive comprehension are exceeded. However, whether this decomposition of intervals into briefer intervals does or does not terminate, far beyond the bounds of intuition, in indivisible points of time is not a matter that can be decided on the basis of what is given in the rejoicing awareness.

There are limitations on the lengths of the intervals that can intuitively appear; the length is determined by the upper and lower limits of my capacity to take in intuitively a stretch of time. Although present intervals can be thought of as ranging from one billionth of a second and briefer to one century and longer, the present intervals I can intuitively feel last somewhere in the vicinity of several seconds or large fractions of a second.

These remarks suggest how the above-described characteristic of the joyously felt fulfillment, its character of being possessed completely and all at once by the world-whole, is to be understood. The world-whole's rejoiced-in fulfillment is not possessed "all at once" in the sense of being possessed literally instantaneously, but in the sense that it is possessed *all at one present*, the present in question being the present interval with which the rejoiced-in fulfillment is identical. The global fulfillment is possessed *at* the present it itself *is*.

IV. 23. *Intuitively Felt Time and the Rational-Metaphysical Theory of Time*

In this section I shall defend the foregoing account of time as it is intuitively felt from some objections based on the predominant alternative conception of time.

Many philosophers have claimed that our so-called "awareness of the present" is in truth an awareness of phenomena related by the relation of simultaneity.[5] If this were the case, there would be no "presentness" in the sense stated in my descriptions and no global importance of fulfillment-of-happening. But I believe there are several reasons to doubt this reduction of presentness to simultaneity.

A *global state* is the state of the whole world at a certain time; it is that which is composed of the state of each world-part, such as the swaying of the trees in the wind, at that time. My joyous awareness is a part of the global state that is simultaneous with my joyous awareness. But this relation of simultaneity is not the presentness of the global state in which I am rejoicing. This is shown by the fact that after the joy burns out, it remains true that the joy bears the relation of simultaneity to the global state of which the joy is a part, but it is false that the joy and the global state to which the joy belong are present. If two states are simultaneous when they are present, they are still simultaneous when they are past — and consequently the presentness of the states is nonidentical with their simultaneity.

The awareness-of-simultaneity with which the above-mentioned philosophers identify the awareness-of-presentness is sometimes specified as an awareness that some phenomenon is simultaneous with my awareness of the phenomenon. This notion is incompatible with the nature of the rejoicing awareness. It is not a reflexive attentional awareness of itself as being related to the world-whole, but an unreflexive attentional awareness of the world-whole itself. The presentness that appears in this awareness is a nonrelational or monadic feature of an interval occupied by the world-whole.

Other philosophers specify the relevant awareness-of-simultaneity as an awareness of the simultaneity of some phenomenon with my utterance of a sentence about the phenomenon. This also is incompatible with rejoicing in the global presentness, for no sentence is uttered during this experience.

Philosophers who endeavor to analyze presentness in terms of simultaneity usually also analyze intervals of time in terms of relations among events. Temporal intervals, they hold, just are physical or psychical events *qua* simultaneous with, or earlier or later than, one another. The implications of this theory are that time is not an original feature of the world-whole, comprised of happenings different from and irreducible to parts of the world, but is nothing other than interrelated and changing world-parts. This reductionist theory has a long history, beginning with Plato's identification of time with the orderly motions of celestial bodies,[6] continuing with Plotinus's identification of time with the sequential acts of the world-soul,[7] Augustine's idea that time is an expanse of the human soul,[8] the variously expressed belief that time is the succession of *ideas* (Locke[9]), *perceptions* (Hume[10]), *representations* (Schelling,[11] Lotze[12]), or *psychical states* (Bergson[13]), and continuing in this century with the various attempts by Russell,[14] Reichenbach,[15] Adolf Grünbaum,[16] and others to identify time with the interrelated physical events postulated by the physical sciences.

The reductionist theory of time is an expression of presuppositions derived from rational metaphysics. It is a central tenet of this metaphysics that being or "what is" in the wide sense is divided into two realms, that comprised of the consequences of the first reason (the whole of created being) and that of the first reason itself (God). This basic ontological division determined the manner in which fundamental categories or phenomena were to be understood and conceptualized; instead of seeking to conceptualize such phenomena in terms of features belonging to the whole of *all* being, one aimed to comprehend them in terms of features unique to each of these two realms of being. Thus one sought to define the basic phenomenon of "the present" in two ways, in terms of a character unique to "the world" or the whole of created being and in terms of a character unique to God. The unique character of "the world" which seemed to correspond in some way to the general sense of "the present" is *change*, and the correlative opposite character of God is *changelessness*. "The present" defined in terms of worldly change is *the temporal present*, and defined in terms of divine changelessness is *the eternal present*. "The concept of eternity derives from unchangingness in the same way that the concept of time derives from change."[17]

This way of conceiving time persisted in the metaphysics of rational meaninglessness, inasmuch as time was still presupposed to be something uniquely characteristic of "the world," where "the world" was still (albeit tacitly) conceived in opposition to the realm of changeless being as "the whole of changing being." Rather than attempt to define "the present" in a new way and from a new perspective, the philosophers in the epoch of rational meaninglessness simply adopted as material for refinement one of the two definitions of "the present" offered in the metaphysics of rational meaning—the one definition, they believed, that could be *known* to have a referent, the definition of "the present" in terms of changing being.

If these two rational-metaphysical presuppositions are rejected, namely the presuppositions that "the world" is the whole of changing being and that time is to be defined in terms of this whole, then it becomes possible to recognize a "world-whole" and a "time" in a different and ontologically unrestricted sense. In particular, it becomes possible to understand "the world-whole" in the absolutely unrestricted sense that corresponds to what appears in our moods and global affects, a sense that is largely indeterminate in its reference and encompasses all that "is" in any sense whatsoever, be these "beings" changing or unchanging. Correlatively, it becomes possible to understand "the present" or "time" in an unrestricted way in terms of this intuitively felt whole.

In the following pages I will show that present intervals in the sense of happenings are change-independent features of the unrestricted whole. The change-independent and global nature of happenings is most clearly apparent in global rejoicings wherein no changing world-parts are being attended to. Consider this instance of such a rejoicing: I am becalmed in a sailboat on a motionless sea on a blue and windless day. Not a sound is to be heard, not a sign of movement is perceptible anywhere. As I open myself to this silent and vast solitude, a rejoicing begins to well up in me, a rejoicing in the happening of everything. I am rejoicing, not only in the happening of these things around me — the still sea and the blue sky — but in the happening of "everything else" as well. I am rejoicing in the happening of the whole that is composed of the sea and the sky and the indeterminately appearing "everything else" that extends beyond the perceptible circumference of the sea and the sky

In this global rejoicing, no movements are appearing to me or are being "measured" in any way. Everything is still. But in this stillness, the enduring of the whole of myself, these-things-and-everything-else is appearing to me, and it is appearing to me more clearly and exclusively than it ever could if my global awareness were distracted by the motions of world-parts around me. In my rejoicing, I transcend the sphere of movements and aim at the being present of the motionless world-whole itself.

It is evident that in this intuition no physical changes are displayed before me as the focus of my rejoicing intuition, and that accordingly the temporal being of the world-whole is manifest in my rejoicing as independent of physical changes. But with respect to this very same intuition it may well be wondered if the temporality of the world-whole is not manifest to me in terms of *psychical* changes. Is there not a "succession of psychical phenomena" passing before my awareness? In particular, am I not apprehending the enduring of the world-whole by means of introspectively observing the successive awarenesses that comprise the synthetic phenomenon of my rejoicing affect?

It is clear that this is not the case. I am not engaged in a reflexive self-awareness wherein I "turn back" my glance and apprehend my rejoicing awarenesses themselves. Rather, I have a straightforward and unreflexive awareness *of* the world-whole's enduring itself. My successive *intuitings* are not what I am aware *of*; rather, I am "living in" these intuitings, and through this "living in" I am aware of what it is that is being intuited, viz., the enduring of the world-whole.[18]

This may be acknowledged, but a further question may present itself. In my rejoicing awareness I may not be intuiting my intuitings, but may I not be apprehending other kinds of psychical phenomena and apprehending the world-whole's temporal being in terms of these psychical phenomena? Am I not aware of certain images, thoughts, feeling-sensations, or bodily processes, and am I not "estimating" the enduring of the world-whole by means of noting the changes in these images, feeling-sensations, etc.? In this case, I would be observing the successively appearing images, bodily processes, etc., and inferring on the basis of this psychical succession that a certain amount of time has lapsed in the world as a whole.

It must be noted to begin with that if I am genuinely rejoicing in the world-whole's enduring, then other images and thoughts are not "floating before my mind." Rather, my attention is entirely absorbed in a captivated intuiting of the world-whole's enduring. However, it is undeniable that I have at least a marginal awareness of my upwardly radiated feeling-sensation of joy, and even more marginally, I may be aware, as James would argue,[19] of such bodily processes as my breathing. But my awareness of such psychical or psychophysical phenomena is not relevant in the sense required to my awareness of the world-whole's temporal being. For I am not aware of these psychical phenomena *as* phenomena *in terms of which* the world-whole's temporal being is appearing to me. These phenomena appear concomitantly with the world-whole's temporal being, but to conclude from this that the world-whole's temporal being is "estimated" or "inferred" on the basis of these appearing phenomena is to draw a conclusion that is in conflict with the appearances themselves. My joyous feeling-sensation, for example, does not appear as a phenomenon whose sequential changes are being used to estimate the world-whole's endurance; rather, it appears as a phenomenon that stands in relation to the world-whole's enduring as an affective response that is engendered by it. And the enduring of the world-whole itself appears as a phenomenon that is immediately and noninferentially apprehended in my rejoicing intuition.

One may respond to this by saying that the world-whole's enduring is "unconsciously" estimated in terms of the changes in the feeling-sensation or in some bodily process, but this would be to resort to empty theoretical constructs that not only remain in principle unverifiable, but which are incompatible with the given fact that the world-whole's endurance is immediately and noninferentially apprehended in the rejoicing intuition itself.

The above explications make it manifest that the happenings are not to be identified with changing physical or psychical world-parts or with their interrelations or features; rather, they originally and directly inhere in the unmoving and unthinking world-whole as features of it. But this "change-independent" nature of the happenings does not of course mean that they can inhere in the world-whole only if no changes are taking place in the parts of the world. As far as we know, some changes are always taking place in some parts of the world. Happenings are "change-independent" in the sense that they can inhere in the world-whole irrespective of whether changes are or are not taking place in its parts. Even if mundane changes are always *in fact* taking place, they do not *need* to take place in order for the happenings to break forth from and into the emptiness as fulfillments of the whole.

Through being change-independent, happenings inhere in eternal beings (if there are any) no less than in changeable beings. This at first sight seems like a contradiction, inasmuch as it belongs to the definition of an eternal being to be "outside of time." However, the "time" that the eternal being is conceived to be outside of is not happening-time but "time" in the rational-metaphysical sense of changing world-parts or their relations or features. To be "in time" in the rational-metaphysical sense means to be changeable, and to be "outside of time" means to be unchangeable. Thus, to be "outside of time" in the rational-metaphysical sense does not entail being "outside of time" in the sense of not happening.

That eternal beings happen is consistent with the characteristics traditionally ascribed to eternal beings. Eternity, like time, is a sort of measurement: "eternity is the measure of unchanging existence [*esse permanentis*], time is the measure of change."[20] The standing now (*nuncs stans*) is the unit in which the unchangeable state of the being is measured. If a being remains in an unchangeable state throughout every happening, the measure of its state is still the *nuncs stans*, for this state *is unchangeable* and the *nuncs stans* is (identically) the measure of such a state.

Eternity is also defined as a simultaneous totality (*tota simul*): no parts of the being have passed away or are still to come.[21] A being can exist as a simultaneous totality in every happening; in each happening, every part of the being is happening, such that no parts are happening-no-longer or not-yet.

The distinction between eternal and "temporal" beings in the traditional sense is still preserved: the former unchangeably and as a totality occupy every happening, whereas the latter are changeable from one happening to the next, such that at any one of the happenings they occupy, some of their parts could be happening-no-longer or not-yet.

Relative to happening, eternity must be understood as a mundane present, a present that belongs only to one part of the whole of all being, the unchangeable part (if there is such a part). Anything that is "present" in the sense of being eternal also is "present" in the sense of happening, but what is "present" in the sense of happening is not necessarily "present" in the sense of being eternal. Accordingly, in order to turn towards the ultimate and truly metaphysical present, one must turn away from the eternal realm and towards the all-embracing realm of that which is happening.

Since the global fulfillment-of-happening is more fundamental than either eternity or "time" in the rational-metaphysical sense, it should not be wholly surprising if this fulfillment-of-happening should prove to be identical with *Existing Itself*. The considerations supporting the idea that "to exist" is "to happen" are the subject of the next sections.

IV. 24. *Fulfillment-of-Happening as the Meaning of Existing*

To say that something exists, existed or will exist is just to say that it *is*, *was*, or *will be*. Existence in its modes is none other than happening in its modes. "To be" in the temporal sense of occupying a present interval is identical with the existential sense of "to be."

That this is indeed the case shall be demonstrated in the following two sections. First let us clarify the sense of the thesis to be established, the thesis that "to exist" means to happen.

In the statement that happening is the meaning of existing, the expression "the meaning of existing" has two senses. In one sense, it is about the referent of the term "existing" ("meaning" here is a synonym for "reference"), and in another sense it is about the importance of existing ("meaning" here is an abbreviation of "felt meaning"). Fulfillment-of-happening is the meaning of existing in both of these senses. The term "existing" refers to happening, and the happening to which it refers is (identically) the importance of fulfillment-of-happening. The importance of existing is not some value intrinsically inhering in existing or added onto existing by human beings; it is not a value or even a feature of existing at all; rather, it is *absolutely identical* with existing. "Fulfillment" is an evocative expression for which "happening" or "existing" is a more exact expression. It can truly be said in an evocative manner that existing is the fullness of which nonexisting is the privation; existing is the positivity of being, of the Is, that is lacked by nonbeing or the Is Not. The Is is lacked relatively by the Was (the Is-no-longer) and the Will Be (the Is-not-yet), and absolutely by the Is Not and Never Was and Never Will Be (the Is-never).

The fullness of existing can be purely appreciated only in the feeling-of-fulfillment, joy.[22] This is why the "problem" of the meaning of existing does not arise in joy, but only in nonjoyous moods and affects. In joy, I intuitively feel the plenitude of existing; I feel in a pretheoretical way that existing is fulfilled and fulfilling in and by itself, and that nothing more than *to be present* is needed to provide myself and others with a meaning of existing. This meaning is wholly realized at each moment of each thing's existing and is not something possessed only piecemeal and in stages, or something that lies waiting for the existent in the future and which can be obtained, if at all, only after a long evolutionary struggle. To existents like ourselves, an *appreciation* of this meaning is granted, although it can be purely experienced only in times of rejoicing. In nonjoyous attitudes, existing in its purity is veiled: I cannot feel its fullness-in-itself, so I may come to think that the meaning of existing must lie elsewhere, outside of the present in which we are all partaking. But no theoretical "answer" to this nonjoyously raised question about the meaning of existing can ever really satisfy me, for no theory can provide me with the intuitive feeling of meaning that is experienced in joy. In joy, the question as an intellectual matter dissolves, for I am elevated to a condition where I can pretheoretically "see" the meaning of existing. But what

I see is so obvious and simple that it can elude my theoretical grasp, for intellectually I may be operating on the false assumption that the meaning of existing must be some highly complex and difficult-to-understand state of affairs. Thus when the joy fades, I may once again resume my theoretical quest, not conceptually realizing that the terminus of my quest had been reached on a pretheoretical level in the joyous affect itself.

It may be said that the real difficulty does not lie in trying to *discover* a meaning of existing that is hidden from us, or in *inventing* a meaning that is not originally there, but in *appreciating* the meaning that existing already and always possesses. Only rarely can this meaning be purely appreciated—hence the seemingly problematic character of our quest for the meaning of existing.

The existing of a thing in its complete character is the thing's occupation of an interval that is acquiring and losing presentness. To say that existing is a feature of a thing amounts to saying that *occupying a present interval* is a feature of a thing. If we wish to consider existing in and by itself, in abstraction from the existents in which it inheres, we shall say that existing itself is the *present interval* that existents occupy.

The meaning of my existing is in one respect identical with that of other world-parts and the world-whole: at any given moment of our existing, the present interval I occupy is identically the same interval that other world-parts and the whole occupy. In another respect it is different: my occupation of the present interval is not any other part's or the whole's occupation of it, for if I cease to exist I shall cease to occupy the interval that is present, while other parts and the whole continue to occupy it.

The conception of existing itself as the present interval occupied by existents is thrown into relief by opposing it to a predominant rational-metaphysical conception of existing itself, according to which existing itself is not a felt meaning but a rational meaning, the first reason for the world. "God is existing itself that subsists by itself [*Deus est ipsum esse per se subsistens*]."[23] For the metaphysics of feeling, existing itself is the temporal present, but for this rational-metaphysical theory, it is the eternal present, for "God is identical with His own eternity."[24] For the metaphysics of feeling, existing itself is known through intuitive feeling, but for this rational metaphysics it is known through logical reasoning, by means of propositional inferences that follow the *via negativa*. And for the metaphysics of feeling, all things "partake of" the one existing in the sense that they *occupy* the same present interval, but for this metaphysics of reason things "partake of" the one existing in that they *imitate* the same eternal present, God.

Is existing itself a rational meaning or a felt meaning, God or fullness-of-happening? It can briefly be shown that existing itself cannot be God. God, if there is a God, is but a part of the world-whole, where "the world-whole" is meant in the absolutely unrestricted sense to include all "things" whatsoever, be they divine or nondivine. The world-whole *exists*, and this existing of the whole cannot be or be an imitation of one of the parts of the whole, God. For a part of a whole is an essential content of the whole; it is part of *what* the whole is, and a part of what something is can neither be nor be like *that* the thing is, the thing's *existing*. The existing of the world-whole transcends God as it does creatures. Existing itself inheres in the world-whole and in each part of the world-whole, and so God, if He is a part of the world-whole, "participates" in this sense in existing itself no less than do His creatures.

But this critical reflection upon this rational-metaphysical theory of existing is not sufficient to substantiate the fact that existing itself is the importance of happening. The identification of existing with happening poses several problems that have not been addressed. Some of these problems follow.

It makes sense to say numbers exist in some way, and yet surely numbers are not in time? Thus does not "existing" have a wider signification than being present in time?

It makes sense to say time exists, but this cannot mean time is present, for some intervals of time are not present. Does not this entail, then, that "existence" cannot be explicated in terms of presentness?

We can distinguish a real happening from an imaginary happening. Is not the "real" in "real happening" what "existing" truly means, so that "existing" means something other than simply *happening*?

Is not time a category, like Aristotle said,[25] and thus a generic predicate? Since, as is commonly acknowledged, existence is a transcendental rather than a genus, does it not follow that time or the temporal present is not existence?

Is not being present in time a real predicate, as Kant implied,[26] and thus distinguishable from existing, which is not a real predicate?

These problems can be resolved if we distinguish the existential sense of "being" from the nonexistential senses (in IV. 25) and explain in what sense existing or happening is a transcendental and is not a real predicate (in IV.26).

IV. 25. The Existential Sense of Being Distinguished from the Nonexistential Senses

A problem that has undermined traditional ontologies is the failure to recognize *the equivocal meaning of "being."* The word "being" has neither a univocal meaning nor a group of meanings that are related by a unity of analogy, but a series of disparate and unrelated meanings, including *identity, inherence, essence, instantiation, truth,* and *existing,* to name most of the central meanings. Not only has this equivocal meaning or sense of "being" not been adequately recognized, but the existential sense of being has not been recognized or distinguished from the nonexistential senses, despite the frequent claims that are made to this effect.

In the following I will distinguish *existing* from the five other senses of "being" mentioned above. This can be done in a very brief manner, simply by showing that these other senses of "being" do not conform to our constant and intuitively based understanding of existing, an understanding that we ordinarily linguistically articulate by means of the term "existing" and its cognates. This term is used to articulate the existing of world-parts and the whole that we marginally intuitively feel on most occasions, and sometimes explicitly and purely feel in joy. It is in reference to this intuitively felt phenomenon of existing that we understand what it means to say "The world exists," "The Devil does not exist," "I exist, but the people who lived during the eighteenth century no longer exist," and "Physical things may have existed ten billion years ago, even though no humans or other mental world-parts existed." Insofar as a sense of "being" does not conform to what we understand in such expressions as these, that sense of "being" must be distinguished from the sense of "being" as existing.

Being as identity. "The world *is* the world" expresses the sense of "being" or "is" as identity. To assert that each thing *is* itself and *is not* things other than itself is to assert that each thing *is identical with* itself and *is different from* other things. It is clear that "being" or "is" in the sense of existing is not identity, for some self-identical things do not exist.[27] It is true that the Devil *is* (identically) the Devil, but the Devil nevertheless *is not*, where "is not" means nonexistent.[28]

Being as inherence. "The world *is* a whole" expresses "being" or "is" in the sense of inherence, i.e., the inhering in something of a feature, where "inhering in" means the linking together or combining of a feature and a thing. Inherence differs from identity, for a thing is identical only with itself, not with any one of its features, and what inheres in a thing is not the thing itself, but only this or that one of its features.

Inherence is evidently not existing, for existing is a feature that inheres in things and thus must be nonidentical with its own inherence in things. "The world *is* existing" expresses (in the "is") the inherence of existing in the world, and this inherence is necessarily nonidentical with that which inheres, existing. Furthermore, evilness inheres in the Devil (the Devil *is* evil) but the evil Devil does not exist.[29]

Being as essence. This sense of "being" is conveyed in the phrase "what it is," where essence is expressed not by the "is" (which here expresses inherence), but by the "what." *What* something is, is comprised of the *essential features* that inhere in it, these essential features being necessary or accidental. In asking "What is it?" I am asking about the thing's essential features, and the question may be answered, "It is a whole," where "It" refers to the thing, "is" to inherence, and "a whole," to an essential feature that inheres in the thing.[30]

Existing is similar to an essential feature in that it is a feature of things (although it is never a necessary feature of things, as I indicate in IV.27.ii). But existing is not an essential feature; it does not comprise *what* something is, but *that* it is. A thing could possess all of its essential features and still not exist. The Devil is *evil, personal, finite, powerful, disembodied*, etc., but nevertheless is not *existing*.

Being as instantiation. In asserting that *"There are* wholes" I am asserting that the universal concept of Wholeness has instances, and in affirming that *"There is* a world" I am saying that the universal concept, World, has an instance. But "there are" and "there is" as expressive of instantiation are not by that fact expressive of existing, for there are instances of universals that do not exist. Some instances of the universal, Human, such as myself, are existing, but other instances, such as those who existed during the eighteenth century, no longer exist.

Moreover, it is possible to argue that there are instances of universals only if classifying minds exist, and that particular physical things could exist even if no classifying minds existed. This can be argued as follows. First, assume that features of particulars are not universals but particulars. Second, assume that universals are formed by minds through abstracting common characteristics from particulars and, consequently, that the universals are mind-dependent. Now if minds ceased to exist, the mind-formed universals would cease to exist, and thus particulars would lose their relational feature of instantiating this or that universal (for a particular can instantiate a universal only if there exists a universal it can instantiate). However, this would not entail that the particulars would cease to exist, for the particulars could still retain their necessary particular features and thus retain all the conditions needed for their existence. If the assumptions of this argument are true, as I shall argue them to be,[31] then it is false to say that existence means instantiation.[32]

Being as truth. "Being" in the sense of truth appears in sentences like "The world *is* a whole!" In this sentence, *"is"* is emphasized and thereby overtly indicated to have a double expressive function, to express both the inherence of a feature in a thing and the truth of this inherence. Truth in such propositions as these means *correspondence*, i.e., the correspondence of *the proposition* asserting the inherence of a feature in a thing to *the featured thing itself*. Since it is true that "the world-whole is existing," i.e., since this proposition corresponds to the existing world-whole, truth cannot be identical with existing, for the correspondence (truth) and that to which there is a correspondence (the *existing* world-whole) are different phenomena.

Nor can existing be plausibly construed as the relational feature things possess of *being correspondents of* true propositions, for some correspondents of true propositions no longer exist, e.g., the correspondents of the proposition, "The people who lived during the eighteenth century are dead."

Moreover, it is possible that physical things could exist even if there were no minds and no true propositions asserted by these minds (as I shall show in Chapter 6).

I will explain in Chapter 5 that a "nominal truth" can be distinguished from propositional truth, nominal truth being the *reference* possessed by nominal senses[33] (the senses expressed by names for things) or the subject-concepts of propositions. False propositions can still have nominal truth in respect of their subject-concepts; "David Hume was a musician" is false, yet "David Hume" is a nominal sense that refers to somebody. Since "the existing world-whole" can be a subject-concept of a proposition, and as such refers to the existing world-whole, its referring cannot be the *existing* world-whole to which it refers. Moreover, the feature of *being referred to* can belong to no longer existing things, e.g., David Hume, and so this feature cannot *be* the feature of existing. And without minds and the referring nominal senses conceived by these minds, there still could be existing physical things.[34]

There is also a prepropositional sense of "truth," which means appearance or "presence" in the apparential sense.[35] But appearance or presence cannot be existing, for it makes sense to say "Ten billion years ago there may have existed physical things, but no humans or other mental world-parts to which these physical things appeared."

Being as existing. The sense of "being" expressed in the sentence "The world is, was, and will be" expresses the existential sense of being; this sentence is equivalent in sense to "The world exists, existed, and will exist." The temporal sense of "being" is (identically) the existential sense of "being."

I stated at the beginning of this section that the existential sense of "being" is that expressed in various sentences—examples of which I quoted—containing the word "existence" and its cognates. We have seen that none of the five aforementioned senses of "being" can be plausibly interpreted as that which is expressed by "existence" in these sentences. However, in each of these sentences, "happening" can be used as a synonym for "existing" without any alteration of sense. Thus, "I exist, but the people who lived during the eighteenth century no longer exist" just means "I am happening, but the people who lived during the eighteenth century are no longer happening."

Furthermore, on each occasion when we distinguished existence from one of the nonexistential senses of "being," the word "happening" could have been substituted for "existence." Thus in distinguishing existing from *identity*, we understand existing as equivalent to happening and can express this understanding by saying, "The Devil *is* the Devil, but the Devil is not happening." And the same is true in regard to *inherence* ("the Devil *is* evil, but the evil Devil is not happening"); *essence* ("the Devil is *evil*, *powerful*, etc., but the evil and powerful Devil is not happening"); and *instantiation* ("*there are* humans, some of whom are no longer happening"). We can also synonymously express the distinction between existing and *propositional truth* in terms of "happening" ("The *correspondence* of 'The world *is* happening!' to the happening world is different from that to which there is a correspondence, *the happening world*, and thus correspondence is different from happening"), and express similarly the distinction between the existing and *prepropositional truth* ("Physical things may have happened ten billion years ago, even though no minds happened to which these things were *appearing*").

The distinction of existing or happening from these nonexistential senses of "being" enables the first three problems raised by my identification of existing with happening to be resolved.

The first problem was formulated thus: "It makes sense to say that numbers exist in some way, and yet surely numbers are not in time? Thus does not 'existing' have a wider signification than being present in time?"

Traditional ontologists have frequently argued that numbers and essences or universals are "timeless" and have a "timeless existence." But the time from which numbers and universals must be excluded is the change-dependent time of rational-metaphysics, the time that is identified with changing world-parts and their interrelations. Numbers and universals do not change; they are intrinsically invariable and thus are not "in time" in the rational-metaphysical sense of this phrase. But this says nothing against the fact that universals happen, for happenings inhere in things regardless of whether they are variable or invariable. I will argue in Chapter 6 that universals happen only while they are being apprehended and thus undergo an external relational change (they acquire and lose the external relational features of "being apprehended"), but universals are invariable in *what* they are (a two cannot become a one or three).

The second problem reads as follows: "It makes sense to say time exists, but this cannot mean time is present, for some intervals of time are not present. Does not this entail, then, that 'existence' cannot be explicated in terms of presentness?"

In reply it can be said that "time exists" does mean time is present, if the latter assertion is understood appropriately to mean time is present in a sequential manner. The assertion that "time is present" is false only if it is misinterpreted to mean the intervals which make up time are simultaneously rather than successively present. "Time exists," properly explicated, means that the intervals of time are present one after the other and that one of these intervals currently is present. Since it is intervals of time whose existence is being characterized, "to exist" does not mean here to occupy an interval which is present, but simply to be present.

The third problem is explained in this way: "We can distinguish a real happening from an imaginary happening. Is not the 'real' in 'real happening' what 'existing' truly means, so that 'existing' means something other than simply *happening?*"

If I imagine a possible but unreal world, say a world composed of ten stars and nothing else, I imagine it to be happening. This imaginary or unreal happening is different from the real happening of the real world. The feature of imaginariness or unreality here means two things: first, an imaginary happening is an *analogue* or *likeness* of a happening, but it *is not* a happening (i.e., it is not identical with a happening); second, an imaginary happening is one that originarily appears only in an imagining awareness and appears as a phenomenon that is formed by this imagining awareness.

The nonimaginariness or reality of a happening is to be understood correlatively. A happening is "real," not in the sense that it has the feature of existing, but in the sense that (1) it is the original of which imaginary or unreal happenings are imitations, and (2) it originarily appears, not in an imaginative and formative awareness, but in a nonimagining *intuitive* awareness (in a "perceiving" in the broadest sense of this term, where "perceiving" means a direct and nonimaginative awareness of the original).

The two other problems that arise from the identification of existing with happening, viz., that existing is a transcendental and not a real predicate, whereas temporal presence seems to be a generic and real predicate, shall be resolved in the following.

IV. 26. Happening Is a Transcendental and Is Not a Real Predicate

Two theses that have played a decisive role in traditional ontological discussions are *being is a transcendental* and *is not a real predicate*. The first thesis was mainly discussed by Aristotle and Medieval ontologists, and the second by late modern and contemporary ontologists.

The use of the term "transcendental" to refer to being (*ens*) first appeared in Roland of Cremona's *Summa theologica*,[36] but the main treatments of the transcendentals can be found in Aquinas's theory of the transcendentals that are coextensive with being (*ens*),[37] in Bonaventura's recognition and explanation of the disjunctive transcendentals,[38] and in

Duns Scotus's fivefold distinction among (1) being, (2) the transcendentals coextensive with being, (3) the disjunctive transcendentals, (4) the pure perfections proper to uncreated being alone, and (5) the pure perfections proper to uncreated being and some created beings.[39] However, the theory of the transcendental character of being was first developed by Aristotle in his *Metaphysics*,[40] *Topics*,[41] and *Posterior Analytics*,[42] and most of the subsequently developed ideas were already explicitly or implicitly present in these works of Aristotle. Accordingly, in the following I will concentrate on Aristotle's explanation of this theory.

In Book 3 of the *Metaphysics*, Aristotle writes:

> But is impossible for either unity or being [*on*] to be a single genus of beings [*onta*]. For the differentiae of each genus must each of them be [*einai*] and be one; however it is impossible for the genus without its species or the species of the genus to be predicated of the differentiae, so if unity or being [*on*] is a genus, no differentia will have being [*on*] or unity.[43]

The reason a genus cannot be predicated of the differentiae is stated by Aristotle in Book 6 of the *Topics*. If a genus were predicated of the differentiae, it "would be predicated of the species a number of times."[44] Aristotle does not spell out the cause or problematic consequence of this repeatable predication of the genus of the species, but the reasons clearly implicit in his theory can be stated as follows.

If the genus were predicated of the differentiae, it would be necessarily predicated, and would thereby belong to the definition of the differentiae. Accordingly, a predication of a differentia of a species would analytically involve a predication of a genus of the species. But this would mean that definition is impossible, for the following reason. In order to predicate the differentia of the species in a way that differentiates the species from the genus, the element in the differentia that is differentiating must be distinguished from the element that is not differentiating, the latter element being the genus that belongs to the definition of the differentia. This differentiating element will then be the true differentia, for it will be what differentiates the species from the genus. But the genus is necessarily predicated of this element, for this element is now *the differentia,* and the genus is necessarily predicated of differentiae. So once again the same problem arises. With each expansion of the differentia into further and further differentiating elements, the differentiating elements that are predicated of the species are increased in number, and since the genus is predicated of each of these elements, the genus "would be predicated of the species a number of times." And this renders definition impossible, for the species can then never be finally differentiated from the genus.

Consequently, "it is impossible for the genus . . . to be predicated of the differentiae." And since being is predicated of differentiae ("the differentiae of each genus must each of them be"), it follows that it "is impossible for . . . being to be a single genus of beings." Being is, rather, a transcendental (although Aristotle himself does not use this word).

However, for Aristotle, time (*chronos*) is a genus, it is one of the ten categories.[45] Unlike being, time is not predicated of each differentia, for some kinds of things, the invariable kinds, are not in time.[46] Thus being is necessarily nonidentical with time.

But this does not mean that being is necessarily nonidentical with happening. For the time that is thought to be a genus is "time" in the change-dependent sense of rational metaphysics. Happening-time is predicated of invariable kinds of things no less than of variable kinds of things and thus, like being, is predicated of the differentiae of each genus. Since happening is a transcendental, it makes sense to say that happening is being, specifically the existential sense of "being."[47]

This correctly implies that there is more than one sense of "being" that is transcendental. Each differentia, for example, not only happens, but also is identical with itself.[48]

The idea that "being" in the existential sense is predicated of the differentiae of each genus can be explained in two ways. A distinction can be made between a "differentia" in the sense of a universal concept and a "differentia" in the sense of an instance of the former. Inasmuch as universal concepts exist or happen *qua* thought-about phenomena, it can be said that the universal differentiae happen *qua* thought-about phenomena. In other words, the universal differentiae happen while and insofar as they are relational terms of an act of thinking.

The second way of explaining the transcendental predication of happening concerns the instances of these universal differentiae. An instance of a universal differentia is a particular feature of something, the "something" being an instance of the species that the universal differentia differentiates. Inasmuch as the instance of the species happens, the particular features that inhere in this instance happen, and since the instance of the universal differentia is one of these features, it happens.

The transcendental predication of happening has a temporal character. "Happening is predicable of each differentia of each genus" means, precisely put, that each differentia of each genus is happening, was happening, or will be happening. Stated otherwise, this means that *at some time* it is true to say of each differentia that "It is happening."

But at this point the question may be raised, Are not some differentiae such that it is *never* true to say that "They are happening," and does not this mean that happening is not predicable of *every* differentia, and consequently that happening is not really a transcendental after all? It seems true to say that the differentiae of absolutely nonexistent things, things that do not, did not, and will not happen, are differentiae that *never hap-*

pen. For example, the Devil never happens, and yet it seems true to say that the Devil has a differentiating feature.

The resolution to this problem is to be found consequent upon the explanation that *being is not a real predicate*.

The discovery that being is not a real predicate was made by Pierre Gassendi in his "Objections" to Descartes's *Meditations*,[49] but the first attempted explanation of the grounds of the truth of this thesis and its accepted phraseology ("being is not a real predicate") were contributed by Kant.[50] That "being is not a real predicate" became a central thesis of most twentieth-century theories of being, from Husserl's[51] and Heidegger's[52] to Russell's[53] and Ayer's.[54] However, interpretations of its sense have diverged widely, and consequently it is best to return to Kant's original explanation of it and to extract the kernel of truth from his remarks.

By saying that "being is manifestly not a real predicate [*Sein ist offenbar kein reales Pradikat*],"[55] Kant means that being is not a predicate that belongs to the concept of an object and determines its content. The concept of an object expresses the object in its possibility; in a concept of a completely determined object, each real predicate, each predicate that determines what the object is, i.e., that determines the content of the object, is contained. "In my concept [*Begriffe*] nothing is missing of the possible real content [*dem möglichen realen Inhalte*] of the thing."[56] Now if I assert that this object actually *is*, I do not thereby add a further determination to the content of the object. For the object *qua* being and the object *qua* possibility must both have the *same* content: "They [the object and concept] must both have the same content, and nothing can have been added to the concept, which expresses merely the possible, by my thinking (through the expression 'it is' [*er ist*]) its object as absolutely given [*als schlechthin gegeben*]."[57]

Why must they have the same content? Because if they did not, the object *qua* being would be a different object (for it would have a different content, one additional determining predicate) than the object of the concept, the object *qua* possibility. And this would entail that I could never assert that the object of my concept *is*, for the object that *is* would in every case be a different object than the object of my concept, the object *qua* possibility. "The object that exists would not be the very same that I had thought in the concept, but something else."[58] But since there are true existential judgements, since on occasion we do truly assert that the object of our concept *is*, it follows that being is not a real or contentful predicate.

But what then is being? Being "is merely the positing of a thing or of certain determinations in themselves [*ist bloss die Position eines Dinges oder gewisser Bestimmungen an sich selbst*]."[59] The content of my concept is "posited as an object that is related to my concept."[60] This positing takes place in connection with our perceptions, such that each thing that is posited is either perceived or is connected with something perceived.[61]

A further explanation of Kant's theory of positing is not necessary in order to bring out the veridical ideas that lie at the basis of his theory. This can be done by answering these questions: Is positing the existential sense of "being," as Kant seems to implicitly think it is? If not, what sense of "being" is it? And if positing is not the existential sense of "being," is it nevertheless true that *existing*, like positing, is not a real predicate?

There are several reasons that warrant the conclusion that existing is not positing. Even within the framework of Kant's ontology it is clear that this must be the case, for it must be true that noumena "exist" in some sense (for if they did not, how would Kant's ontology radically differ from Fichte's?), and yet for Kant only phenomena can be posited.[62] Moreover, it is clear that "to be existent" cannot mean "to be posited," for it is true that an act of positing *exists*; as such, it would itself need to be posited in another act of positing, and this act of positing would in turn need to be posited, and so on to infinity. However, we cannot perform an infinite number of acts of positing; therefore an act of positing "exists" in some other sense than *being posited*.

That positing is not existing can also be shown apart from the framework of Kant's philosophy. I can posit objects that no longer exist, as when I posit an object that is related to my concept of "David Hume." David Hume's *being posited* cannot be his *existing*, for he is no longer existing. Moreover, it is possible for things to exist even if no minds and thus no acts of positing exist, as I shall indicate in Chapter 6.

Positing is not the existential sense of "being," but is related to the sense of "being" as *nominal truth*. A conceptual content, e.g., "David Hume," has nominal truth if there is an object that is related to this content, i.e., if the content *has a referent*. If we say that the content of my concept, "David Hume," is posited as an object that is related to this conceptual content, then we are necessarily implying that the conceptual content *refers* to that object, or *has a referent*.

Given this relation between the notions of positing and nominal truth, it becomes possible to replace the notion of positing, and all the implications this notion has in Kant's transcendental idealism, by the notion of nominal truth and to thereby reformulate in a strictly veridical and non-Kantian manner the thesis "being is not a real predicate." Such a reformulation will enable us to understand in what sense it is true that existing or happening, as well as nominal truth, is not a real predicate.

Precisely understood, "being is not a real predicate" has three senses, what I shall call the widest sense, the narrower sense, and the narrowest sense. The widest sense will be explained first.

Nominal truth involves (at least) the notions of the *referring* of a conceptual content, the *referent* of this content, and the relational feature of *being referred to* possessed by the referent. The widest sense of "being is not a real predicate" can be explained in terms of the notion of *referring*. Referring is not a real predicate because, although predicable of a conceptual content, it is not a part of the conceptual content of which it is predicated. In the concept, "the evil, personal and powerful, etc., Devil," "evil, personal, etc." are parts of the content of this concept, and in this sense are real predicates. If this content *refers*, if there is an evil, personal, etc., Devil that is the referent of this content, then *referring* is a predicate of the content. But this referring cannot be a part of the content that has reference, for the referring is not itself one of the things that refers. It is *predicated of* but is not *part of* the conceptual content — and this we may take as a definition of "being is not a real predicate" in the widest sense.

In this sense, existing or happening is also not a real predicate. Each conceptual content happens while and insofar as I am conceiving it, and thus happening is a *predicate* of the conceptual content. But the happening of the concept is not a part of the concept; e.g., "male," "philosopher," and "lived in the British Isles during the eighteenth century," are parts of my nominally true concept of "David Hume," but that David Hume " is happening" is not a part of this concept. For David Hume *is not* happening. Nevertheless, happening is a predicate of my concept of "David Hume," for my concept *is* happening, it is happening as a relational term of my act of thinking.

The narrower sense of "being is not a real predicate" includes the widest sense, but with the added specification that the "being" that is predicated of but is not a part of a conceptual content is "being" *only in the sense of referring and of the features that inhere in each referring*. Happening is not a real predicate in this sense because it is a feature that inheres in every referring. A concept *is referring* only insofar as its referring is existing or happening.[63]

In this narrower sense in which happening "is not a real predicate," happening has a narrower extension than it does in the widest sense of this phrase. That is to say, every conceived conceptual content, whether it refers or does not refer, *happens*, but only some of these conceptual contents, the ones that refer, have a referring that *happens*.

The narrowest sense of the thesis I am examining is explained in terms of the notion of *the referent* of a conceptual content. "Being is not a real predicate" here means that *being is neither a part of nor a predicate of a conceptual content, but either is or is a feature of every referent of every concept*. It is clear to begin with that a referent of a concept, unlike the referring of a content, is not a predicate of that concept; it is true that a content *is referring*, but false that it *is its own referent*.[64] A referent is, rather, a relational term to which the content is related. One relational term is the conceptual content, the other the referent of the content; the relation between them is the relation of *reference*.

Happening is not a real predicate in this narrowest sense because it is a feature, a temporally modalized feature, of every referent of every concept; every referent either is happening, was happening, or will be happening. Otherwise put, *at some time* it is true to say of every referent of every concept that "It is happening."[65]

In this sense of "being is not a real predicate," happening has the narrowest extension. For while all conceptual contents that are being conceived *are happening*, only some of these concepts have a referring that *is happening*, and of all of the referrings that are happening, only some of them are referrings to referents that *are happening*.

This threefold analysis of the thesis "being is not a real predicate" enables the above-mentioned problem to be solved, viz., the problem that some differentiae, the differentiae of absolutely nonexistent things like the Devil, never happen, and consequently that happening is not a transcendental since it is not predicated of *every* differentiae. The solution may be understood thus: if the Devil absolutely does not exist, this entails that the concept "the Devil" has no referent, i.e., that there does not happen, has not happened, and will not happen a referent of this concept. Nevertheless, the concept "the Devil" *is happening*; it is happening as a relational term of my act of thinking. One of the real predicates that is a part of this conceptual content is the differentiating predicate of the Devil. Inasmuch as the entire content of this concept is happening, each part of this content is happening, and this means that the differentiating predicate that is a part of it is happening. In this sense, then, happening *is* a predicate of the differentiating feature of the Devil.

This can be explained further. When we say that "absolutely nonexistent things, like the Devil, *do have differentiating features*," we mean that differentiating features are parts of our concepts of these things, and "differentiating features" in this sense *do* happen. And when we say that "the differentiating features of absolutely nonexistent things *absolutely do not happen*," we mean there absolutely do not happen any referents of the conceptual contents of which these "differentiating features" are parts.

In terms of the threefold sense in which happening "is not a real predicate," it may be said that in the first sense of this phrase happening *is* a predicate of the differentiating features of absolutely nonexistent things, but in the second and third senses it is not.

The explanation of the senses in which happening "is not a real predicate" also solves the problem that originally motivated the discussion of Kant's thesis that being is not a real predicate, namely the problem that *being* is not a real predicate, but *time* (at least as Kant implies) is. The solution is that "time" in the change-dependent sense is a real predicate, but "time" in the sense of happening-time is not. That something has a changeable nature is a part of the content of the concept of the thing and, moreover, is a part of the conceptual content of some things but not others. Happening-time, on the other hand, is predicable of every concept, every referring of a concept, and every referent of a concept, and as such is not a part of the content of these concepts.

In this section I have aimed to show that happening is a transcendental and is not a real predicate and thus meets two of the criteria for being veridically identified with "being" in the existential sense. In the immediately preceding section, I argued that happening and only happening meets another criterion for being veridically identified with existing, viz., that it is what we intuitively feel to be identical with existing and that we consequently ordinarily express by the word "existence" and its cognates. In Section 24, I described the *pure* intuitive feeling of existing, the rejoicing intuition of fullness-of-happening.

The interconnection of our intuitive feelings, and especially our joyous intuitions of existing, with the theoretical understanding of existing as a transcendental and as a nonreal predicate helps to substantiate one of the main theses of the metaphysics of feelings, that our intuitive feelings are not polarized from our veridical theorizings, but are integrated with them. The foregoing discussions have shown that a reappreciative making-explicit of what is intuitively and purely felt in rejoicing-in-existing gives rise to a concept (fullness-of-happening) that provides a solution to the most complex theoretical problems concerning the meaning of existing. This is only possible if human nature is not dichotomized into "reason" and "feeling," but is comprised of a continuum of feeling-awarenesses, such that the thinking-feelings are more explicit and exact awarenesses of the very same importance (in this case fullness-of-happening) of which the intuitive feelings are more implicit, vague, and holistic awarenesses.

The increase in explicitness and exactness manifested in the thinking-feelings and especially in the concentrative feelings is offset by the loss of the immediacy which is possessed by the intuitive appreciations. Although exactly comprehended only in the thinking-feelings, the importance of fullness-of-happening is directly "seen" and its omnipresence immediately sensuously felt only in the intuitive feelings. Only through experiencing both ways of appreciating this importance, the exact and the immediate, can one *completely* appreciate it.

In the past three sections I have described global rejoicing as the only *pure* immediate appreciation of happening. But why cannot the happening of the world-whole be purely intuited in other global affects?

IV. 27. The Impure Appreciations of the World-Whole's Happening

IV. 27.i. Introductory Remarks on the Pure and Impure Appreciations of the World-Whole's Happening

There has always been a problem in people's minds about which type of affective response a state of affairs truly deserves. Is a certain state of affairs properly apprehended in joy or despair, in tedium or awe? Many people assume that there is no one "true" or "proper" affective response to any given state of affairs and that affective responses are "individually relative" and, in the last analysis, "arbitrary."

Likewise, so this viewpoint holds, the existence of the world does not "truly deserve" any one affective response as opposed to another. Some people may feel joy that the world exists rather than does not exist; others may feel despair, awe, or tedium, but none of these can be said to be the one affect that is truly and intrinsically "demanded" by the world's existing.

This is undoubtedly the objection many people will feel upon reading my description of the world's existing as a state of affairs to which the appropriate reaction is joy. One immediately points to different ways in which people have affectively responded to the world's existing. Does not Schopenhauer write that the truth is that "we have not to rejoice but rather to despair at the existence of the world; that its nonexistence is preferable to its existence; that it is something which at bottom ought not to be"?[66] And does not Sartre, upon encountering the naked existence of the world, feel nausea? Sartre writes:

> Existence [*L'existence*] everywhere, infinitely, superfluous [*de trop*], for ever and everywhere; existence—which is limited only by existence. I sank down on the bench, stupified, stunned by this profusion of beings without origin: everywhere blossomings, hatchings out, my ears buzzed with existence, my very flesh palpitated and opened, abandoned itself to the universal burgeoning. It was repugnant.[67]

There are two responses to this objection to my description of joy as the appropriate affective reaction to the world's existing. The first response is to point out that Schopenhauer and Sartre, and most others who have talked about affective reactions to "the world's existence," are talking about a *different* state of affairs than the one referred to in my usage of the phrase "the world's existence." Schopenhauer and Sartre, for instance, are not describing affective appearances of the *happening* of the *whole composed of myself, these-things-around-me-and-everything-else.* By "the world" Schopenhauer does not mean the unrestricted whole, but the whole of representations that expresses the noumenal will, and by "existence" he does not mean happening or being present, but something else (which he leaves unclarified). The "existence" that nauseates Sartre is not "existence" in the sense of the global happening, but in the sense of being-in-itself (*être-en-soi*), which (if there is such a thing as being-in-itself) is but a part of *the whole* that *happens*.[68]

Thus examples of affects like Schopenhauer's despair and Sartre's nausea do not count as *counterevidence* to my claim that joy is the appropriate response to the world's existence, for these other affects are not responses to what I designate by the phrase "the world's existence" but to something else.

The objection to my claim about joy may be modified accordingly, and the question posed: Cannot one conceive of a despair in what I have described as the world-whole's happening rather than nonhappening, or a nausea in what I have described as the omnipresence of the global happening? Is it not then arbitrary and unjustified for me to talk about joy as the appropriate response to this happening?

The answer to this objection lies in pointing to the phenomena of *pure and impure appreciations*. Joy is the "appropriate" response to happening in the sense that it is the only pure appreciation of happening, and other affects are "inappropriate" and are not "truly or intrinsically demanded" by happening in the sense that they are impure appreciations of happening. A pure appreciation of an importance such as the world-whole's happening is intuitively captivated by this importance alone. An impure appreciation of global happening, on the other hand, feels it to be important, not by itself alone, but *qua* aspect of a broader importance. This impure appreciation has two modes. If we call an importance "A," the pure appreciation of it is the captivation-with-A. One mode of impurely appreciating A is to be captivated with A as having this or that feature; one is captivated with the state of affairs, *A is B* or *A is C*. In IV.27.ii-iii I will show that marvelling and despair are captivated by the global happening as possessing some further determination.

A second mode of impure appreciation is to be captivated by A inasmuch as that of which it is a feature also possesses some other important feature besides A. A is a feature of the world-whole, and X and Y are also global features; there can be a captivation with the fact that *that which is A is also X*, or *that which is A is also Y*. Unlike B and C, X and Y are not features of A, but of that of which A is a feature, the world-whole. In the first mode of impure appreciation, A is felt to be important *qua* aspect of the broader importance, *A-is-B*, and in the second mode it is appreciated *qua* aspect of the wider importance, *that-which-is-A-is-also-X*. In IV.27.iv-vi it is shown that awe, tedium, and peacefulness are appreciations of the world-whole's happening in this second impure modality.

The two modes of impure appreciation are "impure" in the sense that A in its purity, by itself alone, is not appreciated but is appreciated only as A *qua* mixed with other elements, with "impurities" such as B or X.

That global joy is the pure affective appreciation of the world's happening rather than nonhappening has already been implicitly established in the preceding sections. In IV.22, joy was shown to be a feeling of "fulfillment," of something being "fulfilled" rather than being empty or in lack. In IV.24, it was shown that the language of fulfillment is applicable to the world's being present or existing as an evocative description of it. "To be" in the sense of being present or existent is a fullness, a positivity, a plenitude (in evocative terms) in comparison with nonbeing, nothingness. Since the world *is*, rather than *is not*, it is truly evocatively describable as being fulfilled rather than being empty. Now evocative descriptions capture the character of states of affairs as they can explicitly and holistically appear in intuitive feelings. The above evocative description of the world-whole's happening as a fullness brings out the fact that it can explicitly and holistically intuitively appear as a fullness—and it is the intuitive feeling of such a fullness that is uniquely characteristic of joy (for joy, as I stated above, is precisely an intuitive feeling-of-fulfillment).

That this is indeed the case becomes more clearly manifest once it is pointed out that the word "fullness" or "fulfillment" can be used in many different senses and that only one of these is appropriate to rejoicing in the global happening. "Fullness" and its cognates are usually used, whether metaphorically or literally, to refer to *essential* features of things, *what* they are. One says, "The glass is full," or "He is full of surprises," etc. As an evocative signification of global existing, "fullness" signifies an *existential* feature, in fact, *the* existential feature—the existing of everything. It is a "fullness" in this sense that is felt in global rejoicing.

Accordingly, to say that *what* the world is, is "empty" in some sense (e.g., empty of justice), or is such that it does not deserve joy but some other affect, does not touch upon the joyous fullness of the *existing* of the world. In joy, I am not appreciating what the world is, but *that it is*. The "that it is" of any world, regardless of what that world might be, would be a fullness, for "to be" in and by itself, apart from considerations of what it is that possesses this "to be," is a fullness in comparison with "not to be." *Being present* as compared with not being present is *being full*, irrespective of what it is that is present.

It is true nevertheless that in global rejoicing I am rejoicing in *this* world. For I am joyfully intuiting the whole of myself, these-things-and-everything-else. But I am rejoicing in this world, not because it is *this* world (because it has this what-content), but because it *is*, because it has inhering in it *happenings*. I would rejoice in any world that had happenings inhering in it. I rejoice in this world because of all possible worlds it is the only actual one; it is the only one that has *existing* inhering in it.

A further delimitation of the sense that is being expressed in my usage of the word "fulfillment" can be made through noting that I am using this word in a sense uniquely pertinent to what is intuitively felt in joy. "Fullness" can also be used for example to refer to the fact that a spatial region is completely occupied by physical things, but such uses are obviously not identical with the one pertinent to joy. "Fulfillment" in the sense unique to joy can only be defined ostensively by pointing to what intuitively appears in joy. And that existing-rather-than-nonexisting can be purely intuitively felt as a "fulfillment" in this sense can also be shown only ostensively, by pointing to an actual joyous appearance of the world's existing-rather-than-nonexisting. That this is so cannot be "conceptually proven"; it must be experientially verified. Without this experience, one cannot have access to that which is signified by the significations in question. The criterion for verifying these (or any) significations is the *discovery* of the intuitively felt phenomenon they putatively signify. One must discover this intuitively felt phenomenon in one's own experience. I can contribute to this discovery only indirectly. I can through my evocative and exact descriptions attempt to evoke an ignited thinking-feeling and elicit a concentrative insight, in which the reader remembers his own joyous intuition of existing.[69] And at most, my descriptions through being read could provide the occasion for the spontaneous irruption of the joyous intuition.

The demonstration that joy is the only pure appreciation of happening also proceeds through descriptively showing that other global affects are not pure appreciations of this importance. Whereas joy is an intuitive feeling of phenomena that are evocatively describable as "fulfillments," other intuitive feelings are of phenomena that are evocatively describable in different ways. Despair, for example, is an intuitive feeling of *futility* and *emptiness* and is able to intuitively feel in a pure way phenomena that are evocatively describable in such terms. The existing of the world-whole is "empty" and "futile" if it lacks something (is empty) in a way that renders the existing of the whole "futile." These evocative terms are applicable to the state of affairs more exactly describable as the world-whole's *existing without a purpose* (cf. IV.27.iii). Despair, the intuitive feeling of emptiness and futility, is a pure appreciation of the world-whole's existing purposelessly. This means it is an impure appreciation of the world-whole's *existing*, for it is an appreciation of the world-whole's existing, not by itself alone, but insofar as it has the feature of being *purposeless*.

Nausea likewise is an impure appreciation of the world-whole's existing. Nausea is a feeling of the repugnant and ugly. Ugliness implicitly presupposes a sense of "beautifulness" to which it is compared as the opposite. The nausea before existence Sartre describes presupposes implicitly this beauty to be a "rational beauty," the beauty of a complete rational explanation. "That was what irritated me: of course there was no *reason* for it to exist, this flowing larva."[70] "The essential thing is contingency [*L'essentiel c'est la contingence*]. I mean to say that by definition existence is not necessity."[71] By a reason, Sartre means something that makes existence necessary: "But no necessary being can explain existence: contingency is not a semblance, an appearance which can be dissipated; it is the absolute, and consequently the perfectly gratuitous."[72] In relation to this ideal of rational beauty, existence *qua* inexplicable appears to be ugly and repugnant. It is rationally repugnant. Applying this characterization of nausea to global nausea before the world-whole's existing, we can see that global nausea is an impure appreciation of the world-whole's existing. It is not an appreciation of existing *simpliciter*, but of existing as having the feature of being rationally repugnant, of being inexplicable. I feel joy before the world's *existing*, but nausea before the world's *existing contingently*.

But the preceding description of nausea is erroneous inasmuch as it implies that nausea is a real rather than delusory intuition. It can be shown that nausea is unveridical in two senses. First, nausea as Sartre describes it is a seeming intuition of two features of existence that cancel each other out, but which seem in the nausea not to cancel each other out. In his explication of nausea Sartre says that "existence is not necessity"[73] but contingency, and yet that "*it was not possible* for it [the world] not to exist [*il n'était pas possible qu'elle n'existât pas*]."[74] If it is *impossible* for the world not to exist, then the world exists *necessarily*. Existence then is a *necessity*, not a *contingency*. Nausea as Sartre describes it thus cancels out its own intrinsic ground of veridicality: its seeming intuitive awareness of the *contingency* of existence clashes with its seeming intuitive awareness of the *necessity* of existence, and accordingly each of these claims to veridicality is overridden by the other.

The root of the problem is that Sartre was unclear about the difference between necessity as a feature of propositions and necessity as a feature of existence.[75] To say that existence lacks propositional necessity is at bottom to say no more than that existence is not a proposition, and this is both unilluminating and irrelevant to the question of whether *existence itself* is necessary or contingent. Due to his failure to clearly distinguish these two senses of "necessity," Sartre confusedly believed both that (1) existence lacks propositional necessity but is itself necessary and (2) existence itself is contingent.

Let us suppose that a global nausea is experienced that does not cancel out its own ground of veridicality in the above manner; such a nausea would be a seeming intuition (only) of the *repugnant contingency* of the world's existence. But this seeming intuition also is delusory. The world's existence is nonnecessary, and the concept of it as existing necessarily is incoherent (see IV.27.ii). No incoherent concept is intellectually beautiful; quite the opposite, an incoherent concept is "repugnant to the intellect." Thus the world's existing nonnecessarily cannot be veridically appreciated as ugly or repugnant in comparison with the idea of a "rationally beautiful necessary existence," since there is no such idea. There is no veridical basis for a nauseous intuition of the world's existence.[76] The world's existing non-necessarily is appreciated veridically and purely in another affect, that of *marvelling*, as I will show in the following subsection.

In the following five subsections I shall describe five impure appreciations of global fulfillment-of-happening; marvelling and despair are impure appreciations of happening in the first mode of impure appreciation (cf. IV.27.ii-iii), and awe, tedium, and peace are impure appreciations in the second mode (cf. IV.27.iv-vi). These five global affects are directly based on global rejoicing in the sense that they include within themselves as one of their constitutive aspects an appreciation of that which global rejoicing purely appreciates (namely the happening of the world-whole). Global rejoicing is not based on any one of these affects (or upon any other affect) in that it does not include within itself an appreciation of some importance of which some other affect is the pure appreciation. In this sense, joy is the absolutely simple global affect. It is the only pure appreciation that does not include as one of its constitutive aspects an impure appreciation. Joy is *wholly* pure. Every other global affect, by contrast, includes within itself an impure appreciation of the importance of which joy is the pure appreciation.

IV. 27.ii. Marvelling at the World-Whole's Miraculousness

Global marvelling is captivated, not simply by *the happening* of the world-whole, but by this happening *qua* having the feature of being *non-necessary*. *Happening nonnecessarily* is the importance of *miraculousness*, an importance purely appreciated in global marvelling. I will begin the explication of this importance with a few words about the affect of marvelling.

The feeling-sensation of global marvelling has the feeling-flow of being more or less intensely impelled backwards and held in an astonished suspense; the miraculousness of the world affectively strikes me and brings me up short, riveting me in a shocked stillness. I stand before the world dazzled and stunned: Even though it could not be, *it is*! The habitual sense of obviousness and of "taking for granted" that I feel towards the world's happening has been shattered by the sudden unveiling of its utter miraculousness.

The world-whole is miraculous in that at each moment it realizes one of two possibilities, even though it is not necessary for it to realize this possibility rather than the other one. At each moment the world could either *happen* or *not happen*, and I marvel that the world happens, and continues to happen, and avoids the possibility of not happening. At each moment, the world-whole stands before the abyss of nothingness, but it does not vanish into this abyss; it continues, and in so continuing it overcomes again and again the possibility of nonexisting. It is miraculous that the other possibility, the possibility of plunging into nothingness, is not realized, for this is *equally as possible* as the possibility that is realized. There is no feature of the world-whole that shows why one of these possibilities rather than the other should be realized; the nature of the world-whole does not *necessitate* either its happening or its nonhappening, but is compatible with both possibilities.

The importance of miraculousness can be further explicated as follows. If happening or existing necessarily inhered in the world-whole, it would be an analytic part of the content of the concept of the world-whole; it would be analytically true that "the world-whole exists" and a contradiction to assert that "the world-whole does not exist." But it is evident that existing cannot be a part of the conceptual content of the world-whole (or of anything else, including the divine part of the world, if there is one). For assume that existing were such a part; the concept of "existing" would be a part of the concept of the world-whole, it would be a real predicate of the world-whole. But this "existing" *qua* real predicate of the world-whole must be different from the world-whole's *existing itself*, which is not a real predicate. For I could ask of this concept of which "existing" *qua* real predicate is a part: Does it have a reference, does it refer to something that is existing? I am here asking in part if the "existing" that belongs to the conceptual content *refers* to an existing beyond the concept, or if the conceptual content has no referent. This signifies that if "existing" is a part of the world-whole's concept, this does not entail that the world-whole exists, for the entire concept of which "existing" is a part could fail of reference. A concept cannot entail its own reference, for a concept includes or entails only the real predicates that comprise its content; and since reference is not a part of the conceptual content, but a nonreal predicate of it, reference cannot be entailed by the content. Whether or not a concept refers is established empirically or *a posteriori*, by looking beyond the concept to see if there is or is not a referent of the concept.

It might be argued, nevertheless, that in some cases the reference of a concept is itself analytically entailed by the concept itself and as such belongs *a priori* to the content of the concept. The content of the concept of the world-whole would be: "The world-whole exists and is the referent of a concept." Thus it becomes necessarily true of the existing world-whole that it is "the referent of a concept." However, this "being a referent of a concept" belongs to the conceptual content of the world-whole and thus is a real predicate of the world-whole. Consequently, as a part of this conceptual content, it cannot be *the referent* of this conceptual content, the referent that is not a real predicate of the content, but a relational term to which the entire conceptual content is related. This means that the concept of which "being the referent of a concept" is a part *may not refer*, for this concept can entail only real predicates that comprise it and cannot entail anything outside of the concept, such as the referent of the concept. It still remains encumbent upon us, then, to answer in an empirical and *a posteriori* way the question, Does there *exist* anything that is *the referent* of this concept, something that has these real predicates of "existing" and of "being the referent of a concept"?[77]

Thus the nature of the world-whole, that which can belong to its conceptual content, cannot entail that the world-whole *happens*. This nature is compatible with both happening and nonhappening. Both are possibilites; hence, if the world-whole happens rather than does not happen, that is a *miracle*.

We are in a position now to understand how marvelling is an impure appreciation of the world-whole's happening and presupposes the pure appreciation of this happening.

We know that rejoicing is a feeling-of-fulfillment: it feels the happening or existential being of the world-whole to be a positivity and fullness in relation to the emptiness and negativity of being-no-longer, being-not-yet, and being-never. Thus joy is a comparative feeling that the world-whole *is rather than is not.* But the relation of "rather than" that the joy intuitively feels is different than the relation of "could not" that is additionally felt in marvelling. Consider that the world-whole's *being rather than nonbeing* can be apprehended (whether truly or falsely) as an aspect of two opposite states of affairs, one being "the world-whole is rather than is not, even though it could not be" and the other being "the world-whole is rather than is not, and it necessarily is." As I indicated above, the latter state of affairs is an impossibility, but it is sufficient to point it out as a possible datum of a (deluded) global feeling-awareness in order to make clear that "rather than nonbeing" is a different relational fact than "could not be."

Now marvelling is an intuition of the same relational fact of which rejoicing is an intuition, but it also is an intuition of the additional relational fact "could not be." In the joy, I feel the *is* of the world-whole in comparison with an *is not*, and this is why I feel the world-whole to be *fulfilled*. But in the marvelling, I feel the entire *is-rather-than-is-not* of the world-whole in comparison with a *could not be*, and this is why I feel the world-whole to be *miraculous*.

Inasmuch as the marvelling feels this "could not be" in addition to the "is-rather-than-is-not," it is an impure appreciation of the "is-rather-than-is-not." To say the world-whole "could not be" is a different way of saying that its happening-rather-than-not-happening *has the feature of being nonnecessary*, and it is in terms of this latter description that we can understand the impurity of marvelling in terms of the definitions of "impurity" offered above.[78] Marvelling impurely appreciates the world-whole's happening-rather-than-not-happening in the first mode of impurity; it appreciates happening-rather-than-not-happening *qua having the feature of being nonnecessary*.

Marvelling not only impurely appreciates the world-whole's fulfillment-of-happening; it also presupposes its pure appreciation and thus is a less fundamental global affect than is the fulfillment-of-happening's pure appreciation. But this presupposing relation is not a psychological one; it is not as if I must first feel global rejoicing before I am able to feel global marvelling. Nor can it consist simply in a relation of necessitation between the two global importances that are felt. For there is a *mutual* entailment between them; if the world-whole is fulfilled (happens), then it necessarily is miraculous (happens nonnecessarily), and if it is miraculous, it necessarily is fulfilled. In other words, if the world-whole is truly worthy of joy, it necessarily is truly worthy of marvelling, and vice versa.

The presupposing relation in question is based on the fact that *happening* is an aspect of *happening-nonnecessarily*, but happening-nonnecessarily is not an aspect of happening. Rather, happening-nonnecessarily is (identically) happening *plus some feature* in addition to happening, viz., nonnecessariness. Thus, in order to appreciate purely the happening-nonnecessarily of the world-whole, one must appreciate impurely its happening; however, it is possible to appreciate purely the global happening without appreciating at all the nonnecessariness of this happening. And this is what occurs in joy; although the global happening has (and necessarily has) the feature of nonnecessariness, and has this feature while it is being appreciated in joy, the joy does not attend to this feature. The joy intuits happening (more completely, happening-rather-than-not-happening) by itself, in abstraction from the other features it possesses. But marvelling cannot abstract from happening in intuiting miraculousness, for happening is one of the two aspects of miraculousness. Thus, the truth of marvelling presupposes the truth of joy (the intuition of happening-nonnecessarily includes the intuition of happening), but the truth of joy does not presuppose the truth of marvelling (the intuition of happening does not include as one of the aspects of itself the intuition of happening nonnecessarily). In this sense, joy is the unconditionally true global affect; every other affect presupposes its truth, but the truth of joy presupposes no other truth.

IV. 27.iii. Despair at the World-Whole's Emptiness

I am in despair because the world-whole intuitively reveals itself as happening *for nothing, for no purpose whatsoever*. The whole composed of myself, this room, the street and sky I perceive outside of the window, and everything else, manifests itself as continuing on, moment by moment, for the sake of nothing whatsoever. Happenings slide by unceasingly, one after the other, but the whole appears to continue onward and onward through these happenings for no goal and in order to realize no end.

Such global purposelessness leads me to feel in my despair that my own strivings are ultimately *for nothing*. It appears that nothing I or anybody else could do could ever contribute to a purpose of the world-whole itself, since there is no purpose to which we could contribute. We all live, act, and die ultimately for the sake of nothing.

The despairing feeling-flow this global purposelessness evokes in me is not a mere "sinking feeling," as in sadness, but a feeling of "having sunk to the bottom"; I could sink no further. I feel that I am at the bottommost point of the world-whole's abysmal depths. In this respect, despair is the exact opposite of joy, for in joy I am flowingly radiated to the "top of the world."

Despair is an intuition of an all-pervading emptiness, a void in which everything is hopelessly sunken. This global emptiness is the *happening purposelessly* that inheres in the world-whole. Purposelessness inheres in happening (happening is purposeless), and happening inheres in the world-whole (the world-whole is happening) and by means of this purposelessness indirectly inheres in the world-whole (the world-whole is happening purposelessly). The despairing encounter with this global futility is an impure appreciation of the world's happening; it is not a pure feeling of the fullness of the world's happening in comparison with the emptiness of not-happening, but a captivated intuition of another emptiness, an emptiness that comes to appearance when a feature of happening-rather-than-not-happening is attended to in addition to happening-rather-than-not-happening, the feature of purposelessness.

The truth of despair presupposes the truth of joy, whereas the converse is not true. That the world-whole intuitively appears to happen for no purpose presupposes the intuitive appearance of the world-whole's happening, but the intuitive appearance of the world-whole's happening does not presuppose the intuitive appearance of the world-whole happening for no purpose. Thus it may be said that the truth of despair is itself an indication and even a "proof" that the world-whole is also deserving of joy, for the truth of despair includes the truth that *the world-whole happens rather than does not happen*.

The intuitive appearance of the inherence of purposelessness in the world-whole's happening can be made conceptually explicit in the following manner. If there were a purpose for the sake of which the world-whole happened, this would imply that there was some Intelligence (i.e., God) that posited this purpose and caused the world-whole to happen in order that its happening would realize this purpose. But this is impossible, for any whole God creates must be a *part* of the world, never the world itself. God can create only the whole of created being, not the whole of created and uncreated being, the *world-whole* in the unrestricted sense, which is the whole to which He Himself belongs. In order to cause this latter whole to exist, He would have to cause Himself to exist, which is impossible. In order to cause Himself to exist, He must exist *qua* cause. But if He exists *qua* cause, He exists, and thus is not in an existentially lacking condition wherein He is able to receive existence as an effect. No existence could accrue to Him as an effect since He has as causing what would supposedly accrue to Him as an effect.

In order to establish more clearly why God cannot cause Himself to exist, the above remarks can be restated in different and more general terms. In order for something to receive existence, it must not (apart from the received existence) possess existence, for if it did possess existence apart from what it receives, it would be absurd to say that it *receives* its existence. In order for God to receive His existence from Himself, He must not possess existence apart from the existence He receives. But He *does* possess existence apart from the existence He receives, viz., He possesses existence in respect of His act of giving Himself existence.

It might be said that "God's act of giving Himself existence is *identical* with His receiving of this existence." But that is clearly incoherent. To say that giving is *identical* with receiving, that being a cause is *identical* with being an effect, is no more coherent than saying that being active is *identical* with being passive, that being in motion is *identical* with being at rest, and that being straight is *identical* with being curved. In short, one would be saying that each feature is *identical* with its own opposite.

Since God cannot cause the whole world to exist, but only a part of the world, the whole world's existence cannot be created by God in order to realize a divine purpose. The existing of the world-whole is necessarily purposeless and thus is necessarily worthy of despair. Hence, if there is a God, then God, as supremely wise and knowing everything, is necessarily affected by this despair, although His despair is modulated by his knowledge of the other importances of the world-whole.

Global despair stands in two relations to the metaphysics of rational meaninglessness, depending upon how exactly and univocally the expression "the world-whole" is used. In the more vague and equivocal usage, it can be said that global despair is in some agreement with this metaphysics and strengthens its thesis. Global despair and rational nihilism both are in agreement with the fact that there is no knowable cause and purpose of the world-whole. The intuitive evidence of global despair, however, strengthens this thesis by making it clear that there *is no* cause and purpose of the world-whole, not merely that there is no *knowable* cause and purpose. The metaphysician of rational meaninglessness allows that there may be a cause or purpose, but that we cannot know it because there are no true intuition-transcending arguments that could prove its existence, and there are no intuitions or no clearly reliable intuitions of this cause or purpose. But the despairing intuition I have described provides a positive knowledge of the *nonexistence* of such a cause or purpose.

In keeping with this vague usage of the phrase "the world-whole," we may say that global despair differs in a second way from the rationally nihilistic belief. The emptiness and futility of the world-whole appear in despair as a way in which the world-whole is important, and thus as a felt meaning the world-whole possesses. But the rational-metaphysical belief, with its degenerate concept of meaning as a "reason," regards the absence of a cause and purpose as an *absence of meaning*, and as an *absence of importance* in the degenerate sense of "importance" as value.[79] This degenerate sense of "meaning" and "importance" leads the nihilistic metaphysician to the conclusion that the statement of the absence of a knowable cause and purpose is the first and last word in any discourse on metaphysical meaning. If there is no knowable cause and purpose, then that decides the issue of meaning: there is none that is knowable. Global despair, by contrast, is an intuition of a meaning in the nondegenerate sense of a felt meaning and hence enables one to recognize that the causelessness and purposelessness of the world-whole is *a meaning* (not a meaninglessness) possessed by the world-whole and that *other meanings*, meanings that are bases for some other response than despair, also belong to the whole. The world-whole, for instance, also is fulfilled and is intrinsically deserving of joy.

If we use the phrase "the world-whole" in a more exact and univocal manner, we shall have to say that global despair and the metaphysical belief in rational meaninglessness relate to "the world-whole" in different senses of this phrase, and consequently that their relation to each other is to be understood differently than it was in the above discussion.[80] In the metaphysics of rational meaninglessness, the world-whole is thought to be the whole of *what cannot be known to be* created being. There could exist something outside of this whole, a God that creates the whole for the sake of realizing goodness. The cause and purpose of "the world-whole" in this sense are identified with God and goodness. "Global despair," in the sense given this phrase by a metaphysician of rational meaninglessness, would be a despair that the whole of the *possible* consequences of God and absolute goodness cannot be known to be a whole of *actual* such consequences.[81]

Given the unrestricted sense of "the world-whole" that is based upon the moody disclosures and their parallel global affects, the rational-metaphysical identification of God and goodness with the cause and purpose of the world-whole is inapplicable. For God and goodness are *one possible part* of the world-whole in the unrestricted sense and as such are not to be understood as a possible cause and purpose of the unrestricted whole but of *another part* of this whole—the whole of changing being.

Whether God exists or not is *irrelevant* to whether or not the unrestricted world-whole is empty, futile, and intrinsically worthy of despair. For the unrestricted world-whole happens purposelessly irrespective of whether or not God exists and causes one part of the world-whole to happen for a purpose. If God can be known to exist, this terminates the restricted despair of the rational metaphysician, but this knowledge would not save the metaphysician of feeling from his abysmal sunkenness in the bottommost depths of the world. He is saved only by other meanings of the unrestricted whole.

The belief that the restricted despair of the metaphysician of rational meaninglessness is the appreciation of the most important metaphysical fact (that God cannot be known to exist) is based in part upon a failure to recognize that God, if He exists, is *less important* than the unrestricted whole. For besides God (if He exists) there are *other* importances, for example, myself and this shiny pebble on the beach.[82] The whole composed of God and these other importances is more important than God alone. (In fact, if God exists, then His recognition of this fact is a motive for His creation of a whole of changing being.) So if God exists, the *unrestricted whole* is more important than God and is the most important focus of appreciation; if God does not exist, the unrestricted whole is still more important than anything else and is still the most important focus of appreciation. The existence of God is irrelevant to the existence of the most important importance and in this respect is irrelevant to man's true and nondegenerate spiritual life.

These considerations show that despair of the kind experienced by a metaphysician of rational meaninglessness is outweighed in its importance-appreciation by a broader despair in the unrestricted whole's futility *and by a broader joy in the unrestricted whole's fulfillment* (as well as by other global affects). The metaphysician of rational meaninglessness can be saved by *this* knowledge as well as by the knowledge that God exists (but if he is saved by the former knowledge, he is no longer a metaphysician of reason but a metaphysician of feeling).

And in a certain sense that is the *whole point* of this treatise.

IV. 27.iv. Awe at the World-Whole's Immensity

The preceding two subsections were concerned with impure appreciations of fullness-of-happening in the first mode of impurity, wherein happening is appreciated *qua* having some feature, be it nonnecessariness or purposelessness. This subsection and the following two deal with three impure appreciations of happening in the second mode of impurity, wherein happening is appreciated inasmuch as that which possesses it as a feature also possesses some other feature.

In global awe, happening is appreciated inasmuch as that in which it inheres, the world, also possesses the feature of being the greatest and all-inclusive whole. I am in awe of the world because it is the greatest and most inclusive whole that happens.

The feeling-sensation of awe is an *awestruck shuddering back from and below*. This flow of the feeling-sensation correlates to the tonal-flow, which is an *awesome towering above and swelling over me*. In global awe, the absolutely immense world-whole that surrounds and encompasses me is felt to tower over me awesomely from all directions.

Being globally awestruck is the terminus of a process of *becoming* globally awestruck, the latter being the evolution of the pure appreciation of the all-inclusive whole that happens. This evolution of the appreciation is necessary to global awe, for it is demanded by the *all-inclusive* nature of the global importance of which it is the intuition. As all-inclusive, the world-whole includes every other whole that happens within itself, including the whole of my currently perceived hued environment (i.e., the whole of my perceptual surroundings). Becoming awestruck begins through my appreciation of the whole of my hued environment and evolves as I continue to imagine or think of greater and greater wholes in which my hued environment is included, until the very greatest whole is reached and thereby directly appreciated *as* the very greatest whole, at which point I no longer am *becoming* globally awestruck but am *being* globally awestruck. This evolution of global awe can be further explicated in terms of an example.

Becoming globally awestruck originates in a perceiving-feeling of some relatively immense whole, e.g., a mountain range, an oceanic expanse, or a star-spangled sky, that constitutes the whole of my hued environment. I may be perceptually appreciating a brilliant and enormous expanse of stars, when a shudder goes through me as I begin to realize it is *but a part* of an expanding hierarchy of greater and greater wholes that ultimately terminate in an absolutely immense whole. At first, the absolute immensity is felt to be a far-off importance that irresistibly beckons me toward itself, drawing me to imagine or think of the larger and larger wholes that extend between this star-speckled sky and itself. I begin imagining ever larger and more inclusive star-studded wholes, becoming more and more awed the larger the whole I am drawn to imagine. With each more inclusive whole I successively imagine, I retain in my mental grasp all of the preceding wholes I have imagined, as well as the originally perceived starry sky that is still (although less focally) appearing. But this imaginative reeling from one whole to the next and subsequently retaining it in grasp soon reaches its limit, for my imagination can be stretched just so far and no more. At this point, my imagination, strained to the utmost, no longer reels from one star-spangled whole to a larger one, but barely staggers onwards. All the while I am becoming more and more awed by the approaching absolute immensity. Finally, my imagination is overwhelmed and can be drawn on no further; the absolute immensity becomes fully and directly intuitively felt, shattering my imaginative progress and bringing me to a stunning halt. I am completely awestruck by the absolute immensity: I am face to face with the *importance* of the world-whole's all-inclusive greatness, a greatness that towers over me and all around me to ungraspable limits and strikes me back stunned and shuddering before itself. What is before me in all its breathtaking and stupefying tremendousness is the whole composed of the perceived and successively imagined starry wholes and of everything else I am not currently perceiving, imagining, or determinately apprehending.

This importance of *absolute immensity* is comprised of two features, the world's *all-inclusive greatness* and its *happening*. Global awe cannot be experienced if either of these features is not captivatedly intuited. If the world's all-inclusive greatness does not captivatingly appear, and only its happening so appears, then awe becomes a pure feeling of the world's fulfillment-of-happening, i.e., a feeling-of-fulfillment, a joy. And if the happening of the world is not captivatedly intuited, I lose the sense of the *reality* of the greatness I am apprehending, and it is the fact that such greatness actually *exists* that impresses me just as much as the greatness itself (e.g., if I fantasized some *nonexistent* all-inclusive whole, I would not feel overwhelmed by awe, no matter how great I imagined this whole to be).

This shows that global awe incorporates within itself an impure appreciation of the world-whole's fulfillment-of-happening and, as such, presupposes the truth of global rejoicing. But the converse is not true. Global joy *implicitly* apprehends that the world is the greatest and most inclusive whole, for otherwise this joy would not be able to recognize that the whole whose happening it is appreciating is the *world-whole*. But joy is not *captivated* by the all-inclusive character of the whole; it does not "reel through" in imagination or thought the hierarchy of ever more inclusive wholes that terminates in the absolutely towering whole of all wholes. Thus the truth of the joyous captivation does not incorporate within itself as one of its aspects the truth of the awestruck captivation, and in this sense joy is the more fundamental of the two affects.

IV. 27.v. Tedium at the World-Whole's Monotonousness

I am affected with tedium if I turn towards and gaze upon the blankness of the happening world-whole. The world-whole is blank in that no nonexistential processes inhere in it. The world-whole happens, it endures, and in this sense is engaged in a process of existing, but no other processes characterize the whole. It is true that many exciting and interesting processes belong to and are features of *parts* of the world, be these processes physical, ideational, imaginative, or interpersonal, but the world *qua* whole possesses no such features. A part of the world, such as a person, can converse with me interestingly, but the whole world cannot. And a part of the world, like a panoramic sunset or a violent thunderstorm, can keep my senses occupied and stimulated, but the world in its wholeness cannot stimulate my senses. The world-whole does not talk, make noises, or display colors; it does not go fast or slow, rise or fall, or do anything else. Rather it simply *is*, and *continues to be*.

Through focusing on this blankness of the enduring whole, I become oppressed with tedium. It is as if my mind goes "blank" like the world, as if my mind has become a mirror reflecting the nothing-going-on-ness of the whole. For there is just nothing occurring in the whole *qua* whole; it is just *there*: stagnant, inert, an all-encompassing nullity.

The tedious feeling-tonality, like that of its parallel mood, boredom, flows *forwards*, towards me in a *dulling* manner. It does not flow towards me violently or sharply, as does the fearsome or repugnant tonality, but slowly and languorously. The tonal-flow seeps towards me from the globe like a great cosmic fog, deadening my mind, slackening my will, and depleting me of energy.

My tedious feeling-sensation correspondingly flows backwards, although not intensely. It is a largely deadened flow with a barely perceptible backwards movement; I flow *backwards* in a dulled manner, wearied and blunted by the monotony of the whole.

In saying that the world-whole *is happening* and *is blank*, I am mentioning the two features that comprise the global importance of monotonousness. To be monotonous is to be a blankness that endures. This indicates that tedium presupposes the truth of joy, but since I can appreciate the happening of the whole without having to notice its blankness, the converse is not true.

IV. 27.vi. Peace in the World-Whole's Harmoniousness

A harmony that is determinately focused upon in global peacefulness cannot be one of the mundane kinds of harmony, such as the harmonious relations among people or the harmonious arrangements of colors, but must be a *global* harmony. The global harmony consists in the fact that the world is *one whole* in which everything coexists and is unified.

If everything did not belong to one whole, but to different wholes, there would be no global harmony, for all things would ultimately be apart from one another; there would be no overarching unity to bind all things into one whole. There would be multiplicity and segregation, but no unity and integration. But all things, inasmuch as they happen, belong to the one whole of all that happens, and through sharing in this whole they realize a global harmony.

It is impossible for there to be more than one whole that is the-whole-of-all-that-exists, and consequently this whole is necessarily singular and unique. As singular, it is a one, the One of which the many partake. As unique, it is an individual, the Individual of which every other individual is a member. It is the One Individual Whole of all that exists, and it itself exists, and thus is an existent; in fact, it is the Existent, such that only through being a part of It does anything else exist at all.

We can look to a global affect such as peacefulness for an answer to the questions: How can the world-whole both be an existent and be the whole of *all* existents? How can the world-whole be both an individual and the whole of *all* individuals? How can the world-whole be both a thing and the whole of *all* things, an importance and the whole of *all* importances, and a whole and the whole of *all* wholes?

Three possible answers to these questions can be considered. First, one could say (taking for brevity's sake only the example of existents) that the world is the whole of all existents, but is not itself an existent.

Second, one may postulate that the world is both an existent and the whole of all existents, as well as one of the parts of itself.

Third, one may answer that the world is an existent and the whole of all existents other than itself.

In global peacefulness, not to mention global rejoicing and the other global affects, it is intuitively manifest that the world-whole *exists*, so the first possible answer is ruled out. The second answer is ruled out by the transcendence of all parts of the world that is experienced in these affects, especially in the experience of becoming and being globally awestruck, wherein the world-whole intuitively exhibits itself as greater than any one part of itself and thus as nonidentical with any one part of itself. This leaves the third answer, which is indeed what descriptively conforms to the global affective appearances. The world is the One Existent, Individual, Thing, Importance, and Whole composed of *all other* existents, individuals, things, importances, and wholes.[83]

Any thing other than the One That Exists exists only through sharing in the One That Exists. Through sharing in this One Individual Whole That Exists, each thing is *exactly like* each other thing in that each is *a part* of the Existent. Behind all the individual differences and conflicts among the things that exist, there is this ultimate agreement and sameness of things. And each thing is *unified* with each other thing, for each thing is related to the same One to which each other thing is related. The world-whole is the one relational term to which every other thing that exists is related, and is related through the relation of participation.

The pure appreciation of this ultimate agreement and unity of things is a feeling-of-global-harmony, the affect of peacefulness. In global peace, I feel flowingly at rest in the One, calmly reposing in the all-embracing and all-unifying arms of the Individual Existent.

Global harmony differs from global immensity primarily in that the latter involves the world's feature of being *the greatest whole*, whereas the former involves the world's feature of being *one* whole. It is absolute unity, not absolute greatness, that purely evokes a global peacefulness.

Since the singularity and uniqueness of the world-whole are due to its feature of being the whole of all things other than itself *that happen*, happening is an aspect of the harmoniousness of the world and must be appreciated as an aspect of the harmonious importance. In global peace, I am calmly spellbound by the fact that myself, these-things-around-me-and-everything-else are alike and are unified because we all *happen* and thereby are *parts of* the One All-Embracing Individual That Happens. But the truth of global rejoicing does not in turn presuppose the truth of global peace, for although in joy I implicitly recognize the oneness of the world, I am not captivated by it, but am wholly absorbed in the positivity of the *is rather than is not* of the world.

Marvelling, despair, awe, tedium, and peacefulness are five of the global affects that are impure captivated appreciations of the happening of the world-whole and are directly based upon the pure captivated appreciation, joy. A sixth global affect based on joy—global love—is the subject of the next chapter.

CHAPTER V

The Closeness of the World

G lobal loving, like global marvelling, despair, awe, tedium and peace, is directly based upon global joy. Global loving is especially similar to awe, tedium, and peace, for it is an impure appreciation of happening in the second mode of impurity: it is an appreciation of happening as an aspect of a broader importance, the other aspect of this importance being a feature of the world-whole that happens. This feature is the *immediate apparentness*, the *apparential closeness*, of the world-whole.

The present chapter begins with a description of the affect of global love and of the general nature of the importance, apparential closeness, that is disclosed in love (V. 28). There follows a more exact determination of what it means to say that the world-whole immediately or intuitively appears in global loving (V. 29). Immediate appearance must be distinguished from the other ways in which the world-whole appears, its mediate appearances in imagining and thinking, which are apparential distances of the world-whole (V. 30). A second sense in which the world-whole "immediately appears" is then discussed (V. 31), and this leads to a determination of the world-whole's immediate appearance as the ultimate truth (V. 32). Finally, five impure appreciations of apparential closeness are described: global pride, sadness, wonder, desolation, and equanimity (V. 33).

V. 28. *The Loving Response to the World-Whole's Revelation*

In circumstances of a certain sort, a longing for a revelation of the world-whole may arise. This longing can occur when I am tied down to mundane tasks and cares and am unable to free my spirit for an intuitive appreciation of the world in its wholeness. Although the world-whole is always "there" in an immediate way on the horizon of my awareness, I do not feel spiritually free enough to allow it to emerge in its immediacy into the foreground of my awareness, and to let it there captivate me with the importance of its revealedness. The foreground of my awareness is occupied by mundane strivings, affects, and moody mullings; even when

I am free from my obligations, I remain beset by worries and cares about the world-parts with which I am involved and cannot "let myself go" from them and open up to the whole.

But I am at least lifted above mundanity to a degree where I am able to *long for* a revelation of the world-whole. I long to be able to intuit the world-whole in an affective captivation, to stand face to face with the world-whole as it reveals itself to me in an immediate way. I think of and imagine with longing the world-whole in its immediate apparentness. In this longing, I am not apprehending the world-whole in an immediate or direct way, but mediately; I am confined to thinking a *thought* of the world-whole and to imagining an *image* of it (e.g., I may imagine the world-whole as being revealed to me as the whole composed of some fantasized landscape and of the indeterminately manifest "everything else" that extends beyond this landscape). I long to get beyond or do away with these intermediaries, the thoughts and images, and to behold the world-whole itself, in its naked immediacy.

Suppose now that I have been granted a leave or vacation from the mundane obligations that have kept my head bowed to the earth. I journey to the country and climb to the summit of a mountain. Soon I am on the summit: the silver peaks that shine in the distance, the deep blue of the sky, and the sense of vast spaces all cleanse me of my mundane preoccupations and lift and free my spirit. My longing is satisfied as my feelings deepen and broaden in a revelation of the world in its wholeness. The whole that encompasses these distant peaks, this deep sky, and everything else beyond them no longer lies suppressed and obscured on the horizon of my awareness; it flashes forth into the foreground and captivates my attention, engendering in me a feeling of loving illumination.

This flashing forth in an immediate apparentness is the *global revelation*, the revelation of the whole that includes as parts of itself not only myself but also these silver peaks and green valleys and blue sky and the indefinitely manifest "everything else" that extends beyond these perceived parts. In this revelation, the world-whole becomes apparentially close to me; I am no longer apparentially distanced from the world-whole—separated from it, so to speak, by a thought or image—as I was in my global longing. Now there is nothing at all between myself and the world-whole—I am face to face with it, feeling it directly in its intuitive omnipresence. The distant and longed for world-whole is now close to me, flashing forth all around me, from everywhere and everything, and I respond to it with a pure loving feeling-of-closeness.

The appearance of the world-whole in the loving intuition does not imply that all of the *parts* and *features* of the world-whole are determinately and individually appearing in this intuition. All of the individual parts and features of the world-whole cannot be determinately intuited and in-

dividually singled out in any one intuitive feeling, and it is certain that
these parts and features are not apparent in this way in the loving intuition. The world-whole *itself*, which is that which has these parts and
features, is what is immediately apparent in the loving. What engenders
a loving response is that *the whole* which is composed of these parts and
possesses these features is apparentially close to me, and is neither apparen
tially distant from me nor nonapparent to me and incapable of becoming
apparent to me.

This becoming-close of the world-whole is felt not only in the loving intuition, but also in the sensuous feelings that accompany this intuition. A loving feeling-sensation is engendered in me by the coming
close of the whole; a loving feeling-flow is drawn outwards from me and
towards the close whole. I lovingly flow towards the whole in a soft and
effulgent manner, warmly and intimately binding myself together with it.
This feeling-sensation is the pure sensational correlate of the apparentially-
binding-myself-together-with-the-whole, a binding established in my loving intuition of the whole.

The feeling-tonality that is conjoined with this feeling-sensation flows
in the reverse direction, from the revealed whole towards myself. From
the immediate omniappearance of the whole of these mountains-and-
valleys-and-stretching-skies-and-everything-else, there emanates towards
me a soft and vast feeling-tonality of love. Gentle waves of love flow towards
me from everywhere, breaking upon me again and again, bathing me with
an exquisite pleasure and tenderness.

I flow lovingly towards the Omniapparent, and It flows lovingly
towards me. But that the omniapparent whole flows towards me lovingly
does not mean that the world-whole is a person who directs a conscious
act of loving towards me; rather, in my sensuous response to the whole's
flashing forth, *I feel* the whole to have the feeling-tonality of flowing
towards me lovingly. This feeling-tonality is felt by me, not by the world-
whole. It is the way in which I sensuously appreciate the whole's apparential closeness to me.

Moreover, the apparential closeness I sensuously appreciate is no less
dependent upon me than is the loving feeling-tonality. This can be explicated precisely if the following distinctions are made. A relation of *"immediate appearing of"* obtains between the world-whole and myself. I am
experiencing an intuiting or "immediate appearing of" the world-whole,
and this intuiting is a relation whose two terms are the world-whole and
myself. The world-whole as one of the terms of this relation is *the immediately apparent*, and I as the other term am *the immediately appeared
to*. Through being a term of this relation, the world-whole acquires the

relational feature of being *immediately apparent* (*to me*), and I correlatively acquire the relational feature of being *immediately appeared to* (*by the world-whole*).

The global importance of apparential closeness that I lovingly appreciate is the relational feature of immediate apparentness (to me). Since the world-whole has this feature only through being a term of a relation to me, this feature is necessarily dependent upon me.

Analogous remarks hold true for the apparential features the world-whole acquires through being the relational terms of intuitive feelings experienced by other people. The world-whole is immediately apparent to a multiplicity of persons (and perhaps to some nonhuman world-parts as well) in a multiplicity of intuitive feelings (most of them being horizonal intuitions) at the same time and at different times.

But of all these intuitive feelings, it is only in global love that the world-whole's apparential closeness is purely appreciated. One reason for this is that most of these other intuitive feelings are appreciations of some feature of the world-whole that is immediately apparent, rather than the feature of immediate apparentness itself. Take for example global awe, an intuition of the world-whole's feature of being absolutely immense. Now the world-whole's absolute immensity is immediately apparent in this awe, it is being intuited in this awe; but the being intuited of this global immensity is not itself what is being intuited in this awe. I am not in awe of *the immediate apparentness* of the immensity of the world-whole, but of *the immensity of the world-whole* that is immediately apparent.[1]

Global loving, on the other hand, is captivated by the world-whole's very feature of being immediately apparent in the loving intuition. As such, global loving is a *semireflexive* intuition; it is neither an *unreflexive* intuition of some feature of the world-whole, such as immensity, that is immediately apparent, nor a *reflexive* intuition of my relational feature of being immediately appeared to by the world-whole, but a semireflexive awareness of the world-whole's relational feature of being immediately apparent to me. Global loving is not wholly turned back towards myself and my features, as are reflexive intuitions, but is partly turned back towards myself, inasmuch as it is an awareness of the world-whole *qua* related to myself.

There are some other global affects that are semireflexive appreciations of the world-whole's apparential closeness, but only global love is the pure appreciation of this closeness. The impurity of these other affects will be demonstrated in V. 33; here it suffices to elucidate the purity of love.

Global loving is the global *feeling-of-closeness*, just as rejoicing is a feeling-of-fullness, awe a feeling-of-immenseness, and peace a feeling-of-harmoniousness. The closeness felt is the *immediacy* of the world-whole's apparentness. This means that closeness is not a "value" that intrinsically attaches to or is projected upon the world-whole's immediate apparentness, such that this immediate apparentness considered in itself would be a "neutral" feature of the world. Closeness is not something different from or qualifying the immediacy of the apparentness, but *is* (identically) this immediacy. "Apparential closeness" and "immediate apparentness" are phrases that refer to the same feature of the world-whole, except that the former phrase refers to it more evocatively and less exactly.

Global love is the global affect parallel in type to the mood of togetherness. This mood is an unfocused and diffuse feeling of intimacy and togetherness with everything; the whole world is intuitively sensed or contemplated as having a felt closeness to me, although no determinate respect in which the world is close to me is given in this mood. Global loving is a focused intuition of this importance; it discerns a structural content to this closeness.

To say that global loving is a focused intuition of the world-whole's closeness means not only that it is a focused awareness, but also that it is a veridical one as well. For intuitions by their very nature are veridical awarenesses; delusory awarenesses are not intuitions but at best can deceptively seem to be intuitions. That global loving is a seeming intuition that *really is* what it seems to be is evinced by the fact that there are no knowable extrinsic grounds that override its intrinsic ground of veridicality (this intrinsic ground being that it *seems to be* an intuition). Specifically, there are no global intuitions incompatible with this loving, for no feature of the world-whole incompatible with the feature of the world-whole's apparential closeness is ever intuited. Since a global intuition is possible only if the world-whole *immediately appears* in that intuition, any putatively overriding global intuition already presupposes the truth of the loving intuition it putatively overrides, namely the truth that the world-whole is intuitively or immediately apparent.

Nor can any extrinsic mundane ground be found for casting doubt upon the veridicality of this global loving. I will demonstrate this more thoroughly in the next sections, but by way of anticipation it can be noted here that it is an indisputable fact that some world-parts immediately appear. A part of the world-whole can immediately appear as a part of the world-whole only if the whole of which it immediately appears to be a part also immediately appears. Consequently, mundane intuitions likewise presuppose the truth of global loving, that the world-whole *immediately appears*.

Global loving as a *pure* focused intuition of the world-whole's closeness is an *impure* focused intuition of the world-whole's fulfillment. Global loving is based upon and presupposes the truth of global rejoicing. It is an essential ingredient in the feeling-of-closeness that I feel the closeness to me of the *happening* world-whole, not some nonexistent world-whole that is merely the product of my fantasy or thought. It is a characteristic of the *intuitable* world-whole that it be *existing*; I can only be intuitively encountered by a world that exists, and worlds that are merely possible and do not actually exist can never be met with in an intuition. Non-existing but possible worlds can be apprehended in imagining-feelings or thinking-feelings, but precisely because these worlds are *merely imaginary* or *merely conceptual* they cannot appear outside of the imagination or thought and in an intuition. To recognize a world as *intuitively* apparent is by that very fact to recognize it as the *existing* world.

In this way a focused intuition of the world-whole as apparentially close to me involves an intuition of it as happening, and *apparential closeness* considered as a single, complete, and concretely intuited impor-tance includes as one of its aspects the feature of happening. This leads us to distinguish a narrow and wide sense of "apparential closeness" (and "immediate appearance"). In the narrow sense (which is how I have been using this phrase so far), it refers to the previously described feature of apparential closeness that inheres in the world-whole. In the wide sense, "apparential closeness" refers to the complete importance of which hap-pening and "apparential closeness" in the narrow sense are the two aspects. Global loving is the pure appreciation of "apparential closeness" in the wide sense.

For the sake of clarity, I will continue in the following to use "ap-parential closeness" and "immediate appearance" in only one sense, the narrow sense, with the caveat that "apparential closeness" in this sense is always to be understood as a feature of the *happening* world-whole (and accordingly as an aspect, along with happening, of the importance of "ap-parential closeness" in the wide sense).

Global loving is a semireflexive intuition of the happening world-whole's immediate apparentness to me, but global rejoicing is an *unreflex-ive* intuition and as such implicitly apprehends but is not attentionally captivated by the *being intuited* of the whole. This means it does not in-clude within itself as one of its aspects an impure appreciation of the ap-parential closeness of the world-whole. While its truth is included within the truth of global loving, the truth of global loving is not included within that of joy. Rejoicing in this way is the more fundamental of the two affects.

In the above remarks, I have been assuming that we have a clear idea of *the world-whole* that comes to immediate appearance in global loving. But this assumption may have been too hasty, for certainly in some sense of the phrase "the world-whole" it is absurd to say that it can be *intuited*. In fact, philosophers and nonphilosophers alike often say that we can intuit this or that *part* of the world, but to intuit the *whole* world is simply out of the question. It is encumbent upon me, then, to make more explicit and exact what it means to say that "the world-whole can be intuited."

V. 29.   The Immediate Appearance of the Centered World-Whole

In this section I will show that it can be truly said that the world-whole immediately appears in global loving, if by "the world- whole" one means "the centered world-whole." The mediate appearance of the centered world-whole is discussed in the following section.

The first step in making explicit the nature of the world-whole's immediate appearance is to indicate in a general way that a whole can appear only if all its parts appear (where "appear" means "appear in *some* way"). If only some parts of a whole appear, then by that very fact it is unknown whether there are any other parts of the whole (for if these other parts do not appear to me in *any* way, I cannot know if they exist). And if it is unknown whether there are any other parts of this whole, then it is unknown whether there *is* a whole whose composition extends beyond what is appearing. The only whole that is known and appearing is the one composed of the parts that are appearing.

An analogous thesis holds true for the immediate appearance of the world-whole; a whole can immediately appear only if all its parts immediately appear. If only some parts immediately appear, and the other parts mediately appear, the only whole that immediately appears is the one composed of the immediately appearing parts. Thus, in order to show that the world-whole immediately appears, it must be shown that all of its parts appear in this way.

It can be briefly demonstrated that the first thesis, concerning the appearance of a whole in some way, applies to the world-whole. Consider a metaphysical sceptic who acknowledges that there is a world-whole but denies that this whole appears to us in any way whatsoever. "There is a world-whole," he asserts, "but this whole does not appear to us at all." It is evident from this denial, however, that the world-whole is apparent in some way to the sceptic who is making this denial; it is apparent to him mediately and conceptually as that whose apparentness he is denying. The sceptic must in some way be aware of the world-whole in order to deny that it has the feature of "appearing in some way to us," and in this awareness the world-whole is appearing to him. The world-whole mediately appears to him in the subject-concept of the proposition "*The world-whole* does not appear to us at all (not even in the subject-concepts of propositions)."

It is evident, then, that if there is a world-whole, this whole appears to us at least in some way, at least mediately and conceptually. But does it also appear immediately and intuitively?

It could be argued that the world-whole cannot be intuited for two reasons. First, we can never single out in our intuition every thing that exists—and apprehend each of these things in its individual and determinate nature—but can only apprehend in this way the hued things in our immediate surroundings, and the thoughts, images, and sensuous feelings, etc., that we can intuit in our inner sense. Second, we always apprehend the world from a perspective, a point of view, and can never "float above" it and achieve an absolutely objective and nonperspectival intuition of the world.

The response to these two assertions is not to deny them, but to acknowledge their truth and point out that by "the world-whole"and "the intuition of the world-whole" I mean something quite different from what is meant in these assertions. These assertions are presupposing a concept of the world-whole as a *centerless world*, a world that is the totality of existents *as seen from no point of view*. Such a world-whole cannot be intuited by us, for our intuitions in their very essence are points of view, perspectives, and as such necessarily are apprehensions of a *centered world*.[2] "Centered" here means that the world appears as extending out from a "center," this center being one part of the world that is intuitively aware of all the other parts as encircling itself. This can be described more completely in terms of the encompassing character of the centered world-whole. "To encompass"means to encircle and to include. To intuit the world as encompassing me is to intuit it as a whole that includes me within itself and as a whole all of whose other parts besides myself encircle me by extending outwards perspectivally from my awareness.

This encompassing character of the intuited world-whole has already been implied by my previous descriptions of the world-whole as the whole of myself-and-these-things-and-everything-else. The world-whole is not intuitively given as a whole such that each thing in this whole is singled out in its specific nature and made to appear equally with each other thing on a uniform and perspectiveless plane. Rather, the whole is intuitively given first of all in terms of *myself-and-these-things-in-my-surroundings*, e.g., myself-and-these-mountains-and-valleys that belong to my hued environment, or, if we wish to talk of "intellectual surroundings," this-arithmetical-sum-I-am-now-computing, or this-scientific-theory-I-am-now-reading-about.

The world-whole at the same time is given in terms of *everything-else-beyond-myself-and-these-things-in-my-surroundings*. Whereas the things in my surroundings are apprehended in a relatively definite and

individualized way, everything-else appears in a mostly indeterminate way.
All the specific things beyond my surroundings are not singled out in imagination or thought, but appear vaguely and *en masse* as belonging to
a mostly unarticulated totality. Some aspects of this vaguely appearing
everything-else appear with a degree of determinateness; for example, the
world is apprehended to continue in a spatial way beyond my perceived
spatial surroundings into other more distant spatial regions, and to continue through interconnections of sense and essence beyond the theoretical
principles to which I am now directing my attention into a complex network of other theoretical principles. However, these aspects of everything-
else that appear with a degree of definiteness are themselves articulated
segments of a larger totality whose other parts appear as the indefinite
ensemble of "all the remaining world-parts, whatever they may be and
however many they may be."

To be aware of myself, my surroundings, and of what lies beyond
them are necessary aspects of the apprehension of the whole of myself-
and-these-things-and-everything-else, but they are not the sole aspects.
I am also aware of myself, my surroundings, and their "beyond" as *parts
of the same whole*, viz., the whole that is the world, the world-whole.
The world-whole is that to which my self, my surroundings, and their
"beyond" are related by the relation of being "parts of" it. Myself-and-
these-things-and-everything-else appear as *composing* the world-whole,
and the world-whole thus appears to be related to myself-and-these-things-
and-everything-else by the relation of being *composed of* us. The world-
whole accordingly appears as a single whole, as a "one" that is irreducible
to the many parts to which it is related.

This can be made more exactly explicit by pointing out that the
world-whole intuitively appears to be *wholly identical* with all its parts,
but not to be *absolutely identical* with them. That is, the world-whole
is wholly identical with all its parts in that it is nothing more than that
which is composed of these parts. But it is not absolutely identical with
its parts; it is something more than *these parts*. It is not these parts, but
that which is composed of them. In short, the world-whole is not parts
simpliciter, but a whole-of-parts, not a many, but a one-of-many. Thus,
although it is true to say that the world is divided into different parts,
and thus is manifold in respect of these divisions, it is also true to say that
the world, as *that which is divided* into these different parts, is something
unitary.

The idea that the world-whole is not absolutely identical with all
its parts is not to be confused with the notion that "a whole is more than
the sum of its parts." This notion makes sense only if the term "parts"
is used in such a way that the parts of a whole can be distinguished from
the relation the parts have to each other; such a whole is more than the

sum of its parts in that it is identical not just with its parts but also with their interrelations: it is wholly identical with the-parts-as-interrelated. Now in regard to the world-whole, whose parts are all existents other than itself, it does not make sense to distinguish the parts from their interrelations, for these relations — no less than the things they relate — exist and consequently have an equal right to be called "parts" of the world-whole. (But not all relations are parts of the world; some relations obtain, not between parts and other parts, but between parts and the whole. For example, the world is related to its parts through the relation of being composed of them, and the world's *being composed of* parts is not itself a part of which it is composed.) Since relations among world-parts are themselves world-parts, it is false that the world is more than the sum of its parts; rather, it is absolutely identical with this sum. But this sum is not absolutely identical with all the parts, for whereas there is only one sum, the parts of which there is a sum are many. The sum of the parts of the world-whole nevertheless is wholly identical with these parts, for it is nothing other than that which is made up of these parts.

It is worthwhile to dwell for a moment on this distinction between the world and all its parts, for it is crucial to the project of a metaphysics of *the world's* felt meanings to establish that there is such a distinction. Suppose for a moment that the world were absolutely identical with its parts; in that case, there would be no whole of which world-parts are parts; there would be no *world*, no *whole*, of which they would partake and to which they would have the relation of participation. This would mean that world-parts would not really be *parts* at all; there would be nothing more than many existing things. I could never refer to the world, the one world, but only to this and this and this; I would find multiplicity but no unity.

If the world-whole were absolutely identical with all existing things, this would also entail that there would be nothing in which the various *global features* could inhere, and thus there would be no global features. There would be nothing to have the features of being the greatest and most inclusive whole, of being one whole, of being a whole that exists, and exists nonnecessarily and purposelessly, etc.

It might be argued in opposition to this that *all existing things* can serve the function of being *the world* and that in which the global features inhere, and that consequently the world can be absolutely identified with all existing things. But this is impossible for the following reason. There are not many worlds, but one world; the world necessarily has the feature of being one. But all existing things are many, and what is many cannot be one.

If it is said that in truth there is no overarching global unity but only a multiplicity of existing things, I would respond by pointing out that such a state of affairs cannot obtain, for strictly speaking a multiplicity not only implies but *is* a unity; a multiplicity is nothing other than *one* multiplicity, a multiplicity of multiples. The multiplicity, which is one, must be distinguished from the multiples, the items constituting the multiplicity, which are many. If there are eight wolves roaming together, there is a multiplicity of wolves roaming together, a multiplicity that is wholly but not absolutely identical with the eight wolves. There is one wolf-pack but there are eight wolves. Likewise, if there are many existents, then there is a multiplicity of existents, *a world*. But the world differs from multiplicities like wolf-packs, for whereas the wolf-pack is not itself a wolf, the world is an existent. The world is one of those multiplicities that have features that are also definitive of its constituents; the multiplicity of existents is itself an existent — but it is not a constituent of itself. Rather, it is a multiplicity constituted by all existents other than itself (cf. IV.27.vi).

It is also necessary to mention that confusions about the nature of the world's wholeness will arise if one unrestrictedly applies the axioms, theorems, and definitions of contemporary set theory to this whole. Whereas these axioms, etc., are useful in set theory, given its special purposes and assumptions, they are not by that fact reflective of the nature of the wholes found in reality. Take for example Cantor's theorem about power sets. According to this theorem, for each set S there is a larger set PS, the power set of S, whose members are all the subsets of S. For the set S_1, (1, 2, 3), there is the power set PS_1, whose members are the eight subsets of S_1, these subsets being (1, 2, 3), (1, 2), (2, 3), (3, 1), (1), (2), (3), and (0). The (0) is included because one of the axioms of set theory is that the set with no members is a subset of every set. Since each finite set with n members has 2^n subsets, PS_1 has 2^8 subsets, and there is a power set PS_2 containing these subsets as its members, and so on for power sets PS_3, PS_4, etc. One implication of this ascending hierarchy of power sets is that there is no largest set, the set of all sets, because for every power set there is a larger power set whose members are the subsets of the first power set.

Now this theorem is not among those with a verifiable application to real wholes, for power sets are not among the intuitively given phenomena that constitute known reality. It is true that in relation to any whole I can *conceive* of a power set all of whose members are subsets of a set containing all the parts of that whole, but this concept will not be *of* anything disclosed in intuition. I can, for example, take the parts of some intuitively given whole, such as the pages and covers of a book, and sort these parts out *in thought* into various subsets of a set, but this does not show that these parts *in reality* form these subsets, that these subsets exist in the world; indeed, there is no evidence that they do, for all that is met with in intuition are the parts of the whole, the pages and covers of the book.

In reality, each whole but the world-whole is a part of a larger whole, but this ascending hierarchy of wholes is not like an ascent from power set to power set. The whole of a room is a part of the whole of the house, not because the house contains all the (conceived) subsets of the room, but because the house is partially identical with that room and with connected rooms, hallways, staircases, etc., as well. The house in turn is a part of the city block, which is a part of the city, nation, continent, planet, and so on; this hierarchy of wholes continues to ascend until a whole is reached apart from which there is nothing, and this whole will be the whole of all things other than itself.

A further specification of this hierarchical ascent and of the nature of the world's wholeness will be undertaken in the appropriate contexts in Chapter 6. In the context of the present discussion of the world-whole, the explication of this whole as immediately apparent, the most problematic issue concerns if and how it can be both the most inclusive whole and centered. It seems that the centered world-whole cannot be *the one world-whole*, for there seems to be a different centered world-whole for each center. There seems to be a centered world-whole relative to and private to each person ("each person lives in his own world") and to every other globally aware world-part. If this is true, then it cannot be in a centered world-whole that the global features inhere, the features of being the greatest whole, being the one whole of all existents other than itself, etc. Is it not the case that *the world-whole*, that in which these global features inhere, is instead the centerless world-whole? And as such, is not the centerless world-whole the real subject of metaphysics, rather than the centered world-whole given in affective intuitions?

The answer to these questions is that *there is only one centered world-whole*, and that it is not relative or private to this or that particular center. This centered world-whole is *the one world-whole*, the world-whole in which inhere the global features of being the greatest and most inclusive whole, the single whole of existents, etc. The one world-whole is not a centerless world-whole, for *a centerless world-whole does not exist*. This is true because *centers exist*, and if centers exist, the whole of all that exists is *ipso facto* a world-whole that has centers among its parts. Having centers among its parts, it is centered around these parts and as such is a centered world-whole. In the remainder of this section, I will explicate this at some length and then show that the one centered world-whole is immediately apparent in our affective intuitions.

That the intuitively felt whole of myself-and-these-things-and-everything-else is not my private world is indicated in the first instance by the fact that I implicitly apprehend as belonging to this whole *all the other world-centers there are* besides myself. If some other people (or animals, which in varying degrees are more dimly aware of a centered world than are humans)[3] belong to my hued environment, then I will single them out intuitively as belonging to these-things-around-me; at the same time, all the other people and other world-centers are implicitly apprehended as belonging to everything-else beyond what I am singling out in my hued environment.

Furthermore, I implicitly apprehend as world-parts the *perspectival arrangements* these other centers introduce into the world. Each world-center arranges all the things that exist around himself, into these-things-surrounding-him and everything-else. These *relations* that existing things have to his awareness of being centered around it, and the relations they have to each other by virtue of being centered around his awareness (e.g., one building is *in front of* another building and *to the left of* a third building in relation to his perceiving awareness), are themselves *things that exist*. *Qua* existents, these relations are themselves parts of the whole of all that exists. Accordingly, in apprehending everything-else-that-exists-beyond-my-immediate-surroundings, I am apprehending implicitly not only the other world-centers but also the perspectival relations these centers introduce into the world.

This also holds true of the perspectival relations that things have to myself. Inasmuch as I apprehend myself to be a part of the world-whole, I apprehend myself *qua* world-center and the perspectival relations my centering awareness introduces into the world to be parts of the world. I explicitly apprehend myself and these relations in reflexive and semireflexive global intuitions and implicitly in unreflexive global intuitions.

Besides the other world-centers and the perspectival relations that things have to these centers, there also implicitly appears to me the *perspectival appearances* that things in the world exhibit to these centers. If another person is perceiving these mountains at the same time I am feeling lovingly close to the whole they help to compose, the sensuous appearances these mountains are displaying to the other person are different (both numerically and in their exact nature) from the sensuous appearances they are displaying to me. The sensuous appearances of the mountains to him are appearances that are happening, and as such, these appearances — as well as all other appearances that world-parts are currently exhibiting to other world-centers — are implicitly included in the everything-else-that-is-happening besides these mountains and valleys and this sky that I am now singling out intuitively.

The perspectival appearances *to me* exhibited by these mountains and valleys and everything-else are apprehended as existent parts of the world-whole in the very same apprehension wherein I grasp myself and the perspectival arrangements around myself to be world-parts. Thus, strictly speaking, *myself-and-these-things* does not merely include myself, these mountains and valleys, etc., but also the mountains' and valleys' perspectival arrangements around me and their appearances to me. And *everything-else* does not include simply all other physical and psychical, etc., things that I am not intuitively singling out, such as other mountains, stars and spatial regions, and other world-centers and the perspectival arrangements around and appearances to these centers. Everything-else also includes the mostly indeterminate appearances to me exhibited by the above-mentioned things, and the perspectival arrangements around me these things have of extending in different perspectival relationships beyond what I am intuitively singling out.

Thus the centered world-whole I am affectively intuiting is not *my private world-whole*, but *the one world-whole* that includes within itself all world-centers and perspectival arrangements and appearances, as well as all the things that are arranged around and appear to these centers.

It is true that this centered world-whole is centered in different ways around different world-centers, but it is still the same world-whole that is centered in these different ways.[4] "Centered in different ways" means that the perspectival arrangements around and appearances to one center are different than those the world-whole has in relation to another center, even though it is the same world-whole that has these different arrangements and appearances. And it implies that all the arrangements and appearances are manifest at least implicitly to each center,[5] although in each case a distinction is to be made between the arrangements around and appearances to me, and the arrangements around and appearances to other centers, which are some of the things that are arranged around and (implicitly) appear to me.

"The centered world-whole" as I use this phrase thus can mean one of two things: the world-whole centered in different ways around different centers, or, for purposes of exemplification, the world-whole *qua* centered around me in this way at this moment, in which case its current centeredness around me is explicitly referred to and its centerednesses around other centers implicitly referred to (they are implicitly referred to inasmuch as the world-whole that is centered around me includes and implicitly appears to include among its parts the perspectival relations and appearances of things to other centers). In neither case does "the centered world-whole" refer to my private world-whole, my private world-whole being the world-whole thought of in abstraction from its perspectival arrangements around and appearances to other centers and thought of as having only one centered arrangement and appearance — the one it has in relation to myself. This private world-whole is but *one part* of the one world-whole, the other parts of the one world-whole being the other perspectival arrangements around and appearances to other centers, and these other centers themselves. In a *global* affective intuiting, I am not intuiting my private world-whole (intuiting this world-whole would be a *mundane* affective intuiting), but the one world-whole of which my private world-whole and all other private world-wholes are parts.

To render the above descriptions of the centeredness of the world-whole more complete, it should be added that this centeredness includes not only the perspectival arrangements and appearances of things in the world to a world-center, but also the immediate appearance of the world-whole itself, of the world-whole *qua* absolutely nonidentical with all its parts. The immediate appearance of the world-whole itself is a relational feature of the world-whole, the important feature of *apparential closeness*. Hence, in apprehending the world-whole's centerednesses around other centers, I implicitly apprehend not only the perspectival arrangements and appearances things in the world have to these centers, the arrangements and appearances that are themselves *parts* of the world-whole, but also the immediate appearances of the world-whole itself to these centers, these appearances not being parts but features of the world-whole.

So far in this section, I have said that the world-whole that immediately appears in global loving: (1) is centered rather than centerless, (2) is wholly but not absolutely identical with its parts, and (3) is not a private world-whole but the one world-whole that intuitively appears in different ways to its different centers. These distinctions enable the nature of the world-whole's immediate appearance in global loving to be summarily described in a more exact manner than was possible in the last section.

This summary description can be made in reference to my statement at the beginning of this section to the effect that a whole can immediately appear only if all of its parts immediately appear. In light of the fact that the world-whole is wholly but not absolutely identical with all of its parts, this means that the world-whole as absolutely nonidentical with all its parts, and as possessing global features, can immediately appear only if what the world-whole is wholly identical with also immediately appears, what it is wholly identical with being all of its parts. And since the world-whole that immediately appears is centered rather than centerless, "all its parts" are myself-and-these-things-and-everything-else, these parts including not only my private world but also all other world-centers and perspectival arrangements and appearances to these centers. Accordingly, if the centered world-whole is to appear immediately, then all its parts, myself-and-these-things-and-everything-else, must appear immediately.

It may be questioned, concerning this summary account of "the immediate appearance of the centered world-whole," whether it really has been shown that the world-whole *does* appear immediately. Specifically, one may wonder if the appearance of the world-whole is really *immediate* rather than *mediate*. It may be granted that some parts of the centered world-whole immediately appear, namely, myself-and-these-things-around-me,[6] but does not *everything-else* at least appear in a mediate way? And as such, is it not true that only one part, rather than the whole, of the centered world appears immediately?

I can begin to answer this question here, but the complete answer must wait upon the descriptions in the next sections. Let me say that everything-else immediately appears in the sense that everything-else *qua* everything-else immediately appears, although each single thing belonging to everything-else does not immediately appear in the way myself and these-things-around-me immediately appear. (For example, I perceptually intuit these mountains around me, but I do not perceive all the other mountains in the world; the other mountains appear indeterminately as members of everything-else beyond these mountains.) In fact, everything-else cannot immediately appear in the way these-things do, for such a way of immediately appearing is not proper to everything-else. Everything-else is a part of the *centered* world-whole and as such must appear in a way proper for this part of the centered world-whole to appear, this way being a perspectival way, that is, as *arranged* in relation to these-things as their "beyond," as "that which there is besides these-things,"and as *appearing* in a *mostly indeterminate way*. If the things constitutive of everything-else immediately appeared in some other way than this, then these things would not immediately appear as parts of the centered world-whole, and the centered world-whole would by that fact not come to an immediate appearance. For in order for this world-whole to appear immediately, some of its parts *must* immediately appear in this mostly indeterminate and perspectival way as everything-else-beyond-these-things.

It might be said that everything-else beyond what is being perceived is not immediately apparent because it is not sensuously present; only what is perceived is sensuously present and hence is "immediately given." But such a remark construes "immediacy" to mean something else than what I mean by it; I do not use this word as a synonym of "sensuously given," but to mean *given without the intermediary of a concept or image*. In the experience of global loving, I am not running through a series of images of the mountains and other importances beyond the ones perceptually apparent to me; nor am I entertaining concepts of them. Rather, I have a *nonimaginative* and *nonconceptual* awareness of the unperceived things. Exactly how such an awareness is possible will be shown in the following sections, beginning in the next section with a more precise distinction between immediate and mediate appearances.

It would be a mistake to assume that these discussions of immediate and mediate appearances have no crucial spiritual significance. For what is really at stake here is *whether or not there is an ultimate truth* and *what the nature of this ultimate truth is*. What will eventually be shown is that the world-whole's immediate appearance *is* the ultimate truth, the truth that every other truth presupposes but which itself presupposes no other truth. And this will enable us to conclude that even though there may be no "ultimate truth" in the sense of the metaphysics of rational meaning, namely Ideas in God's mind, there is an "ultimate truth" in the sense of the metaphysics of feeling, a sense of "ultimate truth" *more fundamental* than the sense operative in the metaphysics of rational meaning.

V. 30. *The Mediate Appearance of the Centered World-Whole*

The world-whole mediately appears in afterglowing and concentrative reappreciations; in these feelings, there is a mediate "appearing of" the world-whole as it had immediately appeared in a prior intuitive feeling. But not all mediate feelings are reappreciative; in global longing, for example, there is a mediate awareness of the world-whole as it could immediately appear.

What is common and unique to all mediate feelings of the world-whole is an awareness of a *thought* or *image* of the world-whole.

Global thoughts are nominal, like "the world-whole," or propositional, like "the world-whole is one." Nominal thoughts are expressed by a noun or nounal phrase accompanied by a definite article; they function either as the subject-thoughts of the propositional thoughts or appear by themselves—as when I think silently in an afterglowing feeling, "The world-whole!"

Global propositional thoughts have a nominal thought as their subject and a globally predicative thought as their predicate. The nominal thought if true refers to the world-whole, and the predicative thought to some feature of the world-whole, such as its oneness. They are linked by a copulative thought, "the world-whole *is* one," which refers to the inherence of the feature in the world-whole. The *correspondence* of the entire proposition to the world-whole as possessing some feature is comprised of the references of these component parts of the proposition.

The truth of these thoughts is their reference or correspondence; the specification of the nature of this truth-character of thoughts provides us with an understanding of mediate appearances. For a thought to refer or correspond to the important world-whole is for the thought to be a mediate appearance of the important world-whole. The thought itself immediately appears to me; there is no further phenomenon "standing in between"the thought and my awareness of it. However, that of which the thought is a thought, the important world-whole, is not itself immediately apparent; rather, its appearance to me is mediated by the thought; through immediately apprehending the thought I become mediately aware of the world-whole.

If a global thought is not true, it does not refer or correspond; it is merely an immediately appearing thought. But if true, it is also a mediate appearance *of* the important world-whole. All thoughts possess the feature of being immediately apparent, but only true thoughts also possess the feature of being mediate appearances of something other than themselves.

Global images differ from global thoughts in that they are or include *sensuous likenesses* of that of which they are mediate appearances. Although there are no "global images" in the sense of direct sensuous likenesses of the world-whole (for the world-whole is not sensuous and thus cannot be directly sensuously pictured), there are "global images" in two other senses.

First, there are indirect or metaphorical likenesses of the world-whole. If I take a round globe as a metaphor of the world-whole, then through picturing this round globe and taking it as a metaphorical likeness of the world-whole, I am imagining the world-whole itself. In this case, the immediately appearing image of the globe is a mediate appearance of the world-whole.

The second sense of "global image" pertains to memories of past intuitions of the world-whole and fantasies of possible intuitions. My recollection or fantasy involves a sensory picture of hue-displaying configured importances, such that the picturing of these importances is one aspect of my recollective or fantasizing awareness of the whole-of-myself-and-these-configured-importances-and-everything-else-beyond-them. If we use the phrase "imagined state of affairs" in a broad sense to refer to remembered or fantasized states of affairs only one aspect of which is sensuously pictured, then the recollected or fantasized global state of affairs can be said to be imagined. Correlatively, the concrete mediate appearance of this state of affairs, which includes a sensuous picture of these hue-displaying configurations, can be called a global image. The sensuous picture included in this image is a direct sensuous likeness of that which it is a mediate appearance, the hue-displaying configurations.

This account of global thoughts and images enables the differences between immediate and mediate global appearances to be exactly specified. The world-whole's immediate appearance involves one relation between the world-whole and myself, the "immediate appearing of" relation. This relation has two terms, the world-whole and myself, the immediately apparent and the immediately appeared to. The world-whole's mediate appearance, on the other hand, involves three relational terms and two relations. In between one term, the world-whole, and the other term, myself, there is a third term, the thought or image that mediates the world-whole's appearance to me. There is a relation of myself to the thought or image of thinking or imagining it, and a relation of the thought or image to the world-whole of referring/corresponding to it or symbolizing it.

The extra relation and relational term signify that in the experience of a "mediate appearing of" there is a greater apparential distance between myself and the world-whole. Between the world-whole and myself there is a third relational term, and only through the world-whole and myself being directly related to this relational term do we become (indirectly) related to each other. In this sense, mediate appearances are evocatively felt to be apparential distances of the world-whole to myself, and immediate appearances are felt to be apparential closenesses.

Just as global thoughts and images are true in that they are mediate appearances of the world-whole, so global intuitive appearances are true in that they are immediate appearances of the world-whole. *Being an appearance of the world-whole* is the common character of global truths.

The distinction made between immediate and mediate appearances in this section cannot be clearly understood unless we distinguish the above-explained sense of "immediate and mediate appearance" from another and completely different sense of this phrase. This different sense often has been confused with or has not been distinguished from the sense I have assigned to this phrase in the past three sections, and hence it is necessary to distinguish these two senses in order to avoid a hopeless unclarity regarding the immediate and mediate appearances of the world-whole.

V. 31. The Relation of Immediate and Mediate Global Appearances to Universals

It is a widely held belief that all experience involves conceptual mediation, and consequently, that an immediate experience is in truth no experience at all, but a blankness/unconsciousness or a confused chaos of uninterpreted and unrecognized elements. Kant's dictum, "intuitions without concepts are blind,"[7] is the most famous of these assertions, but we can find numerous other statements of this thesis expressed by people from all ranges of the philosophical spectrum. For example, Heidegger avows that all disclosedness involves interpretation, even if it be implicit, wherein something is interpreted *as* something and is so interpreted on the basis of a pre-having (*Vorhabe*), a pre-seeing (*Vorsicht*), and a pre-conceiving (*Vorgriff*).[8] Keith Lehrer states that "experience by itself tells us nothing. The application of concepts to experience is required by any belief or knowledge about the world. Without concepts, cognition is impossible."[9] With regard to affective experiences, mystical affective experiences in particular, Steven Katz asserts this thesis in a bold and dogmatic fashion:

> *There are NO pure (unmediated) experiences.* Neither mystical experience nor more ordinary forms of experience give any indication, or any grounds for believing, that they are unmediated. That is to say, *all* experience is pro-

cessed through, organized by, and makes itself available to us in extremely complex ways. The notion of unmediated experience seems, if not self-contradictory, at best empty. . . . [The mystical] experience itself as well as the form in which it is reported is shaped by concepts which the mystic brings to, and which shape, his experience. . . . There is no evidence that there is any "given" which can be disclosed without the imposition of the mediating conditions of the knower. All "givens" are also the product of the processes of "choosing," "shaping," and "receiving." That is, the "given" is appropriated through acts which shape it into forms which we can make intelligible to ourselves given our conceptual constitution.[10]

What these and other philosophers have in mind is that all experience is "conceptually mediated" in that it involves classifying or interpreting the experienced thing in terms of this or that universal concept. Individual beings are classified or interpreted as falling under this or that universal category, be this category *a posteriori*, like Redness, or *a priori*, like Causality or Readiness-to-hand (*Zuhandenheit*). As H. A. Prichard puts it:

All knowledge requires the realization of two conditions; an individual must be presented to us in perception, and we as thinking beings must bring this individual under or recognize it as an instance of some universal. . . . If we suppose a failure to conceîve, i.e. to apprehend the individual as a member of some kind, we see that our perception—if it could be allowed to be anything at all—would be blind, i.e. indeterminate, or a mere "blur."[11]

This doctrine entails that there are no "pure intuitions," no "immediate appearings of," be they global or mundane, for all "appearings of" in their very essence are acts of conceptual mediation, acts of bringing an individual under a universal.

At first glance, this thesis seems to contradict directly my main contention in the past three sections, namely that there *are* "immediate appearings of" the world-whole. However, the truth of the matter is that this thesis has nothing whatsoever to do with my claim that the world-whole exhibits immediate appearances. For the words "immediate" and "mediate" are here being employed in two distinct senses. By an "immediate" appearance, I mean an appearance that is a relational feature of an appearing thing, a feature based on one relation and two relational terms. By an "immediate" appearance, the proponents of the above-explained thesis mean an appearance of an individual, wherein this individual is not interpreted as an instance of some universal. And by a "mediate" appearance, I mean a relational feature of a thought or image of an appearing thing, a feature based on three relations and two relational terms; they mean an appearance of an individual wherein the individual is interpreted as an instance of some universal. I will elucidate these differences in the following two subsections by showing that a "mediate appearance" in their sense can be either an immediate or a mediate appearance in my sense (V.31.i) and that an "immediate appearance" in their sense also can be either an immediate or mediate appearance in my sense (V.31.ii). Since the demonstration of the latter point, that what they call "immediate appearances" can be either immediate or mediate appearances in my sense, involves not only differentiating their thesis from my thesis but also refuting their thesis (for they would deny that there are any "immediate appearances" that could appear immediately or mediately in my sense), the subsection devoted to demonstrating this point will be substantially larger.

But the demonstrations in these two subsections have a greater significance than merely distinguishing between the two senses of "immediate and mediate appearances." They also aim to show that in global loving and other global intuitions the world-whole is "immediately apparent" in *both* senses of this phrase. The world-whole is apparently close to me, not only in that its appearance to me is a feature that inheres in the world, but also in that the world appears to me *in its naked individuality, with all universal-conceptual mediation stripped away.* In global loving, I behold conceptlessly the absolutely individuated world itself. This expresses a second aspect of global loving, its aspect as a feeling of *individual* intimacy and closeness, and it expresses a second sense in which the world is apparently close to me.

However, in the following two subsections many descriptions and arguments shall have to be presented before we will be in a position to discuss directly this aspect of the loving intuition of the world. For a demonstration that the world is "immediately apparent" in the second sense involves dealing at great length with issues of *universals* and *individuals*. It will be necessary to deal with three of these issues: (1) in V.31.i, I will show that and how universals as well as individuals can be intuited (can be "immediately apparent" in the first sense); (2) in V.31.ii, I first discuss the issue of whether the features of individuals are universals or individuals and argue that they are the latter; and (3) in the second half of this subsection, I examine the issue of whether individuals and their individual features can be apprehended otherwise than as instances of universals. I show that a single individual, specifically, *the world*, and a multiplicity of individuals, specifically *the parts of the world*, can and do appear without the mediation of universal concepts.

In the following I shall, to avoid confusion, use the words "immediate" and "mediate" in the sense I have given them in the last three sections, unless I state otherwise.

V. 31.i Immediate and Mediate Appearances of Instantiated Universals

The word "concept" can mean either a *universal* or a *thought*, be this thought a thought of a universal or an individual. A true thought is a mediate appearance of a universal or individual. Now if an awareness is a "conceptual awareness" in the first sense as an awareness-of-a-universal, it does not mean that it is a "conceptual awareness" in the second sense as an awareness-of-a-thought that refers or corresponds to the universal. For the awareness-of-a-universal could be an immediate or intuitive awareness. This is the case in the normal experiences of classifying or interpreting an individual as an instance of some universal. In cases where the individual is immediately apprehended, e.g., perceived, the entire state-of-affairs, individual-*qua*-instantiating-the-universal, is immediately apprehended. Thus, when I apprehend this hued environment as instantiating the universal, Wholeness, this universal is immediately apparent to me. There is nothing "standing in between" the universal and myself, no thought that mediates the universal's appearance to me.

I will call this intuitive awareness of the universal an *ideative* awareness and the immediate appearance of this universal an *ideational-appearance* of it. The word "idea" can be used to mean the universal-*qua*-exhibiting-an-ideational-appearance.

This ideative awareness of a universal is essentially different from a *thinking* awareness of a universal. In the latter awareness, not the universal but a thought of the universal is the immediate relational term of my awareness, and the universal itself is a mediate term of my awareness. Thinking about universals occurs (for example) when the hued environment is no longer intuitively apparent to me as instantiating Wholeness, and I aim to bring back before my mind in a thoughtful way the hued environment's instantiating Wholeness as it has appeared to me. I form the proposition, "The hued environment immediately appeared to me as instantiating Wholeness," and I affirm this proposition as corresponding to the hued environment's instantiating Wholeness as it had appeared to me. Just as *the hued environment* as it had immediately appeared to me is now mediately appearing to me in the subject-thought of this proposition, so the hued environment's *instantiating of Wholeness* as it had immediately appeared to me is now mediately appearing to me in the predicate-thought of the proposition.

This distinction between intuiting and thinking of universals does not correspond to Husserl's distinction between the fulfilled intuition of a universal and the empty signification of a universal. For Husserl, a universal is intuited if it is apprehended on the basis of and as instantiated by several actual or possible individuals and is emptily referred to if I grasp it by itself, apart from its instantiational relation to individuals.[12] But to my mind, whether we apprehend a universal by itself or *qua* instantiated by several individuals is *irrelevant* to the distinction between intuiting and thinking of a universal. I can intuit a universal by itself no less than I can intuit it as instantiated in several individuals. The universal, Wholeness, is now *immediately* before my mind, although I am not apprehending it as instantiated in this or that individual. And when I propositionally think about this Wholeness as it immediately appeared on the occasion when I apprehended it as being instantiated by the hued environment I was perceiving, I am comprehending this Wholeness as instantiated but am nevertheless *mediately* aware of it. To apprehend the universal *as* instantiated is not by that fact to *intuit* the universal but to apprehend the universal *as related to something other than the universal*, namely some individuals to which the universal is related through the relation of instantiation. The difference between intuiting and thinking of a universal only shows up in such cases as when I form a nominal or propositional thought of a universal as it had immediately appeared to me on a former occasion.

The significance of this conclusion in regard to my descriptions of immediate global appearances can be briefly stated. The world, as I previously indicated, is an individual.[13] Thus, if the thesis that all awarenesses of individuals are classifications of these individuals as instances of universals is true, this means that global loving and other such feeling-awarenesses of the world are classificatory awarenesses of the world as instantiating universals. However, since universals can and usually do immediately appear in classificatory awarenesses, as I have argued in this subsection, the fact that global loving and other such feeling-awarenesses are classificatory would not entail that they are not "immediate appearings of" in my sense. Rather, it would entail that they are *"immediate appearings of" the world as instantiating universals*. In sum, then, the truth of the thesis that all awarenesses of individuals are classificatory would not entail the falsity of the thesis I endeavored to demonstrate in the previous sections of this chapter, namely, that *there are intuitive feelings of the world*.

However, I shall now show that the thesis that all awarenesses of individuals are classificatory *is false*. In particular, I shall show that intuitive feelings of the world and the reappreciative thinking-feelings that belong to their afterglow are nonclassificatory awarenesses. In these awarenesses, *no universals whatsoever appear*.

V. 31.ii Immediate and Mediate Appearances of Individuals

There is a widespread doctrine according to which features of individuals are not themselves individual features, but universals. Thus, the wholeness of the world is not a numerically different feature than the wholeness of a hued environment or the wholeness of a person, but is one and the same wholeness. In fact, it *is* the universal, Wholeness, itself; it is this universal inhering in different individuals.

If this doctrine were true, then every intuition of an individual would involve ideating the universals that are the features of the individual. But if this doctrine were false, and features of individuals were themselves individuals and as such were instances of universals rather than universals, then the intuition of an individual would be only of individuals and would not involve an awareness of universals.

Whether features of individuals are universals or individuals is a matter that can be decided by inspecting the individuals that appear to us. Such an inspection reveals that individual parts of the world, and the world itself, have individual features.

Although I believe an appeal to the intuitive given suffices to decide the issue, many philosophers will find it unconvincing, inasmuch as their theoretical position constrains them to assert that any "appeal to intuition" would decide the issue in their favor and would show that features of individuals are universals. Accordingly, to support and substantiate the truth of my appeal to the intuitive given, I shall offer seven arguments that aim to elicit in the reader a concentrative insight that features are individuals not universals. I intend to make manifest to his concentrative thinking-feelings what I believe is already manifest to him on the pretheoretical level of intuitive feeling. The seven arguments are descriptive explications of the implicitly intuitively felt nature of features *as* individuals; these descriptive explications are not, however, presented as simple descriptions but are moulded into an argumentative form.

In these arguments, the word "thing" or "something" is used as I customarily use it, in the widest possible sense, wherein it refers to whatever happens, be it an individual or universal.

1. It is clear that if A and B possess different features at the same time, then A and B cannot be numerically one and the same thing. For example, if A has the feature of being *all-inclusive*, and B the feature of being *inclusive-of-some* (*but not all*), then A and B are different individuals. Consider now that the wholeness of the world has the feature of being all-inclusive, whereas the wholeness of this panoramically hued environment has the feature of being inclusive-of-some. It follows, then, that the wholeness of the world is a numerically different feature than the wholeness of the panoramically hued environment, and thus that these wholenesses are individual features of the world and the hued environment. This argument can be stated, with suitable modifications, for all features of all individuals.

One may respond to this argument by saying that all it establishes is that wholeness-as-all-inclusive is a different complex feature than wholeness-as-inclusive-of-some. It is true that the argument implies this, but that does not negate the fact that the feature of wholeness that is an aspect of these two different complex features would (on the basis of the theory that features are universals) be itself one and the same universal wholeness. But it *cannot* be one and the same wholeness, for one and the same thing (wholeness) cannot at the same time possess different and opposite features (all-inclusive and inclusive-of-some).

2. Features of hued things can be sensuously perceived, but it is impossible to have a sense perception of a universal. I can smell this fragrance of a rose, but I cannot smell a universal. I can run my hand along a table and feel its smoothness, but I cannot feel a universal with my hand. Universals are not sensible phenomena that my five senses can open onto, but are nonsensible phenomena that can be apprehended only in the mind's eye, in acts of ideation or thinking. Accordingly, sensuous features of hued things cannot be universals, but must be individuals.

This particular argument only applies to some features, sensuous features, and not to nonsensuous features like intelligence and happening. As such, it refutes the theory that *all* features are universals but does not establish (as I do establish in other arguments) that *all* features are individuals.

The proponent of the theory that all features are universals may endeavor to counter this argument as follows. He concedes both that features of hued things are sensuous and that universals *as* universals (which are apprehended in nonsensuous ideation) are nonsensuous. But he would claim that the features of the hued things *are* the universals *as inhering in* the hued things. According to him, there is a difference between Smoothness *as* Smoothness that I apprehend in my mind's eye (and which is a nonsensuous Smoothness) and this same Smoothness *as inhering in* a table (which is a sensuous Smoothness).

This line of thinking, however, is open to the objection that identically one and the same thing (e.g., the universal Smoothness) cannot be both sensuous and nonsensuous. Two phenomena identical with one another cannot have opposite features (sensuousness and nonsensuousness), and so the universal Smoothness I ideate cannot *be* the feature that inheres in the table. Nor can the difference between the two be merely that in one case the universal inheres in the table and in the other case it does not inhere in the table (or in any other individual). For it cannot be identically and numerically the same thing that inheres and does not inhere in the table, since that which inheres in the table is a *sensuous Smoothness*, and that which does not inhere in the table is a *nonsensuous Smoothness*.

Can there be two universal Smoothnesses, one nonsensuous and one sensuous, with the latter being the one that inheres in individuals? I think not, for a universal is that which is or could be "common" in some sense to many individuals. What would be common to many individuals on this theory is the sensuous Smoothness, for it is this Smoothness that inheres in individuals. What, then, of the nonsensuous Smoothness? It could not be a universal, for there are no individuals to which it could be common, since the appropriate individuals (tables, etc.) have inhering in them a different universal, the sensuous Smoothness. We would be left with only one universal, the sensuous Smoothness. The only universal is that which is apprehended through the senses.

But this situation is inadmissible, for it is absurd to say that a certain universal cannot be apprehended in the mind's eye but only through the senses. If anything is evident it is that any universal we care to specify can be comprehended in ideation. I can ideate at this moment the nonsensuous universal, Smoothness, and grasp it as *common* to many individuals. But here "common" cannot mean that *it itself inheres in* many individuals (which it cannot do since it is nonsensuous); rather, it must mean that it is *instantiated by* a number of different sensuous features (individual sensuous smoothnesses) that inhere in individuals.

3. If something is located in space, then it cannot be identical with something not located in space. The wholeness of the sun is located in space, but the wholeness of the world is not. Thus, there are two different wholenesses — one inhering in the sun and one in the world — rather than one universal Wholeness inhering in both.

4. If I destroy something, e.g., an apple, I destroy the thing with all of its features. It is senseless to say I destroy merely a "bare particular," the bare individual in which the features inhere, but not the features themselves. When I hit the apple with a hammer, I am not crushing a bare individual, but an individual *qua* round, red, juicy, soft, two inches in diameter, etc. And when my house burns down, it is not as if a bare individual goes up in flames, and all the features that inhere in the house remain unscathed (which would be the case if these features were universals). Certainly the firemen would not answer the alarm if they knew that all that was really burning was a bare and featureless individual. And certainly, when I sift mournfully through the ashes the next day, I am not mourning the loss of a bare individual, but of my house with all of its features.

But if this is the case, then features of individuals cannot be universals. For the house's feature of wholeness, for example, was destroyed when the house was destroyed, whereas there still exist a wholeness of the world and a universal Wholeness that I am able to contemplate ideationally.

One may argue against this that when my house burns down what occurs is neither that a bare individual is destroyed nor that (universal) features are destroyed, but that the universal features cease to inhere in the bare individual. But in this case there is *nothing at all* destroyed when my house is destroyed, and that is absurd.

It might be said in response that the *inhering in* of features in the bare individual is what is destroyed by the flames. But this cannot be the case, for *inhering in* is not a physical phenomenon, and only physical phenomena can be destroyed by flames. Moreover, this situation would be contrary to what is perceived: I perceive the flames burning and destroying *the physical features* of the house and do not perceive these flames to be burning and destroying any *inherings in*.

5. Universals can be parts of propositions and syllogisms, but such features as the ones possessed by hued things cannot be. The universal, Roundness, is a part of a premise of this syllogism:

> Roundness is a Shape.
> A Shape is a Primary Quality.
> Therefore, Roundness is a Primary Quality.

This syllogism and all of its parts are not in space (although of course the written words that express it are in space). However, the roundness of the sun is in space, and this roundness has a size. Consequently, the universal, Roundness, which is a part of the syllogism, cannot be identified with the roundness of the sun, or with the roundness of any other individual. The universal, then, *is not* a feature of individuals. If it is said that the nonspatial Roundness is a different universal than the spatial Roundness that inheres in individuals, the same problems arise as did in the counterargument to the second argument I presented (which accordingly need not be repeated here).

6. I can alter the features of individuals, but I cannot alter a universal. I can bend the round shape of a clay dish into a triangular shape, but I cannot grab hold of the universal, Roundness, and bend it until it becomes the universal, Triangularity.

The response that in alteration we alter individuals and not their features is unacceptable, for individuals apart from their features are bare individuals and possess no determinations whereby they could be altered from one determinate state to another.

A second possible response, that in alteration we alter the *inhering* of features in individuals and neither the features nor the bare individuals, is equally unacceptable, for *inherings in* possess no alterable determinations (rather, they are the inherings of alterable determinations — features — in bare individuals).

7. The roundness of the sun is in a different place than the roundness of the moon. But a spatial occupant cannot be entirely in one place and at the same time entirely in another place. Consequently, the roundness of the sun must be a different individual roundness than the roundness of the moon.

Some proponents of the theory that features are universals profess to find noncontradictory the proposition that some kinds of spatial occupants (viz., universal features) can be entirely in one place and entirely in another place at the same time. There is little I can say by way of argument in response to such professions; I can only affirm that this proposition *seems to me* to be contradictory and that those who profess otherwise *seem to me* to be deluded in their beliefs.

In order to buttress his belief that this proposition is noncontradictory, a person may argue a related thesis, that the same place can at the same time be entirely occupied by more than one thing. For example, the color, shape, and taste of a hued thing occupy the same place at the same time. This thesis is based on a confusion of configured-importance features with the hues these importances display themselves to be. Color and taste are not located in the space of the configured importance, since color and taste are not physically extended features but apparential features. The configured importance *displays itself* to a percepient as being colored and tasty; displays are appearances, and appearances are not extended (even if they be appearances-of-being-extended). So the color and taste of something are not in the same place as the thing's size.

By means of the above seven arguments I have endeavored to bring the reader's concentrative thinking-feelings into alignment with what I believe to be his intuitive feelings, his intuitive feelings of features *as* individuals rather than universals. These arguments, however, do not suffice to show that individuals can and do appear without universals being simultaneously ideated, for it could be claimed that although features of individuals are themselves individual, they nevertheless are instances of universals and must appear as such. Norman Kemp Smith, for example, espouses such a position: "a particular cannot be apprehended save as an instance of a universal."[14]

It is indeed the case that each individual we apprehend *is* an instance of a universal. However, I believe it can be shown that each individual we apprehend is not *apprehended to be* an instance of a universal. Showing this is essential to the demonstration that global loving and other affects and moods are *immediate feelings* of the world, where "immediate" means "without the mediation of a universal concept." If it can be made manifest that global loving and other such feelings are not ideative awarenesses of the world, then it can be known that in these feelings the world is "immediately apparent" in both senses of this phrase, in the sense that the world's appearance is a relational feature of the world itself, and not of a thought or image of the world, and in the sense that the individual world with its individual features appear without being classified as instances of these or those universals.

The belief that individuals (individuals of all sorts, be they individual features, individual relations, or the individuals that have these features and relations) necessarily appear as instantiating universals is based on a confusion between the concept of an *individual* and the concept of an *in-*

stance of a universal. It has been tacitly assumed that these concepts are identical and that an individual is identically an instance of a universal. But this is not the case. This individual *is* this individual by virtue of being itself, by virtue of being identical with itself. But it is not through being identical with itself that an individual is an instance of a universal; rather, it is an instance of a universal through being related to the universal and related through a relation of instantiation. By virtue of being so related, the individual acquires the relational feature of instantiating the universal, and the universal acquires the relational feature of being instantiated by the individual. It is because the individual has the relational feature of instantiating the universal, and not because the individual *is* an individual, that the individual is called "an instance of a universal."

Consequently, to apprehend an individual as an instance of a universal, it is not sufficient to apprehend the individual *as* an individual. One must also interpret the individual as having the relational feature of instantiating the universal.

Correlatively, to apprehend the individual *as* an individual, it is not necessary to interpret it as having a relational feature of instantiating a universal.

In global loving, to take one case, I implicitly apprehend the world's individual feature of wholeness; I apprehend *the wholeness* of the world. But I do not interpret this wholeness as having the relational feature of instantiating Wholeness, for such an interpretation is unnecessary to my apprehension of *the wholeness* possessed by the world. This is the case, to apply the above considerations to the present example, because the wholeness of the world *qua* the wholeness of the world is not (identically) the relational feature of instantiating Wholeness, but is that which has this feature; consequently, its possession of its self-identity *as* the wholeness of the world is different from its possession of this relational feature. Accordingly, the wholeness of the world can appear as identical with itself, as being the wholeness of the world, without appearing as instantiating Wholeness.

The wholeness of the world intuitively appears without the universal it instantiates appearing, but this wholeness cannot appear unless *all the parts of the world appear*. This fact, which I have earlier discussed, seems to pose a new problem concerning the presence of universal concepts in global feeling-awarenesses. The first problem concerned the appearance of an individual singled out in my awareness. This problem was solved by making it manifest that an individual, in order to be singled out *as* an individual, does not require a universal to be ideated. But our new problem, concerning the appearance of the parts of the world-whole, is a problem about the appearance of *many individuals, each of which is not singled out*. Myself and these-things-around-me are singled out, but each individual constituent of everything-else is not singled out. Everything-else is a mostly unarticulated mass, appearing as all the things beyond the things I am singling out. But how can I apprehend *all*, all other things, if I do not single out each constituent of this all? According to Russell's *Principles of Mathematics*, if I do not single out each member of a class, I must apprehend these members through the mediation of a universal (a "class-concept" as Russell called a universal functioning in this manner).[15] I must apprehend these members as *all the instances of such-and-such a universal*.

Husserl developed this argument at greater length in his *Logical Investigations*, Investigation 2. In order to apprehend many things not individually singled out, there must be a unity (*Einheit*) that unifies the various things one wishes to apprehend and thereby renders them able to appear. This unity is the universal, the species, which I connect to the manifold by means of "the thought-form of allness [*die Denkform der Allheit*]."[16] If A is the species, then I think "All A's" and thereby apprehend the manifold as *all the instances of A*. Applied to the awareness of everything-else beyond myself-and-these-things, this means I would be aware of "All A's," where "A" is the universal, Something-Else (more fully, Something-Else-Beyond-Myself-And-These-Things). I would be ideationally aware of *all the instances of Something-Else*.

However, such an awareness does not in fact belong to the awareness of the whole of myself-and-these-things-and-everything-else. The "unity" manifest in this awareness is not a species but *the world-whole qua* absolutely nonidentical with all its parts. Everything-else does not appear as all the instances of Something-Else, but as *all that resembles what I am intuitively singling out*. Everything-else is manifest as all the relational terms of resemblance relations to myself-and-these-mountains-and-valleys (to use our familiar example). Everything-else resembles myself-and-these-mountains-and-valleys, not inasmuch as myself-and-these-mountains-and-valleys are persons, mountains, or valleys, but inasmuch as they are *things which are happening*. Everything-else appears as all that resembles myself-and-these-mountains-and-valleys in their character as *existents*, as *things that are happening*.

But Husserl says "we cannot predicate . . . resemblance of two things without stating the respect in which they resemble each other."[17] This respect, Husserl continues, is the universal or species of which the two things are instances. Thus, to apprehend all that resembles myself-and-these-things, we must apprehend all that resembles myself-and-these-things *in respect of the universal, Existent, or Something That Happens*.

However, I do not believe that this is the case. The "respect" argument Husserl introduces is traditionally used to refute nominalism and is inapplicable to the theory espoused here. A nominalist holds that the features of things are the resemblances of things to other things, and that the specification of a given feature is tantamount to a specification of one of these resemblance relations. However, since any given thing has several different resemblances to any given group of other things, the specification of any one of these resemblances requires that we specify a *respect* in which the things in question resemble one another, e.g., in respect of existing or wholeness. By specifying this respect, one is *ipso facto* introducing a reference to the very *features* of things that resemblance relations were supposed to explain. And this is why nominalism fails as a theory of the features of things.

But this argument does not apply to the theory being presented here. For this theory recognizes that things have individual features and allows that things resemble one another in respect of these features. If two concrete things are said to resemble one another, one says that they resemble one another in respect of two individual features they possess; e.g., the world and this hued environment resemble one another in respect of their individual wholenesses. With regard to these two individual features themselves, it is senseless to ask about the respect in which they resemble one another, for they can only resemble one another in respect of *themselves*, i.e., in respect of what each of them is absolutely identical with. This wholeness and that wholeness resemble each other in respect of themselves, in respect of being this wholeness and that wholeness.

But Husserl maintains that the respect must be something in relation to which the two things are identical, this identical element being the universal of which the two things are instances. But the issue here is merely terminological. If "respect" is defined with Husserl to mean the universal of which the resembling things are instances and cannot by definition mean anything else, then the conclusion must be that things do not need to appear to resemble each other in any "respect." Some other term or phrase can be introduced to express the specificity of the resemblance, one that is not defined *a priori* to mean a universal, e.g., the phrase "in that." It can be said then that the world resembles this hued environment "in that" the world has an individual feature of wholeness and the hued environment has an individual feature of wholeness, and these two wholenesses resemble each other "in that" they are (identically) two wholenesses.

In regard to the whole of myself-and-these-things-and-everything-else, this means that everything-else comes to appearance as all that resembles myself-and-these-things *in that* they are existents, things that are happening.[18] But this resemblance is a unique one because it is not among individual features or relations, but among *things* and the "*inherings in*" things of one happening. In Chapter 4 it was made conceptually explicit that at any given moment there is only one happening or existing that inheres in the world-whole and in each of its parts. This means that there is not a different individual happening inhering in each thing, such that each thing resembles each other thing in regard to its individual feature of happening. There is only one happening inhering in all things, and the resemblance among things is in regard to the individual "inherings" of the one happening in each thing. Likewise, there is a resemblance among things inasmuch as each thing is a "that in which" the happening inheres; insofar as each is a "that in which" the happening inheres, it resembles each other "that in which" the happening inheres. As a "that in which" the happening or existing inheres, the thing is called *an existent*.

But everything-else does not appear to resemble myself-and-these-things merely in that they are existents in which inheres the same happening that inheres in myself-and-these-things. Resemblance relations also obtain among things *qua* parts of the world. Each existent is a part of the world, and this means it has an individual relational feature of partaking of the world and an individual relation of participation that obtains between itself and the world. As a term of this relation, and as "that in which" the relational feature inheres, the thing is a *world-part*. Thus all world-parts, in regard to these individual relational features and relations, manifest resemblance relations to one another.

Each thing is an existent and a world-part. Everything-else, then, is every-other-existent-and-world-part beyond the ones I am intuitively singling out. They are manifest in the global intuition as *all that resembles* what I am intuitively singling out, myself-and-these-mountains-and-valleys, in regard to the latter's identities as *existents* and *world-parts* (these identities involving the various phenomena I described, the relations, features, inherings, and the "that in which").

This enables us to appreciate the fact that global loving and other global intuitions are nonideative both in their awareness of *the world* and in their awareness of what the world is wholly identical with, *myself-and-these-things-and-everything-else*.

Nevertheless, there is a sense in which universals implicitly appear in global intuitions. For universals do happen, at least while they are being ideated or thought about, and as such they are *existents* and *parts* of the world. They implicitly appear as some of the parts of the whole of all that exists. But as so appearing, they are not being ideated or thought about, i.e., explicitly comprehended and singled out in their determinate nature as this universal and that universal. Rather, they implicitly and indeterminately appear as some of the existent world-parts comprising everything-else beyond what I am currently singling out.

In this connection, it should be noted that there is a broad sense of "individuals" in which these universals themselves are individuals. Anything that is one, that is singular, is an individual. Each universal is one universal and as such is an individual. But such universals are not first-order individuals, such as this mountain or this individual feature of whole-ness. A first-order individual is a single thing that cannot have instances. A universal is instead a higher-order individual, a single thing that can have instances.

In the broad sense of "individual," it can be said that *all the parts of the world are individuals* (as I said in IV.27.vi, "Peace in the World-Whole's Harmoniousness").

The descriptions in this and the previous sections have indicated that global loving and other such feeling-awarenesses are not mediate or con-ceptual awarenesses in *any* sense. The world-whole appears in these awarenesses without the mediation of any thought, image, or universal. But if global intuitions are completely nonconceptual, does this mean the *reappreciative feelings* that are realized in the intuitive *afterglows* are also nonconceptual? Certainly they are "conceptual" in one sense; they are *thoughtful*. But they are not "conceptual" in the sense of being appre-hensions of universals. In these reappreciations realized in the intuitive afterglows, I am inspired to make explicit the intuitively revealed impor-tant world-whole in nominal and propositional thoughts. In the propo-sitional thoughts that are evoked, the world-whole's important features acquire a mediate appearance in the copulated predicate-thought, e.g., "is revealed," "is the greatest whole," "is happening," "is one." Since these features of the world-whole are individual features, the predicate-thoughts in which they mediately appear are *thoughts of individual features*. It is manifest, then, that even the propositional thinking inspired in the intui-tive afterglows is nonconceptual (nonuniversal) in character. And this is exactly how I (implicitly) described this reappreciative thinking in Section 30 of this chapter, for I described the predicate-thoughts that belong to the propositions as mediate appearances of the *features* of the world-whole.

It is only on the third level of the methodological feelings, the reap-preciative concentrating feelings, that universals are ideated. The concen-trating feelings, in explicating the propositions evoked in the second-level methodological feelings, form new propositions. In the first instance, these propositions are new propositions of the same type as the explicated prop-ositions, e.g., propositions about the individual feature of the world-whole that I had affectively intuited and that first came to a mediate appearance in the propositions evoked in the afterglow. In these new propositions, the structural articulation of the individual feature that had been intuited is made more propositionally explicit than it had been made in the prop-osition evoked in the afterglow.

Once these explicative individual propositions have been formed, the concentrative feelings become involved in *generalizing* these proposi-tions. Instead of propositionally thinking about *this revealedness* of the world-whole, I concentrate thoughtfully on *all*, *each*, or *any* revealedness of the world-whole. I ideate the universal, Global Revealedness, or Global Immediate Apparentness, which *this* revealedness instantiated, and make propositional assertions about *all instances* of this universal, or *each* or *any instance* of it. These general assertions are then integrated with the individual assertions in the theoretical exposition of the metaphysics of feeling, the latter assertions often being used to describe concrete examples of the global features generally described in the former assertions.

It is possible that many of these general propositions could be formulated in terms of resemblances rather than instances of universals. I could make an assertion about *all that resembles* this revealedness of the world, "this revealedness" being the one I have intuited and am now mediately singling out in my propositional awareness. All that resembles this revealedness are all the other individual features of revealedness the world-whole possesses. However, such resemblance propositions are not suitable for conveying metaphysical knowledge, as they are not readily comprehensible to other people. Other people have not singled out *this revealedness to me*, and being ignorant of this revealedness to me, they are unable to determine what it is that resembles this revealedness to me. However, they can comprehend and single out the universal, Global Revealedness, and are able to determine what I am talking about when I discuss all the instances of this universal.

Generalizing assertions are not used in regard to each of the global importances. I can talk about all the world's immediate appearances and all of its successively inhering happenings, but I cannot talk about more than one *wholeness* of the world or more than one *unity* of the world. The wholeness of the world is a single and constant individual feature of the world and is manifest at the same and different times to all globally aware world-parts, and as such it need only be made explicit in individual propositions; the same is true for the global unity or oneness.

The conclusion this leads us to is that "concepts" in the sense of universals appear only in *some* of the feeling-awarenesses on the *third* level of the appreciative knowings and are completely absent on the first two levels. Moreover, "concepts" in the sense of thoughts are also completely absent on the first level of these knowings, the intuitive feelings. Our conclusion, then, is emphatic: in both senses of "conceptually mediated," the global intuitive feelings *are not* conceptually mediated. Far from it being the case that "intuitions without concepts are blind," the case is rather that intuitions without concepts *see the whole world*.

The consequences of this conclusion for a metaphysics of feeling, and for the metaphysics of global loving in particular, have a significance that has not yet been made explicit.

In regard to global loving, this brings to light a second sense in which it is a feeling of closeness. Love is a feeling of closeness to and affection for another phenomenon in its unique individuality. In global loving, I am appreciating the world for opening itself up to me in its unique individuality, in its purely individual importance. The world does not disclose to me merely common importances, importances it shares with other individuals, *the universals* that it and other individuals instantiate. It does not appear to me clothed in commonly shared garments, but appears in its naked and resplendent individuality. The individual importances unique to the world are unveiled for me, and I love the world for revealing itself to me in this intimate and individual way.

Global loving is the pure appreciation of the *immediacy* of the world's appearance, in the sense of the freedom of this appearance from universals, an immediacy also experienced but not purely and semireflexively appreciated in other global intuitive feelings. It is in these immediate feelings that the world as a whole is originally *known*. This shows clearly the difference between the relationship to the world that serves as a basis for the metaphysics of feeling and the world-relationship that grounds the metaphysics of reason. The methodological knowing experienced in the metaphysics of rational meaning remains enclosed primarily within universal concepts and the inferential relationships among universal propositions. The world is comprehended in a conceptually mediated manner, in terms of universals and the relationships among universals.

This mediateness of the rationalist world-relationship is manifested in the logicism of its methodology. This method is concerned with *a priori logical reasons* and their *consequences*, the logical reasons being the universal premises of syllogisms and the logical consequences being the universal conclusions of these syllogisms.[19] As the premises, universals are the *reasons* for the truth of the conclusion, its logical grounds. As *logical* reasons, they must be differentiated from the causal and teleological reasons that belong to the world and from the cause and purpose of the world, God and Goodness.[20]

That universals function in rational metaphysics as logical reasons is evinced in the earliest stages of the development of this metaphysics, when Plato in the *Phaedo* identifies universals or essences (*eidei*) with reasons (*aitiai*).[21] In Plato we see the basic spiritual tendency of this metaphysics, the withdrawal from immediate contact with the world, and the engagement in an ideative contemplation of the logical reasons, the *eidei*, that provide the purported universal explanations of the individual world and its individual parts. The world in its immediacy is forsaken for universal reasons.

In the metaphysics of feeling, on the other hand, the world is not there as something to be rationally explained, something to be mediately comprehended in terms of universal reasons and consequences, but as an individual whose individuality is to be appreciated and reappreciated in feeling. "Knowing the world" here means immediately feeling the individual importances of the world, being in direct and conceptless contact with the world *qua* individuated. Only afterwards, in the service of communicating these felt world-importances to other appreciative world-parts, are some of these importances (such as the happenings and immediate appearances) mediately comprehended as instances of universals. But here, these universals are not considered abstractly as logical reasons, but concretely as *importances*. Specifically, they are ideationally appreciated as metaphysically-communicative-importances: they have the importance of communicating to other appreciative world-parts and thereby making available for their appreciation the *individual featural importances of the world*.

The above remarks elucidate the significance of the world's immediate apparentness for the metaphysics of feeling in general and for our descriptions of global loving in particular. The next stage of our investigation, for which we are now sufficiently prepared, is to understand the nature of this immediate apparentness *as the ultimate truth*.

V. 32. *The Ultimate Truth*

One of the strongest and most impelling of our spiritual desires, our desires to know and experience the meanings of the world, is the desire to know and experience the ultimate truth. The ultimate truth is one of the felt meanings of the world, its meaning of being apparentially close. That and how this apparential closeness is the ultimate truth shall be made manifest in this section, but first the connection of this truth with global loving should be made fully explicit.

The desire for the ultimate truth is manifest purely in global longing, wherein I long for the world-whole to offer me a global revelation. The satisfaction of this desire for the revelation *is* the experience of global loving, wherein I am face to face with the ultimate truth itself and feel lovingly illuminated by it and bound together with it. In this loving, the ultimate truth is purely known and purely appreciated in its importance as this ultimate truth.

But how can we ascertain that this global revelation, and not something else, is the ultimate truth? The unveiling of the ultimate truth *as* this global revealedness can best be achieved in an indirect manner, by first considering the nature of ultimate truth as it was conceived in the metaphysics of reason.

The line of reasoning that leads to the ultimate truth in rational metaphysics proceeds as follows. Our notions are true insofar as they are likenesses of the things in the world. But the things in the world are themselves true in a more basic sense; they are likenesses or imitations, albeit imperfect ones, of the Ideas in God's mind. These divine Ideas are *the truth* in the supreme sense, for by virtue of being related to these Ideas everything else has truth. "Whatever is," St. Anselm writes, "is true insofar as it is that which it is in the supreme truth."[22]

This notion of truth had its origins in Plato's *Timaeus*, where Plato developed the theory that the things in the world, and the world itself, were fashioned by God to be likenesses of the divine Ideas. But Plato did not identify God and these Ideas, which implied for later metaphysicians that God was not identical with the ultimate truth—an implication they found unacceptable. However, from Augustine[23] onwards, this identification was made, and various arguments to support it were presented. In the late seventeenth century, Malebranche, equally influenced by Augustine and Descartes, deduced this identity in the following way: "It cannot be doubted that only God existed before the world was created and that He could not have produced it without knowledge or ideas: therefore, the ideas He had of the world are not different from Himself."[24]

The Idea of the world, which is the *the ultimate truth of the world*, is none other than *the unconditioned first reason of the world*. Anselm states this with especial conciseness: "All are dependent upon the supreme truth, but it is dependent upon nothing, nor is it for any other reason than that it is."[25]

For Hegel, this ultimate truth is God or the Absolute Idea: "the Absolute Idea alone is *being*, unending *life, self-knowing truth*, and *all truth*."[26] This ultimate truth is not a mere individuality, for it is "the absolutely *universal Idea*."[27]

As the first quotation from Hegel implies, if the ultimate truth is God, the first reason of the world, then it also is *being itself* and *eternity itself*, for God is (identically) being itself and eternity itself. This identity, which in its classical and nondialectical explanation had been most clearly expressed in the philosophy of Aquinas,[28] indicates that in rational metaphysics the terminus of our spiritual quest for *the ultimate truth, the meaning of being*, and *the real present*, lies in one and the same thing—in the reason that explains the world's existence and nature.

But such a spiritual quest is inevitably doomed to failure and nihilism. For no such terminus of the spiritual quest can be found. There can exist no "God" in the sense of a *reason* for the world, a *necessary existent* that *causes* the whole world to exist in order to realize a *purpose*. That there can be no necessary existent is evidentially revealed in the global affect of marvelling (cf. IV. 27.ii, "The Miraculousness of the World-Whole"), and that there can be no cause and purpose of the world-whole is evidentially disclosed in global despair (cf. IV.27.iii, "The Emptiness of the World-Whole").

However, there can be a "God" in the sense of a nonnecessary existent that causes for a purpose all the parts of the world other than himself (but which does not cause for a purpose the *world-whole*). Such a "God" would be the preeminent world-part, but it would not be a rational meaning of the world-whole. "God" in the traditional sense of a necessary existent that causes for a purpose the world-whole I shall here call *God*; "God" in the sense of the preeminent world-part I shall call *god*.[29] As I indicated in my discussion of mystical feelings, it is possible but not necessary that god is disclosed in these feelings and that he in fact exists. But that he *does* exist we have no conclusive knowledge.

I will show that if god exists, then there is in a sense "an ultimate truth" in that all the parts of the world other than god correspond to Ideas in his mind, but that this truth is not really *the ultimate truth*, but is based upon the ultimate truth, the latter being a *felt meaning of the world-whole*.

An ultimate truth is a truth presupposed by all other truths but which itself does not presuppose any other truth. The uncovering of global immediate apparentness as this ultimate truth begins through elucidating the relationship between immediate and mediate truth in the first sense of immediacy/mediacy discussed in this chapter, the sense in which an immediate appearance is a relational feature of the apparent thing and a mediate appearance is a relational feature of a thought or image of the apparent thing. This relationship is such that all mediate truths presuppose immediate truths, but immediate truths do not presuppose mediate truths. Mediate truths are features of images or thoughts. In order for something to appear mediately in the thought or image, the thought or image and the truth-feature of the thought or image must appear immediately. In this way mediate appearances presuppose immediate appearances, for every mediate appearance, every true thought or image, must — if it is to exist at all — appear immediately.

However, something can appear immediately without also appearing mediately and without the immediate appearance itself appearing mediately. For example, there could be a global intuition which is never reappreciated and made explicit in thoughts or images. And I could perceive some world-part and never subsequently engage in an act of remembering or thinking about what I perceived.

Even in the cases where the intuition of the world-whole and the intuition of a hued thing are subsequently remembered or thought about, *at the time* the intuition is being experienced the intuition exists by itself, unaccompanied by and not requiring for its existence a coexperienced act of thinking or imagining.

The conclusion, then, is that immediate appearances can exist without mediate appearances, but mediate appearances cannot exist without immediate appearances. The next stage in laying bare the ultimate truth is to show that among immediate appearances there is one immediate appearance that all other immediate appearances presuppose, but which does not itself presuppose other immediate appearances. This ultimate immediate appearance is *the appearance of the whole* of myself-and-these-things-and-everything-else.

The first fact to be considered is that no thing can immediately appear unless the world-whole immediately appears. This is true because any given thing either appears immediately as the world-whole or appears immediately as not the world-whole. In the latter case, the thing appears immediately as one part of the whole. For example, I perceive attentionally this lamp on the table. It is immediately apparent to me that this lamp is not the whole of all existing world-parts, but that other things exist as well, e.g., myself, the table, the book on the table, and all that exists outside of this room. But I am not explicitly noticing this, at least not in my usual mundane attitudes. This awareness is tacit. The lamp appears in the foreground of my awareness, and its relational feature of "not being the world-whole, but only one part of the world-whole," appears marginally. In this manner, the world-whole is immediately apparent to me in all cases when I am not attending to the world-whole but am attending to some world-part. Since there are no cases of immediate awareness or appearance besides these two, it is clear that in all cases of immediate awareness or appearance the world-whole is immediately apparent.

Any given world-part cannot appear immediately unless the world-whole appears immediately, but the world-whole can appear immediately without the immediate appearance of any given world-part. Of course the world-whole, as a whole-of-parts, cannot appear immediately unless all of its parts appear immediately, but it is not necessary that this or that part—any given part—belong to the class of all its immediately appearing parts. The world-whole could still be composed of parts, and could still appear as a whole-of-parts, even if this or that part ceased to be among its appearing parts. For instance, the appearance of this room or those clouds is not necessary to the appearance of the world-whole; the world-whole could still immediately appear *as* the world-whole even if this room and those clouds ceased to exist and appear as some of its parts. The difference would be that the world-whole would no longer appear as being partially composed of this room and those clouds, but as being wholly composed of things *other than this room or those clouds*.

The immediate appearance of globally appeared-to world-parts has a distinctive status, however, for these parts are intrinsically constitutive of the ultimate truth. The world-whole's immediate appearance is a relational feature that involves two relational terms and one relation, and one of these relational terms is a globally appeared-to part. The world-whole immediately appears only as the whole-of-myself-and-these-things-and-everything-else, where the "myself" both immediately appears and is the supporter of the world-whole's immediate appearance. Myself and the immediate appearance of myself are thus internally bound up with the immediate appearance of the world-whole.

But the above statement that "the world-whole can appear immediately without the immediate appearance of any given world-part" still holds true. For any given one of these globally appeared-to parts is not necessary to the existence of ultimate truth. I could die, and the world-whole could still immediately appear to some other globally appreciative world-part; the same is true for any other globally appeared-to world-part. What is necessary to the ultimate truth is not *this* or *that* globally appeared-to world-part, but *some* globally appeared-to world-part.

The ultimate truth is an *immediate* appearance of the world-whole in the sense that it is a relational feature of the world-whole itself and not of a thought or image of it. But this ultimate truth is also an immediate appearance in a second sense, in that it is a truth or appearance of first-order individuals, rather than of universals or individuals as instances of universals. The relational feature of apparentness that inheres in the world-whole is an apparentness *of* the individual world-whole with its individual features and not an apparentness of the universals they instantiate. This appearance of global individuality is presupposed by, but does not itself presuppose, the appearance of universals, be these universals instantiated by the world-whole or not instantiated by the world-whole. A universal is a part of the world-whole and as such can only appear if the world-whole appears — the appearing world-whole being the individual world-whole with its individual features. But the appearance of the individual world-whole with its individual features does not require that these features appear as instantiating any universal — as I have shown in the previous section.

The ultimate truth, then, in its complete sense is an *appearance* that is a relational feature of the world and is of the individual world with its individual features.

The ultimacy of this immediate global truth can be further understood if we compare it with the "ultimate truth" that would exist if god existed. The sense in which there is an "ultimate truth" if god exists is that there are Ideas in god's mind, Ideas which all other world-parts, the parts god created, imitate in imperfect ways. But this "ultimate truth" is an "ultimate truth" in a less fundamental sense than is the immediate appearance of the world-whole, for the Ideas in god's mind presuppose but are not presupposed by the immediate appearance of the world-whole. Consider that the Ideas in god's mind are not something of which god is oblivious, but immediately appear to him. And they must immediately appear to him either as the world-whole or as some part of this whole.

Now it is clearly in the latter way that they must immediately appear, for god is well aware that beside these Ideas there exist created world-parts that imitate these ideas. These Ideas immediately appear as a part of the whole composed of the created and uncreated things that exist, and in this appearance the world-whole itself achieves an immediate appearance.

Whereas the world-whole must immediately appear to god if the divine Ideas are to appear immediately, the world-whole is capable of immediately appearing even if no divine Ideas exist or appear. For the world-whole could exist and include parts to which it immediately appears (e.g., humans) even if no god exists (and this may well be what is in fact the case). Thus, divine Ideas presuppose the immediate appearance of the world-whole, but the immediate appearance of the world-whole does not presuppose divine Ideas. The global felt meaning of apparential closeness is *the* ultimate truth, and divine truth, like every other mundane or mediate truth, is absolutely dependent upon it.

The fact that this global felt meaning exists means that we are able to satisfy our spiritual desire to know and experience the ultimate truth. In global loving we experience the terminus of one of our spiritual quests. In global rejoicing, we experience the terminus of two other spiritual quests, our quest for the *meaning of existing* and for the *real present*—fullness-of-happening being the meaning of existing and the real present. But the terminus of the latter two spiritual quests is experienced after a fashion in global loving itself, for global loving is a captivation with the *happening* world-whole's immediate apparentness. The ultimate truth incorporates within itself the meaning of existing and the real present. But this is not to be understood along the lines of the rational-metaphysical theory of ultimate truth, where the ultimate truth is *identified* with the meaning of existing and the real present. Rather, the meaning of existing, which is identical with the real present, is to be understood as an *aspect* of the ultimate truth. And this is to say that the pure appreciation of the ultimate truth is an impure appreciation of the meaning of existing and the real present.

The ultimate truth is purely appreciated in global loving and impurely in certain other global affects. These impure appreciations are worthy of being made explicit on their own account, and I shall now describe some of them.

V. 33. *The Impure Appreciations of the Ultimate Truth*

The descriptions in the preceding sections have made it clear that the ultimate truth is not veiled from us; it is not hidden away from us in a distant and inaccessible Beyond. Rather, it is right here, all around us, omniapparent, and constantly being disclosed to us. It shines towards us from the horizon or focus of our awareness at every moment of our conscious lives. Just as the meaning of existing is always either focally or horizonally displayed before us, so is the ultimate truth.

The ultimate truth can explicitly and attentionally appear only in *foreground* global feelings. But it can do so only in *semireflexive* foreground global feelings, for the unreflexive ones are intuitions of some global feature other than the world-whole's feature of being immediately apparent to me and are only tacitly aware that the world-whole is immediately apparent to me. Among these semireflexive feelings, it is only global loving that *purely* appreciates the world's apparential closeness. Other semireflexive global feelings, like global pride, sadness, wonder, desolation and equanimity, are attentional awarenesses of the ultimate truth, but they do not appreciate it as important in and by itself. It is appreciated as important inasmuch as it is a constitutive aspect of some broader global importance.

These impure affective appreciations of the ultimate truth form a new level of founded affects, after the first level, the latter which consists of loving, marvelling, despair, awe, tedium, peace, and others. The first-level founded affects are directly based on global rejoicing; they are appreciations of the *happening world-whole* in respect of some further feature possessed by this happening or by the world-whole that happens, be this feature immediate apparentness, non-necessariness, immensity, or something else. The second level of founded affects is comprised of affects indirectly based on global rejoicing; these affects are directly based on global loving, which in its turn is directly based on global rejoicing. The affects directly based on global loving are appreciations of the *immediately apparent happening world-whole* in respect of some further feature, be this feature a feature of the immediate apparentness of the happening world-whole or of the happening world-whole that is immediately apparent.

Pride, sadness, and wonder are examples of affects that are captivated by a feature of the immediate apparentness of the happening world-whole, and desolation and equanimity are examples of captivation with a feature of the happening world-whole that is immediately apparent. These are not the only affects that belong to the second level of founded global affects, but an examination of them suffices to elucidate the nature of this level of global affects.

V. 33.i. Pride in the World-Whole's Glorification of Myself

In spiritual pride, I experience a feeling-sensation of inflated rising, of rising up above other world-parts that encircle me. I am exaltantly ascendant because I am a center of the world-whole, and consequently, unlike other world-parts that are not centers but which encircle me, I support and am the source of a centered appearance of the world-whole. I *qua* world-center am responsible for and am the preserver of this centered appearance of the whole of all world-parts.

This centered appearance is an immediate appearance of the happening world-whole. Since the happening whole has this relational feature of immediate apparentness to me only if and when I am intuitively appreciating the world-whole, this relational feature of immediate apparentness itself has a relational feature of being *dependent upon me*. It is this feature, as inhering in the happening world-whole's immediate apparentness, that provides me with a metaphysical glory.

I am soaring in pride because I not only know the ultimate truth, but am in fact the source and sustainer of this truth. I bring this truth into existence through being aware of the world-whole and keep it in existence by continuing to be aware of the world-whole.

In feeling this dependency upon me of the ultimate truth, I feel globally powerful. This is something quite other than mundane power. I do not sustain in existence a social-legal order or a gigantic alteration of a natural part of the world, but instead sustain in existence *an appearance* of the whole world itself. Soaring to the sky in proud exaltation, I feel as powerful as a god; I feel godlike. It is the nature of a god to know and preserve in existence the ultimate truth, and this godlike activity is precisely what I am accomplishing through being intuitively directed upon the whole. I am glorified by the world-whole in that I am allotted the distinction of sustaining in being its very truth.

But I differ in my glorious function from a god in that a god's function is unique; god is usually thought of as the one being who knows and sustains the ultimate (divine) truth, the divine Ideas, such that without this one god there would be no ultimate truth. But my role is not unique; without me, there would still be other world-centers to which the world-whole displayed immediate appearances.

I am aware of this in my exaltation and feel a pride that is both individual and collective. I am exalted, on the one hand, because I am the sole supporter of *this* global appearance. But I am also proud because I belong to the class of globally appeared-to world-parts, *the world-centers*, without which there would be no global appearances *at all*.

My exultant pride extends to my nature as an *appreciator* of the world's importance. The important world-whole, in being immediately apparent in my intuitive feelings, is by that fact *appreciated*. Without me, and world-centers like myself, the world-whole's importance would go unappreciated.

A few words should be said about the difference between exalted pride and loving. In feeling lovingly close to the world-whole, I am captivated solely by the happening world-whole's feature of being apparentially close to me and have no more than a tacit awareness of the feature this apparential closeness possesses of being dependent upon me. Exalted pride, however, is a fascination with the apparential closeness *qua* having this dependency upon me, and accordingly this pride is an impure appreciation of this apparential closeness.

V. 33.ii. Sadness at the Imminent Loss of the World-Whole's Apparential Closeness to Me

The happening world-whole's immediate appearance to me has the feature of imminent cessation; soon I will die, and there will no longer be global appearances to me.

I am globally sad because I will profoundly miss the happening whole's immediate appearing to me. I am a bearer of the ultimate truth only for a little while, and then I bear it no longer. The ultimate truth will then probably be borne by others who will emerge and exist in the whole after me. The world-whole will be centered around other centers, but not around myself.

Wistfully I gaze upon the whole, knowing that soon I shall be able to gaze no longer. Nothingness shall absorb me, as it were, and leave nothing where I, as a globally appeared-to part, had once been. There shall not be an absolute nothing, a nothing of that which happens-never, but a relative nothing, the nonbeing of that which happens-no-longer.

Global sadness, like global pride, is impurely related to the happening whole's apparential closeness to me. In pride I appreciate the global appearance's dependency upon me, and in sadness I appreciate this appearance's imminent cessation. But the impure and sad appreciation of this closeness is a pure appreciation of the impending loss of this closeness, the impending loss of that which I love.

Global sadness is different than global despair. In sadness I am sinking down to the bottom; in despair, I have sunken to the very bottom: I can go no further downwards. All is hopeless in despair; the world-whole is purposeless and my life utterly futile. But in sadness, all is not yet in an absolutely abysmal state. For I am still *sinking down* and have not yet reached bottom. And I am sinking to something other than a state of purposelessness; I am sinking down from my condition of *being present to the whole* to a condition of *no longer being present to the whole*. My life in the world consists in this steady sinking. As time goes on, I come closer and closer to the bottom, and there looms larger and larger the abyss of unalterable nothingness: my everlasting nonpresence to the whole.

Meanwhile, I am here, still happening, still being appeared to. But it feels like I am here *in order to know what I shall be missing forever*.

V. 33.iii. Wonder at the Mystery of the World-Whole

In global wonder, I experience a feeling-sensation of yearning in a questioning way, a yearning to rise upwards and reach outwards into the distance, a yearning, however, that fails to attain the distance and is held back in an unresolved and unacceptable state of unknowing.

In its feeling-tonality, my hued environment is imbued with an aura of wonderment that seems to emanate from the beyond, the global interior. There is felt to be in the far distance something hidden that beckons me to come towards itself, but at the same time I feel that my yearning towards this unknown is resisted by an all-encompassing veil, a veil that shrouds this hidden something from me and prevents me from reaching this beyond whither I am beckoned.

The source of this feeling-tonality of wonderment is the global importance of *mysteriousness*. It is that which beckons me towards itself and at the same time holds me back. As beckoning me, the mysteriousness is a possible hidden global reality; as thwarting my movement to follow the beckoning, the mysteriousness is a veil that hides from me the possible hidden global reality. The veil is an *immediate global appearance*, a global appearing-to-be-so that hides from me a possibly different global really-being-so. The global importance of mysteriousness is this very duality, the reality/appearance that beckons/thwarts me.

A more precise determination of this mystery can be achieved through making it manifest that this mystery does not concern a possible hidden reason for the world-whole's existing. The possible hidden reality cannot be a necessary existent that causes the world-whole for a purpose, for there is and can be no such existent, as is evidentially disclosed in marvelling and despair. The existing of the world-whole is not a *mystery*, but a *miracle*, and a *causeless and purposeless occurrence*. The world-whole exists even though it could not exist, and it exists without its existence being caused or having a purpose. There is nothing here to wonder about, only to *marvel at* and *despair over*.

What I wonder about is not *that* the world *is*, but *what* it *is*. Global wonder does not express itself in the question, Why is it? It expresses itself in the question, What is it? For it is only in regard to what it is that there can be a hidden reality that lies behind the appearances.

What the world *is* constitutes its *being* in the essential sense.[30] The essential features of the world are either necessary or accidental. Necessary features are exemplified by the world's *oneness* and *all-inclusiveness*; accidental features are exemplified by the world's features of *being composed of this dog*, *being composed of those perceptions*, and *being composed of all those galaxies*.

Global wonder is not about the necessary essential features of the world, for these features as necessary could not be otherwise. There are no other possibilities to wonder about. I cannot wonder if the world really only includes some parts of the world rather than all parts, for it is not possible for the world to include only some parts of itself.

The whole is necessarily composed of parts, but it is not necessarily composed of these kinds of parts as opposed to those kinds. It is possible that the world could be composed of kinds of parts other than the ones it appears to me to be composed of. The world's appearing to be composed of *these* kinds of parts could be delusory.

This mystery of the world-whole's accidental composition does not concern this or that thing with which the world-whole is partially identical. For example, I could believe this configured importance I perceive to be a mountain and could be curious about whether it really is a mountain or something else — perhaps a shadow — deceptively appearing to be a mountain. Such a mundane curiosity has little to do with global wonder. Nor does the global mystery concern a kind or class of things that appear to help compose the world; e.g., there appears to be a class of inanimate things that help to compose the world, and I could be curious about whether in reality there is such a class of things or whether all bodies are really animate. The global mystery, rather, concerns the extreme possibility of otherness, the possibility of total otherness. I wonder about all the things in the world, about what the world is *wholly* identical with, and about the most basic determinate features they possess. Myself-and-these-things-and-everything-else could possess in reality radically different features than they appear to possess. The determinately appearing features whose reality I wonder about are the features *I* appear to possess, *these-things* appear to possess, and *the articulated segment of everything-else* appears to possess. The unarticulated segment of everything-else ("and all the other things, whatever they may be and however many they may be") is unknown in a different way — no determinate features of this segment appear at all.

As illustrations of the types of differences that may obtain between any given apparent identity of the world's composition and any given possible real identity, different culturally relative appearances of this identity can be pointed to. The holistic identity the world appeared to have to the Sumerians in 3000 B.C. is considerably different than the identity it appeared to have to the Christians living in the Middle Ages, and this latter identity is in turn quite different than the identity the world exhibits to people living in twentieth-century scientific culture. And again, there are other as yet culturally unrealized possible holistic identities of the world that are just as different from its contemporary scientifically appearing identity as this identity is from the identities that appeared to the Sumerians and Christians.

However, no specific realm of examples is to be taken as adequately illustrating or delimiting the possible types of the world's apparent or real holistic identities. Any such attempt at restriction would collapse in the face of the overpowering and unlimited nature of the mystery itself. For the global mystery consists, not in this or that appearance/reality distinction, but in the *possibility that some such distinction obtains*. More fully, it lies in the fact that it is unknowable if there *is* an appearance/reality distinction, and, if there is one, *which* distinction obtains.

The mysteriousness of the world includes within itself the world's immediate apparentness; the world-whole immediately appears to be wholly identical with myself-and-these-things-and-everything-else *qua* determined in some specific way, and this immediate appearance has the feature of being *possibly deceptive*. This feature of the world-whole's immediate appearance provokes me to wonder about whether this immediate appearance *is* deceptive or not, and if it is deceptive, *how* it is deceptive and what the reality is that is not immediately appearing to me. What beckons me is the unspecified *possible real holistic identity* of the world, and what veils this from me is the *immediate appearance of this specific holistic identity*, a veil I cannot lift because I do not know *if* or *how* it is deceptive, but only that it *may be* deceptive and may be deceptive *in some way* (but which way I do not know).

The possible deceptiveness of this appearance does not impugn the justifiable basis of our belief in the veridicality of the global affects we experience. This is so in two respects. First, the possible deceptiveness concerns the world-whole's accidental compositional features, not its necessary features: so, if an affect is deceived about the world-whole's compositional features it still remains a real intuition of *what the world-whole necessarily is*. Second, the *possibility* of being deceived about the composition of the world does not mean that one *is* deceived. As far as is known, there are no extrinsic grounds that override the intrinsic grounds of veridicality of our seeming affective intuitions of the world's composition. There may be overriding extrinsic grounds, but if there are any, they are unknown. Hence it can be said, as I said in III.20.ii, that there "is no basis for justifiably doubting the veridicality of these affects."[31]

Global wonder is an impure appreciation of the ultimate truth; it is a captivation with the ultimate truth as possessing the feature of possibly being an ultimate falsity. It is not the entire ultimate truth that has this feature, but only the ultimate truth of the world's compositional feature of being wholly identical with parts of a certain kind.

V. 33.iv. Desolation in Face of the Uncaring World-Whole

Pride, sadness, and wonder are examples of global affects that impurely appreciate the world's apparential closeness through appreciating this closeness in respect of some feature it possesses, be this feature its dependency upon me, its imminent loss, or its possible deceptiveness. These three global affects accordingly are impure appreciations of this closeness in the first mode of impure appreciation. The second mode is an affective captivation, not with a feature possessed by the global importance itself, but with a feature possessed by that which has the global importance. That which has the global importance of apparential closeness is the happening world-whole, and a captivation with some feature possessed by the happening world-whole would be an example of the second way of impurely appreciating apparential closeness. Such an example is *desolation*.

Desolation is the global affect parallel to the mood of loneliness. The feeling-tonality of desolation is a feeling of everything around me being *apart* from me, of being *withdrawn* from me. I am left abandoned and forsaken by everything. The desolate feeling-sensation is a sensation of *reaching out into the echoless emptiness*. I feel like I am utterly alone and forsaken in a barren and starless desert. I am reaching out hopelessly into oblivion for contact, all the while realizing there is nothing and nobody on a global scale to notice or care for my existence.

Desolation is the experience of the inevitable failure of the quest for reciprocal global love. I have affectively experienced a love for the world-whole, and have directed a loving awareness towards it, but it has not and cannot return this love. It is utterly indifferent to my love and to myself; it cares nothing for me, for the world-whole is absolutely impersonal and unconscious and cannot care for anybody or anything. It is not a person or mind that could direct towards me an act of loving awareness, or any sort of awareness, but an impersonal whole that blindly happens. I am not illuminated by rays of its loving awareness, but am alone in the oblivion and darkness of its uncaring night.

The implicitly felt nature of the world-whole's impersonality is made conceptually explicit in the following reflections. If the world-whole were personal and mental, it would be either a disembodied mind or an embodied mind. It cannot be a disembodied mind, for (among other considerations) the world-whole includes within itself extended parts, and a disembodied mind possesses no extended parts.

Is not the world-whole, then, an *embodied* mind? How could this be conceived? The world-whole, as the whole of all existents other than itself, includes within itself all configured importances and all innerworldly minds. The whole of all configured importances could be conceived as *the body* of the world-whole, and the whole of all innerworldly minds as *the mind* of the world-whole.

The falsity of such a conception shows itself in several places, for example, in the fact that a whole composed of minds is not itself a mind (no more than the whole of humans — the human race — is itself a human, and no more than the whole of angels is itself an angel). The whole of minds has the feature of *being composed of* various streams of awarenesses, but it does not have the feature of *being a stream of awareness*. This is also true for less inclusive wholes of minds; for instance, the whole of all minds in the classroom who are thinking silently to themselves is not itself thinking silently to itself.

The falsity of this conception of the world-whole as an embodied mind also shows itself in the fact that the whole of all bodies and the whole of all minds are themselves both *parts* of the world-whole; they are parts of the whole composed of the whole of all bodies and the whole of all minds (and whatever other wholes there are). And no parts of the world-whole, not even *all* the parts of the world-whole, can be absolutely identical with the world-whole itself (as I have shown in V.29). Accordingly, even if the whole of all bodies and the whole of all minds were all the parts of the world-whole, they would still not *be* the world-whole, and features of all these parts would not *be* features of the whole.

Could not the world-whole be conceived to have the feature of personality in some other way? Could it not be an act of awareness directed upon all the parts of the world, upon all the innerworldly bodies, minds, and whatever else there is? The answer must be negative: the world-whole is a whole *composed of* extended and unextended parts, and an act of awareness, although *aware of* extended and unextended parts, is not *composed of* them. For, to name only one consideration, an act of awareness cannot contain extended parts. (This conception of the world-whole's personality hence amounts to the first conception of the world-whole as a disembodied mind.)

The world-whole, then, necessarily has the feature of impersonality, and this feature, when purely appreciated, originates a global desolation. This pure appreciation of impersonality is at the same time an impure appreciation of the world-whole's apparential closeness to me. I semireflexively apprehend that the happening world is immediately apparent to me but that I am not immediately apparent to it. It is close to me, but I am not close to it. If my being nonapparent to the happening world is termed the happening world's *obliviousness of me*, then it can be said that the happening world's apparential-closeness-to-me-but-obliviousness-of-me is the importance of *global uncaring* that provokes my desolation. In this affect, apparential closeness is appreciated, not in and by itself, but *qua* aspect of the broader importance of the happening world's apparential-closeness-to-me-but-obliviousness-of-me.

The above description shows that the global importance of uncaringness is in fact the importance of an unreciprocated apparential closeness between the happening world and myself.

Global desolation must be distinguished from the godless desolation I described in III.21. Godless desolation is a seeming intuition of the nonexistence of the preeminent world-part, god, and is not a desolation in face of the uncaringness of the world-whole. Even if the preeminent world-part existed and loved me, I would still be desolate in face of the world-whole's unreciprocated apparential closeness to me. My desire to be appreciated and loved by *the most important importance* would still be hopelessly thwarted.

V. 33.v. Equanimity in the Equilibrium of the World-Whole

I become undisturbed by the world-whole's obliviousness of me, and by anything else that could inflict great pain or pleasure upon me, when I become purely adjusted to the *equilibrium* of the world-whole. To attentionally and affectively partake of this equilibrium is to feel a deep and broad equanimity.

The explication of the determinate nature of the global equilibrium takes its clue from the nature of the equanimous tonality that imbues the world. The equanimous tonality differs from that of peacefulness in that the latter has an upward flowing tendency, a flow of gently gliding upwards, whereas the equanimous tonality is absolutely directionless. It flows neither upwards nor downwards, neither backwards nor forwards. It is absolutely still.

This directionless equanimous tonality constitutes the sensuously felt middle of the world, the sensuous metaphysical region situated in between the joyously radiated top of the world and the despairingly sunken bottom of the world. These sensuous regions have their sources in global importances: a *global fullness* lifts me to the top of the world; a *global emptiness* drops me to the bottom; and a *global equilibrium* holds me halfway between these two extremes, in the middle of the world. A *pure existing* radiates me to the joyous global peaks; a *pure futility* casts me into the abysmal depths; and a *pure centeredness* holds me in the still midlands.

A whole is in an internal state of equilibrium by virtue of a certain relation to and among its parts. Such a relation obtains in wholes that have a central part to which the whole is related and around which all the other parts are arranged. In the world-whole, this relational arrangement has an apparential form: the whole and each of its other parts apparentially converge toward a common center, an appeared-to part. It is my *I* that is this converged-upon center: it is the still point towards which all the apparential lines run and in which they all meet and become one. From the very innermost point of the globe, I look out in all directions and see everything being apparentially balanced upon myself. Everything is in equilibrium through appearing to myself.

Nothing disturbs me while I am in the center of this all-surrounding dome of pure appearance. Each thing that could disturb me becomes undisturbing through *appearing to me* and thereby becoming equipoised with everything else that appears to me; it becomes part of the whole that rests upon me in a state of perfect, apparential equilibrium. I am focused in my equanimity upon the apparential features of the other parts and the whole, their being perspectively apparent to me, and so their other features do not affect me. I am captivated by the perfectly rounded dome of pure appearance formed by the appearance of all these things, and through being spellbound by this dome I am made perfectly still.

That I am unapparent to the world-whole does not disturb me, for the centered appearance to me of the whole and all its other parts is sufficient by itself to bring the whole into equilibrium, and to bring me into its equanimous center.

The world-whole is in equilibrium in that it has the feature of being centered around a center. This feature is complex; it includes both the global feature purely appreciated in global loving and another feature of the world-whole. The world-whole's *immediate apparentness to me*, which is purely appreciated in loving, is one of the features constitutive of the global centeredness; the other is the world-whole's feature of *being composed of parts that are immediately apparent to me*. The distinction between these two features is first made in V.29, where I indicate that the world-whole is not absolutely identical with myself, these-things-and-everything-else, but instead is *composed of* all these things. Accordingly, the immediate apparentness of the world-whole is a different feature than the feature of being composed of immediately apparent parts. It is true that these two features are integrally interrelated, in that the whole cannot be immediately apparent unless all the parts of which it is composed are immediately apparent (as I show in V.29), but it is not necessary to be captivated by both of these features. In global love, I am aware of the immediate apparentness of all the parts, but I am captivated solely by the whole's immediate apparentness, for the latter feature constitutes the whole's closeness to me. But in equanimity, I am captivated by both features, for both features together constitute the *centeredness* of the world-whole. It is not only the whole *as* whole that is apparentially related to me as to a center, but all the other parts besides myself of which the whole is composed.

At the same time these-things-and-everything-else immediately appear to me, I also appear to myself; however, I do not appear to myself as being centered around myself, but as *being* the center around which are centered these-things-and-everything-else and *the whole* that is composed of myself, these-things-and-everything-else.

Just as the world-whole is apparentially close to more than one of its parts, so it is centered around more than one center. It is simultaneously in different states of equilibrium; these states are not unrelated to each other or in conflict, but are *equipoised*. Any given state of equilibrium forms an aspect of each of the other states of equilibrium, and each of the other states of equilibrium forms an aspect of the given state of equilibrium. The centerednesses of the world around all the centers other than myself are some of the things that perspectivally converge upon myself; these other centerednesses are not singled out by me but implicitly and indeterminately appear to me. At the same time, the world's centeredness around myself perspectivally converges upon each of the other world-centers. A vast network of converging and converged-upon centers extends throughout the globe, causing the whole global interior to be reflected again and again in perfect dome after perfect dome. Each dome reflects not only the global interior but each other dome, and each dome is reflected *into* each other dome.

The questions that arise here concern the status of these global appearances. Is the world-whole *in itself* this myriad of reflecting and reflected domes? Can the world-whole exist in domeless darkness, in a state of absolute nonequilibrium? Can it happen centerlessly?

The answer to these questions is provided by a description of what appears in the *opened dome* of global reverence.

CHAPTER VI

The Supremacy of the World

*T*he supremacy of the world is a more complex importance than either the world's closeness or fulfillment. It is directly based on the world's closeness and indirectly on its fulfillment. Just as closeness includes within itself the fulfillment of the world, so supremacy incorporates within itself the world's closeness. The *happening* of the world is an aspect of closeness, and the *immediate appearance of the happening* world is an aspect of supremacy. Supremacy is the *superordination of the happening of the greatest whole to the immediate appearance of this whole*.

Fulfillment is the felt meaning of *time* and *existing*, closeness the felt meaning of *ultimate truth*, and supremacy the felt meaning of the *human-independent absolute reality*. This reality is neither a self-existent uncaused cause nor a noumenal ground that lies behind phenomena, but an infinitely important importance that allows us to partake of and appreciate itself for a brief while. What it means to say that this importance is "human-independent" is a major theme of this chapter.

The importance of supremacy indeterminately appears in the mood of veneration and determinately appears in the parallel affect of reverence. Reverence is a focused intuition of four structural items constitutive of supremacy. These items are given an introductory description in Section 34 and a more detailed description in Sections 35 through 38; some impure appreciations of supremacy are explicated in Section 39.

VI. 34. *Revering the Supreme World-Whole*

I am taking a walk late at night along the deserted streets of a suburb. I feel open to the silent grandeur of everything, of the whole world that stretches far beyond and above me. I feel there to be a solemn and majestic aura that enfolds the rooftops, trees, and the gleaming stars. Soft tremors of reverence arise in me, and I stop and kneel before a fence; I fold my hands and rest them on the top railing. I look up, deep into the starry night. The stars shine in imperial splendor, and beyond them, there is everything else . . . The whole of all these things! Unspeakably august, supreme, surpassing all that I am, so greatly surpassing!

Without this world, I could not be. But it is there, without me, not needing me, so far beyond and above me that its happening does not deign to take into account my happening. It is greater than I, but also greater than every other part of the world. The world-whole embraces within itself every thing other than itself, so that each thing other than the world-whole can happen only as a part of the world-whole. But the world-whole happens without being a part of anything greater.

The whole composed of these rooftops, the dark shapes of these trees, and far above them, the glittering stars and everything else beyond them, is the highest, supreme reality, towering far above me in its unapproachable greatness and majesty. Before this unsurpassably great and imperial whole, I am almost as nothing, utterly subordinated in my reality as a dependent part of it. I bow my head in the hushed silence of reverence.

The supreme whole of myself, these-things-and-everything-else emanates into me a revering feeling-flow. In respect of the revering feeling-sensation, the flow is backwards and downwards in its direction. I do not flow backwards in a cringing manner, as I do in fear. I am not shrinking from a threatening reality, but instead feel myself to be inferior to a supreme and imperial reality. I flow backwards in a respectful and subordinating manner. I intuitively recognize that the greater sublimity and grandeur of the world-whole deserve obeisance and admiration on my part. I flow backwards, not violently, but softly and gently. The feeling-sensation also flows downwards; but its downward flow is not a sagging and drooping, as is the flow of sadness and melancholy, nor is it a plummetting downwards, as is the flow of embarrassed humiliation. Rather, it is a feeling of inwardly "bowing down" before a superior and majestic presence.

The feeling-tonality of the revering is felt to emanate from the supreme whole of these trees and stars and everything else beyond them. From the world-whole a splendor of feeling flows through these-things-and-everything-else, animating them with a sublime aura. This tonal flow has an upward direction; it flows upwards and far above me in an august manner. The supreme world-whole is felt to be "far above me" in its importance, to have a felt remoteness and distance — the distance of the unapproachably great. Through feeling this august upward flow that is emanated through everything around me by the world-whole, I experience a feeling that corresponds to the unapproachable supremacy of the world-whole itself.

The global affect of revering can be internally described in respect of its feeling-flow and externally described in respect of the importance it is captivated by.[1] The importance it is captivated by is *supremacy*. Global revering is the captivated feeling-of-the-world-whole's-supremacy. This feeling-of-the-world-whole's-supremacy can be described in terms of four constitutive items. The following descriptions of these items will be brief and introductory; the detailed explication of the importance of supremacy will be a task of the remaining sections of this chapter.

Revering is (minimally) a feeling that something is *independent of me*. Global revering is a feeling that the world-whole does not need me or depend upon me in order to happen. Specifically, the world-whole is felt to be independent of its appearance to me. By this I do not mean that revering intuits the world-whole to happen *without* appearing to me (which would be impossible, since the world-whole appears to me by virtue of the fact that I am reverentially intuiting it). I mean that it is not *necessary* for the world-whole to appear to me in order for it to happen, and that on some occasions (but not the present one) the world-whole *does* happen without appearing to me.

But this feeling of something's independency of me is not by itself sufficient to constitute a feeling of revering. Many things happen without needing to appear to me: for example, other people. And yet I am not moved to revere other people for their existential independency of me. To feel merely that something is independent of me is not yet to feel a revering.

Revering involves the further characteristic of feeling *subordinate* to something, and correlatively, of feeling the thing to be *superordinate* to myself. Not only is the thing felt to be independent of me, but *I feel dependent upon it*. Global revering is a feeling of the *world-whole's* superordination to myself. In global revering it is felt that the world-whole happens independently of myself and the world-whole's appearance to myself, and also that I am dependent for my happening upon the world-whole. I cannot happen unless the world-whole happens, such that if the world-whole did not happen, I would be nothing.

These remarks can be clarified by formally defining superordination and subordination in the following way:

To be *superordinate* to something is to be independent of a thing that is dependent upon oneself.

To be *subordinate* to something is to depend on a thing that is independent of oneself.

Accordingly, to say that the world-whole is not merely independent of myself, but also superordinate to myself, is to say that in addition to the world-whole's independency of me, there is a dependency of myself upon the world-whole.

A feeling of something's superordination to myself is not, however, sufficient to constitute a feeling of revering. I may feel that air is superordinate to myself and to its appearance-to-me, and yet feel no reverence for air. I may feel that air happens independently of myself and its olfactory and tactile appearance to me, and that I am dependent for my happening upon air (for if air ceased to happen I could no longer breathe and would thus cease to happen myself), but an awareness of this would not constitute a revering of air.[2]

To feel revering, I must also feel that the thing which is superordinate to me is the *greatest thing of its kind*. The nature of the greatness may vary with the kind of the thing that is superordinate to me. For example, I can feel a mundane revering for a king because he is the most powerful leader in the land. And I can revere a wise man for being wiser than any other person I know of. The nature of the greatness that is felt to belong to the world-whole is a *holistic* greatness. The world-whole is the most inclusive whole that happens; everything other than the world-whole is a part of the world-whole, and the world-whole is not a part of any larger whole.

While the feeling of such a maximally great superordinate is very close to being sufficient to constitute a feeling of revering, it is not quite sufficient. For it is possible to conceive of a maximally great superordinate that evokes fear and terror, rather than revering. A maximally great superordinate that is malign, threatening, and demoniac would not inspire a revering, but a trembling in abject terror. A cruel and wicked king would not instill in me a mundane revering, but a fear and loathing. And if the world-whole were, in its very character as a superordinate that is the greatest whole that happens, malign and demoniac, I would not revere it but would feel terror and horror before it.

The maximally great and superordinate thing must have a *positive* and *fulfilled* character in order to evoke a revering. The all-powerful king must, in his very character as a king, be benevolent and just in order to evoke a mundane revering. The world-whole, in order to evoke a global revering, must, in its very character as a superordinate that is the greatest whole that happens, possess a positive and fulfilled feature. That the world-whole does have such a feature was shown in Chapter 4, where I indicated that happening itself constituted a fulfillment of the world. This fulfillment-of-happening belongs to the world-whole in its very character as a maximally great superordinate. The world-whole is superordinate to me in that it *happens* independently of me and in that I am dependent for my happening upon its *happening*. Moreover, the world-whole is maximally great in that it is the most all-inclusive whole that *happens*.

The above four items (independency, dependency, maximal greatness, and fulfillment) comprise the global importance of supremacy, the world's complex feature of being a maximally great and fulfilled superordinate.

The identification of these four items enables us to see more clearly how supremacy includes within itself the less complex importance of closeness. The world's complex character as a fulfilled superordinate includes the two features constitutive of closeness: the immediate appearance and the happening of the world-whole. It is through the happening world-whole being superordinate to its immediate appearance to me that the world-whole is a fulfilled superordinate. To appreciate purely the world-whole's supremacy over me is accordingly to appreciate impurely the happening world-whole's immediate appearance to me.

Supremacy includes not only the world's character as a fulfilled superordinate, but also its character as maximally great. This means that reverence also impurely appreciates the global importance of which awe is the pure appreciation, the *immensity* of the world-whole. The world-whole is immense in that it is the *greatest whole that happens*.[3] Global reverence, then, is directly based on two global affects, love and awe; it is an impure appreciation of the *immediate apparentness* and *maximal greatness* of the *happening* world-whole.

Since both love and awe are directly based on rejoicing, revering is indirectly based on rejoicing; revering incorporates within itself the loving and awestruck impure appreciations of fulfillment-of-happening.

The significance and nature of this hierarchical ordering of joy, love, awe, and reverence will become more apparent in the Conclusion. The task before us now is to make explicit in an exact manner the four items constitutive of supremacy. In each of the following four sections, one of these items is explicated. Since the roles fulfillment and maximal greatness play in constituting the importance of supremacy require less explication than that of dependency and independency, I shall describe them first.

VI. 35. The Fulfillment of the Maximally Great and Superordinate Whole

I noted in the last section that revering is captivated by a fulfillment of the world-whole rather than by a demoniacal or malign character of the world. But is it not true the world has ghastly and evil aspects? If so, how is it that revering is a captivated intuition of fulfillment rather than of these aspects? And if the world is ghastly, how can it be worthy of reverence *at all*?

A reflection on this matter shows that the horrifying and evil phenomena belong to the world in respect of its *parts*, not in respect of its *wholeness*. The numerous instances of cruelty and injustice in human affairs, the suffering and merciless killing involved in the struggle for survival in the animal kingdom, and the crippling diseases and natural disasters that can strike any of us, are one and all parts of the world. They are not features that inhere in the wholeness of the world, but parts that partially compose this wholeness. Now global revering is a global affect, and this means it is an affective response to the world in respect of its global features, and not to these or those parts of the world, be they horrifying or otherwise. This is why the ghastly parts of the world are not captivatedly intuited in global revering. In this way it can be said that *the world-whole,* the world in respect of its *global features,* is worthy of reverence, even though certain parts of the world-whole are not worthy of reverence.

Nevertheless it is true that the horrible parts of the world, like the other parts of the world, contribute in some way to the features that inhere in the world-whole. This follows from the simple fact that they are parts of the world-whole, for it belongs to the nature of any world-part to be related to the world-whole through the relation of *participation.* The world-whole, through being one of the terms of this relation, acquires a *relational feature,* namely the feature of being *a whole that is participated in by the world-part in question,* or, expressed otherwise, *a whole that is partially composed of this world-part.*

The nature of such relational features can be more clearly understood when compared with certain relational features that some world-parts acquire through being related to each other. Take the case of a man and woman who are married; a relation obtains between these two people of *marriage.* And these two people, through being terms of this relation, each acquire a corresponding relational feature. The man has the relational feature of being *the husband of the woman,* and the woman has the relational feature of *being the wife of the man.*

Now a horrible event has the relation to the world of *participation.* Accordingly, the horrible event acquires the relational feature of being *a part of the world,* and the world acquires the relational feature of being *partially composed of that horrible event.* Such a relational feature of the world I shall call a *partial compositional feature,* i.e., a relational feature the world acquires through being a term of a participation relation that obtains between itself and one of its parts. The world has one such compositional feature for each part it is related to in this way, and this means the world has a plethora of such features, for a participation relation obtains between itself and each one of its parts.

It follows from the above descriptions that *the world has features which evoke horror,* viz., features of being partially composed of ghastly events. The world accordingly can give rise to a *global* affect of horror, and not merely a mundane one. A mundane horror is captivated by ghastly events considered by themselves, whereas a global horror is captivated by the world *qua* partially composed of these events. A mundane horror is not horrified at *the world* for being partially composed of evil persons and terrible sufferings, but is horrified at *these people and sufferings themselves.*

Accordingly, my earlier statement that *the world-whole,* the world in respect of its *global features,* is worthy of reverence, cannot be true without some qualification, for some global features are worthy of global horror. But if what is worthy of reverence is not the world in respect of its global features, then what exactly is it that is worthy of reverence? To answer this question several further distinctions need to be made in regard to the world's features.

First, partial compositional features must be distinguished from *collective* compositional features and *distributive* compositional features. The world acquires a partial compositional feature through being related to one of its parts, but it acquires a collective compositional feature through being related to *all* of its parts. For example, all of the parts of the world are quantitatively enormous, enormous in regard to the number of individual parts and the number of the kinds of parts. The world, through being related to this enormous collection of parts, acquires the relational feature of being *collectively composed of an enormous quantity of parts*.

The world acquires a distributive compositional feature through being related to *each* of its parts. "Each part of the world" does not have the same reference as "all parts of the world," for while it is true that each part is one part of the world, it is false that all parts are one part of the world. All parts are quantitatively enormous, but each part is not. An example of a distributive compositional feature can be given if we observe that each part of the world is less important than the world itself. Through being related, through the relation of participation, to each of these lesser importances, the world acquires the distributive compositional feature of being *distributively composed of each lesser importance*. The relation of participation is here "distributed among" the innerworldly importances.

The partial and distributive compositional features differ in that each of the partial compositional features is based on a relation of the world to only one of its parts, whereas each distributive compositional feature is based on a relation of the world to each of its parts.[4]

Distinct from these three kinds of compositional features, the partial, collective, and distributive, there are the *noncompositional* features of the world. These are not features the world acquires through being a term of participation relations to its parts, but are either: (1) nonrelational, (2) relational features the world acquires through being related to that which is other than its parts, or (3) relational features the world acquires through being related to its parts through some other kinds of relation than participation.

1. Examples of nonrelational noncompositional features of the world are *singularity* and *happening*. The world is a single world, it is one; and the world happens, it exists. The feature of happening, to consider one of these, is not a feature the world acquires through being a term of a relation to its parts, specifically, of a participation relation to the things in the world that are happening. The world's feature of happening is a different feature from both the distributive compositional feature of be-

ing a whole composed of each world-part that happens and the collective compositional feature of being a whole composed of all the world-parts that happen. *To be composed* of things that happen is not the same thing as *to happen*. It is true that the feature of happening is dependent upon these compositional features; unless the world were distributively and collectively composed of parts that happen, the world itself would not happen. These compositional features are likewise dependent upon the world's happening, for unless the world happened no parts of the world would happen. But the mutual dependency of these compositional features and the noncompositional feature of happening shows they are different but interdependent features, rather than one and the same feature. This highlights the fact that there is a difference in kind between a relational compositional feature of the world and a nonrelational noncompositional feature of the world.

2. The world also has relational noncompositional features, some of which it acquires through being related to terms other than its parts. Since all the things that happen other than the world itself are parts of the world, these other relational terms to which the world is related cannot be things that are happening. Consider that the world is related to its own *past* and *future*; the world *has* a past and it *has* a future. The past and future of the world are neither things which are happening nor parts of the world; they are relational terms that lie outside of the collection of happening world-parts.

3. The world has relational noncompositional features other than ones of the above-mentioned kind; it also has relational features it acquires through being related to its parts by some other relation than participation. For instance, whenever I am intuitively aware of the world, there obtains between the world and myself an "immediate appearing of" relation. By virtue of being a term of this relation, the world acquires the relational feature of being *immediately apparent to me*. It is manifest that this is a relational feature the world acquires through being related to me in some other way than through the relation of participation, for the relation of "immediate appearing of" that obtains between the world and myself is a relation we have *in addition to* the participation relation that obtains between us. And correlatively, the world's relational feature of being *immediately apparent to me* is a different and additional relational feature to that of being *partially composed of myself*.

Similarly, in respect of the importance of supremacy, it may be observed that the relational feature of being *superordinate to me* is a relational feature the world possesses in addition to its feature of being *partially composed of me*.

The world's relational noncompositional features can also be based on relations to each of or all its parts. For example, although the world is wholly identical with all its parts (i.e., is collectively composed of them), it is not absolutely identical with them. This relational feature of being absolutely nonidentical with all its parts is a noncompositional feature of the world; it is not based on the relation of participation, but on the relation of *difference*.

The compositional and noncompositional features of the world both inhere in *the world*. It may be asked here, What is *the world* in which these features inhere? This is a misleading question, since *what* the world *is* is constituted by its essential global features[5] and cannot be comprised of *that in which* these features inhere. *That in which* the features inhere has no determinations apart from the features that inhere in it, for it is nothing other than *that in which* the features inhere. "The world," if we wish to use this phrase abstractly to refer to the world considered apart from its features, is *that which is* one, the greatest whole, composed of some ghastly parts, etc.[6]

These various distinctions enable us to understand more precisely in what respect the world is and is not worthy of reverence. As we have seen, the world is not worthy of reverence in respect of all of its *global features*, for some of them, the partial compositional features that are based on relations to ghastly events, are worthy of horror. Nevertheless, there is a viable sense in which it can be said that "the world in respect of its wholeness is worthy of reverence." "The world in respect of its wholeness" can be distinguished from "the world in respect of some of its parts" so that the former refers to the world in respect of its noncompositional features and its compositional features that are based on relations to *all* and *each* of its parts, and the latter refers to the world in respect of its compositional features that are based on relations to *some* of its parts. The world is worthy of reference in respect of its *noncompositional and collective and distributive compositional features*; more specifically, it is worthy of reverence in respect of its noncompositional features of *fulfillment* and *superordination* and its compositional features of being composed of *all* things other than itself and of *each* thing other than itself (the latter two features pertaining to the *maximal greatness* of the world).

This provides us with a modified and more exact version of the statement with which this section commenced, namely that although the world in respect of some of its parts is horrifying, the world in respect of its wholeness is worthy of reverence. We can see now that the reverential affect is captivated by the world's *being fulfilled* and not by its *being composed of some ghastly parts*, since only the former feature belongs to the world in its wholeness.

VI. 36. The Maximal Greatness of the Superordinate and Fulfilled Whole

In global revering, the world-whole appears to be maximally great in that it is the most all-inclusive whole that happens. The sense and implications of this maximal greatness can be explicated as follows.

If the world-whole is the greatest whole that happens, then it cannot be a *physical whole*. It cannot be the most all-inclusive physical thing or body extended in space — a physical thing that includes every other physical thing as a part of itself and is not itself a part of any larger physical thing — since the most all-inclusive physical thing that is extended in space does not include the *whole of space* within itself as one of its parts. Instead, it is itself included within the whole of space: it is a body, the largest body, that is extended in space.

This is true if space be absolute or relational, for even space as relational is not absolutely identical with spatially related bodies but also includes the *spatial relations* among these bodies (or among the parts of the maximally great body). If space is relational, then the whole of space is the whole composed of spatial relations and terms of spatial relations.

But the whole of space cannot be the most all-inclusive whole that happens, for some things happen that are neither extended in space nor spatial relations or regions, e.g., awarenesses. Since awarenesses are things that happen (the term "thing" is here being used in a very broad sense), the whole that includes both awarenesses and the whole of space is more inclusive than the whole of space.

However, the maximally great whole also cannot be a *spatial and mental whole*, i.e., a whole of space and awarenesses, for some things that happen are neither spatial nor awarenesses, e.g., *universals, ethical obligations*, and some *relations*. The universal, Redness, the ethical obligation to support art (art-ought-to-be-supported), and the relation "better than," are neither physical things nor acts of awareness.

It may be the case that universals, for example, happen or exist only insofar as and when some mind is aware of them. But this does not mean that they do not happen or that they are the awarenesses directed upon them. Rather, it means that universals are phenomena *of which* there is an awareness and which happen *while* there is an awareness of them.

Since universals, obligations, and some relations happen as well as spatial and mental realities, it follows that a whole including only space and minds is not the most all-inclusive whole that happens.

Could it be the greatest whole that happens is the whole of all spatial and mental realities, universals, ethical obligations, and relations *as well as every other kind of world-part that we know of?* The answer must be negative, for there may be certain kinds of world-parts of which we do not know. There may be "unknown world-parts" in two senses: first, in the sense of parts of whose nature and existence we have no knowledge, and second, in the sense of parts of whose nature we have some knowledge but of whose existence we have none (we know *what* they are, but not *that* they are). Examples of unknown world-parts in the latter sense are other spatial wholes. The one spatial whole we do know to exist is the one that includes the configured importances we perceive as well as all the configured importances spatially related to the ones we perceive. It is possible there are one or more other spatial wholes, wholes that include configured importances none of which are spatially related to the ones we perceive. No matter where or how far we travelled in the spatial whole that includes the configured importances we perceive, we would never come across the configured importances located in these other spatial wholes.

At this point, we are capable of achieving a positive characterization of the maximally great whole that happens. It is the whole of all spatial and mental reality, universals, ethical obligations, and relations as well as all other parts we know to exist and all other things about whose existence, and perhaps nature, we do not know (if there are such things).

But it should be observed that if the world-whole is the most all-inclusive whole *that happens*, it can only include *things that are happening*. Things that are not-yet-happening or no-longer-happening cannot be parts of this whole. These things *will be* parts of this whole or they *have been* parts of this whole, but they *are not* parts of this whole.

This is precisely how global revering is aware of the maximally great whole. In global revering, I feel dependent for my happening upon the most all-inclusive whole that happens. I do not feel dependent upon the whole as it will be happening, say, a thousand or billion years from now, for by then I will no longer be happening. Nor do I feel dependent on the whole as it was happening millions of years ago, for then I was not yet happening. What I feel dependent upon for my happening is the whole *as it is happening*.

The above account motivates the question, If all the above-mentioned things are parts of one whole, then *what is this whole?*

It is clear, first of all, that the whole cannot be a spatial reality, an awareness, a universal, or any of the other kinds of things I mentioned, for if it were one of these kinds of things, it would not include within itself the other kinds of these things. If the world-whole were a spatial thing, for instance, it would not include awarenesses among its parts, and if it were an awareness, it would not include spatial things among its parts. Nor could the world-whole be a universal, for a universal cannot be composed of awarenesses and spatial things. Universals can only be composed of other universals; for example, the universal, Animal, includes as parts of itself the universals, Living Organism, Sentience, and Mobility, but this universal is not composed of the body or awareness of this or that animal. The latter things are individuals, and a universal is related to individuals through the relation of instantiation rather than composition.

What, then, is the world-whole? Is its nature at all similar to the nature of each or any one of its parts?

These questions can be understood in two senses. First, they can be understood in a broad sense as asking *which features* inhere in the world-whole and if any of them are similar to the features that inhere in each world-part. As to which features inhere in the world-whole, we know that compositional and noncompositional features so inhere. Certain of the world's noncompositional features are similar to features that inhere in each world-part. They are the transcendental features: existing, oneness, thingness, etc.[7] The world-whole, like each world-part, is *transcendental*.

In a second and more narrow sense, the above questions can be taken as asking about specifically nontranscendental features. Does the world-whole have any generic features, and if so, does it have any generic features similar to any of the generic features possessed by some of its parts?

The world has one positive generic feature: it is a *whole*.[8] It has this feature in common with such of its parts as myself, this galaxy, and the universal, Animal.

Wholeness is not a transcendental because there are some existents that are not wholes. These are the *simple* parts of the world, the parts not composed of any smaller parts. An example of a simple part is the individual relation "better than" that obtains between two individual relational terms. This relation has terms and it may have features (e.g., it could have the feature of appearing to me), but it does not have parts.

Since wholeness is not a transcendental, the world's feature of being the whole composed of all *wholes* other than itself is not coextensive with its feature of being the whole composed of all *things* other than itself. The feature of being composed of all wholes other than itself is a partial compositional feature, and the feature of being composed of all things other than itself is a collective compositional feature.

To say, then, that the concept of a maximally great whole is equivalent to the concept of a whole composed of all wholes other than itself is not strictly accurate, for an even greater whole is conceivable, a whole composed not only of all other wholes but also of all simple things.

The world's feature of being the *maximally great whole* that is a constitutive item of the importance of supremacy is accordingly to be understood in terms of the collective compositional feature of being composed of all things other than itself, and correlatively in terms of the distributive compositional feature of being composed of each thing other than itself.

VI. 37. The Dependency of Myself upon the Independent, Maximally Great and Fulfilled Whole

The superordination of the world-whole to myself involves both my dependency upon it and its independency from me. I shall consider my dependency upon it in this section and the world-whole's independence from me in the next section.

The explication of my dependency upon the world-whole should be introduced by a few remarks about the nature of the revering intuition of the world-whole.

In global revering, as in all global affects, my intuitive awareness is unifying, not dividing. My awareness is broadened to encompass different things as parts of the One, the Whole. I am focused on the One and am no longer attending to this as opposed to that, to some particular thing among the many things in the world. However, it is not the case that in global revering *only* the One appears. Rather, in revering the One-of-many appears, the whole-of-myself,-these-things-and-everything-else. I feel each thing that appears to me to be a part of the One Thing, the supreme whole.

The revered whole is not somewhere else, in an inaccessible Beyond. Rather it is everywhere, all around me, encompassing and including whatever I think of, imagine, perceive, or introspectively apprehend. The supreme whole is partially identical with each thing that appears to me and wholly identical with all the things, myself, these-things-and-everything-else, that appear to me. Each thing that appears is part of that which is felt to flow upwards in an august and lofty manner; each thing shines softly and majestically with the hallowed light of the supreme.

The revering intuition, then, is not completely oblivious to the things in my surroundings; it does not transcend them and everything else in the world to some putative otherworldly Beyond, but turns towards worldly things as a revering of the whole they compose. The supreme is present to me in each thing. It is present to me in my thoughts and images just as much as in the distant skyline and the farthest star I can see. And it is obscurely present to me in everything else beyond my perceptual horizon, and beyond the horizons of the thoughts and images now appearing to me. The supreme is everywhere, in all innerworldly things, for the supreme is *wholly identical* with all innerworldly things.

This worldly orientation of the revering intuition, however, does not imply that this intuition is captivated by some particular thing within the world with which the supreme is partially identical. Nor is this intuition captivated by all the things, myself, these-things-and-everything-else, with which the supreme is wholly identical. Rather, it is captivated by *that which* is partially identical with each thing and *that which* is wholly identical with all innerworldly things. This *"that which"* is the supreme whole itself, the whole composed of all the things in the world. It is the One that is divided into the many parts of the world, but which is divided into them *with remainder*, for the One Whole is not *absolutely* identical with the many parts of which it is composed.[9] It is *the whole*-of-parts and not simply *the parts*. It remains *the One, the world*, and as such remains different from *the many*, the *things in the world*.

It is this supreme One that I feel dependent upon in my revering affect. I am grateful to it for enabling me to happen. The supreme is the greatest whole that happens, and the happening of this whole is a necessary condition of my happening. I can only happen as a part of the world-whole, such that if the world-whole did not happen, I could not happen.

It may be the case that some things which are parts of certain kinds of mundane wholes could happen even if the wholes they composed no longer happened. For instance, the door of this house can happen apart from this house; I can take the door off its hinges, lay it on the ground, and then burn down the house. In this case, the door will still happen even though the house no longer happens.

However, I myself, as a part of the whole of all innerworldly things, cannot happen unless this whole happens. For, by virtue of being an innerworldly thing that happens, I, along with the other innerworldly things that happen, form a *whole* composed of all the innerworldly things that happen. If I happen with other innerworldly things, then these things and myself necessarily form a *whole*, a whole of myself-and-the-other-inner-worldly-things-that-happen. It is evident that I can only happen if other innerworldly things happen. To begin with, I cannot happen bodily unless a space that contains my body happens and unless such configured importances happen as air, food, shelters, a planet, a sun, and whatever else may be required for me to survive bodily. And I cannot happen mentally, as an awareness, unless there are things my awarenesses are directed upon. Without there being things I perceive, imagine, think about, etc., I cannot perceive, imagine, think, etc. This remains true even if the perceived, thought-about, etc., things happen only while being apprehended by me and are dependent for their happening upon the happening of my feeling-awarenesses. If this situation obtained, then my feeling-awarenesses and the things of which they are the awarenesses would be interdependent. If I and other things are interdependent, this still means that I have a relation to these things of *dependency*, which is all I am concerned to establish at present. In the next section I will show that some things of which I am aware are *not* dependent upon me.

In sum, then, I can only happen if I happen with other innerworldly things that, along with myself, help to form a whole of all innerworldly things that happen.

But my dependency upon the happening of a world-whole extends even further than this. I require not only parts of a world but the world itself to appear in my awarenesses. All my awarenesses either are or involve an awareness of the world as a whole. The world-whole appears in the foreground of my global awarenesses and in the background of my mundane awarenesses. In the latter awarenesses, I never fail to recognize tacitly that the person, artifact, or whatever I am attending to is *only one part* of the whole world; it is this background awareness that orients my behavior towards the person or artifact, my behavior towards the part *as a part* and not as the whole of all parts.

An awareness of the world-whole thus belongs to every awareness I experience. As a globally appeared-to world-part, I am dependent upon an apparent whole, even if the whole that appears is existentially dependent upon its appearing to me. If the world-whole and myself are interdependent, it is still true that *I am dependent upon the world-whole*. But it will be made manifest in the next section that the world-whole is not at all dependent upon its appearing to me.

We are not yet in a position to inquire into the world-whole's independency of me, for the fact of my dependency upon the whole has not yet been fully demonstrated. It could be argued, in opposition to my preceding descriptions, that it cannot be known if *there are* world-parts and a world-whole distinct from myself, be these parts and the whole existentially dependent upon or independent of their appearances to me. It could be maintained that all I can know to exist are *appearances to myself*, and that it is intrinsically unknowable as to whether there exists anything that *does* appear to myself. Such a view would allow that in some sense I have a body, but "my body" is held to be nothing more than an *appearance to me*.

Such a viewpoint I shall call *solipsism*. The implication of this viewpoint is that I am not mentally and physically dependent upon the world; rather, I *am* the world, or, to phrase this more exactly, the only world-whole I can know to exist is the whole-of-appearances-to-me.

I think the falsity of such solipsistic beliefs can be revealed through an accurate description of what appears to us. This can be revealed in the first instance by an accurate description of what appears in global revering. In global revering, I experience or "live through" a revering "appearing of" the world-whole. Through this reverential intuiting of the world-whole, the world-whole becomes apparent to me. Now in this revering, what I revere and feel dependent upon is *the world-whole* that is apparent to me, not *the appearance to me* of the world-whole. There is a reverentially felt difference between the world-whole, which I revere, and its apparentness to me, which I do not revere. The apparentness to me of the world-whole is not the world-whole itself, but a relational feature that inheres in the world-whole, a feature that inheres in the world-whole by virtue of my reverential intuiting of it. In fact, this distinction is at the very basis of the revering, for I revere the world-whole precisely because *it* happens superordinately to its *apparentness to me*. Unless this distinction were explicitly before me and captivating me, I would not be experiencing reverence-of-global-supremacy but some other affect.

But the following objections may be raised. How can I know that the world-whole is something different from its appearance to me? Is it not self-evident that all I can know are appearances to me? Is it not obvious that what is not an appearance to me cannot (by definition) "appear to" me and that therefore I cannot in principle even think of it, let alone know that it exists?

In response, it can be made manifest that in all cases where an awareness is experienced, there is a distinction between *the thing* that appears and the immediate or mediate *appearance* of the thing. It is evident, to begin with, that the appearance of the thing cannot *be* the thing that has the appearance. The perceptual appearance of a deer crossing the road is not itself a deer that is crossing the road. The memorative appearance of a plane which crashed twenty years ago is not the plane which crashed twenty years ago, if only for the reason that memories, unlike planes, cannot crash. Things have certain features that their appearances cannot have. This distinction is manifest even in the awarenesses of unrealities: the unicorn I am imagining is not the image I have of the unicorn, for while the unicorn I am imagining has the feature of galloping across a plain, the image does not. And the pink elephant being hallucinated is not the hallucination of the elephant. The pink elephant is an animal that only seems to exist, but the hallucinatory appearance of the elephant is neither an animal nor a nonexistent; it is a psychical phenomenon that really exists.

What these examples reveal is what any other example would reveal, that an appearance necessarily is an appearance *of* something, such that the thing appearing is nonidentical with its appearance.

It may be concluded accordingly that the reverential feeling of dependency is a veridical feeling: the revered world-whole is not a mere appearance but something that appears, something that my awarenesses cannot exist without.[10]

The preceding descriptions have aimed to establish that I am dependent upon the world-whole in the sense that I cannot exist unless it exists and appears to me. There is also a second sense in which I am and feel dependent upon the world-whole; I feel *I do not produce and sustain in existence* the world-whole. The world-whole appears to exist without being made to exist or brought into being by my awareness of it. But my nonproductive relation to the world-whole does not necessarily mean that the world-whole is independent of me; it could be the case that I and the world-whole exist only as interrelated and yet that neither one of us produces the other. However, if the world-whole is independent of me, then it cannot be produced or sustained in existence by me, for its independency implies that it exists of its own accord, without needing my aid or support. Consequently, to show that I feel dependent upon the world-whole in the sense that I do not produce it is not equivalent to showing that the world-whole is independent of me, but it is a *precondition* of showing the latter.

The nonproductivity of my relation to the world-whole can be elucidated indirectly by way of a critical examination of one of the theses of Husserl's transcendental idealism, the thesis that I *do* have a productive relation to the world-whole. It is Husserl's belief that the world is a sense generated by absolute consciousness: ". . . the whole being of the world consists in a certain "sense" ["*Sinn*"] which presupposes absolute consciousness as the sense-giving field [*Feld der Sinngebung*]."[11] In a later work, Husserl writes: " . . . the world with all its realities, including my human real being, is a universe of constituted transcendencies [*Universum konstituierter Transzendenzen*], constituted in experiences and abilities of my ego."[12]

If such a theory is true, then clearly global revering does not provide us with the final truth about my relation to the world. The feeling of dependency upon the world in the sense of being nonproductive of it would have to count as a "naive" experience of the world based on the perspective of the empirical and natural standpoint. The real truth about my relation to the world would lie elsewhere, in the considerations that form the evidential basis of transcendental idealism.

It is impossible to examine here all the considerations that motivated Husserl to construct a theory of transcendental idealism, but I shall be able to evaluate the one consideration relevant to my present concerns, the consideration that the "appearings of" the world-whole are sense-giving acts that produce the world-whole. If there are such sense-giving acts, then we can allow that the world-whole is a "sense" produced by my awarenesses and consequently I am not dependent upon the world-whole in the sense being discussed. But if there is no evidence that there are such acts, then it should be concluded that there is no basis for doubting the reverential feeling of being dependent in this sense upon the world-whole.

Now these sense-giving acts, as defined in the theory of transcendental idealism, cannot be understood to occur on the natural and empirical level of our mental experience or to be productive in a natural or physical sense.[13] They are productive in the fashion of a transcendental production of senses or meanings, a production whereby the intentional experience — the awareness or "appearing of" — produces *that which appears* in this awareness, that which appears being understood as *the relational term* of this awareness. The question before us, then, is: Do or do not the intentional "appearings of" the world-whole produce, in a transcendental and sense-bestowing manner, the world-whole that appears in these "appearings of"?

Before I examine whether or not there is any *intuitive* evidence for the existence of such sense-bestowing acts, I would like to point out that this issue cannot be resolved by an *a priori* analysis of concepts. The universal concept of an "appearing of" is not identical with and does not analytically contain the universal concept of a (transcendental) producing. *To appear* does not *mean to be produced*, either wholly or in part; it is possible to think the concept of "appearing" without thinking the concept of "producing." "Appearing" and "producing" are both relations; they are not one and the same identical relation, but different relations. Moreover, the relation of "appearing" does not imply the existence of the relation of "producing" in the way, for example, that the relation of "A being to the left of B" implies the existence of the relation of "B being to the right of A." It is a contradiction to assert that A is to the left of B but B is not to the right of A, but there is no contradiction involved in asserting that A *appears* but is not produced by its appearing.

An analysis of the concept of the "appearing" relation can reveal that this concept implies *something that appears* and *somebody that is appeared to* (although it leaves the exact sense of this "something" and "somebody" undetermined). But no amount of analysis of this concept will be able to disengage from it the concepts of producing, product, and producer whereby the *appearing something* would be understood as a product of the appearing, and the *somebody appeared to* would be understood as the producer of the appearing something.

This lack of analytic entailment between the concepts of "appearing" and "producing" signifies that the concept of the "appearing" could be instantiated without the concept of the "producing" being instantiated. It is possible that there could be numerous instances of "appearing" but no instances of "producing." However, there is also no analytic *a priori* incompatibility between these two relations; it is not impossible that an "appearing" relation could be conjoined with a "producing" relation, such that what is a relational term of the appearing relation would also be a relational term of a producing relation. Consequently an *a priori* conceptual analysis can neither confirm nor refute the thesis that "appearing" relations are conjoined with "producing" relations. This thesis can only be established or rejected through a reflexive intuition of "appearing" relations that aims to discern whether these relations are in fact conjoined with "producing" relations.

This recourse to reflexive intuition is not incompatible with what Husserl himself believed to be the method of ascertaining the existence of productive "appearings of." It is true that Husserl never recognized, or at least never mentioned, the fact that there is an analytic *a priori* distinction between the concepts of appearing and producing, but he was emphatic in asserting that we can reflexively intuit intentional acts that are sense-giving (*Sinngebung*), such acts being understood as "appearings of" that involve a producing of that which appears in them. Thus Husserl writes that "consciousness allows itself to be methodically uncovered in such a way that one can directly 'see' it in its performing [*Leisten*], whereby sense is given and is produced [*schaffenden*] with modalities of being."[14] This reflexive "seeing" is achieved through the transcendental-phenomenological reduction, which is the methodological procedure that discloses "appearings of" as sense-giving acts.[15] Can such a transcendental-phenomenological reduction be performed? In particular, can the "appearings of" the world-whole be intuited as "appearings of" that involve a producing of the world-whole?

I believe that no such intuition can be achieved and any attempt to perform the transcendental-phenomenological reduction is doomed to failure. It is possible to intuit an "appearing of" relation that obtains between the world-whole and myself, but not a "producing" relation. The "appearing of" is manifest as empty of any productive character, and no producing relation can be discerned to be conjoined with it. Global "appearing of" relations can be described only as contentless, nonproductive, and diaphanous relations; they are wholly translucent, and all the manifest determinations belong to *that which appears* in these relations. For example, the revering "appearing of" the world-whole does not exhibit any content in itself; all the determinations that appear belong to the apparent world-whole; for example, the world-whole is manifest as happening, as the greatest whole, as superordinate to me, and as having the feeling-tonality of reverential augustness. In reflexion, I "look through" the revering "appearing of," as it were, and my reflexive gaze unavoidably meets with the determinations that appear in this "appearing of"; the "appearing of" itself is manifest only as the translucency *through which* I am reflexively gazing upon the revered world-whole.

The impossibility of achieving a deeper "transcendental" intuition of the revering "appearing of" as a sense-bestowing act still manifests itself if I engage in an eidetic variation upon this "appearing of." I reflect upon a synthetic series of exemplifying revering "appearings of" and attempt to discern the world-whole as a "sense" that is constituted in this series, but no such constitutive relations exhibit themselves in my reflexive intuitings.

What would it be like to intuit the revering "appearing of" as involving a sense-producing relation to the world-whole? It could not be an intuition of the sense of the world-whole as being *emanated out of* or *issuing from* the revering "appearing of," for this "appearing of" has no interior from which the sense could issue. Apparential relations do not have "interiors," even in a metaphorical sense, and as such can neither contain within themselves nor allow to pass through themselves a sense of the world-whole. The world-whole appears in reflexion only as a *relational term* of the "appearing of" relation; it is manifest only as *that which appears* in the "appearing of," not also as *that which issues forth from* this "appearing of" relation.

Although there cannot be an intuition of a relational term emanating out of an "appearing of" relation, there does seem to be the possibility that a relational term could be intuited as being *created* and *sustained as* a relational term of the "appearing of" relation. The relational term would not be intuited as "issuing from" the "interior" of the "appearing of" relation, but as being brought into existence *as* a term of this relation and held in existence *as* a term of this relation, such that from the beginning to the end it remains "exterior" to the "appearing of" relation. It would be created and held in being as *that which appears* in the "appearing of."

That such an intuition can in *some* fashion be achieved is evinced by the experiences of *fantasizing*. I can fantasize an unreal world—for example, a world composed of blue waters undulating endlessly beneath a green sky. This unreal world is a relational term of my fantasizing "appearings of" and is created and sustained in being through being created and sustained *as* a term of these "appearings of." This unreal world *is* only what I fantasize it to be and exists only insofar as and as long as I hold it before my fantasizing gaze. I can alter this world at will or at any moment allow it to vanish into nothingness through ceasing to imagine it. In this manner, it is possible to intuit a "producing" relation that is integrally involved with and coexists with an "appearing of" relation.

However, it is not possible to intuit reflexively a "producing" relation as being involved and coexisting with an "appearing of" the *real* world-whole, the world-whole that we constantly intuit in a horizonal or foreground way in our daily life. These "appearings of" are distinguished from the fantasizing "appearings of" precisely in that they do not involve a "producing" of that which appears in them. The real world-whole appears in these "appearings of" as unproduced by us and as existing of its own accord, without needing to be sustained in being by our "appearings of."

Now a transcendental idealist might respond to this by saying that I am describing only *empirical* "producing" relations. He would say: "Of course on the *empirical* level it is only fantasized worlds that are produced by us, and the real world is not produced. However, if you perform the transcendental-phenomenological reduction, you will be able to intuit a 'producing' in a different sense, a *transcendental* producing, and you will be able to intuit even *the real world* as a transcendental product."

But my response would be that *there is no such transcendental producing that can be intuited.* The only producing that can be intuited is the kind of producing, call it "empirical" if you will, that can be discerned in such cases as fantasizing. The concept of a transcendental producing is an empty theoretical construct that cannot be fulfilled in intuition.

I believe that Husserl was motivated by rationalist-idealist explanatory considerations to develop his conception of transcendentally productive intentional acts, and he was led, in accordance with his methodological maxim to allow as evident only what can be intuited, to assert that such productive acts could be intuited. But I do not believe that Husserl himself ever really intuited such acts. He was able to carry out his transcendental-phenomenological program *as if* he were intuiting such acts because his methodological procedure was primarily to intuit intentional acts and their objects in terms of *fantasized eidetic variations.* "In phenomenology," Husserl writes, "as in all eidetic sciences, representation, or, to speak more accurately, *free fancies*, assume *a privileged position.*"[16] Since the eidetically exemplifying intentional acts and objects he intuited were *intentional products of fantasizing intentional acts*, he could not help but have before his reflexive intuition the *productive features* introduced into these data by his fantasizing intentional acts. It would not be difficult, especially if one were operating upon certain transcendental-idealist assumptions as to what one *should* be intuiting, to take the "being produced" feature that the fantasized intentional objects acquired through being relational terms of the *fantasizing* acts as a feature these objects acquired through being relational terms of the *fantasized* acts. For example, he could produce in his fantasy eidetic variations of a perceived physical thing, and variations of the perceiving act that is directed upon this thing; he could take the "being produced" feature that this physical thing acquired through being fantasized by him as a feature the thing acquired through being perceived by the fantasized perceiving acts, and accordingly he could interpret — in line with his transcendental-idealist assumptions — the perceived physical thing as possessing eidetically a feature of being *transcendentally produced* by the perceiving acts in which they appear.

If transcendental producings are neither intuitable nor analytically implied by the concept of an "appearing of," then there is no basis for the belief that there are such producings. All one can know is that I am an empirical consciousness that participates in the world and is psychophysically dependent upon the world; my "appearings of" do not produce the world but merely *disclose* it. And these truths are precisely those intuitively experienced in a pure form in global revering.

This concludes the account of my reverentially felt dependency upon the world-whole. So far I have described three of the four constitutive items of supremacy: *fulfillment, maximal greatness,* and *my dependency* upon the whole. In the next section I shall make explicit the reverentially felt global independency.

VI. 38. *The Independency of the Maximally Great and Fulfilled Whole*

The reverential feeling-flow of "bowing down" before the supreme whole is instigated (in part) by the immediate appearance of the world-whole's relational feature of being imperially indifferent to my existence. The world-whole appears to be able to happen irrespective of whether or not it is partially composed of or apparent to myself.

If the world-whole were dependent upon me, it seems that it would be dependent upon me as a *globally aware world-part* rather than as a *bodily world-part* or a *mundanely aware world-part*. It is not my body or my awareness of other world-parts that is directly pertinent to the supreme, but my awareness of the supreme itself. It is intuitively evident to me in global revering, however, that the world-whole is not even dependent upon its appearance to myself, but is imperially indifferent to me in that respect as well.

The world-whole is reverentially apparent to me as the whole composed of myself kneeling beside the fence, the surrounding trees and houses, the stars gleaming above, and everything else beyond these things. But the world-whole appears to be able to happen without appearing to me in this way, or in any other way. It is intuitively felt that the noncompositional feature of being immediately apparent to myself is an accidental or nonnecessary feature of the world-whole; the world-whole can be envisaged as happening without this feature inhering in it. Moreover, I feel intuitively that the world-whole could exist without appearing to any of its parts; it can exist even if it has no apparential centers.

I pointed out in the last section that an *appearance* implies necessarily *something that appears.* If this is so, then are not the things that appear necessarily bound up with their appearances? How, then, could the world-whole exist without appearing?

The reply is that not all appearing things are necessarily conjoined with their appearances, even though their appearances are necessarily conjoined with them. A feature, such as an apparential feature, may be unable to exist without the thing in which it inheres, but the thing in which it inheres can exist without the feature. Appearances of the world-whole are like smiles on a global face; the smiles cannot exist except on the face, but the face can exist without smiling.

The reverential intuition of the world-whole's independency implies the following five truths, which I shall explicate in turn: (i) the world-whole can be apparent to me as not being apparent to me; (ii) the world-whole can appear uncentered to a center; (iii) the happening of the nonapparent world-whole can appear to me; (iv) the composition of the nonapparent world-whole can appear to me; and (v) the importance of the unappreciated world-whole can be appreciated by me.

VI. 38.i. The World-Whole Can Be Apparent to Me as Not Being Apparent to Me

The reverential feeling of the world-whole's independency of me involves envisioning the possibility of the world-whole happening without appearing to me. This might seem to be an internally clashing seeming intuition, inasmuch as the world-whole would *be apparent* to me as possibly happening *without being apparent* to me. How can I envisage a nonapparent world-whole if my very envisaging makes this whole apparent?

This seeming internal clash can be resolved if we observe the manner in which we regularly believe the world-whole to have in fact happened without being apparent to ourselves. Consider, for example, our tacit belief that the world-whole continues to happen during our periods of dreamless and thoughtless sleep, when we are not experiencing any "appearings of" the world-whole. We normally believe, on the basis of the testimony of other people who remain awake while we sleep and on the basis of the changes in the world that have taken place while we slept (e.g., the passage from night to day), that the world did not vanish into nothingness when we lost consciousness, but continued to happen.

An examination of these beliefs reveals that we apprehend the world-whole to be apparent and nonapparent *in different respects*. For example, the enduring of the world-whole through my dreamless sleeping last night is apprehended to have been nonapparent to me then, but to be apparent to me at present. This does not mean simply that the world-whole as it endured in the night was not apparent to me, and that the world-whole as it is enduring now is apparent to me. It also means that the world-whole *as it happened during the night* is apparent to me at present. I do not *remember* the world-whole's nocturnal enduring, since memory presupposes a previously apparent state of affairs that is being remembered, and in the present case there is no previously apparent state of affairs that could be remembered. Rather, I *reconstruct* the world-whole's nocturnal enduring and, in this way, bring to the nocturnally enduring world-whole a feature it did not formerly possess, viz., the feature of apparentness to me.

One might wonder how something *past* can acquire *in the present* a relational feature of apparentness to me. But there is no impossibility involved here; in fact, this occurs all the time, in every case of remembering. In remembering a plane crash that appeared to me twenty years ago, this perceived plane crash acquires the relational feature of memoratively appearing to me in the present. The plane crash is a relational term of my remembering awareness and, through being a term of this awareness, acquires the relational feature of being memoratively apparent to me.

Now something past which I do not remember, but which I reconstruct, is a relational term of my reconstructive awareness and as such acquires the relational feature of reconstructive apparentness to me. In this way, the world-whole *in its nocturnal happening* acquires (the next morning) the relational feature of reconstructive apparentness to me. This explains why there is no intrinsic clash involved in experiencing an "appearing of" a nonapparent stretch of the world-whole's duration; the world-whole is not apparent and nonapparent in the same respect, but in different ones. The nocturnally enduring world-whole in respect of its relation to me *qua* sleeping during the night is nonapparent, but the very same nocturnally enduring world-whole, in respect of its relation to me *qua* awake the next morning, is apparent, albeit reconstructively.

These descriptions enable the revering intuition of the world-whole's possible nonapparentness to me to be clarified. The revering affect is not concerned with past or future instances in which the world-whole is nonapparent to me, but with the possibility that *at present* it could happen without being apparent to me. The world-whole *is* apparent to me at present as the whole of myself kneeling beside the fence, these stars, and everything else beyond them, but it is possible that the world-whole could be happening at this very moment without being apparent to me in this way, or in any other way. This revering intuition of the world-whole's independence of me does not clash with itself, for the world-whole is felt to be apparent and nonapparent in different respects: in respect of what is *actually* the case, the world-whole is apparent to me; but in respect of what is *possibly* the case, it is nonapparent to me. That is, the world-whole *qua* possibly enduring nonapparently to me is apparent to me in the present situation that actually exists, but the world-whole *qua* possibly enduring nonapparently to me is nonapparent to me in this possible situation itself.

VI. 38.ii. The World-Whole Can Appear Uncentered to a Center

In global revering, the world-whole appears both as it now is and as it now would be if it were nonapparent to me. The world-whole as it actually is appears to be centered around my revering awareness, but this whole as it would be if it were nonapparent to me appears to lack such centeredness. The world-whole in its possible nonapparent happening is not envisaged as the whole-of-myself-and-these-things-around-me and everything-else-beyond-these-things, but as a perspectiveless whole-of-all-innerworldly-things.

Such a whole cannot be sensuously imagined, for such images involve a perspectival ordering. Sensuous images picture something as it would appear to a perspectival center located at some point in space; for example, a visual image of a house may picture it as it would be seen from some point in space in front of the house. A centerless whole must instead be envisaged nonsensuously. It is in a nonsensuous void that the world-whole's possible nonapparent happening appears to me. I reverentially enter a realm of neither light nor darkness, and therein envision the possibility of the whole-of-all-innerworldly-things existing without appearing to me.

I reverentially envisage the whole as centerless in that it is without the center that *I am*. I believe that there are other world-centers happening at present, and that if I ceased to happen and ceased being appeared to, these other centers could still continue to happen and be appeared to. Thus these other centers are implicitly presumed to be possibly included in the whole-of-all-innerworldly-things I envisage as being able to happen without appearing to me.

Now in apprehending the world as possibly composed of these other centers, I do not envisage in a determinate way how the world would be perspectivally appearing to each of these centers. It would be impossible, of course, for me to envisage concretely how the world would simultaneously appear to billions or trillions of other perspectival centers. Rather, I apprehend in a mostly indefinite way *that* the world could be appearing in different ways to a number of different centers, without attempting to envision in a determinate way *how* it could be appearing to each of these centers.

Nevertheless, it is possible for me to envision determinately how the world could appear to *one* of these centers, specifically, one of the human ones. I could envision the world-whole appearing as the whole of himself, these-things-around-him-and-everything-else, and I could even envision these-things-around-him by means of a sensuous image, if these-things were presumed to be hued things. In such an envisioning, I would be determinately aware of the world at it could happen *nonapparently to me* but *apparently to some other world-center*.

But I do not envisage in this way the world-whole's independence of me in global revering. What I revere for its independency of me is *the world-whole*, not *the world-whole qua perspectivally appearing to this or that world-center*. The world-whole could happen without appearing to this other world-center; thus, to feel that the world-whole's appearance to this world-center is independent of me is not to feel the independency of me that is intrinsic to the world-whole itself. Global revering is an appreciation of the independency of me that belongs to the world-whole considered in respect of its necessary features, i.e., the features without which it could not happen. The world-whole's appearance to another center is accidental or nonnecessary; it is a feature of the world without which the world-whole could still happen. This is true moreover for all of the world-whole's apparential features, for it is not necessary for the world-whole to appear to any of its parts in order to happen.

Accordingly, the world-whole that is revered as intrinsically independent of me can be neither the world-whole *qua* appearing to some other world-center nor the world-whole *qua* appearing in a variety of ways to all the other world-centers. The world-whole that is intrinsically independent of me *may* include other centers to which it appears, but it does not necessarily include them; accordingly, I reverentially envisage it as only *possibly* having the apparential features it would acquire through appearing to other centers. I envisage the world-whole as *necessarily* having only the noncompositional and compositional features without which it could not happen. These include such noncompositional features as happening,[17] oneness, processlessness, purposelessness, etc., as well as certain collective, distributive and partial compositional features.

These remarks raise some further questions. As envisioned to possess necessarily only such features as the above-mentioned ones, the happening world-whole is envisioned as possibly being *without* all its apparential features. But how can I concretely envision the world-whole to have these noncompositional and compositional features and not have any apparential features? In particular, how can I envision the world-whole *to endure* when it does not have features of appearing to parts of itself that *remember, expect* and *present*? And what possible character could I envision the world's *mindless composition* to have? And finally, could I apprehend such a nonapparent world as still having *important* features?

VI. 38.iii. The Happening of the Nonapparent World-Whole Can Appear to Me

I am reverentially envisioning the maximally great and fulfilled whole upon which I am dependent to possibly endure without appearing to myself or any other of its parts. My envisioning is a complex experience comprised of a retaining, expecting, and presenting. It is by means of these time-awarenesses that I can envision the enduring of the world. But could the world really endure *in* the possible situation I am envisioning in my time-awarenesses, a situation in which there are no time-awarenesses? Is the temporal "appearing of" a nonapparent temporality an internally clashing "appearing of"?

That it is nonclashing becomes evident once we clearly distinguish time from *appearances* and "*appearings* of" time. Happenings, happenings-no-longer, and happenings-not-yet are *items which* appear in our retaining, expecting, and presenting "appearings of." Retentional, expectational, and presentational *appearances*, and retaining, expecting, and presenting "*appearings of*" are neither identical with nor parts of the happenings-no-longer, happenings-not-yet and happenings that *exhibit* these appearances in these "appearings of." Nor are they features and relations necessary to and intrinsically constitutive of these temporal moments. Consider a past moment. This moment necessarily is no-longer-a-present, formerly-a-future, continually receding from the present, composed of briefer happenings-no-longer, composed of moments each of which was a happening, and the like. However, the feature, *being a retentional appearance*, and the relation, *retaining "appearing of,"* are items of a different kind entirely. They are *psychical* phenomena, not *temporal* phenomena, and as such they do not comprise the nature of the temporal phenomena *as* temporal phenomena. They are not intrinsically but extrinsically constitutive of temporal phenomena; they are accidental features and relations of temporal moments.

It is through confusing psychical phenomena with temporal phenomena that many thinkers are led to believe that time is mind-dependent. Bergson, for example, writes that "duration . . . is memory . . . a memory that prolongs the before into the after."[18] But we must distinguish here the remembering "appearing of," the memorative appearance (the memory), and that which is remembered. Duration in respect of its "before," the past moments, is not *the memory* but *that which is remembered*. For the memory *is present*, and the "before" that is remembered *is not present*. Duration is not a psychical phenomenon, but something to which psychical phenomena can be related.

Once we recognize that time is neither identical with nor necessarily associated with time-awarenesses and time-appearances, we can discern the answer to the question, How can the world-whole endure in a situation in which it is not being retained, expected, and presented, if in order for it to be envisaged as enduring in that situation it must be retained, expected, and presented? The answer is that the condition of the appearance of the world-whole's duration is not a condition of this duration itself. In order for the world-whole's enduring in a possible situation to be apparent to me in the actual situation, this enduring must be retained, expected, and presented by me. But in order for the world-whole *to endure* in the possible situation it need not in that situation be retained, expected, and presented; it need only have the features and relations intrinsically constitutive of duration itself.

These reflections may not be sufficient to persuade certain philosophers that present, past, and future intervals are independent of their appearances. Many analytic philosophers and most phenomenological philosophers, claiming that the present, past, and future are mind-dependent phenomena, have developed a number of arguments and descriptions to this effect. The principal arguments of the analytic philosophers have been criticized elsewhere,[19] so I shall concentrate on the views put forth by the phenomenologists.

I shall not say much here about Husserl's theory that time is constituted or produced through the intentional animation of temporal *hyle* immanent to consciousness. I have already argued in VI.37 that the producing relation Husserl talks about is not given in reflexive intuition, and in another publication I have demonstrated that Husserl's concept of a *hyle* immanent to consciousness cannot be verified by any intuition.[20]

I shall discuss here Heidegger's, Sartre's, and Merleau-Ponty's theories of the mind-dependence of time. For Heidegger, moments of time or nows are originated in a disclosure of spatial positions that counts these positions. "The making-present [*gegenwartigende*] of the positions of the moving pointer *follows* these positions and *counts* them."[21] The making-present of the traversed positions expresses itself, and the nows are its self-expression.[22]

There are two reasons moments of time cannot originate in this manner. First, the counted spatial positions must already be in time, prior to the counting of them and the self-expression of this counting. What is counted are the successive positions assumed by the moving pointer. The pointer is first at one position and then later at another. The pointer can be at one position later than it can be at another only if it is *in time*, for "later" just means *later in time*. Thus, time already belongs to that which is counted and cannot arise as a result or self-expression of the counting of that which is counted. Second, temporal phenomena, the nows, cannot in principle be the self-expression or self-articulation of a nontemporal phenomenon, the making-present of the counted spatial positions. The making-present of these positions can in its self-expression express only what it itself is, a disclosure of spatial phenomena.

One might object to the second criticism by saying that for Heidegger the making-present *is* a temporal phenomenon: an ecstasis of "temporality" (*Zeitlichkeit*). It is true that Heidegger calls making-present "the present" (*Gegenwart*) in the "temporal" (*zeitlich*) sense,[23] but Heidegger expressly distinguishes the "present, past and future" in the sense of temporality (*Zeitlichkeit*) from the ordinary senses of these terms, which refer to dimensions of time (*Zeit*).[24] The present, past, and future of temporality are modes of disclosure or clearedness. "The ecstases of temporality originally clear [*lichtet*] the 'there' [*das Da*]."[25] The future in the temporal sense is *Dasein*'s clearedness or disclosure of its ability-to-be in the way of *coming-towards itself*; the present is a *making-present*, a letting-oneself-be-confronted-by beings within the world; and the past is a clearedness wherein *Dasein* is what it *has been*.[26]

The making-present, then, is not a making-*present* in the sense of being, making, or disclosing a *dimension of time*, but in the sense of *making-clear* or *disclosing beings within the world*, be they tools or at-hand (*Vorhanden*) beings like the moving pointer of a clock. And as such, there is nothing that it *is*, or that it *clears*, that can be expressed as a dimension of time. In order to express itself in terms of temporal moments, it must when counting the traversed spatial positions, make-present not only the spatial positions, but also *temporal moments*, viz., the temporal moments in which the positions are intuited as earlier and later, and in which they are intuited as past, present, or future. In short, to express itself in the "now," "now-no-longer," and "now-not-yet," the making-present must be a making-present *of* something that *can* be so expressed— the *happenings, happenings-no-longer*, and *happenings-not-yet* in which the spatial positions are located.

A possible source of the seeming plausibility of Heidegger's theory that "the present" in the sense of *the now* is the self-expression of "the present" in the sense of *making-present* is an unrecognized equivocation with respect to the term "present." "Present" has at least three senses. It can mean: (1) *spatial proximity* (as in "He is present at the right spot"); (2) *appearing* (as in "The loud and colorful spectacle was present to my senses"); or (3) *a dimension of time* (as in "The present is earlier than the future"). By the "present" in the sense of the "now," Heidegger means the "present" in the third sense; by the "present" in the sense of "making-present," he means "present" in the second, apparential sense (where "making-present" means making-appear, making-clear, disclosing, letting-oneself-be-confronted-by, etc.). By calling this *appearing* a "present" and this "present" a mode of "temporality," Heidegger creates a merely linguistic connection between *appearing* and *time*. The linguistically based plausibility of Heidegger's theory vanishes when properly *nontemporal* terms are used to describe "the present" in the sense of "making-present," and it is baldly stated that the *present dimension of time* is the self-expression of the *clearedness of* or the *letting-oneself-be-confronted-by counted spatial positions*.

An analogous equivocation is operative in Heidegger's theory that the meaning of Being is "Temporality" (*Temporalität*). The "Temporality" of "the present" in the sense of "making-present" is the horizon of the making-present, this horizon being *praesens* (*Praesenz*) with its two modes, *presence* (*Anwesenheit*) and *absence* (*Abwesenheit*).[27] But *praesens* is a "present" in the second of the three senses I distinguished, the sense of *appearing* or *appearance*, and only by a linguistic similarity to the "present" in the third sense of a dimension of time is it a *"Temporal"* meaning of Being. In truth, it is an *apparential* meaning of Being. *Being and Time* should have been entitled *Being and Appearance*.

This same equivocal use of the term "present" is also what lends the seeming plausibility to Sartre's theory that time originates from consciousness. For Sartre, the present dimension of time is the "reflection [*reflet*] on things"[28] of the original "present," the temporal "present" of the for-itself. In regard to this original "present," Sartre writes: "The meaning of *present* is presence to_____. . . . My present is to be present. Present to what? To this table, to this room, to Paris, to the world, in short to being-in-itself."[29] Sartre clearly explains that by the "present" he means an *appearing of* or an *intentional consciousness of*: "The for-itself is present to being in that it is intentionally directed outside of itself upon being."[30] But the "reflection" of an intentional consciousness or an *appearing of* on things is a *being consciously intended* or a *being apparent*, not a present dimension of time.

Sartre differs from Heidegger in that he attempts to support his account of the mind-dependency of time by means of some arguments. Sartre's first argument concerns the conception of time as continuous, where "continuous" means that between any two temporal moments there is a third moment.[31] The notion that time is continuous, Sartre maintains, leads inescapably to the notion that time *is* the for-itself:

> In the study of temporality in particular, we realize well what service continuity can render us by putting in between the instant a and the instant c, no matter how close together they are, an intermediary b, such that, according to the formula $a = b$, $b = c$, $a \div c$, it [b] is at once indistinguishable from a and indistinguishable from c, which are perfectly distinguishable from one another. It is it [b] which will realize the relation before-after [*avant-après*], it is it [b] which will be before itself inasmuch as it is indistinguishable from a and c. All is fine here. But how can such a being exist? Whence comes its ecstatic [*ek-statique*] nature? . . . Perhaps a more profound examination of the conditions of the possibilities of this being would have shown us that only the for-itself could thus exist in the ecstatic unity of self.[32]

Sartre misunderstands the nature of continuity. If b is after a and before c, it is not the case that it is "equal to" or "indistinguishable from" both a and c and hence "before itself." The continuity of the moments a and c means that if we divide a and c into sufficiently shorter moments, we will discover a moment b of the same length as each of the shorter moments into which a and c have been divided and that is intermediary between a and c. But b is neither a nor c nor any one of the shorter moments that compose a and c; rather, it is a distinct moment *in between* the shorter moments comprising a and the shorter moments comprising c.

This can be illustrated in terms of a continuous number series. If a is one and c is two, b will be a number in between one and two. This number is discovered by representing one as two-halves and two as four-halves; in between two-halves and four-halves there is the number three-halves. Obviously three-halves is equal neither to two-halves nor to four-halves but is perfectly distinct from them.

If b is equal neither to a nor to c, then it cannot be said that since a is before c, then b is "before itself." There is no sense at all in which b is before itself. It is absolutely simultaneous with itself. Accordingly, it does not have an "ecstatic nature" and is not to be understood as the for-itself. The notion that time is continuous does not lead to the notion that time *is* the for-itself, but is *independent* of the idea of a for-itself.

The second argument Sartre propounds to show that time involves consciousness concerns the organization of time. A series of moments organized by before-after relations is an "organized multiplicity." Sartre says that "an organization of multiplicity presupposes an organizing act . . . there is no *given* synthesis."[33] Synthesis is effected by the for-itself.

The idea that organizations presuppose organizers is an unjustified presupposition. The concept of an organization does not entail the concept of an organizer. It is true that a painting necessarily implies a painter, and a building a builder, but there are certain types of organization not necessarily connected to any organizer. These organizations could be such that they *just are*, without being organized by anybody. The organization of nature, for example, could *just be*, without being organized by a god or a transcendental consciousness. And the same is true for time.

Sartre would respond to this by saying that the very nature of time demands that it be organized by consciousness:

> Temporality is evidently an organized structure and the three so-called "elements" of time, past, present and future, should not be envisaged as a collection of "data" for us to sum up—for example, as an infinite series of "nows" ["*maintenant*"] in which some are not yet and others are no longer—but rather as the structured moments of an original synthesis. Otherwise we will meet immediately with this paradox: the past is no longer, the future is not yet, and as for the instantaneous present [*présent instantané*], everyone knows that it is not at all, but is the limit of an infinite division, like a point without dimension. Thus the whole series is annihilated and doubly so since the future "now," for example, is a nothingness *qua* future and will be realized in nothingness when it passes on to the state of a present "now."[34] . . . Thus Time is pure nothingness in-itself [*pur néant en-soi*], which can seem to have *being* only by the very act in which the for-itself overleaps it in order to utilize it.[35]

Certainly the future and past are "nothingnesses" in the sense that they are being-not-yet and being-no-longer. But it is a mistake to regard the present as a nothingness. Sartre does not make it clear what he means by saying that the present is "the limit of an infinite division," but unless he is to be accused of an outright contradiction (in that an infinite division by definition has no limits), his statements can be construed as tacitly applying to time the theory of the convergence of infinite series developed by Augustin-Louis Cauchy in his Lectures of 1821. The simple and instantaneous present accordingly can be represented as the ideal limit approached but unreached by the infinite sequence of divisions of the complex present. But it does not follow from this that the simple present "is not at all." In order for this to follow, an additional assumption is needed—

that something not reached by an infinite sequence of divisions cannot be. But such an assumption is plainly arbitrary: what does being reached or unreached by such a division have to do with being and nonbeing? To specify the instantaneous present as the limit of an infinite division is to ascribe to it the characteristic of being separated from any present interval by an infinite number of briefer present intervals. That is, it is to determine *what* the instantaneous present is, to determine one of its relational features, not *that* it is or is not.

Far from being nothing at all, the simple present is *pure being*; it is a pure Is, unmixed with an Is-not-yet and Is-no-longer. Unlike the complex present—the presentness of intervals—the simple present is not composed of a briefer present and a correspondingly brief past and future that are contiguous with the briefer present; instead, it has no temporal parts at all.

In Chapter 4, I state that it is not disclosed in the joyous intuition of the global presentness whether the intuited present interval is ultimately composed of present, past, and future instants or whether it is composed only of briefer present, past, and future intervals. If the intuited present were composed only of intervals, there would be no pure being in the sense of a simple present, but the present nevertheless would not be a pure nothingness. For within each complex present there is not only a being-not-yet and a being-no-longer, but also a being.

Time, then, whether it contains only intervals or also instants, is not a "nothingness in itself" that requires being-for-itself in order to be realized and sustained. It contains being within itself and does not need to be ontologically supported by anything other than itself.

It is possible to accept that time in respect of its present includes being, but to claim that the very fact that the future and past are nonbeing requires that they be sustained by consciousness. Since the past and future are essential to time, this means that there cannot be time without consciousness. This is the tack taken by Merleau-Ponty in his *Phenomenology of Perception:* "The objective world [*Le monde objectif*] is too full [*trop plein*] for there to be time. The past and future withdraw by themselves from being and pass over into subjectivity in search, not of some real support [*support réel*], but, on the contrary, of a possibility of nonbeing which accords with their nature."[36]

The time that belongs to subjectivity, however, is not an "object of our knowledge, but a dimension of our being."[37] The truth is that "I am myself time [*je suis moi-même le temps*]"[38]; "the subject is temporality [*le sujet est temporalité*]."[39]

Merleau-Ponty's assumption that the world is pure being and that nonbeing can only belong to the subject is not only unjustified but plainly false. Consider the fact that I am born and die. This is impossible if "I am myself time." To be born implies there was a time at which I was not. To die implies there will be a time at which I shall not be. But if I *am* time, and the "was" and "will be" *are myself*, then there cannot be a past and future without myself. There can be no time at which I do not exist. It is impossible for me to begin and cease to exist. I exist at all times. I am an omnitemporal being. But such conclusions fail to conform to the unimpugnable facts that I was born and will die. Accordingly, I cannot *be* time but must *be in* time.

Can the theory that I am time be reconciled in any way with the facts of birth and death? It might be said, for example, that consciousness, upon being born, projects a past behind itself. Sartre attempted to solve the problem of birth in this way.[40] But this solution founders on the reef of incoherency. For a projected prenatal past is a past that never was a present. There never was a time at which this projected past was present, for time first arises with the birth of consciousness. Prior to the projection of the prenatal past, there was no time at which the projected past could have *become past* by first being a future that becomes a present which in turn becomes a past. The projected past first arises *as passed away*. This means that the past is not a present-no-longer—since it never was a present. It is undeniable, however, that a past is *absolutely identical with* a present-no-longer. A past that is not a present-no-longer is a present-no-longer that is not a present-no-longer; that is, it is an impossibility. There can be no prenatal past if time arises with consciousness. It is a fact, however, that consciousness is born; consequently, there is a prenatal past. If there is a prenatal past, then time cannot be consciousness, but must be different from and independent of consciousness.

Several other problems arise if time is identified with consciousness. If it is true that "I am myself time," a theory shared in different ways by Merleau-Ponty, Sartre, Heidegger, and Husserl, then there is a multiplicity of different times, several billion times in fact, for that is how many people there are. Such a theory is incompatible with the intuitively felt state of affairs that I do, say, see, and hear things *at the same time* as others. The phenomenologists claim that each person constitutes a public time. At best, however, each person can only *seem* to constitute a public time. And this seeming is necessarily deceptive. The public time my consciousness constitutes is a phenomenon for my consciousness, and the public time your consciousness constitutes is a phenomenon for your consciousness. The phenomenon of public time I constitute cannot by its very nature be a phenomenon for you, for phenomena consciously constituted can be phenomena only for the consciousness in which they are constituted. If public time is constituted, then there is not one public time but a multiplicity of phenomena of public time. And that is to say there *is* no public time but only private times, although these private times may deceptively seem to the consciousnesses that constitute them to be public times.

This situation brings with it the following problem. Being present in my consciously constituted public time *is not* being present in your consciously constituted public time. Since the only present that is a phenomenon for me and that I can apprehend is the one I constitute, I can never know if what is present in my time is also present in somebody else's time. I live isolated on the island of my own temporality.

Merleau-Ponty seems to be vaguely aware of this problem, but quickly passes over it with the following words:

> Without doubt the other person will never exist for us as we exist for ourselves, he is always a lesser figure, and we never feel in him as we do in ourselves the thrust of temporalization. But two temporalities are not mutually exclusive like two consciousnesses, because each one knows itself only by projecting itself into the present where they can interweave [*enlacer*]. As my living present opens upon a past which I nevertheless am no longer living through, and on a future which I do not yet live, and perhaps never shall, it can also open onto temporalities in which I am not living . . . [41]

Is what Merleau-Ponty assumes here to be true really even *possible*? Is it possible that "my living present" could "open on to temporalities in which I am not living" and therein "interweave" with the other living presents? Let us phrase this question more exactly: is it possible that I could know my living present to be simultaneous with the living present of another temporality?

I could have an experience of seeing and feeling you touch me and of hearing you say, "I am touching you at present." I would experience you to say this at my present. This would not be evidence for the simultaneity of our presents, for your statement could be present in my lived time, but past in your time. Although I am hearing you say this at my present, this interchange could be for you something remembered, succeeded by numerous other experiences, which are all past relative to what you are experiencing at present in your time. In fact, it is possible that at present in my time all other people are past in their time, so that I exist in a world that, for other people, is but a faded and long-ago era.

The absurdity of the phenomenological theory of time is that if this theory were true, then I could never have any evidence for knowing if a scenario such as the above one were real or not. The only present that is a phenomenon for me is my own, and I cannot in principle know if this present is earlier, later, or simultaneous with the presents that are phenomena for others.

But with these remarks we are only beginning to touch the surface of the problematic nature of the phenomenological theory of time. For the very idea that there is a plurality of temporalities implies that these temporalities *are not* temporalities but *mere appearances* located in the one unconstituted time. Let us begin with a scenario such as the above one, where the various living presents are not simultaneous. If your utterance, "I am touching you at present," is present in my temporality but past in your temporality, then my present is simultaneous with your past. But two things are simultaneous only if they *occur at the same time*. This time cannot be my time or your time, but a time in which we both live that is not constituted by either of us.

Consider now a second scenario, where all living presents are simultaneous. If your present is simultaneous with my present, then it occurs at the same time as my present. This means that there is a time in which both presents are located and by virtue of which both presents are simultaneous. But what is *in* time cannot *be* time; since your present and my present are both *in* the same time, they cannot be presents but *appearances-of-present that are present*. There is only one present, the one unconstituted present in which the various constituted phenomena of the present are simultaneous.

Summarily put, if there are several living presents, either these living presents are simultaneous with or earlier or later than one another. In either case, they are simultaneous, earlier, or later *in the same time*, and this time cannot be any one or all of these presents but a time *in which* all these presents are located. As phenomena in time, they are not time but intratemporal phenomena, intratemporal *appearances*.

I shall now take a different critical approach to the phenomenological theory of time. I shall note simply that it is in principle impossible for there to be more than one temporality. For if there were several temporalities, then any given event could simultaneously have opposite and clashing temporal features. In one temporality, the event could *be present*, in another *past*, and in a third *future*. But one and the same event cannot be simultaneously present, past, and future, for this would mean (for instance) its having passed away is simultaneous with its not having passed away, and that is impossible. One and the same event can only be successively future, present, and past.

Let us suppose alternatively that each person's temporal present is simultaneous with each other person's temporal present, so that any given event does not simultaneously have opposite temporal features. Is this situation possible? No, for it would mean that any given event, when it passes away, *passes away several times over*. And an event can pass away only once.

For example, if a flower dies, then it ceases to exist, it passes away. If there are several parallel temporalities, then the flower dies several times over. It does not have only one temporal feature of ceasing to exist—of becoming past—inhering in it, but several such features: one feature for each temporality. That is not possible, though, for a flower can cease to exist only once.

These and other absurdities are entailed by the supposition that there is more than one temporality. I shall not point out the other absurdities but instead note that these absurdities one and all imply that there can be only one temporality not identical with or constituted by any human consciousness. As Kant said, there can only be *one time*.[42] It should be noted, however, that by affirming this Kant refuted his own theory, for Kant held that time is an *a priori* form of a transcendental subject, and there is a plurality of transcendental subjects (a view explicitly espoused in his second critique). If there is only one time, and there are many subjects, then time cannot be *a priori* to each subject. For the *a priori* forms of subjects are the same in number as the subjects; each numerically distinct subject has its own numerically distinct *a priori* form. Time as *one* cannot belong to this form. What belongs to this form is instead a *capacity to be aware of* the one time.

The above criticisms of the theories of the mind-dependence of time have reinforced my initial description of time as it is envisioned in the revering affect, as possibly flowing without appearing to anybody at all. It is only if this description of time is true, and not the above-discussed theories of time, that the world can be worthy of reverence. For if the above-discussed theories are right, the world's enduring is *dependent* upon me; and an essential condition of global reverence is that the world's enduring be independent of me. My conclusion, then, may be stated thus: in opposition to the above-mentioned phenomenological philosophies, I affirm that the world *is*, rather than is not, worthy of reverence.

VI. 38.iv. The Composition of the Nonapparent World-Whole Can Appear to Me

If the world-whole is to be envisioned as happening without appearing to any of its parts, it must be envisioned to possess not only such noncompositional features as happening, but also compositional features. The world must be envisioned as a whole-of-parts, parts with which it is collectively, distributively, and partially identical. How are these parts to be concretely envisioned? What could be the nature of the world-whole's possibly mindless composition?

It can be noted first of all that the world-whole need not happen nonapparently with *any* of the parts known to presently belong to the world-whole. It was pointed out in VI.36 that the world-whole *may* be partially composed of some world-parts of whose determinate nature we know nothing at all, world-parts that are neither physical, mental, universal, etc. Now it is possible that the world-whole could happen as composed *only* of these unknown world-parts; precisely put, this means that if there are some unknown world-parts, and these world-parts could happen without any of the world-parts of which we know, then it is possible that the world-whole could happen as a whole-of-these-unknown-parts such that it would be collectively and distributively identical with these parts alone. Such a world would have in it no space, no configured importances, no mental things, no universals, and no other things about which we know. Such a world cannot be imagined or comprehended in any determinate way, but is nevertheless *possible*. It is true that such a world is not happening at present, but it is possible that such a world could happen in the future or has happened in the past. This is so because no world-parts are necessary existents, things that *must* happen,[43] and this implies that it is possible that all of the known world-parts could cease to happen at some future time and could not have been happening at some past time. At these times, there could exist a nonapparent world wholly composed of the unknown world-parts.

It is also possible, although in a different sense, that the world could happen in this way at present. This possibility is "counterfactual," i.e., it is a possible situation counter to the situation that in fact obtains. It is possible that the world *as it is at present* could have been otherwise. It might have been the case that the world's present composition consisted solely of the unknown world-parts, and that myself, other world-centers, configured importances, and all other things of which we know, did not exist. It is this counterfactual possibility of the world's nonapparent composition that is envisioned in global revering, for revering is captivated, not by the world's intrinsic independency of me at some past or future time, but by its intrinsic independency of me *at present*.[44]

Another counterfactual possibility constitutive of the world-whole's intrinsic independency of me at present is that the world-whole might at present have been composed only of parts of whose nature we do in fact have some knowledge, but of whose existence or nonexistence we have no knowledge.[45] Examples of such parts are spatial wholes other than the one in which we are embodied and in which the configured importances we perceive are located. If these other spaces exist and are not dependent for their existence upon any of the world-parts we know to exist or upon any other world-parts, then it is possible that at present the world might have been composed only of these other spaces.

Among these unknown world-parts that could have solely composed the world at present, god is included. For example, if there is another space, and this space is the space of heaven,[46] then the world-whole at present might have been composed solely of god and this heavenly space.

However, god is a globally appeared-to world-part, and consequently the world through being composed of god acquires an apparential feature. We have earlier seen that apparential features are not among the features necessarily constitutive of the world-whole's intrinsic independence of me;

the world-whole as intrinsically independent may have apparential features, but also may not. This implies that in global revering the intrinsically independent world-whole is envisioned as possibly happening without *any* apparential features. It is this envisioning that I set out to describe in VI. 38. iii-v. The task of this subsection is to answer the question, What possible character could I envision the world's *mindless composition* to have?[47] The envisioning of god (or of resurrected embodied souls, angels, demons, etc.) cannot belong to this envisioning, and accordingly is not to be considered in this subsection.

Concerning the world-whole's mindless composition, there are several possibilities and it is these possibilities that I am concerned to describe. No one of these possible mindless compositions necessarily belongs to the intrinsically independent world-whole, but at least one of them must belong to the world-whole considered as happening without its unnecessary apparential features.

So far I have considered such possible compositions to be wholly unknown world-parts and to be parts of whose nature we have some knowledge but of whose existence or nonexistence we have none. These possibilities are *unsubstantiated possibilities*; that is, they are possibilities not based upon what we know to exist in the world. A possible world-composition that is *substantiated* is based upon what we know to be parts of the world. Are there world-parts with which we are aquainted that could wholly or partly compose a nonapparent world?

Universals are one possibility. In fact, it is sometimes thought that universals *necessarily exist*, such that they are parts of every possible world. But the belief that universals necessarily exist, which has been frequent in the history of philosophy, is based upon a failure to distinguish adequately between what universals are and that they are. A complex universal, such as Triangularity Involving Three-Sidedness, necessarily is what it is; it is impossible that Triangularity could ever involve Two-Sidedness or Four-Sidedness. But this fact is quite different from the fact that the complex universal, Triangularity Involving Three-Sidedness, *exists*. It is possible that the complex universal, Triangularity Involving Three-Sidedness, could not exist. This would not mean that Triangularity would *not* involve Three-Sidedness, but that there would not exist the universal, Triangularity, that could either involve or not involve Three-Sidedness. It is a contradiction to say that Triangularity does not involve Three-Sidedness, but it is not a contradiction to say that the universal, Triangularity, does not exist. In short, the contingency involved in *that* universals are is different from and compatible with the necessity involved in *what* they are.

If this is the case, is it possible nonetheless for universals to exist even if no first-order individuals exist? Could there be a world wholly composed of universals?

It is shown in Chapter 5 that we sometimes ideate and think about universals and sometimes do not. Do universals exist when they are not being ideated or thought about? There is no evidence that they do. The only possible evidence would be that universals, when they appear to us, veridically appear to exist necessarily (and thus to exist whether they are appearing to us or not), but we have seen that universals do not so appear. Without this evidence, all we can say is that as far as we know, they happen only when they are appearing to us.

But *could* they exist without being ideated or thought about? This certainly is possible, for universals do not possess features of being *necessarily* mind-dependent. Triangularity could be completely analyzed and no implication or reference to a mind could be found in it. One could find in it features of Three-Sidedness, Three-Angledness, etc., but not Mind-Relatedness. In this respect, universals differ from phenomena like pains, thoughts, and hallucinations, which necessarily refer to a mind. For example, hallucinations, in regard to what they are, necessarily are *somebody's* hallucinations. The conclusion is warranted, then, that the world-whole at present could have been wholly composed of universals.

Another example of world-parts with which we are acquainted that could compose a nonapparent world is that of *configured importances*. The hue-displaying configured importances we perceptually appreciate appear to be able to exist as configured importances without displaying themselves to us as being hued. A gently rippling and harmoniously round lake I perceptually appreciate is one example. Some of the hues this lake displays itself to be, such as being serenely blue, freshly smelling, quietly lapping, and icily cold, are features the lake possesses relative to one of my five modes of sensory appreciation. Other hues, like being unharmoniously elliptically hued or harmoniously circularly hued are features the lake possesses relative to a spatially perspectival appreciation; for example, the harmoniously round lake displays itself to be harmoniously roundly hued to a person appreciating it from above and inharmoniously elliptically hued to a person appreciating it from one side. But that which displays itself to be hued in these ways, the round lake itself, has configured-importance features it is able to possess irrespective of whether these features are displaying themselves to be hued to this or that percipient. The lake could be harmoniously round[48] and gently rippling even if nobody were present to appreciate its roundness and rippling.

It is worthwhile to consider the reverential envisioning of the independence of these configured importances from their perceptual displays, for, as I shall point out shortly, configured importances are the only world-parts for which there is a *likelihood* (and not merely a possibility) of belonging to the world's nonapparent composition.

It is deep into the night, and I am standing rapt in reverence in a flowery meadow that borders on a lake. The supremacy of the whole composed of myself, this meadow and lake, those glittering stars above, and everything else beyond them, is purely appearing to me. In reverentially envisioning this whole to be intrinsically independent of me, I envisage it as it could have been nonapparentially composed. In this envisioning, I transcend the perceptual appearances of the glittering stars and lake and I transcend all imaginative appearances. I reverentially enter a void of nonsensuousness. This void is not indeterminate, but is a sculptured void. It holds a *titanic hueless configuration*. All configured importances are envisaged to be parts of the one absolutely great configured importance, the one titanic configuration. This configuration is absolutely hueless, not deigning to display itself at all.

The titanic hueless configuration is reverentially envisioned to endure in an absolute silence. No sound exists anywhere at all in this titanically composed world. This silence is not relative, as is the silence of the still lake below the glittering stars. The hueless configuration is not silent relative to louder sounds, but is perfectly soundless in itself. There are no auditory appreciators in relation to which it could display itself to whine, hum, clash, or roar.

This titanic configuration is neither a somber gray nor a violent red; it is neither resplendent in a myriad of rainbow colors nor monochrome. It is absolutely colorless. The absolutely great configuration is *configured*: it has a shape and size and occupies space, but the sides and parts of this configuration are neither hard nor soft, neither sharp nor blunt, neither sticky nor smooth.[49] They are neither freezing cold nor burning hot, nor any degree of warmth or coolness in between. The titanic configuration is absolutely voluminous, but at the same time absolutely intangible. It is a plenum and yet a void.

The parts of this configuration move, but they move neither to the right nor to the left, neither up nor down, neither forwards nor backwards. They move from place to place in an absolutely unoriented space.

What could one of the parts of this titanic configuration be like?

In this soundless world, there may be roses weaving gently in the wind, receiving light from a distant moon. But the roses have no fragrance, and they are not red. The moon is not golden, and its light is totally invisible. The redless, fragranceless roses weave in the silent wind, impinged upon by the invisible light from a colorless moon.

Space is populated with stars, but the starry regions are not dark, like a night sky. Nor are they bright, like the sky of day. Radiating in a space that is neither dark nor light, the stars fling themselves out in an invisible emptiness.

At this moment, one part of this titanic configuration is in fact displaying itself to me; this part is displaying itself to me to be panoramically hued with a darkness speckled with tiny glittering lights. But this display to me is neither a part of nor similar to the hueless configuration that is independent of me, which is beyond anything I could imagine. The counterfactual possibility of this hueless configuration manifests itself purely only in the transcendental void of reverence.

The transcendental envisioning of this hueless configuration has a precedence in global reverence over the envisioning of the other substantiated and unsubstantiated possibilities of the world's nonapparent composition. This is because it is *likely* that the world-whole's nonapparent composition would be a titanic hueless configuration, and unlikely that it would be universals or any one of the other substantiated or unsubstantiated possible compositions. In what sense this is the case can be made explicit through noting, to begin with, that likelihood and unlikelihood are the two modalities of the counterfactual compositional possibilities of the world. The world-whole at present could have had a nonapparent composition, and any given composition it could have had is — given the condition of the world's being nonapparentially composed in some way — either likely or unlikely. This condition, to explicate it more fully, is the world's composition being as it is at present *except* for the absence from this composition of all appeared-to parts and all parts that are existentially dependent upon appeared-to parts. This means, minimally, that such parts as humans and animals, as well as parts like memories, hallucinations, and feeling-sensations, which are necessarily dependent upon parts like humans and animals, would not belong to the world. Other parts *could* belong to the nonapparent world, and of these parts some are *likely* to belong to it and some are not. A part is likely to belong to this composition if it is likely that it would remain in existence if all appeared-to parts departed from existence. I shall show that configured importances, and all world-parts necessarily bound up with configured importances, are likely to continue existing if all appeared-to parts cease to exist, and that all other substantiated possibilities, like universals, and all unsubstantiated possibilities are unlikely to compose this nonapparent world.

The evidence that configured importances are likely to exist in a nonapparent world can be most effectively presented in opposition to some of the doctrines espoused in the debates about "realism" and "idealism" among analytic philosophers. In these discussions, "realism" is associated with the doctrine that physical things are mind-independent. The analytic philosopher who first propounded arguments in favor of realism, Moore, claimed physical things are mind-independent in the sense that they *can* exist without being perceived.[50] He did not attempt to argue that physical things *probably* exist unperceived. But W.T. Stace correctly pointed out in "The Refutation of Realism"[51] that if it is merely possible that physical things exist unperceived, and there is not a shred of evidence to indicate that they probably so exist, then this fact does not support realism but idealism. For it would be tantamount to the assertion that all available evidence indicates that physical things are *probably mind-dependent.*

I believe, however, that there *is* evidence that physical things probably exist unperceived. More exactly, I believe there is intuitively felt evidence that configured importances probably exist while they are not displaying themselves to us as being hued. Consider the following situation.

I am in a room with a grandfather clock. This clock when first looked at reads "1:00 a.m." I look at the clock later (exactly five minutes later according to the wristwatch I am steadily perceiving during this time) and the clock reads "1:05 a.m." There are two possibilities. Either the grandfather clock reading "1:00 a.m." ceases to exist when I stop perceiving it, and springs back into existence, with its hands changed to "1:05 a.m.," when I perceive it again, or the clock continues to exist unperceived during this five-minute interval, with its hands gradually passing through the clock times between "1:00 a.m." and "1:05 a.m." It is implicitly felt, when looking at the clock for the second time, that the second possibility *probably* obtains.

The basis for this feeling is implicitly before me. On past occasions when the grandfather clock was perceived over an interval of time, the clock hands appeared to traverse without break the positions between one clock time and another clock time, and never on any occasion appeared to depart from existence at one clock time and to spring back into existence at a later clock time. Since the clock hands continued to exist and continuously change in all intuitively experienced instances, it is probable that they continue to exist and continuously change in unexperienced instances.

The nature of this probability, the tacit belief in which forms an element of all our relevant perceptual appreciations, can be more generally stated. If a certain configured importance is repeatedly observed to change from state A to state D by first changing to state B and state C, and to change from A to D over similar intervals of time, then in cases when A is first observed and then, after the said interval of time, D is observed (with B and C not being observed), it is likely that A changed to D by first changing to B and C, even though B and C were not observed. In short, B and C probably existed as unperceived states of a configured importance.

It may be objected that considerations of probability apply only to observed changes, and not to unobserved ones. What evidence do we have to extrapolate from observed changes to unobserved ones? But this objection is nonsensical, for probability means just that *unobserved things or processes of a certain kind are probably similar to observed things or processes of that kind.*

It may then be objected that considerations of probability do not establish that unobserved things and processes *exist*, for the existence of unobserved things and processes is not necessarily implied by the existence of observed things and processes. This objection is also absurd, for a "probable connection" means precisely that a *connection between observed and unobserved things and processes is not necessary but probable.*

These remarks can be further clarified by responding to two of Stace's arguments that no probable connection between observed and unobserved things can be known. Stace writes:

> Inductive reasoning proceeds always upon the basis that what has been found in certain observed cases to be true will also be true in unobserved cases. But there is no single case in which it has been observed to be true that an experienced object continues to exist when it is not being experienced; for, by hypothesis, its existence when it is not being experienced cannot be observed. Induction is generalisation from observed facts, but there is not a single case of an unexperienced existence having been observed on which could be based the generalisation that entities continue to exist when no one is experiencing them.[52]

Everything Stace says in this paragraph is true, but it is irrelevant to the inductive evidence we do possess concerning the unperceived existence of physical things. The generalization that entities continue to exist unperceived is not, of course, based on an observation of unobserved entities, which is a contradiction in terms, but on observations of the *changes* entities exhibit when they are observed. If in all observed cases an entity changes from A to D by first changing to B and C, then it is probable that in all cases where A and D are observed but B and C are not observed, B and C existed unobserved.

A second argument Stace propounds concerns processes and laws:

> Why must we believe that causation continues to operate during interperceptual intervals? Obviously, the case as regards unexperienced processes and laws is in exactly the same position as the case regarding unexperienced *things*. Just as we cannot perceive unexperienced things, so we cannot perceive unexperienced processes and laws. Just as we cannot infer from anything which we experience the existence of unexperienced things, so we cannot infer from anything we experience the existence of unexperienced processes and laws. There is absolutely no evidence (sense-experience) to show that the fire went on burning during your absence, nor is any inference to that alleged fact possible. Any supposed inference will obviously be based upon our belief that the law of causation operates continuously through time whether observed or unobserved. But this is one of the very things which has to be proved.[53]

In order to expose the error in this argument, a distinction must first be made between a law and a process. The law of causation is a universal inductive generalization and, as far as we know, mind-dependent (for all universals, be they categories or laws, are not known to exist otherwise than during the times they are being ideated or thought about). A process, on the other hand, is an individual (an individual series of individual states of an individual). Processes of configured importances, such as the burning of a log or a clock hand's gradual change of position, are the individual processes we know to be probably mind-independent. We know them to be so on the basis of the above-mentioned evidence concerning observed states of change.

Is the inference that certain states of change exist unobserved "based upon our belief that the law of causation operates continuously through time whether observed or unobserved"? If it is so based, then the argument, according to Stace, would be a *petitio principii*. However, this inference is not based on a universal law but upon previously observed instances. This is illustrated by an inference drawn about a burning fire. In a certain situation, I may perceive a fire starting, leave the room, come back several hours later, and find ashes in the fireplace. I infer that the fire continued to burn while I was out of room, that the logs became charred (a state of change I did not perceive), and that later embers formed (another state of change I did not see). Although I see only the fire starting and later the ashes, I infer that the logs became charred and embers formed. This inference is not based on the assumption that a universal law of causation operates in things when they are not being perceived, but upon the fact that in previous cases the charring of logs and the forming of embers were perceived to follow the ignition of the fire and to precede the formation of ashes. The assumption refers to previously perceived individual states of change, not to a universal law that obtains in unperceived situations.

Am I assuming, then, not a universal law but a particular proposition that the individual states, *the charring of the log* and *the formation of the embers*, exist unperceived? No, for this is not an assumption of the argument but its conclusion; the assumption refers only to previously observed cases of the ignition of fires being succeeded by, and the formation of ashes being preceded by, the charring of logs and the formation of embers.

It may be concluded, then, that the inference to unobserved states of change is not circular; it does not assume what it is trying to prove.

This may be granted, but a further question may nevertheless be raised. How can a proposition referring to *observed* cases of change entail a proposition referring to *unobserved* cases of change? This question has already been shown to rest on a misunderstanding of probability. Inductive premises do not entail their conclusions; only deductive premises do so. The proposition asserting the unobserved cases is not analytically but synthetically connected to the propositions asserting the observed ones. In other words, the unobserved states of change are not necessarily but probably connected to the observed states of change; there could be no unobserved states of change, but it is likely that there are such states.

To deny that it is even likely that there are unobserved states is to commit a plain error. For this denial is tantamount to denying that there is such a thing as a probable connection, and such a denial conflicts with the fact that probable connections are almost constantly being disclosed to us in our perceptual appreciations. A *doubt* that there are probable connections is even unjustified. For if there intuitively seem to be probable connections, and there are no known extrinsic grounds that override this seeming, then it is justified to believe that there *are* probable connections and unjustified to withhold this belief. This is strictly in accordance with the criteria of intuitional truth.[54]

But is it in accordance with the criterion of propositional truth? A proposition is determined to be true through *discovering* the important state of affairs the proposition putatively signifies.[55] How can a proposition about an unintuited state of affairs be verified if the state of affairs cannot be discovered in intuition?

There is a distinction between a circuitous and noncircuitous discovery of a signified importance. A signified state of a configured importance is noncircuitously discovered if it displays itself to be hued in a perceiving-feeling. It is circuitously discovered if it does not display itself in a perceiving-feeling but the states of the configured importance with which it is probably connected do display themselves in perceiving-feelings. In these perceiving-feelings, a relational feature of the perceived states of the configured importance, the relational feature of *being probably connected to unperceived states*, is intuitively and preconceptually apprehended. Through intuiting this relational feature the proposition about the unperceived states is circuitously verified.

In this manner, propositions about unintuited states of configured importances are distinguished from the unverifiable "intuition-transcending significations" I critically discussed in Chapter 2. The latter significations are not of things probably connected to noncircuitously discovered things, but of things supposedly necessarily connected to noncircuitously discovered things. The "intuition-transcending inferences" are not based on previously intuited processes and things, but upon supposedly universal *a priori* principles, and these inferences are not inductive but deductive. For example, it is assumed *a priori* that every state of change belongs to a finite causal series, the first member of which is an uncaused cause; by means of this principle, the existence of this cause can be "backwardly" deductively inferred in intuition-transcending thinking from the existence of any noncircuitously discovered state of change. This inference is not based upon previous intuitive experiences of the connections among states of change, but upon the purportedly *a priori* assumption that causal series have a first member. This inference transcends that which is noncircuitously and circuitously discovered in intuitive feelings and enters the realm of pure thought-construction.

The preceding reflections enable us to understand the likelihood with which hueless configured importances would compose a nonapparent world. Configured importances are likely to continue to exist when they are not being perceptually appreciated and consequently are likely to continue to exist if all perceptual appreciations and appreciators cease to exist. Correlatively, in the counterfactual situation envisaged in global revering—wherein the world-whole at present is as it is except that it is without all appeared-to parts and all parts dependent upon appeared-to parts—hueless configured importances are likely to exist.

There is no intuitively felt evidence concerning any other type of world-part besides configured importances that shows that type of world-part would probably exist in the envisaged counterfactual global situation. All other substantiated and unsubstantiated possible components of a nonapparent world would *probably not* participate in such a world. For example, it is unlikely that universals would exist in this counterfactual global situation, for all available evidence indicates that they exist only as phenomena of ideation and thought. Universals do not undergo change and hence do not present the same evidence of having undergone nonapparent changes that configured importances do. The evidence for universals' nonapparent existence is nil, and so the probability that they have such an existence is nil. It is *possible but not probable* that they would exist in a world devoid of ideating and thinking parts.

The situation is the same in regard to the unknown world-parts. There is no evidence that they would probably exist nonapparently because there is no evidence that they exist at all. It is possible that they exist and possible that they would exist at present if no appeared-to parts existed, but the likelihood of their existence is nil.

In sum, then, it is possible but not likely that a nonapparent world would consist only of universals, or only of unknown world-parts, or only of universals and unknown world-parts, or only of universals, unknown world-parts, and configured importances (to name some of the unlikely nonapparent world-compositions). It is likely that the nonapparent world would consist *only* of configured importances (and of the parts necessarily bound up with configured importances, such as a spatial whole and certain relations among configured importances).

Configured importances, accordingly, have a precedence in the reverentially envisaged nonapparent world. My envisaging is explicitly directed towards these importances, but only implicitly towards other importances. The titanic hueless configuration appears in the transcendental void of reverence as the likely composition of the nonapparent world.

VI. 38.v. The Importance of the Unappreciated World-Whole Can Be Appreciated by Me

I am at present a part of the supreme whole. It is supreme over me and other appreciative parts of itself in that it is able to withdraw from us and perpetuate itself in an unfelt silence and solitude. In such a solitary existence, would it still be *supreme*? Would it still be *important*? Would it have a *felt meaning* in any sense?

The world-whole if it existed without being appreciated would no longer have the important feature of supremacy, but it would have other important features. In regard to supremacy, the world-whole can be supreme over me only insofar as it is related to me as that over which it is supreme, and it can be related to me in this way only insofar as I happen and am appeared to. It will be recalled that the importance of supremacy has four constitutive items, viz., the world-whole's independency of me, my dependency upon the world-whole, the world-whole's feature as the greatest whole that happens, and its feature of fulfillment-of-happening. Now if I ceased to happen, the world-whole would still be the greatest whole that happens and it would still happen, but it would cease to have relations to me of independency and dependency. Since these two relations are necessary to the importance of supremacy, the world-whole would cease to be supreme over me. If other globally appeared-to world-parts continued to happen, the world-whole would still be supreme over them, but if no appeared-to part happened, the world-whole would not be supreme over any part (for the importance of supremacy involves the world-whole's superordination to its appeared-to parts).[56]

Here I must dispel the seeming paradox concerning the fact that the world-whole's independency of me is dependent upon me. How can the world-whole be independent of me if its independency of me is dependent upon me? The answer is that the world-whole's relation to me of independency is dependent upon me (for this relation cannot obtain unless both of its terms, myself and the world-whole, exist), but that the world-whole which has this relation to me is not dependent upon me. In fact, the very meaning of the relation of independency is that one of the terms of this relation, the world-whole, could happen without the other term of the relation, myself. But this relation itself holds only if both of its terms are happening. If I do not happen, the world-whole is neither happening *independently of me* nor happening *dependently upon me*; rather, it is just *happening*.

Without me and other appreciative parts, the world-whole would not only have the feature of happening, but also the features of being one; the greatest whole; purposeless; nonnecessary; processless; collectively, distributively, and partially composed of parts; and others. But would these features be importances? Would the world-whole still have felt meanings, or would it be *completely meaningless*?

Clearly, it could not have felt meanings if "felt" signifies that these meanings are being affectively or moodily experienced by somebody. For there is no appreciative part of the nonapparent world that does feelingly experience these meanings. But what if "felt meanings" has the sense of meanings that *could be* felt by an appreciative part, even though these meanings are not *in fact* felt by such a part? In this sense the nonapparent world-whole would still have felt meanings. The word "felt," however, like the words "seen," "heard," "touched," etc., implies that something actually is experienced, rather than merely could be experienced, and so a more suitable expression is needed. A meaning that is not being felt but is able to be felt can be called a "feelable meaning." It can be said, then, that the world *in fact* has *felt* meanings, but the world in the counterfactual situation envisaged in global revering has *feelable* meanings.

Does this signify that the nonapparent world-whole is merely able to be important, but is not important? Is an importance a *felt* meaning, such that it must be *felt* in order to be an importance? Or can an importance be *feelable* without actually being felt? In this latter case, an importance would be (identically) a *meaning* that in the factual global situation is felt but in the counterfactual situation is merely feelable.

Confusions will arise in the attempt to answer this question if it is forgotten that "importance" is being used in this treatise in an extra-ordinary rather than ordinary sense.[57] In ordinary usage, some things are called "important" and other things "unimportant." Moreover, in many instances of ordinary usage the word "importance" carries the implication that something is necessarily important *to somebody*. For example, it is said, "If the artifact is not important to anybody, we can throw it away." But in all instances of ordinary usage this is not the case, for we often say such things as "Sunlight is important to plants"; "The heart is the most important organ of the body"; "Planets are more important to the functioning of the solar system than asteroids"; and "The falling of the mountain into the sea was the most important event to occur on the island in years, and yet no one was there to witness it!"

However, considerations of ordinary usage are not directly relevant here, as I am using "importance" in an extra-ordinary sense. In Chapter 2, I listed two characteristics of an importance: it is evocatively and exactly describable and acquires the feature of being a feeling-flow source upon its coming to appearance. It is immediately obvious that if an "importance" is whatever has these two characteristics, then it is quite possible for an importance to exist without appearing and without being appreciated. It is obvious, first of all, that the world-whole as existing nonapparently can be evocatively and exactly described; in fact, the last several subsections have consisted of nothing less than such descriptions. With regard to the second characteristic of an importance, it is to be noted that this characteristic is not that something *has* the feature of being a feeling-flow source, but that it has such a feature if and when it appears. It need not *be a flow-source* in order to *be such that it is a flow-source if and when it appears*. Since the world-whole even if and when it is not appearing is such that it is a flow-source if and when it does appear, it follows that the world-whole as existing nonapparently also has the second characteristic of an importance and consequently *is* an importance.[58]

In the reverential affect, I envisage an intrinsically important whole enduring in absolute silence, appreciated by no one. This whole is important *in itself* and does not need to be important *to* anyone.

But now I can and am appreciating this unappreciated importance. Global reverence is the pure appreciation of the unappreciated importance of the nonapparent world. The world, which is the most important importance, is unappreciated in the envisaged global situation, and that is precisely what I am now appreciating about it. I revere the most important importance for its intrinsical independency of me. These remarks conclude my account of global reverence.

Before I make explicit some of the impure appreciations of global supremacy, I shall compare global reverence with the reverence associated with the metaphysics of reason, which I shall call *religious reverence*. Religious reverence is of the "human-independent absolute reality" in the sense of the metaphysics of reason, viz., the reason for all other reasons that is able to exist without its human consequences. Global reverence on the other hand is of the "human-independent absolute reality" in the sense of the metaphysics of feeling, viz., the importance composed of all other importances that is able to exist without its human parts.

Of these two types of reverence, which one is the appreciation of that which is the *most worthy* of reverence? Is god or the world-whole that which is *unconditionally* deserving of reverence? I will show that by virtue of its supremacy over me the world-whole is more deserving of reverence than god. This is demonstrable in reference to the world-whole's superordination to me, its absolute holistic greatness, and its fulfillment-of-happening.

The world-whole, but not god, is *superordinate to me*; I cannot exist unless the world-whole exists, but I can exist if god does not exist. Indeed, it may very well be the case *in fact* that I myself but not god is existing. Since I am unconditionally dependent upon the world-whole but not upon god, the world-whole in this respect is more worthy of reverence.

As *the greatest whole* there is, the world-whole is wholly identical with all of reality. It is the most real being, the *ens realissimum*, the very highest reality; nothing could possibly be identical with more being than the world-whole. God, if he exists, is merely partly identical with all of reality, and accordingly is ontologically inferior to the world-whole. As such, he is less worthy of reverence than the world-whole.

The world-whole's absolute holistic greatness involves a further respect in which the world-whole is more deserving of reverence than god. God is worthy of reverence because he is (identically) the *highest personal importance*: he is the most wise, powerful, enduring, etc., person. But the world-whole by virtue of its absolute holistic greatness far surpasses this in its importance, for it is partly identical with the highest personal importance (if there is one) and partly identical with every other importance as well. The revered world-whole is thus *more important* than god, and in this respect is a more deserving focus of reverence.

Finally, the world-whole, but not god, can be known to possess a *fulfillment-of-happening*, a positivity of being that by itself is intrinsically worthy of joy and is an integral aspect of supremacy. God, for all we know, possesses an emptiness-of-happening, a nullity of being,[59] and hence is outshone absolutely by the full radiance of the *happening* whole. Concerning this fulfillment-of-happening, god, as far as we know, is not worthy of reverence at all (for a nonexistent god does not deserve to be revered), whereas the world-whole is completely deserving of it.

In response, one may say that there is a sense in which god is "more worthy" of reverence than the world-whole, that god *ought to be revered in preference to* the world-whole. Not only is god a person, and thus in possession of greater ethical dignity than impersonal realities like the world-whole, but he is also the morally best person, and hence is of greater ethical value than any other being whatsoever. God is the one perfectly good person, the person who is just as he ought to be, and such a person ought to be revered in preference to anything else.

This viewpoint, however, collapses in face of the relativity of values. It is not absolutely true that god is the most valuable being, but is true relative to some individual or cultural system of values, e.g., the Christian. Relative to other systems of values, god is a less valuable or even the least valuable being. God *intrinsically* is a person with merely factual features, such as omniscience, omnipotence, and omnitemporality. These ways in which god *is* do not entail either that they are ways in which god *ought to be* or that they are ways in which he *ought not to be*; no matter how long the feature of omniscience is scrutinized, there will never be found in it any reason for the belief that it ought to be or ought not to be. Only by assuming that features of these sorts are valuable can the belief be derived that they are ways in which god ought to be, but this assumption like every other value-assumption is ultimately arbitrary.

A being with such factual features as omniscience and omnipotence may believe that certain factual features ought to be, but *the fact* that such a being believes this does not entail that these features ought to be. That certain features ought to be is not one of the things this all-knowing being *knows*, but is something he merely believes (without justification and without absolute veridicality).

Since value-features are relative features—features things acquire only in relation to some being that is adopting some (ultimately arbitrary) moral perspective on the things—affects that are evaluative are only relatively veridical and, consequently, have no place in an account of the nonrelative affective truths about the world-whole and its parts. Accordingly, if religious reverence is evaluative, it is merely relatively true and cannot be taken as a revelation of what is intrinsic to the divinity.

But it is nonrelatively true that god is the highest personal importance, where this means that god intrinsically has important factual features that are the maximal features in the class of features that can intrinsically belong to persons: the features of maximal knowledge (omniscience), maximal power (omnipotence), maximal duration (omnitemporality), etc. But these maximal features constitute but a part of that which is most important and most worthy of reverence, the supreme world-whole. Only by reverentially transcending god do I meet the genuinely supreme.

VI. 39. The Impure Appreciations of the World-Whole's Supremacy

VI. 39.i. The Place of the Impure Appreciations of Supremacy in the Foundational Order of Global Affects

The impure appreciations of the global importance of supremacy are affective captivations with the most complex of the global importances being described in this treatise. Impure appreciations of the first mode are appreciations of supremacy as possessing some feature; stupefaction at the stunning importance of the world-whole, humility before its loftiness, and apathy before its stultifying importance are impure appreciations of this first mode (cf. VI.39.i-iii). Impure appreciations of the second mode are captivations with a feature of that which possesses the importance of supremacy, the world-whole. Dread of the world-whole's ominousness and quietude in its stillness are impure appreciations of this modality (cf. VI.39.iv-v).

VI. 39.ii. Stupefaction Before the Stunning World-Whole

Stupefaction is directly based on global reverence. That which I revere, considered more fully in its intrinsic nature, is stunning. It shatters and explodes all attempts to envision it. Once my appreciative focus attempts to enlarge, to extend beyond the world-whole's supremacy over me and to penetrate and encompass the complete intrinsic character of the supreme whole, my captivated awareness becomes suddenly blinded and dazed. I am deflected from the globe's suddenly unveiled searing brilliance. My stupefied feeling-sensation has the direction of a forward-tending flow that has come up against a stunning reality that throws the feeling-sensation violently backwards. The sensation of a forward-tending feeling *abruptly and violently thrown backwards* is the sensation-flow of stupefaction. The tonal-flow is *forwards*, towards me from the stunning whole, and it flows forwards in a manner of *violently throwing me backwards*, away from itself.

The stunning importance that throws me back as I try to transcend the revering envisioning includes the supreme importance within itself as well as an additional feature of one of the items constitutive of supremacy, the item in question being the world-whole's intrinsic independency of me. The world-whole is intrinsically independent of me in that it could have existed at present without being apparent to any of its parts. This independency, fully considered, manifests an additional feature: an *infinitude of counterfactual global possibilities that make it infinitely unlikely for the world-whole to be what it in fact inexplicably is, viz., apparent.* This stunning importance can be progressively articulated through beginning with the infinitude of the counterfactual global possibilities.

The description of the world-whole as it is revered showed that the world-whole might have existed nonapparently; it might have been just as it is at present, with the one exception that it would have no appeared-to parts and no parts existentially dependent upon appeared-to parts. In such a world, there would likely exist nothing but a titanic hueless configuration extended in a space that is neither light nor dark. In reverence, I envisage this titanic configuration to be just as it is at present, except that it is not displaying itself to any appreciators. But in stupefaction, I realize this titanic configuration need not have been just as it is at present. It might have differed in any one of innumerable ways from the way in which it in fact is. Besides me there is a lake and a meadow of flowers, and above me there shimmer the stars. The lake could have been smaller or larger than it in fact is; the flowers in the meadow might have been of a more variety of kinds than they in fact are; and the stars, some of which are displayed to me in the night sky, might have been ten times or one-half or one-quarter as numerous as they in fact are. These counterfactual possibilities are not limited. There could have been a world composed of only one colorless star in a vast empty space, or two or three such stars, or one million stars, or one hundred trillion stars, or any other number from one to infinity. This is true for all other kinds of configured importances as well. The world might have been composed of anywhere from one to an infinity of flowers, lakes, trees, rocks, grains of sand, or some other kind of configured importance. Combinations of kinds of things are also possible; the world might have been composed of an infinity of stars, planets, and rocks; or ten thousand stars, forty thousand planets, and ten trillion rocks; or any one of an infinity of other combinations than the ones that in fact obtain.

The laws of nature also might have been different in any one of an infinity of ways. For example, light, instead of propagating at 186,282 miles a second, could have done so at one mile a second or any other number of miles per second up to and including an infinite number of miles (instantaneous propagation).

The *kinds* of configured importances that might have existed could also have infinitely varied. Consider the kinds of configured-importance shapes alone; there might have been a world composed only of three-sided configured importances, or four-sided configured importances, or one-million-sided configured importances, or infinitely sided configured importances, or any one of an infinity of possible combinations of these different types of importances (e.g., four-sided and five-sided importances, or four-sided and one-million-sided importances, etc.).

The above observations imply that there is an infinitude of infinite counterfactual possibilities. There is an infinite number of possible kinds of configured importances, and each kind could have anywhere from one to an infinite number of instances; moreover, there is an infinity of possible combinations of kinds of configured importances and of possible combinations of numbers of kinds and numbers of instances of each kind.[60]

The realization of this infinity of infinities of possible nonapparent world-compositions shatters my envisioning. The stunning infinitude of infinities that belongs to the complete character of the world-whole's intrinsic independence of me sends me reeling back in captivated stupefaction.

But it is not solely this infinite character of the world-whole's independence of me that stupefies me; rather, I am stupefied primarily by a further character of this independency. Through being infinitely independent of its appeared-to parts, the world-whole's being composed of these parts is a state of affairs that, although actual, is infinitely unlikely to be actual. Not only is it *unlikely* that the world-whole in fact appear to me and other parts of itself, it is *infinitely* unlikely. And yet it *does* appear to me and other parts. That is utterly *stunning*.

The infinite unlikeliness of the world-whole's being composed of appeared-to parts can be fully explicated in the following way. If there is an infinity of possible world-compositions, only one of which can be the actual one, then the odds against any one of these compositions *being* the actual one are infinite. And if there is an infinity of possible nonapparent compositions besides the apparent composition that is in fact actual, then the odds against this apparent composition being actual rather than one of the nonapparent compositions are infinite.[61]

But the infinite unlikeliness of the present apparent composition does not fully exhaust the stunning character of the world-whole's independency of me. The stunning importance of the world becomes completely revealed in the recognition that *nothing at all* can explain why among the infinity of possible world-compositions the world has *this* one rather than some other one. Nothing at all could make this apparent composition the one the world-whole *necessarily* has or even is *likely* to have; it is merely one possibility among an infinity of possibilities that just happened — inexplicably — to be the actual world-composition.

It is manifest first of all that it is not *necessary* for this apparent composition to belong to the world. This has already been shown in VI.38 and need only be summarily stated here. No thing necessarily exists[62]; consequently, the things that do in fact compose the world might not have existed. Possible things that do not in fact compose the world *might* have composed the world instead; it is no more necessary for these nonexistent things to *not exist* than it is for the existent things to *exist*.

Not only is it not necessary for the world to have this apparent composition rather than some nonapparent composition, it is not even *probable*. Probability is based on observed states of existent things. A statement of probability has this form: since these existents occurred in a certain way in observed cases, it is likely that they occur in that way in unobserved cases. In considering the possible compositions of the world, we are not concerned with existent and observed cases, but with the intrinsic nature of the possible compositions that could make their existing probable or improbable. Now it is precisely because we are not concerned with existent and observed cases that these compositions *cannot* reveal any probability of existing. For probability cannot be established in relation to a possible composition's nature but only in relation to existent and observed cases. For example, if a composition has existed and does exist, certain observations of it may show that it is likely to *continue* to exist, but if we abstract from the observed existence of the composition and consider only its nature, there can be nothing to show that it is likely to exist. The nature of the composition reveals no more than the possibility of its existence, and in this respect the actual composition evinces a warrant to exist equal to the warrant to exist evinced by each of the unactual compositions.

But there is evidence to show that any composition is *unlikely* to exist, although this evidence cannot be found within the nature of the composition in question. It is found by comparing the composition in question to each other possible composition. Besides any given composition, there is an infinity of other possible compositions. Since only one of these can be actual,[63] the odds against any one of them being actual are infinite.

Considerations of a *cause* of a world-composition are no more applicable than are considerations of the necessity or probability of a composition. No possible world-composition can be caused to be actual. A cause can at best cause all parts of the world other than itself to exist; it cannot cause itself to exist[64] and so cannot cause the entire composition to which it belongs to exist. Thus, if any world-composition is actual, it is actual without being caused to be so.

Observe further that it is not at all necessary that there exist a world partly or wholly composed of causes. There might have existed a world composed solely of empty spaces or universals. That there *does* exist a world composed of causes is not due in any way to the causal activity of the causes that belong to this world; rather, it is due to *nothing at all*. No possible world-composition can make itself actual (for there can be no self-causes), and no possible world-composition can be made actual by anything lying outside of itself (for everything that exists either belongs to this composition or is the whole that is wholly identical with this composition). It is sheer chance that a possible world-composition containing causes, rather than some world-composition not containing causes, is the actual composition. This composition exists nonnecessarily, improbably, and causelessly. It exists *for absolutely no reason at all*. It is *inexplicably* and *stunningly actual*.

The full import of the stupefying character of the world can be grasped if we compare stupefaction with marvelling. Stupefaction bears some relation to marvelling, but is more extreme. Global marvelling is at *a* world existing rather than not existing, even though the nonexisting of a world is no less of a possibility than the existing of a world. Global marvelling compares the actual situation, the *existing* of a world, to *one* other possible situation, the *nonexisting* of a world. Stupefaction, on the other hand, is not about the existing of a world, but about its *composition*, and it compares the actual situation, the world as apparentially composed, not with one but with an infinity of other possible situations, the infinity of nonapparent compositions the world could have had. The odds against *a* world existing are not infinite, but one to one (existing vs. nonexisting), whereas the odds against *this* world existing rather than some other nonapparent world are infinite.

The full realization of this stunning importance of the world-whole breaks apart any attempt to *envision* this importance. The stupefied captivation *is* this very explosion of the envisioning. There is an infinitude of infinite counterfactual nonapparent world-compositions, and it is *infinitely infinitely unlikely* the world would have this one rather than any one of the nonapparent ones. And yet it *does* have this apparent composition! And it has this one rather than one of the other ones *for no reason at all*! The impact of this captivated realization upon me is overwhelming. I am completely stunned. I take a few dazed steps in the dark meadow, and fall among the flowers. I lie stupefied, whirling without comprehension in this world through numberless worlds other than this one.

VI. 39.iii. Humility Before the World-Whole's Loftiness

Humility differs from the affect of embarrassed humiliation; the latter affect has a sensation-flow of suddenly and sharply plummeting downwards, an unwelcome experience that disposes me unfavorably towards the source of the humiliation. Humility, on the other hand, is a gentle and welcomed feeling of lowering myself beneath a reality I intuitively feel to be absolutely above me. Humiliation is painful, but humility has a pleasurable quality. I want and deserve to put myself beneath this highest reality; I want to be in its intuitive presence, and the proper way to be in its presence is through humbly flowing down beneath it.

Humility is somewhat similar in its feeling-flow to reverence, but there are noticeable differences. The revering feeling-sensation flows downwards and backwards in a deferential and respectful manner, and the reverential tonality flows upwards in an august manner. The humble feeling-sensation does not flow backwards but only *downwards*, in an *abasing* manner. It is a more self-lowering feeling than reverence. The feeling-tonality of humility that flows from the Highest has a reverse direction and manner; it flows *upwards* in an *exalted* manner. This is similar to an extent to the reverential tonal-flow, except that the humble tonal-flow is such that it *deflects* me from the exalted presence; I feel as if I am unable to "look up" at the higher reality, as I do in reverence, but am instead impelled to "look down" and experience the unworthiness of my self in face of the Highest. The exalted flow flows too far above me — it flows absolutely above me, at an unreachable height — to allow me to "gaze upon" the exalted source. I can only feel its height indirectly by experiencing the extent of my own lowliness. In reverence I directly gaze up at It, but in humility I gaze down at myself and see Its height reflected in my comparative lowness.

The source of the exalted tonal-flow is the global importance of *loftiness*. This importance includes my *subordination* to the world-whole and the superordinate whole's feature of being the *greatest whole* that is *happening*. These items completely constitute the supremacy of the world-whole but incompletely constitute its loftiness. The latter importance possesses the additional feature of the greatest superordinate whole that happens being *absolutely more important than myself*. This feature attaches specifically to one of the items of supremacy: the item of holistic greatness. I humbly feel that I am absolutely surpassed in importance by the greatest whole; the world-whole is not only more important than myself, but is unrestrictedly so. Moreover, it is felt that if I exist it is not accidental, but necessary, that the world-whole is absolutely more important than myself.

The phrase "more important" can have several different senses, but only one of these corresponds to the "absolutely more important" that is felt in the humble affect. Five senses (which do not exhaust all possible senses) of this phrase can be specified, but only the last pertains to global humility:

1. "More important" can mean *ought to be preferred to*; used in this way, the phrase refers to only some of the features that are "important" in the sense proper to the metaphysics of feeling: the ethical features that are some of the ways in which some phenomena can be sources of feeling-flows. This ethical sense of "more important" is inapplicable to the humbly felt world-whole, for rankings of phenomena according to ethical values have no necessity but are relative to this or that (ultimately arbitrary) cultural or individual moral perspective. The world-whole may be regarded as the most valuable ethical phenomenon, but it just as well— with equal arbitrariness—may not be. The intrinsic features of the world-whole are ways in which it *is*, and these and all other features that *are* do not entail either that they ought to be or that they ought not to be.

2. "More important" may mean *more indispensable*. The heart is more important to the functioning of the body than are the fingers, in that the body's functioning is less impaired by the loss of the fingers than by the loss of the heart. Relational features of being more or less dispensable to something are only some of the features that can be sources of feeling-flows. The world-whole has a relational feature of being indispensable to me, for I could not exist without it; but it is not more indispensable to me than anything else is, for I also could not exist without certain world-parts, e.g., the spatial whole, and if two items are such that I could not exist without either of them, then they are equally indispensable to me.

3. "More important" can mean *a source of more intense feeling-flows*. This is not the relevant sense, for although it may be the case that I feel more intense feelings about the world-whole than about anything else, it also may not be the case.

4. "More important" can mean is *a source of more affective responses*. This sense also is inapplicable, for although the world-whole may engender more affects in me than any world-part, it need not do so.

5. "More important" in the sense relevant to global humility means *wholly identical with more evocatively and exactly describable possible sources of feeling-flows*. The world-whole is humbly felt to be *absolutely* more important than myself in that it is wholly identical with more possible flow-sources than is anything else that is wholly identical with more

possible flow-sources than I am. Some other world-parts, like the human race, are relatively more important than myself; the human race is wholly identical with more importances than I am, but the world-whole is absolutely more important than myself in that it is wholly identical with more importances than is the human race or any other whole that is more important than I am. If I exist, it is necessary that the world-whole be absolutely more important than myself in this sense, for the world-whole is the greatest whole of importances and hence cannot be surpassed in the amount of importances with which it is wholly identical.

The absolutely more important importance is superordinate to me. This does not mean that the world-whole's being absolutely more important than myself is superordinate to me (for this relational feature cannot exist without the relation to myself upon which it is based), but that *that which* is absolutely more important than myself is superordinate to me. The *world-whole* that is lofty in relation to myself (and each other appeared-to world-part) can exist without being related to myself (or any other appeared-to part), but I (and each other appeared-to part) cannot exist without being related to it.

That the relational feature of loftiness cannot exist without myself (or some other appeared-to part) is compatible with the humbly felt necessity of this feature, for this necessity is felt to be conditional; only if I (or some other appeared-to part) exist must the world-whole possess this feature.

VI. 39.iv. Apathy Before the Stultifying World-Whole

Apathy, like humility, involves a sense of my insignificance in face of the supreme whole. But the insignificance felt in apathy is of a different kind than that provocative of humility; I feel insignificant in being stymied and stultified by the supreme whole.

The stultifying whole is the source of an apathetic tonal-flow that is basically inert and directionless, but which has a slight downward tendency. It is directionless in a *stagnating* manner and has a downward tendency in a manner of *hanging down lifelessly from everything*. The apathetic sensational-flow likewise stagnates in me, hanging down from my ego lifelessly.

In global apathy I feel mired in a thick global heaviness that penetrates and fills me and weighs me down. I do not sink, plummet, or flow downwards in an abasing manner, but remain as if paralyzed.

The gray languorous skies lie low and heavy upon the earth; nothing moves, lassitude overtakes everything. The whole composed of myself, these gray skies over the earth, and everything else, is revealing itself purely as a stultifying whole. The world-whole stultifies me in that it destroys my incentive to act or move by rendering in advance all my possible global behaviors intrinsically inefficacious. The world-whole stymies my possible behaviors by being utterly indifferent to me. This indifference is something else than the uncaring character of the world-whole that purely evokes desolation. To not care for me is to not appreciate and love me; to be indifferent to me means here that I am not needed by the world-whole. I am not necessary but accidental to the whole; I am a gratuitous lump on the blank surface of the globe.

To be indifferent to me means that I make no difference to the existing and necessary features of the world-whole; the world-whole can exist and be one, the greatest whole, composed of parts, etc., regardless of whether I happen to exist and participate in this whole. My appreciations of the whole are not needed; whether I experience global intuitive feelings and explicate them in afterglowing and concentrative reappreciations, and thereby develop a global philosophy or art, is a matter of indifference to the world-whole. It need not be appreciated immediately or mediately by any of its parts.

If I am not needed, if nothing I can do or feel makes a difference, why bother to act or appreciate? Why strive to explicate the world-whole in concentrative reappreciations? Why open myself affectively and intuitively to the world-whole? I collapse into apathetic sluggishness, inertly captivated by the great stultifying morass of being.

If I and other appreciative parts were necessary to the world-whole, if the Greatest Importance needed us in order to *be* the Greatest Importance, then my apathy would vanish and I would be stirred to vigorous life by the powerful incentive of my global responsibility. I would be responsible for the existing of the Most Important Importance, and would thereby have an impelling motive to open myself intuitively to the whole and to strive to explicate it in concentrative reappreciations. But instead I am completely dispensable; whatever effects I could bring about are *absolutely ineffective* in terms of the intrinsic nature and existing of the Most Important Importance. It *is*, and *is what it necessarily is*, irrespective of what I do or whether I live or die. The world-whole renders intrinsically inefficacious any possible state of change I could undergo, be this state psychical or physical.

If the world-whole is worthy of apathy, then it is also worthy of reverence, and if it is worthy of reverence, then it is also worthy of apathy. For if I were indispensable to the world-whole, it would be dependent upon me and hence not worthy of reverence. It is worthy of reverence only if it is independent of me, and this independency brings with itself the additional feature of *rendering intrinsically inefficacious my possible global behaviors*. This feature, which attaches to the world-whole's independency, does not captivate me in reverence but is captivatingly apparent in apathy. This feature and the four items that comprise supremacy completely constitute the importance of stultification.

The global affect of apathy is parallel in type to the mood of *indifference*, which I earlier described by saying that "in global indifference, I feel indifferent to the world as a whole in that it does not have the kind of importance that 'makes a difference' to me."[65] The determinate nature of this lacked importance that "makes a difference" to me is not disclosed in the mood of indifference; but in the global affect of apathy, it is revealed as the supreme whole's lacked feature of rendering intrinsically efficacious my possible global behaviors. This important feature "makes a difference" to me in the sense that it is felt to be the condition of my engaging in global actions. I shall move myself to global actions *only if* my actions intrinsically affect the world-whole.

This makes it implicitly clear that three senses of "indifference" are involved in the complete apathetic experience. First, the world-whole is "indifferent" to me in the sense that I am accidental to it. The consequence of this is that the world-whole is "indifferent" in a second sense: it lacks the feature that "makes a difference" to me, the feature of rendering intrinsically efficacious my possible global behaviors. The consequence of this second sense of "indifference" is the third sense of "indifference"; I *feel* indifferent (apathetic) towards the world-whole because it lacks the feature that "makes a difference" to me.

The apathetic feeling is somewhat similar to global tedium, which I made explicit in IV.27.v. But there are significant differences. In tedium, the world-whole *dulls* me; by virtue of its monotonousness its makes me flow slowly *backwards* in a dulled manner. In apathy, I do not flow backwards from the whole but am wholly paralyzed by it, rendered stagnant and inert. I am weighed down by a great stagnating flow. Moreover, there is nothing about the world-whole that dulls or "bores" me in apathy; I am not in apathy because of the monotonousness of the world-whole's processless enduring but because of the bearing the world-whole has upon my global life—its stultification of this life. Tedium is unreflexively captivated by the pure blank enduring of the world-whole; this monotonousness is an intrinsic feature of the world-whole and not a relational feature it acquires through being related to myself.[66] In apathy, on the other hand, I am semireflexively captivated by the world-whole's stultification of myself; this stultification is a relational feature the world-whole acquires through being related to myself and my possible global behaviors. In tedium, I am unconcerned about my life and completely absorbed in the wearying, mesmerizing global blankness; but I am in apathy precisely because my life is stultified by the whole.

Is there any escape from this apathy? Is the *intrinsic* efficaciousness of my possible global behaviors the *only* condition of my engaging in global behaviors? Is there another global condition that also "makes a difference" to me and *does* belong to the world-whole? If so, this condition would

306 Part Two: The Basic Felt Meanings of the World

belong to a more complex importance than stultification and would be appreciated in an affect that discerns *more* of the world-whole's features than does apathy. The explication of this condition shall be presented in the Conclusion of this treatise, in the discussion of the *global summons* and the *extrinsic* efficaciousness of my possible global behaviors.

VI. 39.v. Dread of the World-Whole's Ominousness

Dread is the affect parallel to the mood of anxiety. The feeling-sensation of dread has a suspended flow; I am quavering helplessly over a bottomlessness in my ego. It is imminently possible that I shall plunge down this abyss and become extinguished as a self. The dreadful feeling-tonality imbues everything about me; everything about me is suspended quivering over a dark world-gulf, as if a terrible global bottomlessness has suddenly opened up.

The source of this tonal-flow is the *ominousness* of the world-whole. The global importance of ominousness involves a distributive compositional feature of the world, this being a feature that the world has by virtue of being related to each of its parts through the relation of composition. The specific distributive feature that is an aspect of ominousness is based on the fact that each part of the world has the feature of being *precarious*. The world-whole is distributively composed of precarious parts. Each part is precarious in that it could behave in the future in a way that is improbable but nevertheless possible. In the past, certain regular ways of behaving have been noted; trees and buildings remain standing unless destroyed by superior natural forces or man-made machines; the moon continues to revolve about the earth; people are usually civil and are not murderous in their conduct; the ground does not cave in beneath my feet, etc. But all this could change at any moment. Trees and buildings could begin toppling all about me, the moon could plummet towards the earth, people could madly attack me and each other, and the ground could cave in beneath my feet.

This pertains to thoughts and images as well; they could suddenly flash in unorganized ways through my mind, or some thought could suddenly become fixed in my mind, so that I could not help but think it.

The world-parts far distant from me or wholly unknown by me could also behave in strange new ways; they could suddenly exert new and even deadly effects on myself and my surroundings.

There are several different ways in which each world-part could behave improbably, and some of the ways in which some world-parts could behave improbably are harmful to or destructive of me. A sense of imminent danger belongs to the dreadful feeling of the precariousness of the world's composition. To dread the unknown future of the world is to dread that *each part of the world could behave in improbable ways, with some*

*of the improbable ways of behaving of some of the parts being harmful
to or destructive of me.*

The distributive compositional feature of being composed of each
precarious part of the world is one of the aspects of the importance of ominousness. The other aspect is the importance of supremacy. Ominousness
is a complex importance that includes both supremacy and the distributive
compositional feature; supremacy and this compositional feature are interrelated in that the compositional feature is a feature of that which has
the importance of supremacy, the world-whole. I dread the supreme world-
whole because it is distributively composed of precarious parts.

These reflections can be developed if we note in particular that a
feeling of the world-whole's superordination to me is essential to dread.
I would not be in dread unless I were wholly dependent upon the world-
whole and hence could be affected or even destroyed by the improbable
changes that might take place in it. If I were independent of the world-
whole, I could remain unharmed by any improbable change that took place
in it, no matter how severe the change. But instead I am psycho-physically
at the mercy of the world-whole.

Equally essential to my dreadful feeling is the sense that the greatest
whole that happens is *independent* of me. Because the world-whole could
happen without me, it could destroy me with impunity. I am accidental
to the world-whole, and whether or not I am destroyed by any improbable
change that might take place in the world-whole is a matter to which the
world-whole is indifferent. Because of this, the range of improbable changes
that could take place in the whole is not restricted to those which are
harmless to me. I could just as well be annihilated as left unaffected by
an improbable change.

Through being accidental to the world-whole, I could also destroy
myself and leave the world-whole intrinsically unaffected. It is improbable
but possible that an irresistable urge to commit suicide could suddenly
arise in me; I could suddenly and without warning be compelled to leap
out of a window or to asphyxiate myself.

There is no shelter or haven of safety in which I could find protec-
tion from the global peril. There is no place I can go and nothing I can
do. I am completely exposed; I stand naked and defenseless before the
imponderable might of the globe. This exposure to the strange and perilous
unknown is the very condition of my participation in the world-whole.

Surrounded on all sides by the ominous and filled from within by
the ominous, I am suspended helplessly in dark dread.

VI. 39.vi. Quietude in the Stillness of the World-Whole

The global affect of quietude has a feeling-sensation that flows slowly
and softly inwards; it flows backwards into my ego, towards a still and
quiet region deep inside myself. The feeling-tonality that imbues each

thing also flows inwardly; each thing is felt to flow away from me and other things and towards a still and quiet region deep inside itself. I and each other thing flow toward a silence that is interior to each of us. I and each other part of the world partake of a Perfect Stillness. The one whole of which we all partake persists in unblemished self-sameness throughout the variations that we ourselves undergo. This global self-sameness can be discerned if we isolate it from the two principle respects in which the world-whole undergoes changes.

The features of the world-whole are either compositional or noncompositional. Due to the various alterations that take place in the things that compose the world—alterations in place, size, quality, rate of motion, existence and nonexistence—the world's compositional features themselves alter. At one moment, the world-whole is composed of certain things in certain states, and at a later moment it is composed of things and states some of which are different than those that composed the world-whole at the earlier moment. Although the world-whole always has compositional features, it does not have identically the same compositional features from one moment to the next. *Being composed of a, b, and c* is a different compositional feature than *being composed of a, b, and d*, although both features *resemble* one another in that they are both compositional features.

Many of the world-whole's noncompositional features are also changing. At each moment, a different *happening* inheres in the world-whole, and the world-whole at different moments has different features of *being apparent* to different parts of itself.

If the world-whole is variable in respect of these compositional and noncompositional features, in what respect is it invariably self-same? The steady self-sameness of the world-whole can be discerned through focusing, not upon any compositional or noncompositional feature that inheres in the world-whole, but upon *that in which* these compositional and noncompositional features inhere. The old global features cease to inhere in *that which* the new global features begin to inhere in. This "that which" persists as the self-same "inhered in"of the successively arising and vanishing global features. If the expression "the world" is used to designate that in which the global features inhere, then it can be said that *the world* remains unchangingly *the world* throughout all the alterations in the features that inhere in *the world*.

That in which the global features inhere is also that in which the world-parts participate. That to which each world-part is related through the relation of participation is *the world*, i.e., that in which the compositional and noncompositional global features inhere. Each world-part participates in *that which* is the greatest whole that happens, that which is one whole, that which is immediately apparent in global intuitions, and that which has all the other global features.

It can be said, then, that the world *is* the world throughout all the changes in the features and parts of the world. The "is" in the phrase "the world *is* the world" expresses "being" in the sense of *identity*.[67] The world is (identically) the world through all the differences in its features and parts.

The globally *inhered* and *participated in* persists in self-sameness. The Unchanging One is omnipresent, encompassing every innerworldly change that occurs. It is the unvarying backdrop of all variations, the changeless condition of all changes. Transcending and yet permeating the hustle and bustle of the parts of the world, there is a great untouchable Stillness, the stillness of the world itself.

A constitutive aspect of the importance of stillness is the importance of supremacy. The global stillness is comprised of the enduring self-identity of that which is the greatest whole that happens. And that which endures in self-sameness is superordinate to me. Its unchanging self-identity implies that it is independent of the coming-to-be and ceasing-to-be of its appeared-to-parts; *the world* remains identically *the world* regardless of whether I live or die. And through my dependency upon the unchanging, the unchanging is always and necessarily there for me, always available for me to turn towards and quietly repose in. An ingredient of my affective quietude is the certainty that no matter what, the Stillness will be there as a resting place, a spiritual home, for my intuitive gaze.

CONCLUSION

Implications of the
Metaphysics of Feeling

Concl. 40. The Foundational Order of Global Importances

In Part 2, I have described global importances on four levels of complexity, ranging from the simplest (fulfillment-of-happening) to the most complex (the five importances described in the last section). The completion of my descriptions raises certain questions.

One set of questions concerns the exhaustiveness of my explications. Have all the importances on these four levels been described? And are there higher levels of importances besides the four discussed? (See Concl. 40.i.)

Another set of questions concerns the relation of the importances on these levels to the affects they originate. Can each important feature originate only one pure affective response? And can each type of affective response be purely related to only one important feature? (See Concl.40.ii.)

A third set of questions concerns the possibility of other foundational orders besides the one described in Part 2. Are there other foundational orders? If so, how are they related to the one I have explicated? (See Concl.40.iii.)

Concl. 40.i. Global Importances and Levels of Global Importance Other than the Ones Explicated in Part 2

In Chapters 4 through 6, I explicated eighteen global importances, fulfillment and five importances directly based upon it, closeness and five importances directly based upon it, and supremacy and five importances directly founded upon it. These importances are not the only ones; there are other noncompositional importances and other collective, distributive, and partial compositional importances. I will illustrate these other importances in terms of partial compositional importances, none of which were among the eighteen importances described in Chapters 4 through 6.

A partial compositional importance is a relational feature the world-whole has by virtue of being composed of some part of itself. Some partial compositional importances concern beauty, ugliness, justice, and injustice.

310

The world-whole is partly composed of beautiful things (a feature purely appreciated in global enchantment), and the world-whole is partly composed of ugly things (the pure appreciation of which is global repugnance or nausea). And the world-whole is partly composed of unjust events (a feature purely appreciated in global indignation), and of just events (global approbation being the pure appreciation of this feature). Nor are these the only partial compositional features. In fact, the world-whole has one such feature for each importance that is a part of itself. This implies there is a plethora of important global features that have not been described in this treatise.

Do all these important features that have not been described belong to one of the four levels of global importances that have been described? The four levels are:

1. Fulfillment
2. Closeness, Miraculousness, Emptiness, Immensity, Monotonousness, Harmoniousness, etc.
3. Supremacy, Glorification, Imminent Loss, Mysteriousness, Uncaring, Equilibrium, etc.
4. Stunning, Lofty, Stultifying, Ominous, Still, etc.

It is certain that there are more than four levels, but the issue of exactly how many more levels there are requires for its resolution more extensive investigation than can be achieved within the limits of this subsection. I can, however, briefly show that there is at least a fifth level of global importances. This is demonstrated by presenting in outline form a description of a global importance directly based on one of the importances on the fourth level.

The importance of the *global summons* is directly based upon global loftiness, the important feature purely appreciated in humility. The importance of *summoning* includes the lofty importance and an additional feature of the world-whole. The supreme world-whole that is absolutely more important than myself has the further feature of unconditionally demanding my present and future appreciations. The world-whole as summoning me purely evokes an affect of *devotion*, which flows forwards and upwards towards the whole that summons me. I feel called to devote myself throughout my existence, to the extent of my capacity, to the immediate and mediate appreciation of the world-whole. This demand is unconditional; it takes precedence over any mundane demand upon my appreciations. Through feeling that the world-whole is more important than any part of itself, I feel this whole to be more worthy of appreciation than any part of itself; and through feeling the world-whole to be absolutely more important than myself, I feel this whole's demand upon me to outweigh any contrary or selfish desire I may have. It is true that I cannot live without engaging in mundane appreciations, but I feel enjoined from allowing these appreciations to take precedence in my feeling-life over my intuitive, afterglowing and concentrative appreciations of the world-whole.

Certainly much more could and needs to be said about this summoning importance,[1] but the above explication is sufficient to illustrate briefly the fact that there are global importances on higher levels than the four described in Chapters 4 through 6.

Concl. 40.ii. The Relation between Global Importances and Their Pure Appreciations

One of my aims in Part 2 was to show that features of the world-whole and global affects are not arbitrarily related, but that each feature of the world-whole is appropriately responded to in one type of affect and not in others. I demonstrated this by distinguishing between pure and impure appreciations, between these appreciations and incomplete ones,[2] and by applying these distinctions to the eighteen global affects and importances discussed in Part 2. I will not repeat these distinctions here, but shall add a few remarks about some of the general principles involved.

Each type of affective response is a pure appreciation of something truly evocatively describable in one way and not in others. That of which awe is the pure appreciation is truly evocatively describable as immense and stupendous, but falsely describable as monotonous, futile, or uncaring.

Each such evocative description is truly applicable to some exactly describable phenomena and not to others. The evocative term "immense" is truly applicable to the world-whole's feature of being the greatest whole that exists, and to some mundane phenomena, such as an infinite number series or the distance of the earth to the moon as compared with the distances between places on earth. But "immense" does not evoke such exactly describable realities as the world-whole's feature of happening purposelessly or appearing immediately rather than mediately, or such mundane phenomena as a house of a certain size compared to another house of the same size, or such events as a man stubbing his toe.

These two principles constitute the basis of the connection between global affects and global importances. Each global afffect is a response to something evocatively describable in one way and not in others, and each evocative description is applicable to some exactly describable global features and not to others. If these two principles did not obtain, then any evocative description could be arbitrarily connected to any affect and to any exactly describable global feature. Such descriptions as the following one would be no more or less plausible than the ones presented in the preceding sections:

"The world-whole is immense! It is immense in that it happens processlessly. And that is why I am outraged at it!"

Compare this description with the following one:

"*The world-whole is immense! It is immense in that it is the greatest whole that happens. And that is why I am in awe of it!*"

The fact that the second description rings true, and the first seems false or even incoherent, illustrates the nonarbitrary character of the connection between affects, evocative explications, and exact explications.

In the above elucidation of the correlation between certain evocative and exact global descriptions, I said that "each evocative description is applicable to some exactly describable global features and not to others." This implies that more than one exactly describable global feature can be suggested by the same evocative description, and hence that the same type of global affect can be a pure appreciation of more than one exactly describable global feature. This is true because a global affect is a pure appreciation of something that can be evocatively described in a certain way (e.g., as "immense") and not in others; and if more than one exact global feature can be evocatively described in the way in question (as "immense"), then the global affect can be a pure appreciation of more than one exact global feature. Since this implication was not discussed in the preceding sections of Part 2, it is worthwhile to develop it here.

In Chapter 4 global joy was described as a pure appreciation of a global feature evocatively articulable as a "fulfillment-of-happening" and more exactly articulable as a "complex happening composed of briefer happenings, happenings-no-longer, and happenings-not-yet." The fullness-of-happening I explicated is a noncompositional feature of the world. But the world also has compositional features analogous to this noncompositional feature. It is not only true that *the world-whole happens*, it is also true that the world-whole is collectively composed of parts *all of which are happening*, distributively composed of parts *each of which is happening*, and partially composed of *this or that part which is happening*. Each of these different features correlates to one of the different but mutually consistent ways of exactly explicating the world-whole's evocatively describable fullness-of-happening. In chapter 4, I exactly explicated it in terms of a noncompositional feature of the world; the evocative phrase "the world is full-of-happening" was analyzed in terms of a feature of fullness-of-happening inhering in the world-whole itself. "The world is full-of-happening" can also be analyzed as meaning that the world is composed of parts all of which are full-of-happening (or each of which is full-of-happening, or some which are full-of-happening).

Correlating to each of the different noncompositional and compositional features this same evocative description can suggest, there is a distinct joyous pure appreciation. Each of the different compositional and noncompositional modalities of rejoicing-in-the-global-fullness-of-happening has the same feeling-flow (upwardly radiated), but a somewhat different feeling-awareness (a feeling-awareness of the world-whole as full-of-happening, or a feeling-awareness of the world-whole being collectively composed of parts which are full-of-happening, and so on).

This analogy among the noncompositional and compositional features suggested by the description "the world is full-of-happening" does not pertain to each of the global importances. "The world is harmoniously one" suggests the noncompositional feature of being *one, a single individual*, but there is no corresponding collective compositional feature it could suggest (for it is not the case that the world is collectively composed of parts all of which are one—rather, all the parts of the world are *many*).[3]

The different compositional and noncompositional ways of precisely explicating such suggestive descriptions as the "the world is full-of-happening" are based on analyses of the "is," the copula that refers to the inherence of a feature in the world-whole. For example, "The world *is* full-of-happening" can be precisely analyzed as meaning that a certain collective compositional feature inheres in the world, such that this phrase is understood to mean "The world *is-collectively-composed-of-parts-which-are* full-of-happening." Or the "is" can be taken as referring to a noncompositional feature: "The world *is-itself* full-of-happening."

Besides these divergent ways of precisely explicating the "is," there are various ways of exactly explicating the global predicates, such as "fulfilled," "empty," or "harmonious." In Chapter 4, I explicated "fulfillment" more precisely as a "fulfillment-of-happening" and, more precisely still, as a "complex happening composed of briefer and briefer happenings, happenings-no-longer and happenings-not-yet." However, "fulfillment" can be made exact in other ways as well. Most, if not all, of these ways concern partial compositional features of the world. Different parts of the world on different occasions can be joyously felt as "fulfillments." The victory of the best political party, the recovery of the full bloom of health after a long illness, the return of a beloved, and the attainment of success are all events that can be appropriately evocatively described as joyously feelable "fulfillments." For instance, the return of my beloved "fills up the void of my life" that had been created by her absence and gives me a feeling that my life is once again complete, a plenitude, and no longer empty of her loving presence. The world-whole, through being composed of one of these parts, has the partial compositional feature of being composed of that fulfilled part. If the "is" in "the world is fulfilled" is explicated as referring to the inherence of a partial compositional feature in the world, and the "fulfilled" is explicated as the return of my beloved, then "the world is fulfilled" can be made explicit as *the world's being partially composed of the return of my beloved*.

In the appropriate sense of "global joy," it can be said that each of these partial compositional features of fulfillment, as well as each of the noncompositional and compositional features of fulfillment-of-happening, is purely appreciated in the same type of global affect, viz., *global joy*. "Global joy" signifies in this context an affect with an upwardly radiated feeling-flow and a captivated feeling-awareness of the world-whole as possessing a feature of fulfillment. The distinction among different global joys arises when we take into account the different exactly determinate fulfillments the world-whole possesses.

The multifariousness of the ways of exactly explicating the "fulfillment" of the world extends to each of the other global importances as well. This multifariousness consists almost exclusively in the range of partial compositional features the world possesses. Nevertheless, it is not impossible that some noncompositional features and some collective and distributive compositional features, features other than the ones I have discussed, can be evoked by the terms "fulfillment," "emptiness," "harmoniousness," etc.

The recognition that an evocative term used in one evocative sense can suggest more than one exactly describable global feature must not be confused with the idea that an evocative term can be used in different senses and can in this way also suggest different exactly determinable global features. The term "emptiness" used as an evocative description of what is intuitively felt in despair has a different evocative sense than this same term used to suggest what is intuitively felt in tedium. As suggestive of a despairingly felt world, "empty" belongs with such evocative terms as "futile" and "pointless"; as associated with tedium, it is connected with terms like "monotonousness" and "dullness."

Now the thesis I expounded above that the same evocative description can suggest different exactly describable global features does not claim that the same evocative words can be used in different evocative senses, but that the evocative words used in the same sense can evoke different exactly describable global features. It means, for example, that "emptiness" in the evocative sense associated with despair can suggest the world-whole's happening purposelessly as well as other exactly describable global features, e. g., the world-whole being partially composed of a human race whose spiritual achievements will be annulled consequent upon this race's eventual extinction. This eventual annullment does not comprise a "global emptiness" in the sense of a monotonousness and dullness but in the sense of a futility and pointlessness.

This univocity of the evocative terms used in the preceding sections of Part 2 must be kept in mind if the correspondences among the affects and the evocative and exact descriptions I presented are to be correctly understood. It would be a mistake to object to my claim that despair is the pure appreciation of the global emptiness by pointing out that tedium also is a pure feeling of the global emptiness, for they are appreciations of "emptiness" in different senses.

Even if this univocity of the evocative terms is kept in mind, it still may be difficult to determine in some cases the appropriate connection among the affects and the evocative and exact descriptions. Two or more affects may be somewhat similar to each other, and the importances of which they are the pure appreciations may also be somewhat resemblant. In such a case, the evocative descriptions of each importance will not obviously differ from one another and could seem to be wholly or in part interchangeable. This is true for the affects of awe, reverence, and humility, as well as their corresponding importances: immensity, supremacy, and loftiness. At first glance, it seems no less plausible to say (for example) that awe is the pure appreciation of global supremacy or loftiness than to say that it is the pure appreciation of global immensity. Similarities also hold between the affects of peacefulness and equanimity, tedium and apathy, marvelling and stupefaction, as well as among despair, sadness, and desolation. However, these affects and their corresponding importances are not *perfectly* similar; although the affects' qualitative-flows may be largely alike, and the evocative descriptions of the importances may be somewhat resemblant, there are detectable nuances among them, however subtle these nuances be. That there are such differences is a fact I have endeavored to establish in my explications of the above-named affects and importances in the preceding sections.

The clarification of the relation between pure affective appreciations and global importances undertaken in this subsection points to a third respect in which my explications in Part 2 are incomplete, in addition to the two respects noted in the last subsection. It is not merely the case that higher levels of importances and importances of different evocative articulations (like global beauty and ugliness) were not described, but also that exactly determinate importances of the same evocative articulations as those I did explicate were not described.

I also endeavored to show in this subsection what will become more apparent in the next subsection, that my explications although incomplete are not of arbitrarily selected connections between importances and affects.

Concl. 40.iii. Foundational Orders Other than the One Explicated in Part Two

The foundational order made explicit in Part 2 has fulfillment-of-happening at its lowest level and the stunning, lofty, stultifying, ominous, and still importances of the world at its uppermost level. Is this order the only possible order of global importances?

There can only be the first two levels I described, but there are also other levels parallel to and compatible with the third and fourth levels. It has already been shown how and why every other importance but fulfillment-of-happening includes fulfillment-of-happening within itself as a constitutive aspect,[5] so I shall concentrate on elucidating the singularity of the second level and the multiplicity of the third and fourth levels.

There can only be one second level of global importances because there is only one importance on the first level, fulfillment-of-happening. An importance belongs on the second level if it includes fulfillment-of-happening within itself, as well as a feature of fulfillment-of-happening or a feature of the world-whole that is full-of-happening. I articulated six such importances (closeness, miraculousness, emptiness, immensity, monotonousness, and harmoniousness). Any other importance that includes fulfillment-of-happening and an additional feature also belongs on this second level, not on some *different* but *parallel* second level of importance.

What does it mean, then, to constitute a different but parallel level of importance? This can be seen in relation to the third and fourth levels, which do have different but parallel levels. The importances on the third level (supremacy, glorification, imminent loss, mysteriousness, uncaring, equilibrium, etc.) are directly based on *one* of the several importances on the second level, the importance of *closeness*.[6] A different but parallel third level of importances would be comprised of importances directly based on some other second-level importance, for example, the importance of miraculousness or emptiness. These importances would include, say, the importance of miraculousness as well as a feature of miraculousness or a feature of the world-whole that is miraculous. In this way, there is a different third level of importances for each of the importances on the second level. Moreover, if we take into account the importances (like supremacy) based on two or more of the second-level importances, further third levels arise. Similar considerations apply to the fourth and higher levels of importances.

These remarks make it clear why there can only be one second level of importances; since there is only one importance on the first level, fulfillment-of-happening, there is only one importance available for a second level of importances to be based upon.

It should be implicitly apparent from the preceding considerations that the foundational order of importances I have described in Part 2 is valid only insofar as each of the importances is exactly explicated in the way I have explicated it. "Fulfillment" is the fundamental importance only insofar as it is exactly understood as a noncompositional fulfillment-of-happening. "Fulfillment" explicated, for example, as the world's being partially composed of the return of my beloved, is obviously not the most fundamental global importance. The same considerations hold for closeness, supremacy, and the other importances.

The fact that there are other parallel third and fourth levels of importances does not annul or impugn my explications of an order of global importances in Part 2, but shows merely that the order I presented is one of several orders. The explication of any of the orders of global importances must include an exposition of the first and second levels I examined (since there are only one of each of these levels) but need not include the specific third and fourth levels included in my descriptions. It can be said, then, that my descriptions of the first and second levels were necessary, but my descriptions of the third and fourth levels were only exemplifications of some of the third and fourth levels of importances.

A central motive for explicating one of the orders of global importances was expressed in the Introduction. I stated there that one of the tasks of the metaphysics of feeling is to discover "the basic way of being important that underlies every other way."[7] Through describing the world-whole's fulfillment-of-happening and showing that the other levels of importances are based upon fulfillment-of-happening, I aimed to establish that *to be filled with happening* is the ultimate way in which the world-whole is important. Beneath all the global complexities, there lies a simple joyous truth—*that a world is existing*.

Concl. 41. *The Importance of a Metaphysics of Feeling*

The importance of a metaphysics of feeling has a dual aspect, one related to humans and the other to the world-whole. The true significations it aims to develop are important to ourselves as an impetus to and aspect of our spiritual or global salvation, and it is importantly related to the world-whole as a response to its unconditional demand to be mediately as well as immediately appreciated. These two intertwined aspects of the importance of a metaphysics of feeling deserve to be elucidated.

Global salvation must be distinguished from mundane salvation. Mundane salvation is worldly happiness; it is comprised of phenomena like a successful career, a harmonious love relationship and family life, the respect and acceptance of other members of society, and material comfort. Through acquiring such things one is saved from a worldly unhappiness: career failure, loneliness, and physical discomfort.

The need for spiritual salvation emerges consequent upon the experience that mundane salvation is by no means sufficient to quell one's yearning for meaning. Spirituality is the needful quest for a meaning of a *wholly different order* than that exemplified by career success, harmonious family life, and the like. The meaning for which one yearns is not of this or that part of the world-whole, but of *the whole itself.* One yearns to be saved through being inwardly related to a meaning of the whole. The spiritual condition in which this yearning is present but unsatisfied is *nihilism*: the belief that there is no global meaning or no knowable global meaning to which one can be related.

In our present spiritual-historical situation nihilism is the condition that prevails. Our nihilism has the particular form of a belief that there are no knowable reasons that explain why the world exists and has the nature it possesses. Salvation from this nihilism does not lie in knowing the reasons—for there *are* no knowable reasons—but in recognizing that the needful quest for such reasons is a degenerate form of spirituality. It has been the major aim of the metaphysics of feeling to show that this is the case and to explicate in a positive way the nondegenerate form of spirituality, that of *feeling*. Salvation from the prevailing nihilism is achieved through *spiritual regeneration*, through inwardly adopting an *appreciative* rather than *explanative* relation to the world-whole. One is saved from the hopelessly frustrated desire to explain the world in terms of rational meanings by immediately and mediately appreciating the world's felt meanings.

A metaphysics of feeling is important to us in that it makes available an essential ingredient of our salvation—the evocative and exact mediate appreciations of the global importances—and provides an impetus or occasion for the experience of the immediate appreciations, the moody and affective intuitions. A metaphysics of feeling thus is important to us not because it satisfies our "intellectual curiosity" or solves certain "philosophical puzzles" that may bemuse us, but because it is *instrumental to our spiritual salvation*. It differs, however, from religious scripture in that it does not present to us a putative global meaning in which we are to have faith, but a real global meaning that we are to evidentially know.

The motive for being spiritually saved is not, however, *to be saved*, but transcends all considerations of myself and my conditions. This seemingly paradoxical motivation for spiritual salvation is in truth not paradoxical at all, for the experience of being saved is not of doing something *for myself*, of serving myself by satisfying one of my needs, but is an ego-transcending experience of serving something greater than myself, of something before which my ego pales in importance. To be saved is precisely *not* to live for myself or for this or that other part of the world, but to live *for the whole*.

The motive for spiritual salvation is to *carry out the global summons*, the summons to enhance the importance of the whole by endowing it with the important features it can only acquire through being appreciated. The reference to this summons brings us to the second respect in which a metaphysics of feeling is important. Being important to ourselves as an instrument of our salvation is at the same time being important to the whole as a way of increasing its importance. For through being instrumental to our salvation, a metaphysics of feeling is instrumental in providing the world-whole with the important features it can only acquire through being appreciated by spiritually saved world-parts.

The global summons is purely appreciated in global devotion, which has been partly described in the last section. It can be more fully explicated here through tracing the following connections. Something is *worthy of appreciation* if it is "noteworthy" in the sense illustrated in Chapter 2; appreciationworthiness is a feature a thing possesses if it can "demand" to be appreciated, if it is able to attract and hold directed upon itself a feeling-awareness. A feeling-awareness is an awareness of something as an evocatively and exactly describable source of flowing pleasure or pain. Something is *more worthy of appreciation* than something else if it is wholly identical with more possible relational terms of feeling-awarenesses than the other thing, and hence is able to demand more appreciations. The world-whole is more worthy of appreciation than any of its parts in that it is wholly identical with more possible demands for appreciation than is any world-part, and in this sense *is more demanding* of appreciation than any world-part. The world-whole is absolutely more worthy of appreciation than I am in that it is identical with more possible demands for appreciation than is anything else more important than I am. The world-whole is unconditionally demanding of appreciation: no condition could make the world-whole less demanding of appreciation than anything else.

The global summons is *the supremely and absolutely important whole's unconditional demand to be appreciated*. Through being purely captivated by this summons in global devotion, I am inspired to devote my life unreservedly to carrying out the summons.

But this devotional experience is not sufficient to ensure that my life shall be given over to the fulfillment of the global summons. The devoted affect is but one global affect among others, and as such my *being devoted* to the world-whole is but one among many of my affective responses to the whole. In a different affect, this devoted commitment to the whole will not be experienced. How then can my devotion to the summoning world-whole be anything more than temporary, lasting only as long as the devoted affect lasts?

The devotional commitment can be lasting if it can be reinstituted in a freely repeatable experience that is not one global affect (or mood or striving) among others but is a global feeling of a different kind. Such a feeling interconnects and unifies all my global affects, moods, and strivings. It is a feeling of *global resoluteness*.

Global resoluteness is not an anxious disclosure of various situational possibilities, but an iron-hard determination to do one thing, to carry out the global summons intuitively revealed to me in global devotion. Resoluteness is a mediate rather than immediate "appearing of" the global summons: it voluntarily induces the reappearance of the summons that had involuntarily and captivatingly appeared in the devoted affect.[8] Resoluteness brings the summons to reappearance, not in order to make it evocatively and exactly explicit (this is properly achieved in the devotional afterglow and concentrative reappreciation), but to freely reinstill in myself the commitment to carry out the summons that had originally been involuntarily instilled in me by the devotionally captivating world-whole.

The resolute feeling-sensation flows forwards in a powerful, unbendable, and determined manner. Its texture is firm, unyielding, and iron-hard. It is not engendered or "made to flow" forward by the world-whole but is engendered and "made to flow" forward by myself. I induce and sustain in myself an unbreakable and unconditional resolve to carry out the global mission, come what may. No obstacle can deter or weaken my resolve, and no sacrifice is too great. The pure granite strength of my willing is invincible, unshatterable; it is a willing-unto-death, a determination to fulfill the global mission or perish in the attempt.

My spiritual willing is an invisible power I generate that extends outwards to all corners of the globe. My unconditional willing imbues things with a feeling-tonality of being overpowered and rendered incapable of weakening or destroying my resolve. I may be destroyed, but as long as I am alive my *resolute determination to carry out the mission* shall never be destroyed.

The global mission I am determined to carry out unifies all my global affects, moods, and strivings. It establishes them as realizations of the mission to enhance the world-whole's importance by enabling it to have the additional important features that accrue to it from *being appreciated*.

This mission appears in the resolute feeling-awareness to be implicitly articulated into interior and exterior realizations. Interiorly, I resolve to allow my global affects and moody contemplations and their reappreciations to take precedence over my mundane feelings. This involves allowing myself to become more attached to the whole than to any part so as to enable the whole to engender more affective responses in me than any given world-part. I resolve to avoid being completely absorbed in any part of the world, and to remain somewhat interiorly detached from this or that part so as to remain relatively unaffected by these parts and reserve my primary affectively responsive capacity for the captivating appearances of the omnipresent global importances. I do not resolve to attach myself completely to the whole, since it belongs necessarily to my nature as a human world-part to be at least partially mundane and not to be completely spiritual.

The interior commitment also involves determining to realize the potential for global contemplation offered to me in my moods, and to realize the potential for reappreciating the whole in the afterglows of both moods and global affects.

Global feelings that are within my capacity to originate voluntarily at any given time are global strivings. These are the concentrated strivings to make exactly explicit the global importances that have intuitively appeared to me. The concentrative knowledge of these importances is always "on the way," in respect both of its extension and perfection. I am resolved to continue extending and developing the precise global explications and to reexamine and improve the exact explications already developed. In regard to these latter explications, it is possible that some of them which had previously seemed to be true or complete could, upon further analysis or upon acquisition of further evidence, be discovered to be untrue or incomplete and to warrant reformulation or expansion. My unconditional will is not to be overcome by the enormous difficulties and problems inherent in the attempt to make the world precisely appreciated, but to pursue the truth unflaggingly and to the end.

The evocative explications are also subject to extension and improvement; the latter involves making these explications more and more evocative and more and more appropriate to the global importances they are designed to evoke. These explications not only form a part of metaphysics but are of the essence of global art (linguistically articulated evocations constitute global poetry and literature, and visually and auditorily symbolic evocations constitute global painting, sculpture, and music).

By these means I aim to realize interiorly the global mission. My affective and moody appreciations enhance the whole by endowing it with the important features that inhere in it when it is being *immediately appreciated*, and my afterglowing and concentrative reappreciations enhance the whole by providing it with the important features that accrue to it when it is being *mediately appreciated*.

In connection with the evocative and exact explications of the important whole, the *exterior* realization of the mission is resolved upon. This exterior realization concerns the important features that inhere in the whole through being appreciated by spiritual parts other than myself. This is achieved in personal communication (e.g., in global rather than mundanely motivated conversation or teaching) and in metaphysical treatises and art works.

This exterior realization of the mission involves spiritually saving others, but the motive for this realization is not to *save others* (which would be doing something for other world-parts and thus would be mundane) but *to enhance the importance of the world-whole*. The conventional and mundane alternative of doing something *for myself* (selfishness) or *for others* (altruism) is here overcome by doing something *for the whole in which I, other people and everything else participate* (global resoluteness). The capacity to engage in this spiritual mission is not, however, possessed by all appreciative parts of the world and is possessed in different degrees by the parts that do have this capacity.

The central obstacles to this exterior realization of the mission are the *complacent mundanity* of most human life and culture, and the historically entrenched habits and beliefs of *rational spirituality* in the spiritual enclaves of culture that resist being reexamined and questioned. The human race is imperfectly spiritual and hence is largely resistant to the global mission.

Global resoluteness is akin to fanaticism in the unconditionality of the determination with which the mission is resolved upon. The resolute one and the fanatic mirror one another in respect of their pure willing-unto-death. They differ in that the basis of the fanatical willing is a *faith* in the truth of the mission and consequently a *closure* to all evidential criticism and questioning of the basis and validity of the mission. The globally resolute one, by contrast, resolves upon the basis of evidential knowledge. Furthermore, one of the things the resolute person resolves upon is the perpetual reexamination of the basis and intent of the resoluteness itself. Through resolving to pursue the global truth unconditionally, he resolves to change his resolution if need be in order to accord with the truth.

The global mission upon which I am resolved is a magnetizing importance, in fact the unconditionally magnetizing importance. A magnetizing importance is made exactly explicit as a purpose or end. The unconditionally magnetizing importance is thus a global purpose. But how can it be so if the world-whole is empty-of-purpose, as is purely revealed in global despair? The purposelessness revealed in despair pertains to the *existing* of the world-whole; the world-whole exists, and continues to exist at each new moment, for the sake of nothing at all. The purpose constitutive of the global mission, however, is a purpose of the *appreciative parts* of the world. It is not a purpose for which these parts came into existence (they came into existence accidentally and for no purpose), but a purpose they are able to adopt once they do exist. It is a purpose to which the purposelessly existing world-whole unconditionally summons its purposelessly existing appreciative parts to devote themselves to realizing.

This can be elucidated further. The world-whole does not exist and continue to exist *in order to* be appreciated. And the human race did not come into existence *in order to* appreciate the world-whole. But the world-whole is the most important importance and as such is that which is most worthy of being appreciated. If the world-whole accidentally happens to include among its parts appreciative parts, they can recognize this and be motivated to commit themselves to this appreciation as their *adopted* unconditional purpose.

Through this purpose being attained the world-whole is extrinsically affected. It acquires new features through being appreciated by its parts. The acquisition of these features is extrinsical to the world-whole in that these features are accidental; the world-whole could exist without having any of the features that inhere in it through being appreciated.

This is how devotion and resolution are compatible with the apathetic captivation with the world-whole's stultifying character. I am in apathy because I am purely appreciating *intrinsical efficaciousness* as a condition for global action; I feel stultified because nothing I can do makes a difference to the world-whole's existential or necessary importance. Devotion, on the other hand, is a pure appreciation of extrinsical efficaciousness as a condition for action. I feel devotionally inspired because I can do something that makes a difference to the world-whole's nonnecessary importance. Extrinsical efficaciousness is the *only* motivating condition of global action. It is the only global condition that when purely appreciated *summons* me to act.

In global resoluteness, I unify apathy and despair with my other responses to the whole by establishing them as *realizations* of the extrinsical global mission. Apathy and despair realize this global mission in that they are immediate appreciations of the world-whole and as such enhance its extrinsical importance. They enhance the world-whole's importance through rendering purely appreciated its features of being purposeless and intrinsically unsummoning of global action.

Through taking up within himself this extrinsical global mission, the resolute person endeavors to make the world-whole more adequately responded to both by himself and others. He aspires to elevate humans as much as possible from a mundanely to a globally appreciative existence, and to regenerate the spiritual aspect of human culture from its present epochal condition of rationalistic nihilism to a new spiritual-historical epoch based upon appreciative feeling. By this means he aims to render the world-whole spiritually appreciated not merely by himself but by the successive members and generations of human culture as a whole. But if due to the prevailing mundanity and spiritual degenerateness his mission seems to be failing, at first or even later, he will not falter or succumb. He shall never grow deaf to the global summons but shall keep willing unconditionally and to the end.

Notes

Introduction

1. Plato, *Phaedo* 97C.
2. Plato, *Laws* 894E–896C.
3. Plato, *Republic* 504E–511E.
4. Plato, *Timaeus* 30, 32D–33A. An analogous connection is made in *Laws* 903B–D.
5. Aristotle's conception of this teleological order is evinced in brief remarks made in different treatises. Cf. *Metaphysica* 1072A18–1072B29, 1073B25, 107512–24; *Meteorologica*, I, 9; *De Generatione et Corruptione*, II, 10; *Ethica Nicomachea*, X, 7, 8; *De Anima*, II, 4. The statement of the purpose of humans is first made in his Platonic period. Cf. *Protrepticus* 16, 19.
6. There were a few exceptions to this tendency, the most noteworthy being the theory of purpose developed by Moses Maimonides in *The Guide for the Perplexed*. He argued that each thing existed for its own sake, not for the sake of man. Cf. *Moreh Nebuchim*, III, 13.
7. Boethius, *Quomodo substantiae in eo quod sint bonae sint cum non substantialia bona*. The implication of this distinction can be inferred from Augustine's earlier *De doctrina Christiana* XXXII, but Augustine himself did not develop this distinction.
8. Aquinas, *Summa Theologica*, Ia. V. 1.
9. *Ibid*.
10. Leibniz, *De Rerum originatione radicali*. GERH. Vol. VII, p. 302.
11. *Ibid*. p. 305. For the following explanation of Leibniz's theory, see *De Rerum originatione radicali; Principes de la Nature et de la Grace* VII–XVIII; *Discours de Metaphysique* XXXV, XXXVI.
12. The essence/existence distinction is arguably implicit in previous theories, e.g., in Aristotle's *Analytica Posteriora* 92B4–93B27, and in Plotinus's *Enneads*, V, 5 (32), 6, but Avicenna was the first to make it clearly and to recognize its metaphysical significance.
13. Ibn Sina (Avicenna), *Danish Nama-i 'ala i (Ilahiyyat)*, XIX–XXXVII.
14. "The thing in itself is a presupposition without which I cannot enter into Kant's system, but with which I cannot remain there." Jacobi, *Werke* (Leipzig, 1815) II, p. 304. The contradiction is that the categories of the understanding are inapplicable to noumena, and yet the category of causality is applied to noumena.
15. Hegel, *Vorlesungen uber die Geschichte der Philosophie*, Bd. III, in *Sämtliche Werke* (Stuttgart: Fr. Frommanns Verlag, 1959), Neunzehnter Band, pp. 689–90.

16. Schopenhauer was the first philosopher of the epoch of rational meaninglessness; he argued that there is no knowable and unconditioned causal or teleological reason for the will and its phenomenal manifestation. See especially *Die Welt als Wille und Vorstellung*, Vol. II, Ch. L, where Schopenhauer indicates that his "philosophy does not presume to explain the existence of the world from ultimate reasons."

17. Although it falls beyond the purview of this Introduction to analyze the expression of rational-metaphysical beliefs in nonwestern cultures, a few brief remarks can be made. A belief in a causal and telic reason for the world has prevailed in most nonwestern cultures, including Indian, Chinese and African cultures, among many others. In Hinduism, for instance, *Brahman* was conceived as the causal reason for the world (the classical expression of the Hindu version of the metaphysics of rational meaning can be found in Sankara's *Commentary on the Vedanta-Sutras, Atmabodha*, and other writings). In Mahayana Buddhism, *tathatā* (Suchness) or *śūnyatā* (Emptiness) are often conceived as the reason for *samsara* (the world of change). The classical expression of this Buddhist version of the metaphysics of rational meaning is Asvaghosha's *Mahayana-sraddhotpada-sastra*. In China, *Tao* is frequently conceived as the first reason for the world. Thus in the Neotaoist school of *Hsüan-hsüeh* (dark learning), *Tao*, in its aspect as *pen-wu* (original non-being), is conceived to be the cause of *yu* (being), which in its turn is the cause of the world. (See for instance Wang Pi's *Lao Tzu chu* and *I ch'uan*.)

However, a belief in a rational meaning of the world is not confined to cultures with literary traditions. The African Zulus have no theoretical literature, and even no religious scripture of any form, but they nevertheless have worked out a conception of a first reason of the world. The first reason of the world, called by the Zulus *Unkulunkulu*, the "Great-great one," is conceived as an uncaused cause of the world whose essence is identical with His existence. *Unkulunkulu* is conceived as "He Who is of Himself"; that is, as an existent that requires no cause for His existence, as He exists through his own nature. Cf. John Mbiti, *African Religions and Philosophy* (Praeger Publishers, 1969), Ch. 4; Mbiti, *Concepts of God in Africa* (New York: Praeger, 1969); and Smith, ed., *African Ideas of God*, 2nd rev. ed. (London, 1961), p. 109.

These cultures, unlike the West, are not in the throes of metaphysical nihilism, with the exception of cultural tendencies that result from the import of western theories, such as Marxism. A case in point is Fung Yu-lan, the leading Chinese philosopher of the 20th century; he advocated a metaphysics of rational meaning derived from Neoconfucianism in his *Hsin li-hsüeh* (1939), but repudiated it in favor of Marxism in 1950 (in his "I discovered Marxism-Leninism," *People's China*, 1, 1950, no. 6).

The basic difference between western and nonwestern metaphysics of rational meaning is that the latter are less based on logical argumentation and more based on mystical intuition. Since mystical feelings are types of feeling, it falls within the province of a metaphysics of feeling to determine whether or not such feelings reveal a rational meaning of the world. In Chapter 3, it is shown that mystical feelings cannot be known to reveal such a meaning.

18. These studies were first published in 1882–83 in his *Grundlagen einer allgemeinen Mannichfaltigkeitslehre* and in his essays in *Acta Mathematica*, Vol. II.

19. Russell, *Our Knowledge of the External World* (New York: Mentor, 1960), Lectures VI and VII.

20. Edwards, "The Cosmological Argument," in *The Cosmological Arguments*, ed. D. Burrill (New York: Anchor Books, 1967), pp. 101–23.

21. Hick, *Arguments for the Existence of God* (New York: Herder & Herder, 1971), pp. 37–52.

22. Matson, *The Existence of God* (New York: Cornell University Press, 1965), pp. 58–61.

23. Kupperman, *Philosophy: The Fundamental Problems* (New York: St. Martin's Press, 1978), p. 184.

24. Frege, *Die Grundlagen der Arithmetik* (Breslau: Wilhelm Koebner, 1884), p. 65.

25. Smart, "The Existence of God," in *New Essays in Philosophical Theology*, eds. Flew and Macintyre (London: SCM Press, 1955), pp. 28–46.

26. Alston, "The Ontological Argument Revisited," *Philosophical Review*, 69 (1960), pp. 452–74.

27. Shaffer, "Existence, Predication and the Ontological Argument," *Mind*, 71 (1962), pp. 307–25.

28. Strawson, *The Bounds of Sense* (London: Methuen, 1966), p. 225.

29. Swinburne, *The Coherence of Theism* (Oxford: Clarendon Press, 1977), pp. 254–80.

30. Heidegger, *Die Grundprobleme der Phänomenologie* (Frankfurt am Main: Vittorio Klostermann, 1975), pp. 35–67.

31. The two philosophers who first propounded a critique of this idea are Hume (cf. *Dialogues Concerning Natural Religion*, IX) and Kant (cf. *Kritik der reinen Vernunft* A592/B620–A602/B630). But only in the last 100 years or so has this critique become widely accepted. An example of this is that when Norman Malcolm published (in *Philosophical Review*, Vol. 69, 1960, pp. 41–62) a rare defense of this concept, it was met the very next year by six different articles refuting his arguments (see *Ibid.*, Vol. 70, 1961, pp. 56–111).

32. Strawson, *The Bounds of Sense, op. cit.*, p. 225.

33. Nietzsche, for example, in *Jenseits von Gut und Böse*, #186–203.

34. Sartre, *L'Être et le Néant* (Paris: Librairie Gallimard, 1943), pp. 127–39.

35. Westermarck, *Ethical Relativity* (London, 1932).

36. Ayer, *Language Truth and Logic* (New York: Dover, 1952), Ch. VI.

37. Stevenson, *Ethics and Language* (New Haven: Yale University Press, 1944).

38. Carnap, *Philosophy and Logical Syntax* (London: Routledge, Kegan Paul, 1936), Ch. 1, Sc. 4.

39. Wittgenstein, *Logisch-Philosophische Abhandlung*, 6.41 and 6.432. Also see his *Notebooks, 1914–16* (eds. von Wright and Anscombe), where he writes that "good and evil are somehow connected with the meaning of the world. The meaning of life, i.e. the meaning of the world [*den Sinn der Welt*], we can call God." Cf. p. 73 of his *Notebooks*.

40. *Ibid.*, 6.41.

41. Ayer, *Language Truth and Logic, op. cit.*, p. 31.

42. Carnap, *"Uberwindung der Metaphysik durch Logische Analyse der Sprache," Erkenntnis*, Vol. II, 1932.

43. Heidegger, *Sein und Zeit* (Tübingen: Max Niemeyer, 1972), p. 88.

44. *Ibid.*, p. 135.

45. *Ibid.*, p. 276.

46. In his discussion of truth, Heidegger also writes: " 'In itself' it is quite inexplicable *why* beings are to be uncovered, *why* truth and Dasein must Be." *Ibid.*, p. 228, my italics.

47. *Was ist Metaphysik?* (Frankfurt A.M.: Vittorio Klostermann, 1955), p. 41. The character of *Dasein* as reasonless or *Abgrund* is discussed more fully in *Vom Wesen des Grundes* (Frankfurt A.M.: Vittorio Klostermann, 1965), pp. 53–54.

48. *Die Grundprobleme der Phänomenologie, op. cit.*, p. 318.

49. Jaspers, *Philosophie* III (Berlin: Springer-Verlag, 1958), p. 235.

50. Sartre, *L'Être et le Néant, op. cit.*, p. 713.

51. *Ibid.*, p. 715.

52. Merleau-Ponty, *Sens et non-sens* (Paris: Nagel, 1958), p. 168.

53. But there are a few exceptions to the general acceptance of this belief, e.g., the early Scheler and Von Hildebrand among the phenomenologists, and Charles Hartshorne and Alvin Plantinga among the (post-positivist) analytic philosophers. My contention about the epoch of rational meaninglessness is that the overwhelming majority (but not necessarily *all*) of the philosophers living in that epoch share the belief that the world has no knowable reason. The same holds, *mutatis mutandis*, for my characterization of the epoch of rational meaning.

54. Most of the positivist and phenomenological philosophers do not deal specifically with the claim that so-called "mystical experiences" can function as verifying intuitions of a reason for the world, but some philosophers have presented considerations showing that it is impossible to infer justifiably from the existence of a mystical experience that seems to be of a reason for the world to the existence of this reason itself. See for example C. B. Martin's "A Religious Way of Knowing" in *New Essays in Philosophical Theology*, eds. Flew and MacIntyre; A. MacIntyre's "Visions," *Ibid.*; R. Gale's "Mysticism and Philosophy" in *Philosophy and Religion*, ed. Stephen Cahn; N. Melchert's "Mystical Experience and Ontological Claims," *Philosophy and Phenomenological Research*, June 1977, pp. 445–63; and other works. For further discussion, see III.21.i.

55. Wittgenstein, *Logisch-Philosophische Abhandlung*, 6.41.

56. *Ibid.*, 6.432 and 6.4321.

57. Heidegger, *Einfuhrung in die Metaphysik* (Tubingen: Max Niemeyer, 1966), p. 8. Heidegger also discusses this question in *Was ist Metaphysik?* (1929) and in *Vom Wesen des Grundes* (1929).

58. *Einfuhrung in die Metaphysik*, p. 25.

59. *Ibid.*, pp.5–6.

60. *Ibid.*, p. 2. My italics. Also see p. 22.

61. *Ibid.*, pp. 24–25. But Heidegger allows that this reason *may* be Being itself. Cf. *Ibid*.

A somewhat analogous approach to this question is worked out by Milton Munitz in his *The Mystery of Existence*, although in non-Heideggerian categories. For Munitz, we cannot know if there is a reason-for-the-existence-of-the-world, or if there is one, what kind of reason it is.

62. Heidegger, *Einfuhrung in die Metaphysik*, p. 25.

63. It is worth noting that the later Heidegger, in a reinterpretation of his earlier thinking, thought of a new and quite different sense that this question ("Why is there being and not rather nothing?") could have, a sense, however, that there is no textual indication that he had recognized in 1928–29 or in 1935. He writes in the introduction (1949) to *Was ist Metaphysik?* that this question could have the sense: "How did it come to pass that beings everywhere take priority and

lay claim to every 'is', while what is not a being is understood as nothing, though it is Being itself, and remains forgotten?" *Was ist Metaphysik?, op. cit.*, p. 23.

The issue of the later Heidegger's rejection of "metaphysical thinking" can also be touched upon here, at least to indicate that by "metaphysical thinking" Heidegger did not mean "rational-metaphysical thinking" in the sense given to this phrase in the present treatise, the sense namely of thinking about reasons and reasonlessness. By "metaphysical thinking" the later Heidegger meant a representational-calculative thinking that objectifies beings into at-hand (*Vorhanden*) objects. Although the later Heidegger does not engage in this thinking, he does engage in "rational-metaphysical thinking" in the sense this phrase has in the present work. For example, a study of *Der Satz vom Grund* (Pfullingen: Neske, 1957), pp. 203–11, would show that Heidegger therein engages in a meditative thinking about Being as the reasonless (*Ab-grund*).

64. Thomas Pynchon, *Gravity's Rainbow* (New York: Bantam, 1974), p. 4.

65. Descartes, *Meditationes de prima philosophia*, 1642 (2nd Latin ed.) Med. VI, p. 78.

66. Descartes, *Principia Philosophiae* IV, CXC. (*Oeuvres* ed. Adam-Tannery, Vol. XIII.)

67. Spinoza, *Ethica Ordine Geometrico Demonstrata*, Pars III, Defs. 1–3. (*Opera* II. Heidelberg, 1925. P. 139.)

68. Leibniz, *Principes de la Nature et de la Grace, op. cit.*, n. 17.

69. Spinoza, *ibid.*, Pars II, Props. 24–40; Pars III, Defs. 1–3, Props. 1–3; Pars V, Prop. 3–20. (*Opera* II, pp. 110–22, 139–45, 282–94.)

70. Malebranche, *De la recherche de la vérité*, Bk. I, Ch. 1, Sc. 2. (*Oeuvres complètes*, ed. A. Robinet, Vols. 1–2, 1962.)

71. Hegel, *Die Philosophie des Geistes*, #441, Zusatz, in *Sämtliche Werke* (Stuttgart: Fr. Frommanns Verlag, 1958), Bd. 10, p. 298.

72. Aquinas, *Summa Theologica*, 1a. LXXX. 2.

73. Kant, *Kritik der praktischen Vernunft* in *Kants gesammelte Schriften* (Berlin: Preussische Akademie, 1900-1942), Vol. 5, pp. 71–89.

74. Aquinas, *Summa Theologica*, Ia. LXXX. 3.

75. Aristotle, *Ethica Nicomachea*, VII, 3, 6 and 7.

76. The rational standard of metaphysical truth is being understood here as the standard for obtaining an *a priori* demonstrative knowledge of the existence and nature of God and goodness.

77. Leibniz, *Principes de la Nature et de la Grace*, GERH. Vol. VI, 602. n. 7.

78. Wittgenstein, "Lecture on Ethics," *Philosophical Review*, Vol. LXXIV, 1965, p. 8.

79. Wittgenstein, "The Lecture on Ethics," *op. cit.*, p. 11.

80. "If I want to fix my mind on what I mean by absolute or ethical value [I think of my experience] of *wonder at the existence of the world*." *Ibid.*, p. 8. In addition, this experience "is, I believe, exactly what people were referring to when they said God had created the world." *Ibid.*, p. 10.

81. *Ibid.*, p. 13 (original German) and p. 15 (Max Black's translation).

82. Heidegger, *Sein und Zeit, op. cit.*, p. 137.

83. *Ibid.*, pp. 186–87.

84. *Was ist Metaphysik? op. cit.*, p. 42.

85. *Ibid.*

86. A feeling is "global" if it is about the whole of the world, and "mundane" if it is about parts or a part of the world.

87. The early Fichte and the early Schelling used the phrase "the Absolute Ego" rather than the term "God" to refer to the first reason for the world; this reason is the referent of the primary and self-evident proposition, "I am I" (*Ich bin Ich*). Cf. Fichte, *Grundlage der gesammten Wissenschaftslehre* (1794), and Schelling, *Vom Ich als Princip der Philosophie* (1795).

88. By a "state of affairs" I do not mean a proposition or an abstract object, but something (be it abstract or concrete) *qua* possessing some feature. A global state of affairs is the world-whole *qua* possessing some feature.

89. These logical reasons must be distinguished from causal and teleological reasons. Logical reasons are propositions, and causal and teleological reasons are, of course, causes and purposes. The *method* of the metaphysics of rational meaning involves logical reasons and logical reasoning (inferring), but the *subject-matter* of this metaphysics is the unconditioned cause and purpose of the world. The distinction between logical and causal/teleological reasons was first clearly made by Leibniz (cf. *Monadologie*, No. 32; *Theodicée*, No. 44; and his fifth letter to Clarke, No. 125), but more systematically made by Wolff (cf. *Philosophia prima*, No. 70ff.); Baumgarten (*Metaphysica*, No. 20–24 and 306–13); and Schopenhauer (cf. *Uber die vierfache Wurzel des Satzes vom zureichenden Grunde*).

Chapter I

1. Descartes, *Les Passions de l'Ame* I, 27.

2. A clarifying note is required here concerning the phrases "the world," "the world-whole," and "world-part." Unless I expressly indicate otherwise, or it is clearly indicated otherwise by the context, I shall henceforth use "the world" to refer both to the world as a whole and to the world in respect of its parts (i.e., in respect of each, some, or any of its parts). Accordingly, to say that "sensuous feelings can be features of the world" means that they can be features of the world-whole and can be features of a part of the world. If I wish to refer exclusively to the world as a whole, I shall use "the world-whole," and if to a part of the world, "world-part."

In saying that "sensuous feelings are features of the world as well as features of the I," I am really saying—to put it exactly—that they are features of the world-whole and of world-parts other than the I, as well as of the I, for the I too is a part of the world.

3. Affects are distinguished from moods in Chapter 3.

4. See *Politica*, VIII, 7, 1342A, 8 and *De Memoria et Reminiscentia*, I, 450B, 1 for the assertion that affects are "movements of the soul." For the statement that they involve pleasure or pain, see *Ethica Nicomachea*, II, 5, 1105B, 22–23, and *Ethica Eudemia*, II, 2, 1220Bff, *Magna Moralia*, I, 7, 8, 1186, and *Rhetorica*, II, 1, 1378A, 20–21. The theory that pleasure and pain are complements of a function is developed in Book X of *Ethica Nicomachea*.

5. Aristotle does not, however, consider these three items to exhaust the possible ways in which affects can be defined. Affects can also be defined, for instance, in terms of a material reason (*aitia*). Thus the material reason for anger is blood boiling about the heart. Cf. *De Anima*, I, 1, 403A–403B. I distinguish physiological disturbances from feeling-sensations in 1.7.

6. Aristotle, *Rhetorica*, II, 8, 1385B, 13–14.

7. *Ibid.*, II, 10, 1387B, 23–24.

8. Hume, *A Treatise of Human Nature*, Selby-Bigge edition (Oxford: Clarendon Press, 1888), Book II, Part I, Section 2, p. 277.

9. Spinoza, *Ethica Ordine Geometrico Demonstrata*, Pars III, Def. 6, in *Opera* II, *op. cit.*, p. 192.

10. *Ibid.*, Pars III, Prop. 30, Sch. (*Opera* II, p. 163). I am following the Dutch version in reading "internal cause" rather than "external cause."

11. Spinoza, *Ethica, op. cit.*, Pars III, Prop. 56. (*Opera* II, p. 184).

12. *Ibid.*, Pars III, Prop. 56, Dem. (*Opera* II, p. 185).

13. Wenger, "Emotions as Visceral Action: An Extension of Lange's Theory," in *Feelings and Emotions*, ed. M. Reymert (New York: McGraw-Hill, 1950), p. 5.

14. Brentano, *Vom Ursprung sittlicher Erkenntnis*, Appendix IX.

15. Scheler, *Der Formalismus in der Ethik und die materiale Wertethik* (Halle: Max Niemeyer, 1921). Pt. II, Ch. 5, Sc. 2, pp. 262–65.

16. Sartre, *L'Être et le Néant, op. cit.*, Pt. III, Ch. 2, Sc. 1, pp. 396–400.

17. Buytendijk, "The Phenomenological Approach to the Problem of Feelings and Emotions," in *Feelings and Emotions*, ed. M. Reymert, *op. cit.*, pp. 127–41.

18. Scheler, *Der Formalismus in der Ethik und die materiale Wertethik, op. cit.*, p. 262.

19. *La Transcendance de l'Ego* (Paris: Librairie Philosophique J. Vrin, 1966), p. 57.

20. *Ibid.*, p. 61.

21. This is explained by Sartre as follows: The ego is "the ideal unity of all the states and actions. As something ideal, naturally, this unity can embrace an infinity of states. But one can well understand that what is offered to the concrete and fulfilled intuition is only this unity *insofar* as it incorporates the present state. By virtue of this concrete nucleus [*noyau concret*], a greater or lesser number of empty intentions (by right, an infinity of them) are directed toward the past and toward the future, and aim at the states and actions not presently given." *Ibid.*, p. 69.

22. The "I" that feels is also neither a soul nor a substance. Nor is it the "person" Scheler conceives, which is the personal unity, not of individual intentional acts, but of the essential kinds of intentional acts; such a "person" is in truth a theoretical construct.

23. *The Principles of Psychology*, Vol. II (New York: Dover, 1950) pp. 450–51.

24. Kant, *Kritik der Urteilskraft*, #3, in *Werke*, Band V (Berlin, 1922), ed. Cassirer, p. 275.

25. Aristotle, *Politica*, VIII, 1342A, and *De Memoria et Reminiscentia*, I, 450B,1.

26. Cicero, *Tusculan Disputations*, IV. v. 10.

27. Plato, *Philebus* 41C–42B.

28. Hume, *A Treatise of Human Nature, op. cit.*, p. 276.

29. Wundt, *Grundzüge der physiologische Psychologie* (Leipzig: W. Engelmann, 1908–11).

30. See for example E. B. Titchener's criticisms in *Lectures on the Elementary Psychology of Feeling and Attention* (New York, 1908), pp. 125–68.

31. Kenny, *Action, Emotion and Will* (New York: Humanities Press, 1963), p. 61.

32. Strasser, *The Phenomenology of Feeling* (Pittsburgh: Duquesne University Press, 1977), trans. Robert Wood, p. 188.

33. Certain remarks in Sartre's *L'imaginaire, psychologie phénomenologique de l'imagination* (Paris: Gallimard, 1940), Pt. II, Ch. 2, suggest that he also was aware of some nontypological characters of feeling-tonalities, but Sartre also did not expressly acknowledge them to be *sensuous* feeling-characters or to be different from the nonsensuous affectively apprehended properties like "injustice" or "dangerousness"that he discussed in his *"Une Idée fondamentale de la phénomenologie de Husserl: l'intentionnalité"* (in *Situations* I, Paris: Gallimard, 1947) and in his *Esquisse d'une théorie des émotions* (Paris: Hermann, 1965), Pt. III. Some of Sartre's ideas pertinent to the issue of feeling-tonalities are further explored in Quentin Smith, "Sartre and the Phenomenon of Emotion," *The Southern Journal of Philosophy*, Vol. 17, No. 3, Fall 1979, pp. 397–412; "Sartre and the Matter of Mental Images," *The Journal of the British Society for Phenomenology*, Vol. 8, No. 2, May 1977, pp. 69–78, esp. pp. 74–78; "Sartre's Theory of the Progressive and Regressive Methods of Phenomenology," *Man and World*, Vol. 12, No. 4, Fall 1979, pp. 433–44, esp. pp. 438–43; "A Contradiction in Sartre's Theory of Freedom," *The Personalist*, Vol. 60, No. 4, October 1979, pp. 369–72. The standpoint adopted in these early articles, however, is not one to which I still completely subscribe.

34. Husserl, *Logische Untersuchungen* (Halle: Max Niemeyer, 1913), Zweiter Band, V. #15B, p. 394.

35. For a further account of Husserl's theory of feeling, see Quentin Smith, "Husserl and the Inner Structure of Feeling-Acts," *Research in Phenomenology*, Vol. 6, 1976, pp. 84–104; "On Husserl's Theory of Consciousness in the Fifth Logical Investigation," *Philosophy and Phenomenological Research*, Vol. 37, No. 4, June 1977, pp. 482–97; "Husserl's Early Conception of the Triadic Structure of the Intentional Act," *Philosophy Today*, Vol. 25, No. 1/4, Spring 1981, pp. 82–91. Some of the criticisms in these articles presuppose a view of feeling I no longer share.

36. Other feeling-characters like the feeling-colors are nontypological in nature for another reason as well. Not only is there not an individual feeling-color, for example, corresponding to each feeling-quality, but even the individual correspondences that do obtain are not unique. One feeling-color may correspond to different qualities (as a feeling-color of blueness is present both in serenity and sadness) and one quality may be experienced as having one or the other feeling-color (as a sadness or depression can be felt either as a blueness or as a blackness). Individual feeling-flows, on the other hand, uniquely correspond to individual feeling-qualities, and vice versa.

It may be objected that feeling-flows are culturally and individually relative, since people express their sensuous feelings in different ways. But feeling-flows are neither to be identified with their expressions nor to be correlated in a necessary way with any given mode of expression. If the Japanese express joy by crying and Westerners express sadness by crying, that does not mean that the feeling-flow of the joy felt by the Japanese is the same as the feeling-flow of the sadness felt by the Westerners. For crying can express either an *upwards radiation* or a *downwards sinking*, and each of these feeling-flows can also be expressed in some other way than through crying.

37. Aristotle, *Poetica*, Chs. 21–25, and *Rhetorica*, Bk. III. Also see Cicero, *De Oratore*; Horace, *Ars Poetica*; Quintilian, *Institutio Oratorio*; and Longinus's treatise on the sublime.

Some progress has been made in criticizing this tradition, and in offering, although in different ways, a positive account of metaphor by I. A. Richards,

Monroe Beardsley, Max Black, Philip Wheelwright, Paul Ricoeur and others, but its fundamental and distinctive *metaphysical* role in reappreciative feeling-afterglows and concentrative feelings has not been explored.

38. But not all verbal significations in a metaphysics of feeling are metaphorical. In particular, global importances reveal themselves to be more susceptible to an exact and detailed explication in literal terms than do the sensuously felt features of the world. The relationship between the evocative and exact explications of the world as felt is discussed further in Chapters 2 and 3.

39. Hegel, *Die Philosophie des Geistes*, #400, Zusatz, in *Sämtliche Werke*, *op. cit.*, Bd. 10, p. 124.

40. Some of these mundane importances, however, are sensuous, especially the importances of a part of the surface of the world. These importances include hues, which are described in Section 13 of the following chapter.

Chapter II

1. The issue of whether some importances can exist without appearing, and hence without being the source of a feeling-flow, is discussed in Chapter 6. If there are such importances, and if a reference to them is to be included in my preliminary characterization of importances, this characterization would read: an importance is whatever, if and when it comes to appearance, acquires the feature of being a feeling-flow source.

2. The phrase "an importance" can be used to refer to the concrete thing that is important, or to a feature of the thing which is one of the ways in which the thing is important.

3. The most significant of these articles are "The Conception of Intrinsic Value" and "The Nature of Moral Philosophy" in *Philosophical Studies* (1922) and "Is Goodness a Quality" in *Philosophical Papers* (1959).

4. Moore, *Principia Ethica* (Cambridge University Press, 1971), No. 13, p. 17.

5. *Ibid.*, No. 36, p. 60.

6. *Der Formalismus in der Ethik und der materiale Wertethik*, *op. cit.*, p. 166.

7. *Ibid.*, Ch. IV, Sc. 1, pp. 163–206.

8. *Ibid.*, pp. 185–86.

9. *Ibid.*, Ch. I, Sc. 1, pp. 7–19.

10. *Ibid.*, Ch. II, B, 2, p. 79.

11. For a further exposition, see Quentin Smith, "Max Scheler and the Classification of Feelings," *Journal of Phenomenological Psychology*, Vol. 9, Nos. 1–2, Fall 1978, pp. 114–38; "Scheler's Critique of Husserl's Theory of the World of the Natural Standpoint," *The Modern Schoolman*, Vol. 55, No. 4, May 1978, pp. 387–96; "Scheler's Stratification of Emotional Life and Strawson's Person," *Philosophical Studies* (Ireland), Vol. 25, 1977, pp. 103–27; "Alfons Deeken's 'Process and Permanence in Ethics: Max Scheler's Moral Philosophy,' " *Philosophical Studies* (Ireland), Vol. 28, 1981, pp. 403–6. Also see "Franz Brentano's 'The Origin of Our Knowledge of Right and Wrong'," *Ibid.*, pp. 406–10. The critical standpoint I adopted in these early articles remained within the phenomenological fact/value and feeling/nonfeeling dichotomy, and is defective in this regard.

12. Scheler, *"Ordo Amoris,"* Sc. II, in *Schriften aus dem Nachlass*: I, *Zur Ethik und Erkenntnislehre*, 2d ed. rev., ed. Maria Scheler (Bern: Francke Verlag, 1957), pp. 347–76.

13. Whitehead, *Modes of Thought* (New York: The Free Press, 1968), p. 11.

14. Von Hildebrand, *Ethics* (Chicago: Franciscan Herald Press, 1953), p. 34.

15. *Ibid*, pp. 79 and 139.

16. This is discussed further in Quentin Smith, "On Heidegger's Theory of Moods," *The Modern Schoolman*, Vol. 58, No. 4, May 1981, pp. 211-35.

17. A neutral phenomenon in the ordinary sense is correspondingly regarded as a phenomenon that is not a source of sensuous feeling and which is solely exactly describable.

18. "Phenomenon" ordinarily has several senses, one of them being for example that an event or state of affairs is unusual and warrants special attention. The ordinary sense I have in mind in the present discussion is the one that philosophers have traditionally been concerned with and have endeavored to make precise in various ways, "phenomenon" in the sense of an appearance or something that appears.

19. In regard to such affective reactions as these, it should be noted that in some cases the same words can be used to describe the perceived importance and the feeling it emanates. A calm day can be a source of a calm feeling, a gloomy day of a gloomy feeling. These words, nevertheless, have different referents: "gloomy" in "gloomy day" refers to a panoramic hue displayed by a configured importance that is a source of a feeling, whereas "gloomy" in "gloomy feeling" refers to a feeling-sensation and feeling-tonality emanated from an important source.

20. Some other sorts of flowing importances, such as dogs and monkeys, are also embodied in thingly parts of some surrounding configured importances.

21. Some aspects of Democritus's theory of this distinction are preserved in Theophrastus, *de Sen.* 49 ff. *Dox.* 513; Claudius Galenus, *de Elem. sec. Hipp.* I, 2, among other places.

22. Aristotle, *De Anima*, 426A, *Metaphysica*, 1010B.

23. Locke, *An Essay Concerning Human Understanding*, Bk. II, Ch. VIII.

24. Descartes, *Meditationes de prima philosophia*, Meds. II, III, VI and *Principia Philosophiae* Pars I, XLVII, LXVI–LXXI, Pars II, I–IV, and Pars IV, CLXXXXIX–CCIII.

25. Hobbes, *Leviathan*, Pt. I, Ch. I.

26. Galileo, *Il Saggiatore*, in *Opera* VI (Edizione Nazionale), ed. Antonio Favaro, 1896, p. 232.

27. *Ibid.*, p. 348.

28. Geometrical features represented by rational numbers also cannot be discovered, for it is necessary to measure them to an infinity of decimal places (e.g., an infinity of zeros).

29. We must distinguish here *the thinking, the thought* (the signification), and *the phenomenon of which there is a thought* (the signified phenomenon). These and other distinctions, such as that between nominal and propositional significations, are discussed in Chapter 5.

The word "signification" can also be used to refer to the linguistic signs that express the thoughts (as I did sometimes in Section 5 of the Introduction), but in the present and ensuing discussions I am using this word to refer solely to the thoughts.

30. Ideative feelings are discussed more fully in Chapter 5. Other issues touched upon in the ensuing discussion are also treated more fully in Part 2.

31. *Vide*, Mach, *Die Analyse der Empfindungen*, Jena, 1886. However, a phenomenalist theory of science is at least clearly implicit in the writings of George Berkeley and Hume, and especially in those of Mill.

It should be noted that there are differences between phenomenalist and operationalist theories of science, and between different versions of phenomenalism and operationalism, but it is not necessary for my present purposes to take these differences into account.

32. I shall also make clear how my conception of these importances differs from the philosophy of science espoused or suggested by phenomenologists like Husserl, Heidegger, Sartre, and Merleau-Ponty. My emphasis on intuition as opposed to empty thought does not imply a commitment to phenomenological idealism in some form or the other, wherein perceptible beings are conceived as constituted by or dependent upon transcendental consciousness, *Dasein* or the for-itself.

33. This substitution has been reflected upon by some philosophers, although these philosophers did not also reflect upon—but instead tacitly presupposed—the divorce of the empirically exact from the evocative concepts. Cf. Husserl, *Der Krisis der europaischen Wissenschraften und die transzendentale Phänomenologie* (The Hague: Martinus Nijhof, 1954), Pt. II and Appendixes; Russell, *Human Knowledge* (New York: Simon and Schuster, 1948), Pt. IV; Toulmin, *The Philosophy of Science* (London: Hutchinson's Univ. Library, 1953), Ch. III, Sec. 3.

34. One of the motives for this exact-neutral conception of phenomena that will not be discussed in the next section is the mistaken belief that evocative descriptions of phenomena are one and all individually relative, whereas universal and intersubjective agreement can be reached about some exact descriptions. I shall show in Part 2, in my theory of pure and impure appreciations, that universal intersubjective agreement can also be reached about some evocative descriptions. Cf. IV.27, V.33, VI.39, and Concl. 40.

35. Although the unconditioned purpose (which is divided into the purpose of the world's existence and the purpose of its nature) explains why the first cause causes the world, this purpose does not explain why the first cause exists. The latter explanation is that it is the first cause's essence to exist.

36. In terms of the model of explanation, this means that premises function as the logical *explanans* (that which explains) and signify the causal or telic *explanans*, and the conclusion functions as the logical *explanandum* (that which is explained) and signifies the causal or telic *explanandum*.

37. This global importance is thematically discussed in IV.27.iii.

Chapter III

1. Aristotle, *Rhetorica*, II, 10, 1387B, 23–24.
2. *De Anima*, I, i, 403A23–24.
3. Descartes, *Les Passions de l'Ame* II, Art. LI.
4. It should not go without notice that Hegel talks of "moods" (*Stimmungen*) in his *Die Philosophie des Geistes*, #392 and *Zusatz*, and the *Zusatz* to #401, and means by them feelings of the changes in the seasons and hours of the day (the lower form of moods) and the feelings evoked by outer sensations but wherein we are not yet conscious of an object distinct from ourselves (the higher form of moods).

5. *An Outline of Philosophy* (New York: Meridian Books, 1960), Ch. XXI, pp. 226–27.

6. Cf. Husserl, *Logische Untersuchungen*, Inv. V, sec. 15. Husserl's conception of a sensation of feeling that is "referred merely to the feeling-subject" represents an incipient version of Scheler's "feeling-states" (of which moods are one type).

7. Scheler, *Der Formalismus in der Ethik und die materiale Wertethik, op. cit.*, p. 263.

8. Von Hildebrand, *Ethics, op. cit.*, p. 191. There are some differences between Von Hildebrand's and Scheler's theories. For instance, while Von Hildebrand claims that affects are intentional acts that mean their objects, Scheler denies this and asserts they only have an immanent directedness towards their objects. Cf. *Formalismus*, p. 266.

9. Heidegger, *Sein und Zeit*, secs. 29, 30, and 40.

10. *Vide*, Bollnow, *Das Wesen der Stimmungen* (Frankfurt A.M., 1941).

11. Strasser did not present his theory as a critique of Scheler and Von Hildebrand, but it can be understood as such.

12. *Phenomenology of Feeling, op. cit.*, p. 190. I have substituted "mood" for "disposition" in this and the following passage.

13. *Ibid.*, p. 188.

14. Paul Ricoeur, *L'Homme faillible*, Ch. IV, Sc. 2, in his discussion of *Tonalities*.

15. Solomon, *The Passions* (New York: Anchor Books, 1977), p. 133.

16. The immediate awareness of the world-whole is more fully discussed in Chapter 5.

17. Aquinas, *Summa Theologica*, I, Q. 5, A. 1.

18. Insofar as an awareness of "distinctionlessness" in some sense is associated with mystical feelings, this awareness is discussed in III.21.i.

19. *Physical efforts* are one of the three kinds of feeling of striving, along with *mental concentrations* and feelings of voluntarily *adopting an interpersonal pose* (such as deliberately "putting on a cheerful face" in order to greet the arriving guests).

Feelings of striving are a distinct class of feelings from moods and affects. They are gravitationally attracted ways of appreciating magnetizing importances (Cf. II.14). A partially complete exact explication of feelings of striving and magnetizing importances is developed in my "Four Teleological Orders of Human Action," *Philosophical Topics*, Vol. 12, No. 3, Winter 1981, pp. 213–30.

20. On indifference as an appreciation of importance, see II.11.

21. I am not claiming, however, that my usage of these terms to designate the parallel types of moods and affects corresponds exactly to the ordinary ways in which these terms are used.

22. Of course "causes" in the rational metaphysical sense are not manifest at all in the felt world. Cf. II.14.

23. On the unfocused character of moods, see III.16.ii.

24. The global importance of monotonousness is further discussed in IV.27.v.

25. In the discussion of these terms in Intro.5, I was characterizing them as inexact and suggestive terms, and thus understanding them in relation to the importances as they appeared in global affects.

26. The word "amazement" is often used to refer to an affect that is different in its quality and flow than awe, and these connotations must be avoided.

27. The nature and criterion of significational truth was first discussed in II.14.

28. It cannot be the case that only *some* seemings are intrinsically veridical, for there can be no grounds for distinguishing between those that are and those that are not intrinsically veridical (for all seemings are internally alike in being *seemings*). Extrinsic grounds may determine some seemings to be nonveridical, but that is irrelevant to the fact that considered solely *intrinsically*, as *seemings*, seemings do not differ from one another.

29. *Śvetāśvatara Upanishad*, I, 11.

30. *Bṛhadāranyaka Upanishad*, IV. IV. 13.

31. *Chāndogya Upanishad*, III. XIV. 1.

32. *Śvetāśvatara Upanishad*, IV. 9.

33. Sankara, *Atmabodha*, #63.

34. *Ibid.*, #64.

35. Plotinus, *Enneads*, VI, 9, 3.

36. *Ibid.*, VI, 7, 5.

37. *Ibid.*, VI, 9, 10.

38. *De mystica Theologia*, Ch. 2.

39. *Meister Eckhart*, trans. Raymond Blakney, Sermon 7, p. 135.

40. *Ibid.*, Sermon 28, p. 231.

41. *Ibid.*, Sermon 27, p. 226. Also see *Tractate* XIX.

42. *Ibid.*

43. A somewhat analogous doctrine can be found in Sankara, Ruysbroeck, Sri Ramakrishna, and others. An interpretation and comparison of Eckhart's and Sankara's doctrine can be found in Otto's *Eastern and Western Mysticism*.

44. In Margaret Smith, *Readings from the Mystics of Islam* (London: Luzac & Co., Ltd., 1950), p. 21.

45. *Ibid.*, p. 100.

46. *Ibid.*, p. 99.

47. In F. C. Happold, *Mysticism: A Study and Anthology* (Baltimore: Penguin Books, 1963), p. 228.

48. Among the Christian mystics, Eckhart evinced the greatest tendency to talk of an identity with God rather that a "likeness."

49. Margaret Smith, *op. cit.*, p. 100.

50. *Ibid.*, pp. 100-1.

51. *The Collected Works of St. John of the Cross*, trans. Kavanaugh and Rodriguez (Washington: ICS Publications, 1973), p. 116.

52. *Ibid.*, pp. 100–101.

53. Cf. Gershom Scholem, *Major Trends in Jewish Mysticism* (New York: Schocken Books, 1941), and my discussion of Taoism in the Introduction.

54. See the *Samyutta-Nikaya* and the *Questions of King Milinda*.

55. D.T. Suzuki has argued in his *Mysticism: Christian and Bhuddist* (1957) that even Theravada Buddhism conceives of enlightenment as an experience of the world's first reason. He claims enlightenment is an experience of the Creator (the absolute ego, *Ātman*) of the relative and empirical egos (each of which he calls a *gahakāraka*). However, the Theravada Buddhists unequivocally denied the existence of *Ātman*. Suzuki acknowledges this, but asserts, without any real attempt at textual justification, that by "Ātman" the Theravada Buddhists meant the empirical self, not the absolute self; but the evidence of the Pali Canon indicates otherwise, as has traditionally been recognized.

56. *Mahayana-sraddhotpada-sastra* (the reconstructed Sanskrit title of *Ta-ch'eng ch'i-hsin lun*), Pt. 3.

57. See for example, Suzuki, *Zen Buddhism* (New York: Doubleday, 1956), Ch. 9.

58. Inge, *Christian Mysticism* (New York: Meridian Books, 1956), esp. Lecture I, pp. 5–9.

59. Underhill, *Mysticism* (New York: E.P. Dutton & Co., 1961), esp. pp. 103–4.

60. Jones, *Studies in Mystical Religion* (London, Macmillan, 1923), esp. p. xv.

61. Otto, *Das Heilige*, Ch. 1.

62. Stace, *Mysticism and Philosophy* (New York: Lippincott Co., 1960), esp. p. 181.

63. Zaehner, *Mysticism: Sacred and Profane* (Oxford: Clarendon Press, 1957), esp. p. 204.

64. One of the exceptions to this tradition is James, who broadly defined mystical experience as any experience which is: (1) ineffable, (2) noetic, (3) transient, and (4) passive. This definition entails, as James himself affirms, such consequences as "the drunken consciousness is one bit of the mystic consciousness." *Vide, The Varieties of Religious Experience* (London: Collier, 1961), p. 305.

65. Nevertheless, most metaphysicians of rational meaning did not base their metaphysics upon mystical intuitions but upon intuition-transcending thinking.

66. *Das Heilige*, Ch. 1

67. *Ibid.*, Ch. 4, Sc. 2.

68. *Ibid.* Another significant way of conceiving these two aspects of the first reason is Sri Ramakrishna's, who writes in the *Prophet of New India*: "When I think of the Supreme Being as inactive—neither creating nor preserving nor destroying—I call him *Brahman* . . . the Impersonal God. When I think of Him as active—creative, preserving, destroying—I call him *Sakti*, or *Maya*, or *Prakriti*, the Personal God. But the distinction between them does not mean a difference. The Personal and the Impersonal are the same thing. . . . It is impossible to conceive one without the other." (Quoted from Stace's *Mysticism and Philosophy*, p. 166.)

69. *De Ornatu Spiritalium Nuptiarum*, in *Opera* (England: Gregg Press Limited, 1967), pp. 303–72.

70. In the Introduction it was necessary to use the phrase "the world-whole" in a relatively inexact and suggestive sense, as only in this way could a historical discussion of the various and divergent metaphysical theories of "the meaning or meaninglessness of the world-whole" have been undertaken. The expression "the world-whole" had to be sufficiently fluid to be able to be used to refer to such divergent conceptions of the world-whole as Aquinas's, Hegel's, Heidegger's, and Wittgenstein's. But it is the task of the metaphysics of feeling, in Parts 1 and 2 of this work, to give an exact and unambiguous sense to this phrase through explicating and articulating what intuitively appears in moods and global affects.

71. I will show in Chapter 4 that "the world-whole" in the unrestricted sense *cannot* have the relational feature of *being an effect of God*, even if God exists.

72. In order to avoid ambiguity, I shall henceforth use the expressions "world-whole," "world-part," "global affect," and "mundane affect"only in the unrestricted sense.

73. In the following is the discussion promised in Intro.2, n.54.

74. Swinburne, *The Existence of God* (Oxford: Clarendon Press, 1979), p. 270.

75. *Ibid.*, pp. 254–55.

76. Swinburne might object to this on the basis of his assumption that God is not a publically observable object (*Ibid.*, pp. 248–49) and does not reveal Himself to everybody. Along these lines, Swinburne might argue that God has good grounds for concealing Himself from an atheist's intuition, an atheist being a person with a prior conviction of God's nonexistence. (These good grounds would be that an atheist "does not deserve" a divine revelation.) God has good grounds, so this argument would go, for revealing Himself only to persons who genuinely wish to see Him and/or who have a prior faith in His existence.

The above argument, however, even if true does not eradicate the evidentiality of the desolate affect. For this affect can be experienced by people who (prior to the experience of this affect) are agnostics who genuinely desire to see God and who hope or wish that He exists. The desolate affect can also be experienced by people who prior to this desolate intuition have faith in the existence of God but lose this faith consequent upon this intuition. These latter persons are in the same category as the mystics (people who have a prior faith in God and who desire to intuit Him), and as such would have the same grounds for being granted a vision as would the mystics.

77. The term "existence" is being used here in the sense or senses it has in existential philosophy, and is not being used in the sense I will give it in Chapter 4.

78. *L'Être et le Néant, op. cit.*, p. 66.

79. *Philosophie*, II (Berlin: Springer-Verlag, 1956), p. 266.

80. *Ibid.*

81. *Ibid.*

82. *Repetition*, trans. W. Lowrie (New York: Harper and Row, 1964), p. 78.

83. *Ibid.*, p. 79.

84. *Ibid.*, pp. 125–27. But Kierkegaard distinguishes this from the "true repetition," which is "eternity," and is not to be obtained in this life.

85. *Repetition, op. cit.*, p. 125.

86. *Also sprach Zarathustra* (Berlin: Walter de Gruyer & Co., 1968), II, "*Das Tanzlied*," p. 137.

87. "*Nachtrage zur Lehre von der Nichtigkeit des Daseins*," in *Sämtliche Werte, Zweiter Band, Parerga und Paralipomena*, pp. 305–6.

88. *Formalismus, op. cit.*, pp. 355–57.

89. *Sein und Zeit, op. cit.*, p. 53.

90. *Ibid.*, p. 186.

91. *Ibid.*

92. Cf. *Philosophie*, II, *op. cit.*, Ch. I, "*Existenz*."

93. Cf. *L'Être et le Néant, op. cit.*, p. 514.

94. *Sein und Zeit, op. cit.*, p. 137.

95. Heidegger discusses this whole of being in *Vom Wesen der Wahreit*, Sections 4–8, *Was ist Metaphysik?*, "*Die Ausarbeitung der Frage*" and "*Die Beantwortung der Frage*," and *Vom Wesen des Grundes*, Chs. 2 and 3.

96. *Was ist Metaphysik?, op. cit.*, p. 31.

97. Strictly speaking, however, Heidegger's *angst* is not even fully revelatory of the ontological whole, for Being-in-the-world as a whole does not even

exhaust *Dasein*'s ontological constitution: "Being-in-the-world is of course a necessary *a priori* constitution of *Dasein*, but it by no means is sufficient for completely characterizing *Dasein*'s Being." Cf. *Sein und Zeit*, p. 53.

98. See for example his *Grundlegung zur Metaphysik der Sitten* (Rosencranz and Schubert edition, 1838), ftn. to page 22.

99. *Philosophie der Geistes*, #401, *Zusatz*.

100. Note that the phrase "essence thing" is not meant to imply that essences are eternal and mind-independent; a mind-dependent essence is still "something."

101. "A Free Man's Worship" (1903), in *The Basic Writings of Bertrand Russell*, eds. Egner and Denonn (New York: Simon and Schuster, 1961), p. 67.

102. *Ibid*.

103. *Ibid*.

104. "Nature" (1854), in *Essential Works of John Stuart Mill* (New York: Bantam, 1961), p. 380.

Chapter IV

1. This character of rejoicing is somewhat analogous to the joyous feeling of possessing an "instantaneous totality" that Sartre describes in Part III of *The Emotions: Outline of a Theory*. But Sartre considered only senses of this "instantaneous totality" that are mundane and deluded.

2. The term "emptiness," which can be used as an evocative term for many different kinds of phenomena, is used here to evoke the nature of the happenings-no-longer and -not-yet in comparison with the nature of the happenings. This is a different sense of "emptiness" than that which is pertinent to global despair. Cf. IV. 27.

3. This possibility is discussed elsewhere. Cf. Quentin Smith, "Kant and the Beginning of the World," *The New Scholasticism*, Vol. LIX, No. 3, Summer, 1985.

4. On the possibility that time begins, see Quentin Smith, "On the Beginning of Time," *Noûs*, Vol. 19, No. 4 (1985). On the possibility that time is infinite, see my "Infinity and the Past," *Philosophy of Science*, forthcoming.

5. Cf. Russell, "On the Experience of Time," *Monist*, 25 (1915); Hans Reichenbach, *Elements of Symbolic Logic* (New York: Macmillan Co., 1947) #51; Nelson Goodman, *The Structure of Appearance* (Cambridge: Harvard Univ. Press, 1951), Pt. 3, Ch. XI; Smart, *Philosophy and Scientific Realism* (London, 1963), p. 134; D.C. Williams, "The Sea Fight Tomorrow" in *Structure, Method and Meaning*, ed. P. Henle *et al.* (New York, 1951); B. Mayo, "Events and Language," in *Philosophy and Analysis*, ed. M. Macdonald (Oxford, 1954).

6. Plato, *Timaeus* 37–39.

7. Plotinus, *Enneads*, III, 7, xii.

8. St. Augustine, *Confessions*, Bk. XI, Ch. 28.

9. Locke, *An Essay Concerning Human Understanding*, Bk. II, Ch. xiv.

10. Hume, *A Treatise of Human Nature*, Bk. I, Pt. II. Sc. 3.

11. Schelling, *System des transcendentalen Idealismus, Sämtliche Werke*, Vol. III, p. 487.

12. Rudolf Lotze, *Metaphysic*, Sc. 154.

13. Bergson, *Essai sur les données immédiates de la conscience, Oeuvres* (Paris: Presses Universitaires de France, 1963), p. 67.

14. Russell, *Human Knowledge*, Pt. IV, Ch. 5.

15. Reichenbach, *Philosophie der Raum-Zeit-Lehre*, Chs. II-III.

16. Grünbaum, *Philosophical Problems of Space and Time*, Pt. II.

17. Aquinas, *Summa Theologica*, 1A. 10, 2.

18. I do have an implicit awareness of my ego as one of the parts of the world-whole, but I am not intuiting in a captivated way either my ego or its feeling-awarenesses, but the happening of the whole of which they are parts.

19. *The Principles of Psychology*, Vol. I, *op. cit.*, p. 620n.

20. Aquinas, *Summa Theologica*, 1a, 10, 4. Strictly speaking, eternity is the measure of an unchangeable state, not a contingently unchanged state.

21. Cf. Aquinas, *Summa Theologica*, 1a, 10, 1; Boethius, *De Consolatione*, V, prosa 6; Augustine, *De Trinitate*, Bk. XV, Ch. 7; Plotinus, *Enneads*, III. 7, 3.

22. Cf. IV. 27.

23. Aquinas, *Summa Theologica*, 1A. 4, 2. Also see *ibid.*, 1A. 3, 4; *Comm. in Libr. de causis*, Lectio 6; *De Potentia*, VII, 2, ad 9m; and *In I Perihermeneias*, Lectio 5, n. 22.

24. *Summa Theologica*, 1A. 10, 2.

25. *Categoriae*, Ch. 9. 11b, 10–14.

26. Cf. *Kritik der reinen Vernunft*, A30/B46–A41/B58, A218/B265–A226/B274, and A598/B626–A602/B630.

27. The sense in which "there are" nonexisting things is explicated in IV. 26.

28. "Being" in the sense of identity played a decisive role in Plato's ontology, wherein forms (*eidei*) are held to be the "really real" or the "beingliest being" (*ontos on*) in that they persist in a constant and absolute self-identity. Sensible things which are becoming themselves and ceasing to be themselves have less "being" in that they are imperfectly self-identical. Cf. *Republic*, V, 476–80; *Phaedo*, 78D and 80B; *Timaeus*, 27D–28A; and other passages in these and other dialogues.

29. "Being" in the sense of inherence formed the core of Joseph Owen's theory of "being" as a synthesizing. "The cat *is* black" means that blackness inheres in or is synthesized with the cat. Owens's mistake was to try to equate the sense of "being" as existence with "being" in the sense of inherence or synthesis. See his *An Interpretation of Existence*, Chs. 1–3.

30. "Being" in this sense flourished in Aristotelian and medieval philosophy. Of the four senses of "being" Aristotle distinguishes, accidentality, truth, potentiality/actuality, and the categories (cf. *Metaphysics*, VI, 2. 1026a31), it is the latter sense that is the focus of his ontology. In this sense, "being" (*on*) means essent (*ousia*, "substance" in the usual translations) and the essential features of an essent. An essent is a "what it is" (*ti esti*) (*Topics*, I, 9, 103b20 and *Metaphysics*, V, 7. 1017a25) and in the primary sense is an individual and an ultimate subject of essential predication. Essents are that of which essential features are features, such that every essential feature is either present in or predicable of an essent, whereas an essent is neither present in nor predicable of anything else (cf. *Categories*, Ch. 2).

Near the beginning of medieval philosophy, Boethius asserted that *esse* (being) is the form expressed by a definition (cf. *In Isag. Por.*, IV, 14, editio secundi; CSEL 48, p. 273, lines 13–15), but the principal discussions of *esse* and *essentia* did not begin until Avicenna's works were translated into Latin. In these translations the view is expressed that *essentia*, taken in itself and in abstraction from its *esse* in things and its *esse* in the human mind, has an *esse* of its own (cf. Avicenna's *Metaphysica*, V, 1C; fol. 87rl).

This paved the way for the subsequent distinctions of *esse essentiae* (essential being) from *esse existentiae* (existential being), a distinction first made by Henry of Ghent (cf. *Quodl.* I, 9 [Paris, 1518], fol. 7r), and later made by such philosophers as Godfrey of Fontaines (cf. *Quodl.* III, 1; ed. de WulfPelzer, in *Les philosophes belges* [Louvain, 1904], 11, 304), Duns Scotus (cf. *Op. Ox.* 1, 36, 1, no. 11; ed. M.F. Garcia [Quaracchi, 1912] I, 1177 (no. 1084) and Francisco Suarez, (cf. *Disputationes Metaphysicas*, XXXI; *Opera Omina* [Paris: Vives, 1856–77], XXVI, 224b.)

Aquinas was the principal scholastic who denied that there is an *esse* of *essentia* (cf. *De Ente*, cap. 3; ed. Roland-Gosselin [Paris: Vrin, 1948], p. 26II. 8–10).

31. Cf. Chapters 5 and 6.

32. The instantiational theory of being was first explicitly formulated by Frege in his *Begriffsschrift* (1879) and later writings, and later became the predominant ontological theory in analytic philosophy due to its development and propagation by Russell (see especially his *Principia Mathematica*, Vol. I, 15 and his "The Philosophy of Logical Atomism," Ch. V).

33. It should be noted that I am here dissassociating myself, in more than one way, from Frege's doctrine that names, rather than the senses expressed by names, possess *Bedeutung* (reference). Cf. Frege "*Ueber Sinn und Bedeutung*," *Zeitschrift fur Phil. und phil. Kritik*, vol. 100 (1892), and V. 30.

34. I shall explain below that Kant's theory of being as "positing" is based on "being" in the sense of nominal truth.

The same is true, although in a different way, for Munitz's idea that existence is a semantical index of a singular term. "Existence" in this sense means that the singular term to which it is affixed refers to a part of the universe, rather than merely expresses a sense (cf. *Existence and Logic*, Ch. 7).

Developing the notion of a "part of the universe" and "the universe," Munitz unsuccessfully argues in Chapter 8 that "Existence" can be understood in a language and mind-independent sense (cf. pp. 197–98). He states that Existence is an "aspect of The Universe" (p. 205), its aspect as "undifferentiated and utterly unique" (p. 205). The Universe, however, is an "individual whole" (p. 186), and individuals are individual wholes only if they are the "*designata* of individual names" (p. 175), rather than merely a sense expressed by a name. For example, Socrates and The Universe of which Socrates is a part are individual wholes because they are referents of names, whereas Pegasus and the imaginary universe of which Pegasus is a part are not individual wholes because they are but senses. Accordingly, being an individual whole analytically entails being a referent of a name. Since Existence is an aspect of The Universe, and since The Universe is an individual whole and as such necessarily is the referent of a name, Existence is an aspect of a referent of a name (e.g., the name "The Universe"), and hence is dependent upon a name and language users that employ this name. Clearly, then, "Existence" in Munitz's sense cannot be *existence itself*, for it is possible for physical things to exist even if no language-users and thus no names exist that are able to be employed to refer to these physical things (See Chapter 6 of the present treatise.)

However, Munitz can be credited with a very spiritually profound conception of what is ultimately implied in the notion of a referent of a name, especially in regard to his explication of these implications in terms of the idea of a *mysterium tremendum et fascinans* in Ch. 8, Sec. 6. In fact, 8.6 of *Existence and Logic* is one of the most spiritually profound pieces of writing produced in the tradition of analytic philosophy, ranking on a par with Wittgenstein's *Logisch-Philosophische Abhandlung*, 6–7 and "Lecture on Ethics"—and also with Munitz's earlier *The Mystery of Existence*, Part Four, and his later *The Ways of Philosophy*, Ch. 14.

    35. This sense of truth, as well as the propositional and nominal senses, will be explicated further in Chapter 5.

    As is indicated primarily in *Der Grundprobleme der Phänomenologie*, the early Heidegger conceived of Being (*das Sein*) in terms of *praesens* or "presence" in the apparential sense. The later Heidegger also conceived of Being in this sense, a conception that is expressed most evocatively in *"Der Spruch des Anaximander"* (*Holzwege*, Frankfurt, 1950), and most exactly in *"Zeit und Sein"* (*Zur Sache des Denkens*, Tübingen, 1969), where Being is articulated as the presencing (*wesen*) to *Dasein* of the past present and future.

    But it should be noted that the early Heidegger vacillated between his identification of Being with truth and a recognition of a more fundamental sense of "Being," one that is *Dasein*-independent, and this produced an inconsistency in his ontology, as William Vallicella has demonstrated in "The Problem of Being in the Early Heidegger," *The Thomist*, Vol. 45, No. 3, July 1981, pp. 388–406 and "Heidegger's Reduction of Being to Truth," *The New Scholasticism*, Vol. 59, No. 2, Spring 1985. Compare *Sein und Zeit*, pp. 183, 212 with *Die Grundprobleme der Phänomenologie*, pp. 313–17, 419.

    This vacillation is also manifest in the later Heidegger, as he wrote in the Postscript to the 1943 edition of *Was ist Metaphysik?* that Being can be (*west*) without beings, and thus without *Daseins*, but changed this to assert otherwise in the fifth and later editions, Cf. *Was ist Metaphysik?* 5. Auflage. (Frankfurt am Main: Vittorio Klostermann), p. 46.

    36. *Summa Theologica*, Paris, Mazarine Mss. 795, fol. 7vb. For a further discussion, see H. Pouillon, "Le premier traite des propriétés transcendentales," *Revue Néoscolastique de Philosophie*, XLII (1939), 44, and Allan Wolter, *The Transcendentals and Their Function in the Metaphysics of Duns Scotus* (Washington, D.C.: The Catholic University of America Press, 1946), pp. 1–2.

    37. *Quaestio disputata de Veritate*, quaest. 1, art. 1.

    38. *Quaestio disputata de Mysterio Trinitatis*, q. 1, art. 1.

    39. *Opus Oxoniense*, lib. 1, dist. 8, quaest. 3 nn. 18–19, 597b-598b.

    40. *Metaphysica*, III, 998b, 20ff, and VIII, 1045b6, and XI, 1059b 26–34.

    41. *Topica*, VI, 6, 144a32–b11.

    42. *Analytica Posteriora*, II, 7, b14.

    43. *Metaphysica*, III, 3, 998b, 20–27.

    44. *Topica*, VI, 6, 144b1.

    45. *Categoriae*, VII, 11b, 10–14.

    46. Cf. *Physica* IV, 221 b, 1–6.

    47. Aristotle expressed an awareness of the existential sense of "being," at least implicitly, in *Posterior Analytics*, II, Chs. 7–9, but did not take it into account in his theory of being in the *Metaphysics*.

    48. However, identity, like happening, was not one of the four senses of "being" he dealt with in the *Metaphysics*, which are "being" in the sense of the categories, potentiality/actuality, truth and accidentality, and did not play a part in his conception of being as a transcendental.

    49. Gassendi asserted that existence is not a "perfection." Cf. *The Philosophical Works of Descartes*, eds. Haldane and Ross, Vol. II, (Cambridge: University Press, 1972), p. 185.

50. *Vide, Der einzig mogliche Beweisgrund zu einer Demonstration des Daseins Gottes,* and *Kritik der reinen Vernunft,* A218/B265–A226/B274, and A598/B626–A602/B630.

51. *Logische Untersuchungen,* Vol. II, Inv. 6, ch. 6, sec. 43.

52. *Die Grundprobleme der Phänomenologie,* Pt. I, Ch. 1, and *"Kants These uber das Sein,"* in *Existenz und Ordnung, Festschrift fur Erik Wolf zum 60,* Geburtstag, Frankfurt.

53. "The Philosophy of Logical Atomism," Ch. V, in *Logic and Knowledge.*

54. *Language Truth and Logic,* Ch. 1, p. 43.

55. *Kritik der reinen Vernunft,* A598/B626.

56. *Ibid.,* A600/B628.

57. *Ibid.,* A599/B627.

58. *Ibid.,* A600/B628.

59. *Ibid.,* A598/B626.

60. *Ibid.,* A599/B627.

61. *Ibid.,* A601/B629. It should be noted that "positing" in Kant's discussion in A598/B626 to A602/B630 is tacitly being used in the sense of the positing of actuality (*Wirklichkeit*), which along with the positing of possibility and necessity are the three "modes" of positing. Cf. *Ibid.,* A600/B628–A602/B630, A218/B265–A226/B274, and *Kritik der Urteilskraft,* #76.

62. *Kritik der reinen Vernunft,* A219/B266-7 and A601/B629.

63. The same remarks hold true of the *being referred to* that is a relational feature of the referent.

64. I am not considering here unusual and problematic cases in which a concept supposedly includes itself as one of its referents, as with the concept of all concepts.

65. The referents of concepts of happening, happening-no-longer, and happening-not-yet are exceptions to this rule; the referents of these concepts are *existing* and its privative modes, not items that are, have been, or will be existing.

66. Schopenhauer, *Die Welt als Wille und Vorstellung,* Vol. II, Ch. XLVI.

67. Sartre, *La Nausée* (Gallimard, 1938), p. 187.

68. See my discussion of Sartre in III.21.ii.

69. On ignited and nonoriginative concentrative thinking, see II.13.ii.

70. Sartre, *La Nausée, op. cit.,* p. 190.

71. *Ibid.,* p. 185.

72. *Ibid.* In *Being and Nothingness* Sartre writes that "being [*l'être*] can neither be derived from the possible nor reduced to the necessary. Necessity concerns the connection between ideal propositions but not that of existents [*existants*]. An existent phenomenon can never be derived from another existant, insofar as it is an existant. This is what we shall call the *contingency* of being-in-itself." Cf. *L'Être et le Néant, op. cit.,* p. 34.

73. Sartre, *La Nausée,* p. 185.

74. *Ibid.,* p. 190.

75. See my quotation from *Being and Nothingness* (n. 72) in context with my above quotations from *Nausea.*

76. But there is a veridical nausea at the world-whole for being composed in part of ugly things. Cf. VI.40.

77. These same considerations also pertain to God's existing. If "existing" belongs to the conceptual content of God ("If God is God, God is [*Si Deus est*

Deus, Deus est]," Bonaventura, *De myst. Trinit.* I, 1, 29, t.v., p. 48), and if "being the referent of a concept" belongs to the conceptual content of God (God must be "conceived as existing in reality [*esse in re*]" as well as in the understanding, Anselm, *Proslogion*, II), it still remains possible that this conceptual content fails of reference, and hence that God does not exist. God's existence is no more necessary than the world-whole's.

78. Pages 177-78.

79. Cf. II. 14, p. 106 and the preceding discussion of the degeneration of feeling into reasoning.

80. The difference between these two senses of the phrase that I discuss in the following was first explicitly mentioned in III.21.i.

81. A "global despair" in this sense was discussed in II.11, p. 66.

82. See the discussion in III.17.ii.

83. In the preceding portion of this work, I have consistently talked of the world-whole as the whole of *all* existents, things, importances, etc. In these discussions, "all" was used as an abbreviation for "all other." A similar interpretation is to be given in the appropriate contexts to my usage of "everything" and "each thing."

Chapter V

1. I am referring here to the experience of *being* globally awestruck, not *becoming* globally awestruck, for the latter is essentially a mediate awareness of ever greater world-parts.

2. However, although a centerless world cannot be intuited, the *possibility* of such a world can be. Cf. Chapter 6.

3. If animals like humans are intuitively aware of a centered world-whole, then what is distinctive to humans is the three-tiered character of their global awareness, as intuitive feelings/afterglowing reappreciations/concentrative reappreciations.

4. The evidence for this is that it intuitively seems to me that the world-whole centered around me is the same world-whole that is centered around others, and that there are no known extrinsic grounds that override this intuitive seeming. According to the criteria of intuitional truth (cf. III.20.ii), this evidence justifies a belief that the same world-whole *is* centered around each of us.

5. If they are not at least implicitly manifest, the world-center in question is not really a "world-center," i.e., a world-part that is intuitively aware of the world-whole, the whole composed of *all* parts that exist, including all centers, arrangements, and appearances.

6. That my ego and configured importances *are* immediately apparent is made evident in this way: the "I that feels" and configured importances *seem* to be immediately apparent (this was shown in I. 7 and II.13.i). Since there are no known extrinsic grounds that override this seeming, it follows (in accordance with the criteria of intuitional truth elucidated in III.20.ii) that it is a justified belief that the "I that feels" and configured importances *are* immediately apparent.

7. Kant, *Kritik der reiner Vernunft*, A51/B75.

8. Heidegger, *Sein und Zeit*, Sec. 32.

9. Lehrer, "Skepticism and Conceptual Change," in *Empirical Knowledge* (Englewood Cliffs: Prentice-Hall, Inc., 1973), eds. Roderick Chisholm and Robert Swartz, p. 49.

10. Katz, "Language, Epistemology, and Mysticism," in *Mysticism and Philosophical Analysis*, ed. Steven T. Katz (New York: Oxford University Press,

1978), pp. 26 and 59.

11. Prichard, *Kant's Theory of Knowledge* (Oxford: Clarendon Press, 1909), pp. 28–29. This is one of the few instances in which Prichard expresses an agreement with a Kantian doctrine.

12. Husserl, *Logische Untersuchungen*, Inv. VI, esp. Ch. 6, Sec. 52, and *Erfahrung und Urteil*, Pt. III, Ch. 2, Secs. 86–93.

13. Cf. IV.27.vi, "Peace in the Harmoniousness of the World-Whole," and Section 29 of this chapter.

14. Norman Kemp Smith, "The Nature of Universals, Part III," *Mind*, Vol. 36, (1927), p. 410.

15. *The Principles of Mathematics* (New York: Norton & Norton), 2nd ed., Pt. I, Chs. 5 and 6, pp. 53–81.

16. *Logische Untersuchungen*, *op. cit.*, Zweiter Band, Inv. II, Ch. I, Sc. 4, p. 115.

17. *Logische Untersuchungen*, *op. cit.*, Sc. 3, p. 112.

18. "All" in this context means "all but the world-whole," for the world-whole does not belong to everything-else, even though it resembles myself-and-these-things in that it is an existent.

19. In dialectical reasoning, universals function in the thesis, antithesis, and synthesis. Cf. Intro. 5.

20. In Hegel's system, which culminated the metaphysics of rational meaning, logical reasons were identified with the causal and teleological reasons of the world. Ultimately, God relates to the world as a thesis to its antithesis and synthesis; Nature is the antithesis of the thesis, God, and Spirit, in which the highest stage is the purpose of the world, is the synthesis of God and Nature.

21. *Phaedo* 99D, ff.

22. St. Anselm, *Dialogus de Veritate*, Ch. VII, in J.P. Migne *Patrogia Latina*, Vol. 158, col. 467–86.

23. Cf. St. Augustine's *De Vera Relig.*, and *De. Trin.*

24. Malebranche, *De la Recherche de la Vérité*, Bk. III, Pt. II, Ch. 5.

25. St. Anselm, *Dialogus de Veritate*, *op. cit.*, Ch. X.

26. Hegel, *Wissenschaft der Logik*, Vol. Two, Sec. Three, Ch. Three.

27. *Ibid.*

28. Cf. Aquinas, *Summa Theologica*, 1a, Qs. 15 and 16, and *De Veritate*, Qs. 1–4.

29. In previous chapters, however, I have expressed both senses of the divinity by the capitalized word.

30. On being in the sense of essence, see IV.25.

31. A justifiable doubt is based on a *knowledge* of extrinsic grounds that clash with global affects, an unjustifiable doubt is based on the *mere possibility* that there be such grounds. Global wonder involves a doubting of the latter kind.

Chapter VI

1. See I.6 for this distinction between internal and external descriptions of feelings.

2. It should be noted that in mundane affects of revering, dependency and independency are not always felt to be characterized in terms of *happening*. For example, an ordinary person can revere a wise man for being superordinate in respect of his *knowledge*. The ordinary person could feel that whereas the wise man is independent of the ordinary person in respect of his (the wise man's)

knowledge of the truth, the ordinary person is dependent for his own knowledge of the truth upon the wise man.

3. Cf. IV.27.iv.

4. It should be noted that in using "being part of" and "being composed of" to refer to relational features, and "participation" to refer to a relation, I am making terminological distinctions not made before, for in preceding discussions I also used "being part of" and "being composed of" to refer to the relation between parts and wholes. (See for example V.29).

5. On "being" in the sense of essential feature, see IV.25. The essential global features are all its compositional features and some of its noncompositional ones, like singularity.

6. The world so considered is a "bare individual" in the sense given to this phrase in V.31.ii.

7. A transcendental feature inheres in all existents, a generic feature only in some existents. Cf. IV.26.

8. The world also has several negative generic features, such as being processless (see IV.27.v) and impersonal (see V.33.iv).

9. See V.29 for a more complete explication of the difference between "absolute identity" and "holistic identity." In reference to my distinctions in VI.35, it can be noted that *holistic* identity is the same thing as *collective* identity, and the world's *collective identity* with its parts is equivalent to its being *collectively composed* of its parts.

10. It is worth noting that in some sense of "appearance" the world-whole can be called an appearance (or phenomenon). We often designate a thing that has an accidental feature with a noun that is derived from the adjective or verb that refers to its accidental feature. For example, a person who runs is called a runner. Likewise, things whose appearances are accidental features can be called appearances or phenomena. Since it is true, as I shall argue in the next section, that the world-whole's appearances are accidental features, the world-whole can be called an appearance or phenomenon in this accidental sense.

11. Husserl, *Ideen au einer reinen Phänomenologie und phänomenologischen Philosophie*, #55. *Husserliana*, Band III, 1 (Den Haag: Martinus Nijhoff, 1976), pp. 120–21.

12. Husserl, *Formale und transzendentale Logik*, #99. *Husserliana*, Band XVII (Den Haag: Martinus Nijhoff, 1974), p. 258.

13. Husserl, *Formale und transzendentale Logik*, #63. *Husserliana*, Band XVII, *op. cit.*, pp. 175–77.

14. Husserl, *Formale und transzendentale Logik*, #97. *Husserliana*, Band XVII, *op. cit.*, p. 251.

15. Cf. Husserl, *Formale und transzendentale Logik*, #102. *Husserliana*, Band XVII, *op. cit.*, pp. 274–78.

16. Husserl, *Ideen au einer reinen Phänomenologie und phänomenologischen Philosophie*, #70. *Husserliana*, Band III, 1, *op. cit.*, p. 147.

17. The world does not necessarily have the feature of happening (see IV.27.ii), but *if* it is to happen, *then* (as is tautologically obvious) it must have the feature of happening.

18. Bergson, *Durée et Simultanéité* (1922), Ch. III.

19. Quentin Smith, "The Mind-Independence of Temporal Becoming," *Philosophical Studies* (U.S.A.), Vol. 47, No. 1, January 1985, pp. 109–19.

20. Quentin Smith, "A Phenomenological Examination of Husserl's Theory of Hyletic Data," *Philosophy Today*, Vol. 21, No. 4/4, Winter 1977, pp.

356–67. The later Husserl abandoned his early theory of a temporal *hyle*, but still claimed that time is produced.

21. *Sein und Zeit, op. cit.*, p. 420.

22. This is the *explicit* origination of the *pure* nows; nows as dated, spanned, made public and significant, originate in the self-expression of our caring-for (*Besorgen*) to-hand (*Zuhanden*) beings. The problems I shall point out in regard to Heidegger's conception of the origin of the pure nows also pertains, *mutatis mutandis*, to his conception of the origin of these nows.

23. Cf. *Sein und Zeit*, p. 326. The expression "making-present" is used to refer to the "temporal" present formally understood, and to this present in its specific inauthentic mode. Cf. *Ibid.*, p. 338.

24. *Ibid.*, p. 326.

25. *Ibid.*, p. 351.

26. *Ibid.*, pp. 325–26.

27. *Die Grundprobleme der Phänomenologie, op. cit.*, sec. 21A, pp. 431–45.

28. *L'Être et le Néant, op. cit.*, p. 265.

29. *Ibid.*, p. 165.

30. *Ibid.*, p. 166.

31. Most contemporary philosophers use the term "density" to refer to this character of time, and employ the word "continuity" to refer to the fact that moments can be understood in terms of irrational numbers. In the following, I adopt Sartre's usage.

32. *Ibid.*, p. 180.

33. Sartre, *L'Être et le Néant, op. cit.*, p. 181.

34. *Ibid.*, p. 150.

35. *Ibid.*, p. 267.

36. Merleau-Ponty, *Phénoménologie de la Perception* (Paris: Librairie Gallimard, 1945), p. 471.

37. *Ibid.*, p. 475.

38. *Ibid.*, p. 481.

39. *Ibid.*, p. 487.

40. Sartre, *L'Être et le Néant. op. cit.*, pp. 184–85.

41. Merleau-Ponty, *Phénoménologie de la Perception, op. cit.*, p. 495. The idea of a future in which I shall never live is incoherent if "I am myself temporality." For this future can never become present if I am not there to *live* it. Since a future is absolutely identical with a becoming-present, a future that cannot become present is a becoming-present that is not a becoming-present, i.e., an impossibility.

42. Kant, *Kritik der reinen Vernunft*, A31–32/B47.

43. Cf. IV.27.ii.

44. See VI.38.i. Concerning the world's intrinsic independency of me, see VI.38.ii.

The other two possibilities, that at past and future times the world could have been composed solely of these unknown world-parts, can be called "factual" possibilities, in that they are consistent with rather than counter to the situation that in fact obtains at present.

It is to be noted that I am here using the term "counterfactual" in a narrower sense than those given to this term by some contemporary philosophers.

45. These parts of course are known or unknown only in relation to the factual global situation; in the counterfactual global situation they are neither known

nor unknown, since there are no minds in relation to which they could have these features.

46. According to some theologians, resurrected bodies would occupy a heavenly space; these bodies would not be spatially related to the bodies we perceive in the space in which we ourselves are embodied.

47. Cf. p. 271.

48. The configured-importance feature of harmonious roundness is not the hue of being harmoniously round the configured-importance feature displays itself to be when appreciated from above. Cf.II.13.i.

49. I am using these words to refer to tactile hues.

50. Moore's arguments first appeared in "The Refutation of Idealism," *Mind*, N.S. Vol. XII, 1903. However his arguments in this essay were fallacious, inasmuch as he argued that (in my terminology) the hues configured importances display themselves to be, such as the hue of blue, could exist without being displayed to a percipient. That is impossible, for displays are necessarily connected to displayed-to beings.

This mistake was corrected in his "A Reply to My Critics," when he allowed that hues are mind-dependent and that the configured importances which display these hues are mind-independent. Moore writes: "As an argument for my present view I should give the assertions that a toothache certainly cannot exist without being felt, but that, on the other hand, the moon certainly can exist without being perceived." Cf. *The Philosophy of G.E. Moore*, ed. Paul A. Schilpp (Chicago: Northwestern University Press, 1942), p. 653.

Moore does not notice that this mistake also infects his essay "A Defence of Common Sense" (first published in 1925). He argues in this essay that facts like "That mantelpiece is of a light colour" are mind-independent. Cf. *Philosophical Papers* (New York: Collier Books, 1962), p. 45.

51. Stace, "The Refutation of Realism," in *Readings in Philosophical Analysis*, eds. H. Feigl and W. Sellars (New York: Appleton-Century-Crofts, Inc., 1949), pp. 364–72. This essay was first published in *Mind*, Vol. LIII, 1934.

52. Stace, "The Refutation of Realism," in *Readings in Philosophical Analysis, op. cit.*, p. 367.

53. Stace, "The Refutation of Realism," in *Readings in Philosophical Analysis, op. cit.*, p. 369.

54. Cf. III.20.ii.

55. Cf. II.14 and V.30.

56. Cf. VI.34.

57. See II.12.

58. This was first suggested in Chapter 2, n.1.

59. On the ontical status of nonexisting things, see IV.26.

60. Since it is improbable that universals would exist in this world, these "kinds" and "instances" must be understood in terms of resemblance relations among individuals. See V.31.ii.

61. Of course there are other possible apparent compositions besides the actual one, but it is not necessary to take these into account in order to realize that it is infinitely unlikely that there be *this* apparent composition (the one that is in fact actual) rather than one of the nonapparent compositions.

62. Cf. IV.27.ii.

63. There can be only one actual composition, for a composition if actual includes within itself *all existents* other than the whole they compose.

I have discussed elsewhere a current cosmological theory that worlds other than our own exist, but in this theory "world" is used in a restricted sense to refer to a causally independent physical system. Cf. Quentin Smith, "The Anthropic Principle and Many-Worlds Cosmologies," *The Australasian Journal of Philosophy*, Vol. 63, No. 3, Sept 1985,

64. Cf. IV.27.iii.

65. II. 11, p. 66.

66. "Monotonousness" accordingly has to be divested of the associations it sometimes has in ordinary usage of being a mind-dependent feature of things.

67. Cf. IV.25.

Conclusion

1. In the next section I will discuss the relation of this importance to the importances of stultification and emptiness-of-purpose, which are respectively appreciated in apathy and despair.

2. Cf. IV.27.i for the distinction between pure and impure appreciations. An incomplete appreciation is a captivation with some but not all the aspects of a certain global importance. Joy is an incomplete appreciation of closeness in that it is captivated with the feature of *happening* that constitutes this global importance but not with the other feature that constitutes it, *immediate appearance*. Cf.V.28.

3. Cf. IV.27.vi and V.29. But of course *each* part of the world is one individual.

4. Some of the conditions that must be met in order for something to be truly evocatively describable as a joyously feelable "fulfillment" are discussed in IV.22.

5. Cf. IV.27, V.28, V.33, VI.34, and VI.39.

6. Supremacy is based on two of the second-level importances, closeness and immensity, but this can be ignored for the moment.

7. Intro. 4, p. 20.

8. Concerning the involuntary nature of global affects, see III.19. "Involuntary" does not mean *against* my willing (which would be "antivoluntary") but *without* my willing.

Index